DAVID FELLMAN
Vilas Professor of Political Science
University of Wisconsin
ADVISORY EDITOR TO DODD, MEAD & COMPANY

INTERNATIONAL POLITICS TODAY

INTERNATIONAL POLITICS TODAY

DONALD JAMES PUCHALA

Columbia University

DODD, MEAD & COMPANY
NEW YORK   1971   TORONTO

TO JEANNE

PREFACE

LIKE most textbooks in political science, *International Politics Today* was born and nurtured in a university lecture hall. Its chapters are records of attempts to confront and acquaint students with the political world they live in—a world their generation did not make, but one they will be forced to cope with nonetheless. If this book aids even a modicum in their coping, its prime purpose will be fulfiled.

International Politics Today is intended first as a contribution to the general literature of international politics. Each textbook in a given field represents a particular author's attempt to define, delimit, capture, and command the length and breadth of a subject, and to correspondingly display his "world view" before a readership of colleagues and students. This textbook therefore describes the world of international politics as I see it and explains this world as I understand it. If my images and understanding of international politics differ in significant ways from those of other generalists in our field, so much the better. Surely, no one has yet said the last word about international politics, and students gain in perspective and insight by comparing and combining diverse views.

Beyond fulfilling my desire to set my world view in juxtaposition to that of other authors, *International Politics Today* in certain specific ways is intended to fill some notable gaps in the existing textbook literature in our discipline:

First, strictly speaking, this book was written to buttress intermediate-level undergraduate as well as introductory graduate courses in international politics, courses for which an appropriate textbook is presently needed. To be sure, this text will serve well as core reading for a first course. It has much to offer to the beginning student. Nonetheless, I intended from the outset that *International Politics Today,* would offer more than a basic survey of the elements of world affairs. It will carry the student from fundamental topics on toward the challenging empirical and theoretical frontiers of the international relations discipline. While, admittedly, I do not always succeed, I try to maintain a level of discourse somewhat removed from the day-to-day substance of international affairs. Furthermore, I treat the rudimentary concepts of international political analysis unconventionally and diplomatic history quite sparingly. My purpose here is to encourage the student already versed in history, current events, and political analysis to synthesize and generalize, and to approach international politics as a field of causally accountable and causally interrelated behavior patterns. In short, above the elementary level, studying international politics should involve theory-building—and much of this book does. Wherever possible, discussion moves from the known to the unknown, so that students are implicitly or explicitly challenged to step beyond current research frontiers.

Second, as noted already, treatment of certain topics in *International Politics Today* is unconventional. Approaches ranging from foreign policy via cybernetic modeling, to goal-resource balancing via simulation flow charts, to "security" via differentially skewed statistical distributions, and to other topics via similarly irregular paths, are exhibited in this book not because I choose to pose as a "young Turk" in the international relations discipline, but rather because I want this book to reflect some of the most outstanding results of recent research. The last fifteen years have been ones of exciting leaps forward in our abilities to cope with international politics both empirically and theoretically. These years, for example, saw the publication of Morton Kaplan's *System and Process in International Politics,* Thomas Schelling's *The Strategy of Conflict,* Raymond Aron's *Peace and War,* Karl W. Deutsch's *The Nerves of Government,* Sprout and Sprout's *The Ecological Perspective on Human Affairs,* Ernst B. Haas's *Beyond the Nation-State,* Herman Kahn's *On Thermonuclear War,* Richard Rosecrance's *Action and Reaction in World Politics,* and many more provocative works that all but revolutionized our thinking about international politics. Lamentably, very little of this new and exciting work has as yet been reflected in standard textbooks (with some notable exceptions, of course). Very little of it, consequently, enters into undergraduate instruction. In light of this, *International Politics Today* is specifically intended to diffuse the ideas, findings, and provocations of the young Turks of the 1950's and 1960's, among the younger Turks of the 1970's.

A final difference between this book and the existing textbook literature is evident in the inclusion of lengthy passages that cannot be called discussions of international politics by conventional definition. Segments of Chapters 5, 6, and 9; large parts of Chapters 2 and 11; and almost all of Chapter 8 are concerned with internal politics within states rather than international politics among them. There are several reasons for this poor "boundary" maintenance. First, as a result of predispositions I bring to the study of international politics, I cannot convince myself—and hence, I surely could not convince my readers—that interactions among governments can be explained without also explaining the policy contexts that produce states' international behavior. Nor, for that matter, can I conceive of looking at international politics in terms of states' impacts upon the international system, without at the same time noting the system's impacts upon states. In effect, I see no boundary between internal and external politics; I rather see important linkages.

More important, with regard to this last point, much of the emphasis upon internal politics in this book represents deference to the fact that the "third world" is an arena in contemporary international politics. The international political roles and actions of the new states must be analyzed and understood, for a variety of factors visible today indicate that world history during the last decades of this century is likely to be made in the non-Western world. At present third-world countries affect international politics rather minimally, but, at the same time, *they are greatly affected by international politics*. Therefore, appropriate questions to ask about international politics and the third world concern how and why the creeds, myths, institutions, and technologies of the global environment penetrate and affect the less developed states. In such states these necessarily become questions about internal affairs, but even so they are among the most relevant "international politics" questions we can ask today.

In *International Politics Today* I make no attempt to hide or disguise my values concerning certain ideas, countries, men, issues, and events. Normative considerations must remain as prominent in international political analysis as empirical rigor. Otherwise, we foster a sterile science. Nevertheless, accepting particular value positions is certainly not prerequisite to grappling with either international politics or with the contents of this book. All the reader need bring to this book are a moderate capacity for abstract thinking, an active curiosity about international affairs, and a sincere concern for the fate of our troubled, but improvable, world.

Creating a book is an intellectual and technical task that no author attempts alone. This book reflects the intellectual influence and technical efforts of many individuals. The reader will immediately become aware that my thinking about problems in international politics has been greatly influenced by Karl W. Deutsch, my former teacher and present colleague. From William T. R. Fox I gained insight into subtleties of international political behavior that only a man with keen awareness and long experience can sense. Other colleagues whose influence upon my thinking undoubtedly enriched this book include, Hayward R. Alker Jr., Annette Baker Fox, Leland M. Goodrich, Ernst B. Haas, Morton Kaplan, Catherine M. Kelleher, Richard L. Merritt, Bruce M. Russett, and Warner R. Schilling. Added and special thanks are extended to Catherine M. Kelleher, who read my manuscript, commented extensively upon it, and thereby contributed immeasurably to improving the final version. Preparation of the manuscript was superbly handled by Mrs. Mary Stevens. Magnanimously patient editors at Dodd, Mead & Company guided *International Politics Today* to publication.

D.J.P.

CONTENTS

FIGURES

TABLES

INTERNATIONAL POLITICS TODAY

CHAPTER ONE
INTERNATIONAL POLITICS
AND ITS SETTING

STUDYING international politics means studying patterns of political interaction between and among states. Understanding international politics means understanding how, when, and why such states are born; how, when, and why they perish; and how, when, and why they rise or decline in power, wealth, and status. To understand international politics also means tracing the reasoning behind foreign policies and discerning why some policies succeed while others fail. Beyond this, it means answering "how," "when," and "why" addressed to wars fought or avoided, treaties concluded or broken, coalitions formed or dissolved, and world leaders famous or notorious. Finally, at abstract levels above specific phenomena and personalities, understanding international politics means understanding the geography of interstate conflict and cooperation, the economics of national development and defense, the anthropology of cultural interaction, the social-psychology of international integration, the psychology of coercion and compliance, and the history of statecraft. Given the immensity of the subject, no single book on international politics can do more than point the way toward understanding. This book pretends to do no more.

There is presently no single method for ordering the subject matter of international politics that is wholly satisfactory, since no theory of international politics yet proposed, nor any particular approach to the study of the subject yet devised, adequately takes full account of the range and complexity of phenomena that occur in relations among states. For this reason this book's framework for the study of international politics rests upon an eclectic foundation. The descriptions

and explanations that emerge in succeeding chapters have been arrived at by juxtaposing the findings, insights, and approaches of many
scholars and statesmen who have separately broadened our understanding of particular aspects of international affairs. Hence, this book
is, as a textbook should be, primarily an attempt at synthesis.

A FRAMEWORK FOR INTERNATIONAL POLITICAL ANALYSIS

No effort at theoretical synthesis can be successful unless separate
ideas, theories, findings, and insights are fitted into a central framework
or design. Accordingly, the design for this book is built about three
propositions concerning the fundamental nature of international politics. Explaining these propositions is the purpose of this chapter.
Elaborating upon them is the task of the book.

Proposition I: International politics are, by definition, *politics.*
Therefore, strategies, processes, and patterns observable in international politics are similar in fundamental ways to strategies, processes,
and patterns characteristic of politics generally. The one distinctive
difference between international politics and politics generally is that
most political processes commonly take place within systems framed
by governing institutions, regulated by administrative authorities, and
grounded in accepted rules and laws. In contrast, international politics
is politics without government. The international political system is
made up of multiple, autonomous policy-making centers that are
neither responsible to any central authority, nor even necessarily
responsive to one another. Nor finally, does any comprehensive body
of law exist at the international level to lend order or predictability to
interstate relations.

Proposition II: International politics, or relations among states, take
place within a world social, economic, cultural, technological, and
psychological setting or *environment.* While "politics" aptly describes
the *form* of relations among states, as will be shown below, problems
and opportunities created by prevailing conditions in the world environment constitute the *substance* of such relations. States interact
politically over economic, social, technological, ideological, cultural,
and other substantive issues. Characteristics of the world environment
change, of course, with time. But at all times, satisfactions or dissatisfactions with conditions prevailing in this environment define states'

international political goals and motivate their international political actions. In general, states seek either to preserve characteristics of the world environment which they deem favorable, or else they seek to alter characteristics which they find detrimental. The attempts of particular states to preserve or alter the characteristics of the world environment, and the reactions of other states to such attempts form the dynamics of international politics.

Proposition III: International political action, as all political action, requires the investment of resources both human and material. No state can hope to preserve or alter the world environment, or to combat others' attempts to do so, without setting men, money, and materials to the task. Therefore, a state's endowment of resources combined with statesmen's talents for using these define its capabilities for international political action. Understandably, states with greater capabilities hold greater potential for international political accomplishment. In international politics capabilities are the links between motivation and action.

In general then, "politics" defines the *form* of interaction among states in the international system. Conditions prevailing in the world environment lend *purpose* to state actions and *substance* to interactions among states. Capabilities link motivation to accomplishment. Understanding this trilogy of themes is the formula for mastering this book. But more important, grasping relationships among these themes and their implications is the key to understanding international politics.

POLITICS IN GENERAL AND INTERNATIONAL POLITICS IN PARTICULAR

Politics are those varieties of human interaction that, in Harold Lasswell's words, decide *who gets what, when, and how.*[1] Political behavior is goal-seeking behavior; and politics result whenever, and wherever, men, groups, or organizations interact in their goal-seeking pursuits. The "whos," "whats," "whens," and "hows" of politics vary with time, place, and situation; but the basic goal-seeking nature of political interaction remains constant.

Moving one step further, a *political system* can be defined as a collection of men or groups who interact in their goal-seeking pursuits.

1. Harold D. Lasswell, *Politics: Who Gets What, When, How* (Cleveland: The World Publishing Company, 1958).

According to this definition there can be an extensive variety of political systems characterized by collections of different kinds of political actors, pursuing an almost infinite variety of specific goals, using various means under varying circumstances and conditions. Political systems could, for example, include individuals interacting in pursuit of influence in any organization, in interest groups, or in parties interacting in pursuit of influence over governments, and could include states interacting in the pursuit of influence over the world environment.

Several analytical characteristics of the *international political system* are noteworthy. First, as mentioned above, the components or basic units of the system are states, sometimes many or sometimes few depending upon historical era and the strength of pressures toward either international amalgamation or fragmentation. Second, the international political system assumes various structures according to the number, relative size, relative might, and relative influence of various component states. These too vary with time, with the fortunes of states, and with pressures for amalgamation or fragmentation. Analysts see the contemporary international political system as *loosely bipolar* in structure with essentially two centers of world power, influence, and attention—the United States and the Soviet Union—and possessing clusterings of client states about the centers, and a scattering of non-aligned states ranged between poles. Alternative structurings for the international system might include a *tight bipolar* configuration, wherein the nonaligned states gravitate toward alignment; a *multipolar* configuration, where power and influence are nearly equally shared by several major states; or a *unipolar* configuration, where one major state successfully maintains world ascendance.[2] Variations of all of the polar configurations are of course possible, and many are historically observable. Third, the international political system, as do most political systems, passes through phases of *stability,* wherein actors remain viable, their actions remain generally predictable, and their interactions buttress (or at least do not threaten) normal systemic structure and processes. The international political system is also susceptible to phases of *instability,* wherein some actors may lose their viability, actions become generally unpredictable, and inter-

2. Morton A. Kaplan, *System and Process in International Politics* (New York: John Wiley, 1950), pp. 21–53.

actions threaten the continuity of the system. Instability in an international system sometimes precedes *systemic transformation,* in which a new system with new structure and new patterns of interaction among components replaces an older, undermined system. Instability and systemic transformation, for example, marked the passage from the multipolar system of the nineteenth and early twentieth centuries to the contemporary loose bipolar system. Some argue that sources of instability in our own system may be driving international politics back into a multipolar configuration.

More will be said later in this book concerning stability and instability in international systems. It is essential at the outset, however, that the student and reader acquaint themselves with some of the vocabulary of systems analysis used above. The terms will recur. They have precise meanings in the study of international politics.

Patterns of Political Interaction. There are three common varieties or patterns of political interaction observable in all political systems. First, politics may be, and often are, reflected in *competitive interaction,* in which the attainment of goals by one political actor is incompatible with the attainment of goals by other actors in the political system. Second, politics may be, and surprisingly often are, reflected in *cooperative interaction,* in which goal attainment is facilitated or expedited by the complementary efforts of different political actors. Finally, and most realistically, politics may be reflected in *mixed competitive/cooperative interaction,* in which actors pursue multiple goals, some of which are incompatible and give rise to contention, while others are compatible and are therefore sought through complementary efforts.[3]

1. Competitive political interaction takes the form of a "zero-sum game," in which, at the outcome, one actor clearly "wins" and others clearly "lose." A national presidential election in the United States, for example, approximates a case of purely competitive political interaction. All candidates seek the same single office, so that goal-attainment by one must be incompatible with goal-attainment by others. Hence, in attempting to "win," each candidate must adopt a competitive strategy wherein he strives to enhance his own standing with the electorate while striving to undermine the standing of his opponents.

3. Thomas C. Schelling, *The Strategy of Conflict* (Cambridge: Harvard University Press, 1960), pp. 83–118.

In countries where political competition for the office of chief executive results in absolute power for the "winner" and political banishment (or worse) for the "loser," the intensity of the political contest may readily escalate to armed violence.

In international politics, interaction of the "pure competition" variety is observable in arms races, in which each contender's striving after military predominance is incompatible with the similar striving of others. Competitive interaction is also part and parcel of contests for ideological influence, in which adherence to one "political faith" is taken as incompatible with adherence to another. Certainly, pure competition in international politics is also to be found in the process of total wars, in which victors acquire empires and the vanquished lose their existence as autonomous political entities. Because the stakes in international competition can be very high (sometimes literally life and death) and because conflict control mechanisms are either weak or lacking in the international system, political competition at the international level frequently assumes violent forms.

2. While the image of "politics as competition" is readily accepted by student, journalist, and man-in-the-street, the fact that *cooperation* is also a political process is sometimes overlooked. Cooperation is a central part of politics. In contrast to the zero-sum form of the competitive political game, cooperative interaction produces mutual rewards from joint efforts toward goal attainment—i.e., all players can "win." Legislative outcomes in the United States Congress, for example, follow quite directly from patterns of cooperation among individuals, factions, and voting blocks. Similarly, in multiparty political systems such as those in Italy, the Netherlands or Japan, control over the national government depends upon the ability of factions to cooperate in forming governing coalitions. Here, failure to cooperate can result not only in undermining opportunities of reluctant groups for greater influence, but also in critical governmental instability.

Cooperation takes many forms in international politics. This process is at the heart of alliance formation, wherein states attain greater security collectively than would be attainable by any state acting alone. Relatedly, international political cooperation is also at the heart of regional integration, wherein separate states merge to form military units more powerful, economic units more prosperous, and political units more influential than any of the smaller national components.

Further, international cooperation is central to arms control, in which states enhance their mutual security by reducing the danger or destructiveness of war between them. Less spectacularly, international cooperation also includes expressions of diplomatic support, the offering of foreign aid, the sharing of world communications facilities, and the prosecution of various joint technical programs. Thus, while newspaper headlines may not show it, international cooperation is a major, meaningful, and growing dimension of international politics.

3. While the descriptions "competitive" or "cooperative" characterize particular varieties of political interaction among actors in a political system, the full scope of relations between any pair of actors can best be described as a *mixture of cooperation and competition.* It is rare when political actors either compete or cooperate *all the time.* More often, and more realistically, we can expect to observe political actors continually pursuing multiple goals, simultaneously competing to attain some of these and cooperating to attain others.

An example of mixed competition and cooperation in American politics was observable during the late 1940's and early 1950's, when strong interparty rivalry and contests concerning domestic economic ·and social issues contrasted markedly with bipartisanship in foreign policy. More generally, mixed competition and cooperation is the hallmark of most constitutionally based political systems, in which actors compete incessantly over specific issues and policy goals, but simultaneously cooperate in limiting their competition to constitutionally prescribed channels and constitutionally acceptable means.

What is true of domestic politics with regard to modes of mixed competition and cooperation is certainly true also of international politics. For example, if "peaceful coexistence" is at all descriptive of American-Soviet relations at present, what it means is that both states will compete with gusto in furthering their basically incompatible world goals. But, at the same time, they will cooperate in limiting their competition to the realm of nonviolence, or at least to levels of violence below the nuclear threshold. Despite sharp disagreements about the desirable future of the world, the superpower antagonists apparently share the goal of preserving civilization and interact cooperatively in pursuing this goal. Another, and even more explicit, example of mixed competition and cooperation in international politics is to be found in the case of limited wars of the Korean War variety. Here the actors have competed violently for control over a specific territory. But, here too, contenders have also cooperated in limiting their competition to that specific territory.

The point here of emphasizing the importance of conceiving political relations as mixtures of competition and cooperation—not to belabor the obvious—is made to alert readers to some of the complexities of international political analysis which become keys to understanding in later chapters. Perspective can be lost when political relations are approached in "either-or" terms. As noted, specific interactions between or among states may be either competitive or cooperative. But modes of political relations among states are seldom either *wholly* competitive or *wholly* cooperative. They are usually a bit of both. Hence, analyzing political relations always involves examining both their competitive and their cooperative aspects.

Finally, and importantly, it must be remembered that political interaction is a prevailing form of human behavior. In value it is neither necessarily "good," nor necessarily "bad." Competitive and cooperative goal-seeking are simply parts of human social dynamics. Globally, barring the emergence of complete abundance and universal idyllic satisfaction, or barring total nuclear war and no world at all, there are always going to be values and goals that men and states are going to seek, and they are going to compete or cooperate to reach them. International politics, then, are unlikely to disappear.

This final point is put forward strongly here in part to combat the common belief that politics are the roots of all evil, and in part to expose the misconception that achieving world peace will follow from dispensing with international politics. Certainly, the results of intense political competition can bring tragedy. But the results of world political cooperation can bring global, social, and economic betterment. Dispensing with politics, or at least with competitive politics, at the international level might bring world peace. But, realistically, is it possible to dispense with politics, to curtail human goal-seeking, or to make everyone's goals always compatible? The obvious negative answer to such questions clearly suggests that moving toward world peace, both within and among states, requires *controlling political competition* rather than eliminating politics. Hence, no matter how the reader may be attitudinally predisposed toward international politics and no matter how the author may feel during his lapses into whimsy, analysis and criticism in this book will continue to rest upon the proposition that political behavior is an ineradicable aspect of human behavior and on its corollary, that the only realistically conceivable world peace is one that somehow accommodates international politics.

SOME DISTINCTIVE FEATURES OF INTERNATIONAL POLITICS

Recognizing and pointing out similarities between international politics and politics in general, as in the preceding section, is important first because these similarities are sometimes overlooked in approaches to the study of international politics, and second because looking upon international politics as politics opens the way to studying interactions among states by using standard tools of political analysis. On the other hand, searching out similarities between international politics and domestic politics must not blind one to significant differences between them.

The most important differences between international and domestic politics stem from the fact that no central institution or set of institutions or practices exist in the international system to perform the allocative, regulatory, and arbitrating functions that governments perform in domestic systems. In short, international politics is politics without government. Relations among autonomous states, then, approximate a politics of anarchy. The impacts and implications of the absence of central government in the international system lend a distinctive flavor and style to international political interaction.

In a typical domestic system, the government normally performs a variety of allocative and regulatory functions. A government may, for example, allocate wealth by distributing and redistributing income; it may allocate enlightenment by offering public education; it may allocate influence and status by favoring or suppressing the aspirations of certain individuals and groups. Similarly, a government may regulate and control a range of social, economic, and political activities by supporting or suppressing social mobility, by intervening to contain economic fluctuations, or by acting administratively or coercively to limit political competition to constitutional channels and nonviolent means. The government thus makes rules for society, enforces these, and adjudicates disputes about them. It is able to act effectively first because individuals and groups in society accept its activities as legitimate and therefore comply with its decisions. Ultimately, however, a government is effective because it generally holds a monopoly or near monopoly over the instruments of coercion available in society. It can enforce compliance if it must.

Looking more closely at the role of government in a typical society, it becomes clear that governing institutions and processes function as arbiters among political interests. In a democratic pluralist system, for example, institutions and processes of government normally provide mechanisms for the expression of common interest among groups, and for the conciliation and compromise of their differing interests. Government in an authoritarian system, on the other hand, provides the mechanism whereby the interests of a dominating group are imposed upon a society and whereby interests of dissenting groups are suppressed. Hence, a government may be a just or biased arbiter. But, no matter which, as an arbiter it becomes the ultimate center for building political consensus and resolving political conflicts in a society. In all but revolutionary situations, governments can successfully act to settle, or at least control, political disputes arising from clashes in goal-seeking among individuals and groups in a society.

But what happens to allocation, regulation, and arbitration when central government is absent? Clearly, the political system is transformed from one endowed with a single center of consensus formation, conflict resolution, and rule-making, into one characterized by basically uncontrollable, multiple, autonomous political groups. What must emerge in the absence of government is an "every actor for himself" political world. In such a world, no single actor may act to perform the allocative and regulatory functions performed by a central government. Instead, each separate political group acts independently, through competitive and cooperative interaction with others, to allocate rewards and regulate behavior in the overall system in ways favorable to itself. Therefore, distributions of rewards in such a system follow from groups' successes or failures at advancing self-interest rather than from consensus generated or compromises reached through processes of government.

More than this, in a system of autonomous groups, actions undertaken by one group are not necessarily (and indeed are very often not at all) viewed as legitimate by other groups. Therefore, effecting allocation or regulation by voluntary compliance in the normal manner of a government, is uncommon in a system of autonomous groups. In such a system one group's ability to influence others depends either upon its leaders' skills in demonstrating mutual self-interest, or, more often upon their ability and willingness to credibly threaten and actually employ coercion. Fundamentally, in the absence of government, the only way that one political group may ultimately influence a second resistant group is by imposing its will by force. Fundamentally too, the only way a group can ultimately resist another's influence in such a system is by defending its positions with force. Therefore, resort to violence as a form of conflict resolution tends to be much more common in a system of autonomous groups than in one controlled by a central government. In the ungoverned system no accepted or imposable central mechanism exists to guide or force groups into nonviolent conflict resolution. No center holds a monopoly over coercive instruments, and hence no center can deter violence among groups by threatening overwhelming counter-violence. Ultimately, no center can act to preserve the overall political system if the autonomous groups that compose it act to destroy it.

The international political system (or a domestic system on the brink or in the throes of revolution) approximates the model of politics among autonomous groups. In international politics, each state acts in its own self-interest in trying to allocate rewards or regulate behavior in the larger international political system. Moreover, in the international political system there is no universally accepted or imposable mechanism for nonviolently reconciling conflicting interests among states in the interest of stability or continuity for the larger system. No state that chooses not to be influenced by another can in fact be influenced except by defeat on a battlefield. All states possess and intermittently wield instruments of violence in pursuing their self-interests. Hence, the absence of central governing institutions and processes defines both the distinctiveness and the dilemma of political relations among states. International politics are politics without government. But without government, international politics readily become a politics of inherent violence.

Several factors, however, modify the prevailing anarchy of international politics to make political life at the interstate level something less than the "nasty, brutish and short" existence postulated in the Hobbesian "state of nature."[4] First, as noted already, international interaction is as often characterized by the pursuit of mutual or compatible self-interests among states—i.e., cooperation—as it is by the pursuit of conflicting self-interests. Second, although self-interest is the prime stimulus behind international political action, considerations concerning the stability and continuity of the larger international system do frequently complement, influence, or modify states' self-seeking pursuits. Students of the eighteenth- and nineteenth-century European "balance of power," for example, point out that preserving the balance, and hence the stability, of the larger international system weighed equally or identically in certain statesmen's calculations with the pursuit of more specific *national* interests. Similarly, it might be suggested that the restrained use of violence by a number of states at present stems first from fears of nuclear annihilation, but also from desires to preserve contemporary civilization. In short, the ungoverned separate and independent pursuit of self-interests characteristic of international politics need not be dysfunctional to the stability of the international political system. Third, in the actual playing out of the international political game, diplomacy rather than military action is the preferred means for resolving conflicts of interest. Moreover, diplomacy more often succeeds than fails since few states prefer warfare as long as concession and compromise remain possible. Hence, while the international system is structured for a politics of confrontation, this structure does not preclude consensual processes.

Fourth, though nothing resembling a world government exists to overarch and integrate the international political system, there exists a fragmentary body of universally recognized and accepted international law, and there also exist several regional and universal international organizations that exercise some allocative and regulatory control over some facets of relations between and among states. International law and international organizations exist, of course, because states see the existence of such bodies as complementary to their self-interests. Nevertheless, international organizations do exist and operate; they are accepted and often respected; and they do restrain international anarchy to a certain extent.

4. Kenneth N. Waltz, *Man, the State, and War* (New York: Columbia University Press, 1959), pp. 159–186.

Finally, in a normative dimension, in all eras in international political history, and perhaps particularly in our own, there has intermittently appeared a universalism in recognition of a common humanity that supersedes political divisions among states. At certain times this universalism has been more loudly proclaimed than at others, and indeed at no time has the voice of world community ever been terribly effective. Nevertheless, advocates of world community do succeed in raising inescapable normative questions about the morality of narrow self-interestedness in international behavior, the excusability of resorts to violence, and the rectitude in empire. Few statesmen have been able to completely ignore the moral questions and implications of their international political actions, or to completely circumvent the moral dilemmas generated in the juxtaposition of national interests and larger human concerns.[5] The student of international politics, therefore, cannot help but note that many instances of restraint in international behavior, instances of self-abnegation, and other deviations from the expected anarchy of international life, must be explained at least partly in terms of statesmen's sensitivities to morality. The structure of international politics condones an amoral game, but the players are, after all, men.

POLITICS IN THE INTERNATIONAL ENVIRONMENT

Thinking about international politics in terms of the fundamental nature of politics and in terms of the structure of the international system helps to establish a partial framework for analysis by focusing attention on the political game and the way it is played. Still, such game theoretic thinking falls short of explaining what the game is all about. Knowing that international politics means states interacting in the pursuit of goals, is not the same as knowing which states are likely to interact in pursuing which goals and why. Answering these more specific questions requires an exploration of the relationships between peoples' values and characteristics of the international environment. As noted earlier, the *processes* of international politics are competition and cooperation. But the *substance* of international politics is in

5. Arnold Wolfers, *Discord and Collaboration* (Baltimore: The Johns Hopkins Press, 1962), pp. 47–66.

states' attempts to preserve or acquire that which they value, and to alter that which they abhor.

The International Political Environment. An omniscient observer, surveying the world in any given period in time, might make the following observations. First, with the aid of a map, he might note that the territorial space and population of the globe are subdivided into reasonably distinct units of varying size. By observing communications cables and transportation lines, he can conclude that the peoples within the different territorial units communicate with one another, and, by tapping the content of their communications, he can conclude that they sometimes cooperate with one another. He also observes, however, that armies periodically move across the demarcation lines separating the territorial units, and, at these times, tiny bits of metal fly profusely through the air. From these observations he can conclude that the different peoples do not always cooperate with one another—indeed, they sometimes attempt to destroy one another. So far our observer has gained a view of the international political game in operation.

But he is also likely to see a good deal more than a collection of states cooperatively and competitively interacting. He might, for example, note that the collection of states includes a variety of internal political systems; a variety of social systems and social structures; a variety of economic systems; and a variety of cultural, philosophical, and ideological systems. In addition, he might further note that the collection of states comprising the international political system forms a number of hierarchies structured according to states' endowments of material and nonmaterial attributes. Here, for example, he can observe that states differ according to relative military might, according to wealth, according to technological advancement and accomplishment, and according to the relative respect and prestige they accord to one another. The exact ranking of the different states in the various hierarchies tends to be blurred. But, in most cases, those states near the top, those clustering about the middle, and those lying near the bottom are distinguishable. In all, the political, social, economic, cultural, and ideological diversity, and the hierarchies and distributions structured according to endowments of material and nonmaterial attributes that our observer notes, together constitute the international political environment. This is the setting for the international political game.

The most important relationship between the international political environment and the behavior of states in international politics lies in the fact that satisfactions or dissatisfactions with the environment, or aspects of it, provide motivations for international political action. To be more explicit, goal-seeking in international politics reduces conceptually to statesmen's attempts to preserve or alter characteristics of the world environment in order to bring about a consonance or compatibility between their values, or the values of their societies, and the external environment surrounding them. Practically, this means that states negotiate, bargain, entice, threaten, or fight in order to nurture or preserve the kind of world they would like to live in. This, in a nutshell, is what international politics are about! The ideologically bound Communist, for example, likely feels uncomfortable in a world environment characterized by a diversity of political-economic systems. He would probably be more comfortable in a world of communist states, and, correspondingly, he would be prone to act in international politics to nurture a world environment more consonant with his ideological values. Similarly, the statesmen and peoples of emerging nations may well believe that a world environment characterized by a gaping and growing "have-have not" split critically threatens their well-being and status. Accordingly, they may seek to act in international politics in efforts to narrow disparities in the world distribution of wealth. As noted in a later chapter, states' international political preferences in general (i.e., the characteristics of worlds they would wish to live in) can be topically categorized under self-preservation, security, prosperity, and prestige. Beyond this, the values of any given people are embodied in their political creeds or traceable in the philosophical roots of their society and culture.

Objective and Subjective Factors in the Environment-Goal Relationship. For several reasons, examining the environment of international politics and the relationship between environmental characteristics and political action turns out to be a more complicated undertaking than it might at first appear. As noted earlier, the world environment, to an omniscient observer, appears as a set of diversities and distributions in such factors as political, economic, and social systems; cultural patterns; military and technological capabilities; and the like. Hence, upon *objective* observation, our contemporary world environment would be characterized by a great many autonomous political units of varying size, with great diversity in governmental structure, ideological adherence, economic system, cultural patterns and norms, and social structure. At the same time, objective observation would show our world essentially bipolarized in military capability, wealth, technological advancement, and international prestige. By similar objective assessment, the late eighteenth- or early nineteenth-century world environment would undoubtedly be very differently described; and, in all likelihood, the world environment of the twenty-first century will differ considerably from our world environment today. The point here is that the world environment can be *objectively* described as it exists at given points in time. Here the social scientist can assume the role of omniscient observer, if he so desires, by reconstructing and mapping the world environment from data presented in statistical yearbooks and other national and international reference works.[6]

But while such objective reconstructions of the world environment may be generally enlightening, they are of limited usefulness for explaining goals and motivations in international political behavior. There are at least two reasons for this:

First, statesmen seldom observe their environment in a strictly objective manner. For many reasons, having to do with cultural conditioning, ideological indoctrination, and psychological gratification or avoidance, men's perceptions of their environment tend to be somewhat incomplete, often inaccurate, and usually biased in some way by personality factors.[7] Therefore, the world perceived by international political actors may differ markedly from the environment perceived by an objective observer. In such a case, the objective characteristics of the environment would provide rather poor guides to explaining actors' behaviors. More meaningful here would be attempts to reconstruct the international environment *as perceived* by particular statesmen.

Some examples display this point. If Chinese Communist literature is accepted as a guide, we can conclude that the Peking Government's perception of the world environment differs greatly from "objective reality," or at least from our own perceptions. For one thing, the government of the Chinese People's Republic tends to perceive all of the

6. See, for example, Bruce M. Russett, *et al., World Handbook of Political and Social Indicators* (New Haven: Yale University Press, 1964), *passim.*

7. Ralph K. White, "Images in the Context of International Conflict: Soviet Perceptions of the U.S. and the U.S.S.R.," in *International Behavior,* Herbert C. Kelman, ed. (New York: Holt, Rinehart and Winston, 1965), pp. 236–276.

Western countries, the United States especially, as rent by extreme class conflict and working-class alienation. While this characteristic of the Chinese Communist world view may have little basis in fact, this aspect of the world *as Peking sees it* may provide insights into and explanations for Chinese international behavior—i.e., the Chinese attempt to exploit class conflicts in the West because the Chinese "see" class conflicts in the West. On the other hand, simply pointing out the objective fallacy in the C.P.R. view would leave one puzzled as to why the Chinese are behaving in a particular manner. Similarly, while Nasser's perceptual subdivision of the world political-ideological environment into "imperialist" and "anti-imperialist" forces may again have had little foundation in objective reality, explaining the former Egyptian leader's international political behavior might here again pivot on reconstructing the world *as Nasser saw it*. That is, a key to Nasser's behavior was in the way *he* perceived the world regardless of the accuracy of his perception. Hence, for purposes of international political analysis one must go well beyond viewing the world environment as it exists in fact. *What is important is how statesmen see the world.*

Second, and relatedly, even in cases where statesmen perceive characteristics of the international environment relatively accurately, the key to their probable behavior is not as much in what they see as in how they interpret their observations. Again, meaningful analysis drives one toward looking at the world through statesmen's eyes. For example, while both Western and Eastern statesmen can observe the United States in the top position in the international military hierarchy, the former might assess this as a highly satisfactory state of affairs, while the latter would undoubtedly evaluate the situation negatively. Consequently, the West would likely want to act to preserve the observed military hierarchy; the East, on the other hand, would likely wish to alter it. Clearly, what is important for understanding the environment-goal relationship here is that *observed characteristics of the world environment were evaluated by statesmen, and our predictions concerning behavior follow from knowledge concerning both their observations and their evaluations.*

Though it may appear as dwelling on a relatively minor point, emphasis here upon subjective factors in the environment-goal relationship is deliberate. The point, simply summarized, is that different people perceive and react to the world around them in different ways.

This being the case, it is essential for the student of international politics to develop facilities for observing the world through statesmen's eyes, and for shifting and sorting world views as analytical attention moves from actor to actor. A central question in international political analysis is: "How does the world look to *him,* and how does *he* feel about what *he* sees?" This question will be raised recurrently throughout this book. It is a key to understanding international politics.

CAPABILITIES FOR INTERNATIONAL POLITICAL ACTION

While examining the international political environment helps to explain goals and motivations in political behavior, it is unrealistic to suppose that statesmen actually move to pursue all of the goals that their satisfactions or dissatisfactions with the environment prompt. More realistically, we can assume that statesmen normally pursue only those objectives which they are capable of pursuing. Political action requires and consumes resources—men, money, materials, and the like—and the scope of a given state's operations tends to be delimited by resource availability. Therefore, control over adequate resources becomes the link between motivations toward international political action and the action itself.

Since an entire section of this book will later be devoted to taking inventory of capabilities for international political action, it is unnecessary to go into particulars at this point. Still, a number of general observations concerning capabilities for international action should be made in this introduction.

First, as noted earlier, the pursuit of any goal—social, economic, or political; individual, organizational, national, or international— requires an investment of human and material resources. Pointing out this relationship between action and resource consumption possibly belabors the obvious. Yet, the point is so basic to understanding international political behavior that it must be underlined. Whenever states act in the pursuit of international objectives, they consume resources: men are paid, materials are allocated, time is spent, and reputations are tested. Consequently, the quantities and qualities of resources available to states for foreign-policy purposes index their capabilities for international political action.

At the same time, it should be noted that measuring a state's capabilities in terms of resource endowments accurately gauges its abilities to act only if it is assumed that resources are controlled and allocated with maximum efficiency. That is, ability to act depends both upon possessing resources and upon using them appropriately and efficiently. History shows many instances where states wasted large, high-quality resource endowments to the detriment of international goal attainment, as well as instances where states used relatively small resource endowments with high efficiency to attain major international goals.

Second, while part of the relationship between states' goals and their capabilities has to do with adjusting objectives to match resources, states are rarely so well endowed with resources that they can act to fashion exactly the kind of world they would most like to live in. The ancient Romans perhaps approached such a situation for a short time during their ascendance. But no state since ancient times has been able to shape the world exactly to its liking, because no state has been able to muster, control, and allocate the resources that would be required for such an undertaking. In actuality, most states' international activities would have only minimal impacts upon the overall world environment even if these states allocated all of their resources to international political ends. Therefore, for most states, goal-seeking in international politics is a process of seeking the most favorable environment attainable with limited means. In short, goals are adjusted to suit resource availabilities.

Third, allocating resources to support pursuits, and adjusting objectives to match available resources both involve establishing priorities in goal-seeking and hierarchies among goals. Not only do states rarely have the capabilities to impose their grandest designs upon the world environment, but they also often lack sufficient capabilities to simultaneously pursue all of their more limited goals with equal vigor. Hence, statesmen tend to assign priorities to their pursuits in the international arena, with the result that limited resources are allocated to objectives in order of urgency or salience. Relatedly, resource constraints often lead to phased international programs in which short-run activities are directed toward enhancing capabilities so that these may be used in later phases for more ambitious international undertakings. The point here is to underline again that actors' motivations, intentions, and objectives can be restrained by their capabilities. As noted in this section, available capabilities limit both the ambitiousness of goals and the number of goals that may be pursued simultaneously.

Fourth, and finally, any discussion of capabilities for action in international politics, as well as any attempt to analyze the role of capabilities in international political behavior, must take account of the fact that *perceived* capabilities may differ considerably from actual capabilities. Most important, statesmen tend to match goals with capabilities *as they perceive them;* and errors of overestimation and underestimation have had markedly dramatic impacts upon the history of international politics.

If statesmen were always able to assess their states' capabilities, their friends' capabilities, and the enemies' capabilities with perfect accuracy, international politics might approximate a logical pattern in which political strategy would become a science; each actor would pursue only those objectives he was capable of pursuing; and actors seldom would make strategic mistakes, seldom bring disaster upon themselves, and seldom fall short of their goals. Such a "logical" pattern is clearly not the case in international politics (at least not very often), and an important reason why it is not is that statesmen often misperceive both their own capabilities and the relative distribution of capabilities among other actors in the international system. Since resources for international political action include many intangibles such as national morale, character, and endurance under duress, it is understandable that no wholly accurate assessment of a given state's capabilities can be made. That is, capability for international political action is essentially unmeasurable. Hence, in this sense, the difference between the successful and the unsuccessful statesman may reduce to their differential abilities to make judgments about the intangibles of international political capability. Leaders of the German Empire during World War I misassessed the United States' capabilities. Frenchmen in World War II misassessed both their own capabilities and those of Germany. The Japanese in the same war underestimated American resilience and determination. Americans in 1949 misperceived the relative capabilities of Nationalist and Communist forces in China. Arab leaders surely overestimated their own capabilities and underestimated Israeli capabilities in the summer of 1967. In nonmilitary affairs, optimism about economic development in emerging nations

voiced by Western leaders during the 1950's reflected an underassess-
ment of resources required for development and an overassessment of
industrialized countries' abilities to provide these.

In sum, then, international political action follows from objectives
that statesmen *think* they are able to pursue. Therefore, success or
failure in international goal-seeking follows to a considerable extent
from the accuracy of statesmen's capability assessments. By the same
token, depth in understanding concerning action in international
politics builds from students' facilities for assessing states' capabilities,
and for ascertaining the accuracy of statesmen's estimates of their own
and their neighbors' abilities to act internationally.

SUMMARY AND CONCLUSION

Understanding the general theoretical overview of international
politics offered in this chapter is pivotal to understanding the structure
and development of this book. In brief review, international politics
should be looked upon as goal-seeking behavior (i.e., political behavior)
pursued by political units (i.e., states) competitively and cooperatively
interacting in a political system characterized by the absence of strong
central institutional, constitutional, or normative restraints. The numbers, configurations, and identities of international political units, and
their goals and fortunes all change with time. But the basic competitive
and cooperative goal-seeking nature of the international political
process remains constant.

Goals pursued in international politics emerge from consonances
or dissonances between the social, cultural, economic, and political-
ideological values of peoples, or their leaders, and the social, economic,
political, ideological, cultural, and technological characteristics of the
overall world environment. Motivations to act in international politics
are, basically, drives to preserve or alter characteristics of the world
environment. The varieties of goals that states pursue in international
politics change with time as characteristics of the world environment
change from the impacts of modernization or other secular or cyclical
forces, and from the impacts of states' successful efforts to bring about
environmental alterations.

Finally, action in international politics follows from capabilities as
well as from motivations. Resources and talents for their efficient use

are prerequisites for international political action. Hence, motivations inspired by reactions to the world environment become international political goals, and goal-seeking becomes manifest action when re-sources are available and allocated to international pursuits. When two or more states interact in their goal-seeking pursuits, episodes in international politics are born.

The abstract features of international politics described in this chapter, and the explanations for the dynamics of international be-havior offered here, will become major topics for detailed and more substantive discussion in later sections and chapters:

Characteristics of international political units will be explored in Part I. Discussion here moves from a classical treatment of the state as the fundamental acting unit, to an investigation of kinds of states and of institutions and men that represent states in international politics. Finally, analysis in this section turns to foreign-policy formulation and to the processes and politics that produce demands for and drives toward international political action.

The focus in Part II is upon goals and motivations in international politics and, relatedly, upon relationships between environmental conditions and drives toward political action. Discussion in this sec-tion moves from more or less conventional attempts to take inventory of varieties of goals that states customarily pursue in international politics, to explorations of motivating forces that produce such differ-ing international political phenomena as wars, acts of imperialism, patterns of cooperation, and intermittent peace.

In Part III, attention is turned to questions of capabilities for inter-national political action. This section opens with a definition and discussion of power in international politics, and later includes an inventory of resources requisite for international political action. Ex-position here, however, moves rapidly beyond conventional "basic factors" considerations and into discussions of certain intangible, but centrally important, aspects of international political capability such as nationalism, emotional mobilization, and information handling. Efforts are made throughout Part III to explore perceptual as well as objective links between international political capabilities and international political behavior.

The substantive rewards from the theoretical elaborations of Parts I–III come in Part IV, where attention is focused upon international politics in the contemporary world environment. Here, the analytical tools fashioned and sharpened through most of the book are used to explore, describe, and explain international politics since World War II, and particularly since 1960. Changes in the structure of the international political system, evolutions and revolutions in the world environment, and changing distributions of international political capabilities become keys in Part IV to analyzing and explaining the course of the Cold War, movement toward and later away from political-military bipolarity, the practice and sophistication of nuclear deterrence, the new salience of arms control, the emergence of the "third world" and its impacts upon international politics, and the enhanced role and efficacy of international organization.

As noted earlier, this book is intended as a guide to the conceptual analysis of international politics. My purpose in it is to provide the student and interested reader with a framework for understanding international politics, within which it may become possible to organize, and evaluate the facts of day-to-day international political developments. If the framework presented here at times seems lacking in substance, this is only because priority was allotted to developing the conceptual structure. With this as the primary goal, time and space limitations necessarily had to limit the substance. In addition, the substance of international politics—the actions, reactions, interactions, and events in relations among states—change rapidly, so that contemporary substantive analysis offered today may very well turn out to be historical analysis when read tomorrow. Therefore, rather than to offer a chronology and interpretation of events, I think it more important to offer a set of concepts and tools for analyzing such events. Hence, reading and studying this book is not going to result in a detailed descriptive understanding of contemporary history. Nor will it substitute for reading, say, the last ten years' *New York Times*. However, if it provides the reader with a perspective for understanding the international political events of the next ten years, then my goal in writing it will be fulfilled.

PART ONE
ACTORS IN
INTERNATIONAL POLITICS

CHAPTER TWO
STATES AND STATESMEN
IN INTERNATIONAL POLITICS

ANSWERING "who" questions is a central and basic part of political analysis. In international political analysis such answers lead to identifying world political actors, examining their characteristics, and noting relationships between their characteristics and their behavior.

Since the sovereign state is conventionally, and accurately, considered the primary actor in international politics, it is appropriate to begin an analysis of actors with a discussion of the origin and characteristics of the sovereign state. Still, any discussion of actors that began and ended with the state would be lacking in depth, for the state, after all, is an abstraction. States as such neither act nor react, perceive or communicate, succeed or fail in international politics. The men who represent states in making and executing foreign policies, and the men who influence foreign policy-makers, are the true actors in international politics. Consequently, emphasis in this chapter is upon groups and individuals participant in typical tasks of policy formation and statesmanship.

ORIGINS AND CHARACTERISTICS OF THE MODERN STATE

A survey of world history reveals that the modern state, as we know it, is of relatively recent origin. Some historians date the emergence of the state in the seventeenth century. Others set this date either somewhat later or somewhat earlier. Even dating the emergence of the state from the early sixteenth century, however, leaves a broad span of time in which world political interaction was between units or forces that could not be called "states" in the modern sense. A long era of European political history, for example, is more appropriately characterized as a period of interactions among cultures, religions, or princes, rather than among states. Similarly, Renaissance and Ancient Greek political history is better characterized as a history of interactions among cities or principalities rather than states. Much of Oriental political history is the story of interactions among great cultures, and Ancient Mediterranean political history is the story of interactions among powerful tribes. Hence, the first questions we must ask about the modern state are: What is it? and What are its origins? These questions answer each other.

The modern state is best defined as "a sovereign territorial political unit." [1] This definition will be derived in a moment. Suffice it to say at this point that *sovereignty* implies external autonomy, and it also implies internal order and control over means for maintaining this order. *Territoriality* denotes a geographic perimeter or unit, and territoriality linked with sovereignty implies that external autonomy and internal order are characteristics of geographically defined units. *Political,* as explained in Chapter 1, implies interaction in goal-seeking behavior, so that the sovereign territorial political unit—the state—is, in the abstract, an externally autonomous, internally ordered geographic unit that interacts in its goal-seeking behavior with other such units. It becomes more meaningful to talk about states after we place people within the geographic perimeter and charge some of them with responsibility for maintaining external autonomy and internal order. But for the moment let us preserve the abstraction.

Tracing the emergence of the modern state helps both to clarify the meanings of "sovereignty" and "territoriality," and to pave the way for discussing the international political implications of these characteristics of states. The modern state is European in its origin. Its emergence was largely the product of the related supersession of central government over feudal decentralization and state autonomy over transcendent religious and secular authority in Europe during the sixteenth and seventeenth centuries generally, and during the Thirty Years' War, 1618–48, in particular. R. R. Palmer, in his *History of the Modern World,* descriptively captures the emergence of the modern

1. John H. Herz, *International Politics in the Atomic Age* (New York: Columbia University Press, 1959), pp. 39–61.

state system in two passages that amount to a "before and after" comparison of political organization in Europe at the beginning and at the end of the Thirty Years' War. Remarking in the first passage upon conditions at the outbreak of the war, Palmer notes that:

The Wars of Religion despite the religious ferocity shown by partisans of both sides, were no more religious than they were political. . . . [They] were essentially a new form of the old phenomenon of feudal rebellion against higher central authority. "Feudal" when the word is used of the 16th, 17th or 18th centuries, generally refers not to nobles only, but to all sorts of component groups having rights within the state, and so including towns and provinces, and even craft guilds and courts of law, in addition to the church and the noble class. It remained to be seen whether all these elements could be welded into one body politic. If the reader will recall how hard it is in the Twentieth Century to unify an army, navy and air force, or form a tariff union between two states, not to mention the problem of international government, he may be less puzzled as to why the history of Europe, for centuries, seems to consist of struggles between "feudal decentralization" and "central power."[2]

States existed territorially in medieval Europe, but these were seldom political units internally ordered under the authority of central governments or ruling houses. Instead, the predominant units of political organization in medieval Europe were feudal units smaller than medieval states—baronial fiefs, walled towns, monasteries, tradesmen's guilds, secular and clerical social classes, and the like—*and these units were often completely autonomous within their domains within the states*. Central authorities in the medieval states were often deficient in legitimacy, and, consequently, kings and princes could influence or control the activities of autonomous feudal groups only to the extent that they were willing and able to bring force to bear. Medieval history records numerous instances in which the coercive capabilities of central authorities were markedly inferior to the capabilities of feudal groups within their states. Hence, the picture that Palmer paints of feudal groups within states warring with central authorities and with one another for autonomy and aggrandizement is an accurate and vivid picture of relative anarchy within medieval states. This is a far cry from the internal order and central governmental control generally characteristic of modern sovereign states.

Just as internal order was not characteristic of the medieval state,

2. R. R. Palmer, *A History of the Modern World,* 2nd ed. (New York: Alfred A. Knopf, 1957), p. 114.

neither was external autonomy. During the medieval era, all states were formally, and from time to time actually, under the transcendent dominion of both a Holy Roman Emperor, charged with the maintenance of European political unity, and a Pope, responsible for the spiritual orthodoxy and unity of Christendom. Therefore, the external autonomy of medieval states was at least formally controlled and constrained by the efforts of temporal and religious authorities charged with overseeing different aspects of interstate relations. Even as internal control in the medieval era depended on force and the ability to use it, the influence of transcendent authority over medieval states depended largely upon the military capabilities of these higher authorities. States maneuvered and fought to thwart external control, and Holy Roman Emperors and Popes maneuvered and fought to impose and exercise overarching control. This struggle between local and transcendent authority became another phase of medieval political interaction. Palmer captures this phase and its outcome in a passage describing the conference at Westphalia that marked the end of the Thirty Years' War in 1648:

The Peace of Westphalia marked the advent in international law of the modern European system of sovereign states. No one any longer pretended that Europe had any significant unity, religious, political, or other. Statesmen delighted in the absence of any such unity, in which they sensed the menace of "universal monarchy." Europe was understood to consist in a large number of unconnected sovereignties, free and detached atoms, or states, which moved about according to their own laws, following their own political interests, forming and dissolving alliances, exchanging embassies and legations, alternating between war and peace, shifting position with a shifting balance of power.[3]

Hence, two developments combined during the sixteenth and seventeenth centuries to destroy the medieval state and feudal system, and to initiate the rise of the modern state and the modern state system. First, central authorities within medieval states succeeded, after decades or even centuries of civil strife, in undermining and dashing the political and military autonomy of feudal units within their domains. Next, and relatedly, these same kings and princes managed ultimately to seal their states against the demands and incursions of secular and religious transcendent authorities.

To elaborate the many reasons why central authorities were ulti-

3. *Ibid.*, p. 130.

mately able to gain superiority and impose order within their territorial domains is beyond the scope of this discussion. A deeper treatment, however, would have to take account of such factors as accretions in wealth in central treasuries from exploration and exploitation in the New World, improvements in military technology—in artillery especially—which rendered baronial castles and walled towns vulnerable, improvements in central administrative organization and efficiency, and impacts from religious schism that enhanced the legitimacy of secular authority.[4]

For purposes of this discussion, the impacts of internal consolidation in the medieval states are more important than the causes, because these impacts led directly to the enforcement of external autonomy and the emergence of the modern international system. One of the most important results of the internal consolidation of princely authority in medieval states was greatly increased power in the hands of central governments. In effect, the victory of "central authority" over "feudal decentralization" transferred absolute control over the human and material (and hence military and economic) resources of territorial units to the authorities governing these units. With the exception of the tiny German states, most of the newly ordered territorial units were sizable and therefore usually well endowed with resources that could be transformed into central governmental power.

New power was wielded by governments first to irreversibly complete their internal ascendancy, and then to exert and enforce their independence from transcendent authorities. New capabilities under the control of central governments served to render their territorial domains defensible against, and largely impermeable to, military thrusts directed by Holy Roman Emperors and Popes seeking to extract tribute or to otherwise realize their nominal hegemonic control. The result was that the imperial claims of these transcendent authorities were undermined; and in consequence, the international order of Europe was changed, *de facto,* from mythical unity in a Holy or Holy Roman empire, to fragmentation and a system of internally ordered and externally autonomous territorial political units. By the time the medieval jurists met at Westphalia in 1648, state sovereignty had become a fact. The modern state system had emerged.

4. Carl J. Friedrich, *Constitutional Government and Democracy* (Boston: Ginn & Company, 1950), pp. 5–100.

IMPACTS AND IMPLICATIONS OF STATE SOVEREIGNTY

A number of important analytical implications follow from this descriptive history of the emergence of the modern international system of sovereign states. These have to do first with the definition of sovereignty as "an objective state of affairs"; second, with the kind of international politics that results when political actors are sovereign units; and third, with relations between citizens or subjects, their governments, and the international order in a system of sovereign states.

First, it must be emphasized that the expression "state sovereignty" is descriptive of an objective state of affairs. The predominant actors in the international system *are* sovereign states. "State sovereignty" therefore is neither a creation of international lawyers, nor simply a phrase in legal jargon. It refers to internal order and external autonomy, and it suggests that international political interaction must be conceived and perceived in terms of a system of ordered, autonomous political actors. Not all states participating in international politics at the time of the Treaty of Westphalia, nor, surely, all states participating in international politics today are fully sovereign in an ideal sense. But if political units were located in two-dimensional space along continua that ran from "ordered" to "anarchic" and "autonomous" to "dependent" respectively, it could be observed that most political units actually participating in international politics are those that cluster in the "ordered-autonomous" quadrant. Units falling into other quadrants would be either unable or unwilling to participate. Hence, sovereignty has an operational meaning; a "sovereign state system" does in fact exist; and international politics acquires a number of notable characteristics as a result of the fact that "players in the game" are sovereign states.

Questions about the kinds of politics that result when sovereign states are the primary acting units were largely answered in Chapter 1 under the heading, "Some Distinctive Features of International Politics." As suggested there, politics among sovereign states amounts to a politics of anarchy in an arena where violence becomes the only tool ultimately available for exerting influence, and where warfare becomes the ultimately available means for settling disputes. As John Stoessinger tells us, "it is sovereignty more than any other single factor that is responsible for the anarchic condition of international relations." [5] Where each unit is legally autonomous, and where many units are able to preserve and protect their autonomy with military might, there is no reason why any unit should bend to the will of any other *when it does not wish to.* Neither is there any way to make such a unit submit short of demonstrating the inferiority of its military forces or actually defeating them in battle. To be sure, this is a rough and painful way to run a world. But it is the way the world of sovereign states has been running for centuries, despite noble and impressive attempts to change it.[6]

A world of sovereign states and a resultant politics of anarchy suggests a world of jeopardy for citizens residing within states. Since attack remains the ultimate instrument of international political persuasion, citizens may never completely alleviate the dread that a foreign government might attempt to violently exert its will. Moreover, though it is argued that nuclear weaponry and mutual deterrence have lowered probabilities of major war to near zero, few citizens in the West or the East are fully convinced that "the other side" is actually deterred, and few of us can help wondering about our fates in the event of a nuclear war. As Harold Lasswell suggests most eloquently, world politics is a continuing source of personal insecurity.[7]

Furthermore, personal insecurity may be compounded by the internal characteristics of state sovereignty. The state, by virtue of its sovereignty, is, *de facto,* the final arbiter over the life, death, or livelihood of every person residing within its territorial domain. The autonomy of the state means that there is no secular court of individual appeal above or beyond the government of the state. In consequence, citizens may be commanded or otherwise compelled to suffer for their states, to fight for them, and even to die for them. Flight from one state to another amounts simply to movement from one governmental jurisdiction to another, and flight from international politics seems impossible as long as one remains on this planet. For these reasons state sovereignty has traditionally been the target of anarchists, and

5. John G. Stoessinger, *The Might of Nations,* 3rd ed. (New York: Random House, 1969), p. 10.

6. F. H. Hinsley, *Power and the Pursuit of Peace* (Cambridge: The University Press, 1967), pp. 13–152.

7. Harold D. Lasswell, *World Politics and Personal Insecurity* (New York: McGraw-Hill, 1935).

the system of sovereign states has been a prime object of pacifists' outcryings.

But, while "world politics and personal insecurity" is surely a valid theme, it must also be pointed out that the emergence of the sovereign state has, in one important sense, heightened personal security. A world of sovereignties is nonetheless a world of relative order *within* states. History shows that the rise and predominance of the centrally governed state has considerably reduced the scale of world anarchy. As noted earlier, the age prior to the rise of the modern state was characterized—in Europe at least—by continual civil warfare, baronial feuding and by general internal disorder. When every feudal lord thought himself sovereign in his own domain, and when literally thousands of tiny sovereignties were scattered across Europe, the probability of continual violent conflict was extremely high; and the scale of anarchy increased in direct proportion to the expanding number of miniature feudal units. Constant civil turmoil took frightfully heavy tolls of civilian populations. On the other hand, the enforced civil order that followed the consolidation of major states drastically reduced the frequency of internal warfare, and consequently injected an element of relative security into citizens' lives. Hence, a world of sovereign states is at least a world where citizens within states are relatively protected from one another.

PEOPLE AS ACTORS IN INTERNATIONAL POLITICS

One cannot talk at any length about actors in international politics without introducing *people* into the discussion. While the general characteristics of states give abstract form to the international system, the characteristics and behavior of the men who represent states in international politics are the real keys to understanding states' actions. International political moves are acts of human behavior, principally determined by men's motivations, perceptions, decisions, and directions. Analysis in international politics, therefore, must come rather quickly to questions about the men who act for states in world affairs concerning their characteristics, their behavior, and the reasons for their behavior. Answering these questions is the object of this book. Beginning to answer them is a goal of this chapter.

National Elites and International Action. To make a first approximation, one might assume that those men who govern states generally are those who speak for states in international politics. Social scientists call such groups "political classes," "influential strata," or *elites*. The political elite in any state is a relatively small group. Those directly influential in policies of government seldom number more than 5 percent of a state's population, and in some cases political influence is the privilege of far less than 1 percent. In short, "government is always government by the few, whether in the name of the few, the one, or the many." [8] Furthermore, in most states the political elite tends to be characteristically unrepresentative of the total population. Elite members are generally wealthier, more highly stationed socially, better educated or technically trained, more endowed with administrative, symbol manipulating, persuasive and coercive skills and talents, and more respected than average citizens or subjects in their states. Ascent to elite status may be by ascription or achievement or both; and personal distinction may be either a pathway to political elite membership, or a reward flowing from it. In sum, as Lasswell notes, "the influential are those who get most of what there is to get. . . . Those who get the most are the elite; the rest mass." [9]

Needless to say, there are no hard and fast "laws" linking elite characteristics to governmental behavior. Elites in different countries are so diverse in structure, membership, attitudes, and behavior, that elite study has not as yet produced very many analytically useful generalizations. Still, a number of findings are especially relevant to international political analysis. These deserve emphasis:

1. LINKAGES BETWEEN ELITE STRUCTURE AND FOREIGN POLICY BEHAVIOR. At the risk of considerable oversimplification, it can be said that two general models of elite structure and elite-mass interaction emerge from the theoretical literature of elite study. Let us call these the *monistic* and the *pluralistic* elite models.

One group of social theorists—including such nineteenth century figures as Karl Marx, the early twentieth century sociologists Gaetano Mosca and Vilfredo Pareto, later C. Wright Mills and his followers, and most recently social analysts of the New Left—perceive a hier-

8. Harold D. Lasswell, *Politics: Who Gets What, When, How* (Cleveland: The World Publishing Company, 1958), p. 168.
9. *Ibid.*, p. 13.

archical and markedly stratified socio-political structure within states (i.e., a socio-political pyramid with a small elite at the apex, and with the mass population filling a huge base). The most important feature of this socio-political structure is that the elite at the apex is a *unified ruling class*. Common elite interests in preserving power and tenure, in maintaining lines of socio-political stratification that separate rulers from ruled, and in retaining near monopoly over values and rewards in the society, tend to override any intra-elite differences of interest, and to cancel possible differences in members' origins. Characteristically, the predominant direction of political communication in the monistic system is from the apex downward. Commands and directions flow from elite to mass in profusion. But demands flow effectively upward only when the elite chooses to make itself accessible (and this may be seldom). In addition, in the monistic system, elite status tends most generally to be conferred either by ascription or co-option, so that class integrity and patterns of stratification are perpetuated.

By contrast, other social theorists, including the American political scientists Harold Lasswell, Robert Dahl, and Gabriel A. Almond, have suggested that while the monistic model may have historical, and admittedly also some contemporary, empirical significance, an alternative model more accurately describes elite structures and elite-mass interaction in many modern states.[10] In this alternative or pluralistic model, the hierarchical structure of society and polity are taken as given. However, elite cohesion into a unified ruling class, rigid socio-political stratification, and unidirectional political communication from the top downward are all dropped. Instead, the structure of society and polity are described in terms of multiple pyramids representing the numerous social, economic, political, and cultural sectors and interests typical in modern states. Business, labor, the military, elective politics, education, and the church are but a few of these sectors. A leadership group occupies the apex of each of the pyramids; and the citizenry, represented in the combined bases of the pyramids, is subdivided into differentiated constituencies for the various elites. Political communication in the pluralist society characteristically flows in three directions: (1) from mass constituency to elite leadership, in

10. Robert A. Dahl, *A Preface to Democratic Theory* (Chicago: University of Chicago Press, 1956); Gabriel A. Almond, *The American People and Foreign Policy* (New York: Harcourt, Brace, 1950).

the form of requests and demands for policy action; (2) from elite faction to elite faction, in a search for convergence and consensus among differing viewpoints; and (3) from elite leadership to mass constituency, in the form of government policies and directives. Recruitment to elite status in the pluralist society varies among sub-elites. Election, ascription, achievement, and co-option all are pathways to leadership. Generally though, elite status and tenure tend to be much more closely linked to constituency approval in the pluralistic system than in the monistic one. In sum, the pluralist society has no ruling class and no masses as in the Mosca-Pareto tradition. The governing group is a constellation of factions or sub-elites; the citizenry have differentiated interests in supporting the fortunes of various leadership factions; government amounts to accommodating different factional viewpoints rather than imposing the singular will of a ruling class.

It must be borne in mind that the two models elaborated here are ideal types. No state matches either model exactly. But all states, past and present, can be located along a continuum that runs between monistic systems at one end and pluralistic ones at the other. Every state therefore can be described in terms of degrees of monism or pluralism reflected in its socio-political structure.

Moreover, while the monistic and pluralistic models correspond roughly to the more popular classifications of states into "authoritarian" and "democratic" categories, one must be cautious about loose uses of these latter terms. The Soviet political structure, for example, contains elements of pluralism that are essential both to the functioning of the Soviet governmental process, and to our understanding of it. If one rests content in describing the U.S.S.R. as a "totalitarian Communist dictatorship," resultant understanding of Soviet policy-making will be superficial. For that matter, much the same can be said about the American system, with themes reversed. Myths about populist democracy and extreme elite pluralism blur elements of monism in certain policy areas in American government. Relatedly, it is tempting in our egalitarian age to think of monistic systems as "bad" and pluralistic ones as "good." Such attributions are dashed empirically as soon as one notes, historically, that aggressive behavior, imperialism, diplomatic folly, and domestic injustice and upheaval have been widely distributed all along the monism-to-pluralism continuum.

Elite structure, however, does hold clues to international behavior.

First, with regard to international political style, monistically structured states are able to act and react in world affairs more rapidly and more flexibly than pluralistically structured ones. Since intra-elite factionalism is minimal in the ideal monistic system, minimal policy-making time need be expended in intra-elite dialogue and consensus-building. Furthermore, the monistic elite need neither inform nor respond to public opinion on policy issues. Hence, avenues are open to swift decisions, abrupt turnabouts, and generally opportunistic international behavior. Some analysts have pointed out that the flexibilities that follow from monistic elite structure lend such states a definite edge in international bargaining and negotiation.[11]

On the other hand, there is something to be said for the learning capacities and long-run adaptability of pluralistic systems. In these systems, intra-elite and elite-mass dialogues and debates can expose much wider ranges of policy alternatives to serious consideration than can be the case in monistic systems, where policy debates may amount simply to tactical discussions among like-minded men all committed to nearly identical ends. Furthermore, as a result of wider perspectives, gained through variances in perception and aspiration among different elite factions, a pluralistic system is better equipped than a monistic one to monitor and analyze social, economic, political, and other changes that could have bearing on state security and survival. Where monistic systems with limited perspectives have a tendency to lose touch with changing reality and to lapse into paranoid-like behavior, pluralistic systems are more adaptive to change, albeit slowly and haphazardly. In general, the more diverse the meeting of minds in policy councils, the higher the probability that great challenge will be met with creative response.

Some of the most promising work to date on linkages between elite structure and international behavior is that presented by Morton A. Kaplan in his *System and Process in International Politics*.[12] Kaplan's work is deductive and abstract, and as yet more theoretically suggestive than empirically validated. Still, Kaplan insists that we can know a good many things about a state's probable international behavior when we know where it stands along the monism-to-pluralism

11. Fred Charles Iklé, *How Nations Negotiate* (New York: Praeger, 1967), pp. 225–256.

12. Morton A. Kaplan, *System and Process in International Politics* (New York: John Wiley, 1950), pp. 54–88.

continuum. For example, if we assume other factors equal or constant, we can postulate that:

A. Monistic actors will be able to allocate proportionately more attention to international pursuits than pluralistic actors, since the former are freer from internal constraints than the latter.

B. Monistic actors, much more often than pluralistic ones, will subordinate international stability to national goal-attainment.

C. Monistic actors, much more often than pluralistic ones, will ally themselves with small states "whom they can dominate and possibly absorb or with large (pluralistic) actors who can be outmaneuvered later." [13]

D. Pluralistic actors, as a rule, will not join blocs or alliances led by monistic actors, although the reverse is not true.

E. In a polarized world with a universal organization such as the United Nations, all states will subordinate the interests of the organization to the interests of their bloc, and all, too, will subordinate the interests of their bloc to their national interests. This pattern of priorities, however, will be much more pronounced for monistic actors than for pluralistic ones, since elite responsiveness to mass pacifism in the latter would force some deference to international organization. Moreover, among actors who are not bloc members, priority will be allotted to international organizational interests over rival bloc interests, but organizational interests will still be subordinated to national interests. But, here again, this pattern of priorities will be much more pronounced for monistic actors than for pluralistic ones.

2. LINKAGES BETWEEN ELITE ATTITUDES AND FOREIGN-POLICY BEHAVIOR. Needless to say, knowing something about a particular elite's attitudes, predispositions, and aspirations adds considerably to any knowledge gained from studying its structure. To be sure, there are no direct relationships between men's perceptions and their behavior, and certainly no direct links between elite perceptions and governmental behavior. Nevertheless, elite members do have perspectives and preferences, and—other factors being equal—these suggest something of the kinds of policies they will advocate and support.

Generally speaking, national elites can be distinguished attitudinally by differences in ethos or "world view." As a result of common backgrounds and experiences, elite members tend to share values and con-

13. *Ibid.*, p. 67.

victions about "right" and "wrong," "good" and "bad," desirable and undesirable, attainable and unattainable, etc., with regard to social, political, and economic processes and outcomes, including international outcomes. Moreover, as a result again of common socialization, elite members also tend to share satisfactions or dissatisfactions about their international environment, expectations or apprehensions about its impacts upon them, and preferences for preserving or changing it. With regard to the international environment in particular, elite members in a given country are likely to share perceptions of threats, perceptions of the international-status hierarchy, and perceptions of structure and process in the international political system. Therefore, as a group, an elite may be conservative with regard to preserving the world status quo, reactionary with desires to restore past conditions, or revolutionary with aspirations to make the world over into conformity with their utopian images. As a group, too, an elite may be optimistic or pessimistic about attaining its international ends, just as it may also be secure or apprehensive about maintaining its internal tenure. Finally, an elite may be collectively predisposed toward favoring certain procedures for goal-seeking and rejecting others. International cooperation and conciliation are differentially valued among national elites and, similarly, violence and war are differentially eschewed.

The elite ethos forms the attitudinal environment for governmental policy, and characteristics of elite thinking heighten the probabilities of certain kinds of governmental behavior and lower the probabilities of others. Certainly, it is not possible to predict exactly how a government is going to behave in a specific situation on the basis of elite ethos alone, since any predisposition may suggest a range of behavior. Certainly too, when pluralistic elites are under study, the analyst must take into account that different factions may have very different—and indeed sometimes incompatible—world views, so that the relative influence of the different subgroups must be weighed. By and large, however, ethos factors do relate to broad patterns of international behavior that develop over extended periods in time. Chinese Communist international behavior during the last twenty years, for example, has been highly, and quite openly, consistent with the revolutionary ethos of the CCP leadership. Some analysts suggest, moreover, that Soviet behavior over the past fifty years has closely followed changes in elite ethos away from revolutionary preferences toward status quo satisfactions.[14] Then, too, alterations in emphasis in American foreign policy always reflect the changes in world view that result when Republican administrations are replaced by Democratic ones and vice versa.

In addition to sharing general world views, elite members (or members of sub-elite factions) also share specific attitudes about particular day-to-day issues and problems. These follow, at least theoretically, from the more general characteristics of group ethos. What is important is that specific elite positions, expressed in journalists' editorials, political oratory, and private communications, often become inputs into policy-making processes. In pluralistic systems, such interpretations and preferences become the stuff of intra-elite dialogue and debate, and in monistic systems they mark the range of alternatives available for the political leadership's choice. Analytically, information about elite positions and preferences on policy issues can add greatly to understanding and predictability concerning particular states' international behavior. In recent years, therefore, there has been a thrust in social science research toward elite-attitude surveys and careful content analyses of elite publications and oratory in many countries of the world.[15]

3. LINKAGES BETWEEN ELITE SOCIO-DEMOGRAPHIC ATTRIBUTES AND FOREIGN-POLICY BEHAVIOR. Harold Lasswell and several other pioneers in elite study based much of their initial research on the assumption that elites differentially composed of various kinds of men would behave in ways that reflected their compositions. Hence, for example, an elite composed primarily of men of military background would behave differently from an elite made up mainly of businessmen and industrialists, and an elite of executives and administrators would behave differently from an elite of political activists and party organizers. In the same way, elites recruited primarily from the countryside would behave differently from elites recruited from the cities; those recruited mainly from upper social classes would behave differently

14. George K. Schueller, "The Politburo," in *World Revolutionary Elites,* Harold D. Lasswell and Daniel Lerner, eds. (Cambridge: M.I.T. Press, 1966), p. 140.

15. Karl W. Deutsch, *et al., France, Germany and the Western Alliance* (New York: Charles Scribner's Sons, 1967); Robert C. Angell, Vera S. Dunham, and J. David Singer, "Social Values and Foreign Policy Attitudes," *Journal of Conflict Resolution,* VII, No. 4 (December, 1964) entire issue.

from those recruited from middle and lower classes; and those drawn primarily from intellectual circles would behave differently from those composed largely of less formally educated men. Numerous attempts at "elite profile analysis" followed from these assumptions. None, however, were very successful.[16]

It is true that elites of different socio-demographic composition do behave differently in their handlings of both domestic and international affairs. The problem, however, is that there do not appear to be any direct and generalizable links between certain types of elite composition and certain types of behavior. For example, a military regime in Turkey would likely behave quite differently from a military regime in Peru, and a predominantly intellectual elite in India would likely behave very differently from an intellectual elite in Tunisia. Much the same can be said for any cross-national similarities in the socio-demographic composition of elites. Hence, there is really no basis for international generalization.

Elite profiles are, however, useful for gauging and predicting evolutions in policy within particular states. Noticeable shifts toward international conservatism, for example, have coincided with the gradual replacement of "old Bolshevik revolutionaries" by administrator-bureaucrats in the Soviet political elite. Shifts away from international adventure and involvement toward domestic problem-solving follow patterned elite changes in new nations, where the activists and intellectuals who lead movements for independence are ultimately replaced by grass roots politicians more interested in domestic development than in continuing anti-colonial world crusades. In American foreign policy over the years, changes in emphasis and direction have coincided with shifts in regional, rural-urban, and civilian-military elite composition. While it is most often impossible to say exactly what kinds of policy change will follow alterations in elite composition, continually monitoring elite compositions in different states may nonetheless alert analysts to probable policy movements and thereby focus analytical attention.

Age is one aspect of elite composition that has been relatively overlooked analytically until recently. Promising study by Karl Deutsch,

16. Note, for example, difficulties encountered by Lasswell and his associates in attempts to generalize from elite characteristics to states' patterns of foreign policy. See Lasswell and Lerner, *World Revolutionary Elites, op. cit.*

Ronald Inglehart, and others during the last several years, however, suggests that changing age composition within elites may be an important clue to evolving policy.[17] "Age Cohort" analysts base their work upon the assumption that different generations tend to experience different—oftentimes radically different—political socializations. Therefore, each new generation enters politics with different outlooks, ambitions, and expectations from older generations; and as it rises toward positions of political responsibility, it carries with it its particular ethos. Policy becomes increasingly reflective of new-generation influence. Ultimately the new generation dominates. But then this influence wanes as still another generation begins to exert its political will. None of this is to say that generations *must* differ in their perspectives, or that aims and expectations formed during youthful socialization necessarily persist over time. Nevertheless, climactic events such as world wars, revolutions, defeats, victories, diplomatic triumphs and follies, national ascents to grandeur, and plunges toward oblivion, do leave their lasting impressions upon whole generations. Moreover, these impressions may well enter policy as lessons learned, drives for revenge, emphases upon caution, or accents on adventurism, when power comes eventually into the hands of the new generation. Age Cohort analysis, when refined, may become a powerful predictive tool in international studies.

STATESMEN AS ACTORS IN INTERNATIONAL POLITICS: FOREIGN POLICY DECISION-MAKERS

While political elites *influence* foreign policy, statesmen *formulate* and *execute* it. The men who actually direct states' actions in international politics can be theoretically identified with varying degrees of specificity. Ivo Duchacek, for example, in his *Nations and Men*, defines the actors in international politics as "those men who have the authority to commit their national communities to a given course of action."[18] Here authority and autonomy become the criteria for isolating and defining the key figures in foreign policy. Similarly, Richard Snyder in his *Decision-Making as an Approach to the Study of Inter-*

17. Karl W. Deutsch, *et al., France, Germany and the Western Alliance*, pp. 14–19.
18. Ivo D. Duchacek, *Nations and Men* (New York: Holt, Rinehart and Winston, 1966), p. 2.

national Politics looks upon official decision-makers as those "whose authoritative acts are, to all intents and purposes, the acts of the state." [19] In a more detailed definition, using "role" criteria, Robert North and his colleagues point out that:

> . . . a state is defined as the sum total of those major decision-makers who are empowered to make policies which are binding on the government. Monarchs, and elective heads of state, prime ministers, foreign ministers, under secretaries of state and military chiefs of staff are designated as *bona fide* decision-makers.[20]

One might wish to broaden North's functional definition somewhat by adding civilian defense and intelligence chiefs and by making provision for autocrats in nonmonarchial, nondemocratic states. But, the focus on "top" men with explicit foreign affairs responsibilities and authority should remain. Analytically, we can label these men who speak and act for states in international politics, *foreign policy decision-makers*.

It should be pointed out that the analytical label, "foreign policy decision-makers," is adopted here in deference to convention. The term is widely used in the literature of international politics, and it is certainly meaningful as long as a number of qualifications and cautions are observed. First, describing the official actors in international politics as foreign policy *decision-makers* must not blur the fact that a significant proportion of statesmen's activities may consist in avoiding, delaying, and circumventing decisions rather than making them. Pacifists and anti-Communist activists may debate about whether we should better be "Red or Dead." But responsible officials in charge of foreign policy may work to avoid the need for such a choice. Moreover, it must be borne in mind that the *decision-making* procedure in foreign policy seldom approximates the process of "rational choice among alternative courses of action" suggested in many formal decision-making models.[21] For one thing, human emotion and irrationality cannot be written out of foreign policy formulation. For another, that

19. Richard C. Snyder, H. W. Bruck, and Burton Sapin, *Decision-Making as an Approach to the Study of International Politics* (Princeton: Foreign Policy Analysis Series No. 3, 1954).

20. Dina A. Zinnes, *et al.,* "Capability, Threat, and the Outbreak of War," in *International Politics and Foreign Policy,* James N. Rosenau, ed., 1st ed. (Glencoe: The Free Press, 1961), p. 472.

21. Thomas C. Schelling, *The Strategy of Conflict* (Cambridge: Harvard University Press, 1960), pp. 3–52.

imperfect information is used (almost always the case in international political situations) makes foreign policy formulation much less a process of rational calculation and much more a process of semi-informed guessing and hoping. Then too, selecting a course of action in international politics frequently amounts to reacting to current situations in "conditioned response" fashion based upon past experience. Here, rather than weighing options and scanning for alternatives, statesmen confront developing situations with the question, "what did we do the last time, and did we succeed or fail?" Recalls of success in the past raise the probability of certain responses to present situations regardless of what other, and perhaps more productive, options might be open. Finally, *fait accompli* is employed in international politics with surprising frequency. Its object is to limit a political opponent's range of alternatives to the point where calculated decision-making becomes impossible. In sum, the term "decision-making" can be used to describe policy formulation (or, "what statesmen do") only if the term is used rather loosely. The foreign policy decision-maker may at times resemble the *homo diplomaticus* maximizing his accomplishments through rigorous and accurate ends-means calculations.[22] But, more often, he better resembles the harassed statesman operating on judgment, emotion, experience, and intuition in a political environment of great uncertainty.

Some Characteristics of Foreign Policy Decision-Makers. Using the definitions offered here, the group of men arrived at that may properly be described as foreign policy decision-makers is necessarily very small in any given state. It is far smaller than the political elite as a whole, and it usually excludes much of the formal foreign affairs establishment, whose prime responsibility it is to execute rather than formulate policy. In fact, history records a considerable number of cases where the determining of the international behavior of a state was one man's prerogative. Absolute autocracy is, however, increasingly rare; and in most states foreign policy decision-making rests ultimately in the hands of a group of senior civil servants, experts, and executive advisors. As noted, a checklist of officials likely to participate directly in foreign policy decision-making would include a state's chief executive, minister for foreign affairs, minister for defense, military chief of staff, and perhaps also the state's intelligence chief, some second-

22. Raymond Aron, *Peace and War* (Garden City: Doubleday, 1966), p. 91.

echelon people from the ministries of foreign affairs and defense, and perhaps, finally, some special assistants and advisors. The size and composition of the foreign policy decision-making group of course vary from state to state according to such factors as the degree of pluralism and structural differentiation in the state's political system and government, degree of the state's involvement in international politics, and cultural and ideological traditions. The checklist of officials reported here would, for example, be quite inappropriate if applied to the Communist systems, in which foreign policy decision-making rests with the highest organ of the Communist Party, well beyond the control of government ministries. Then too, the size and composition of the foreign policy decision-making group vary with the nature of the problem requiring decision and policy action. Oftentimes, foreign policy decisions originate with *ad hoc* groups of officials assembled for their expertise in particular issue-areas. In any case, the group of those men who have the authority to commit their states to courses of international political action is never very large.

Foreign policy decision-makers are generally recruited from political elite strata in their societies and they therefore resemble typical elite members with regard to general ethnic-cultural background, and social, economic, professional, and occupational characteristics, attributes, and skills. In monistic systems, foreign policy decision-makers are generally typical members of the unified ruling class, while in pluralist societies, they tend to be recruited from elite factions dominant at particular times. More important than the socio-demographic similarities between foreign policy decision-makers and broader political elites is the fact that foreign policy decision-makers also tend to share the ethos, the values, the goals, the hopes, and the apprehensions of the broader political elites from which they are recruited. These officials hence inject the values, goals, hopes, and fears of the political elites of the state into their policy formulations.

Various scholars and observers in many writings have attempted to isolate and define the distinguishing individual qualities of statesmen. The net result of these works, however, has been to demonstrate that statesmen actually come in a great variety of intellectual and emotional (and physical) shapes and sizes. In fact, at the personal level, there is really no way to distinguish between international political actors specifically and political actors generally. All are *political men,* constantly under the crossfire of pressures from manifold sources. Consequently, few officials are allotted the privilege of complete autonomy in decision-making and action. Unless one is endowed with charisma, the most that can be hoped for is some choice among pressures to bow toward, some means for reconciling cross-pressures, or, barring these, some pathway to triumphant rather than disgraceful political suicide.

Beyond a commonalty in all being politicians under continual pressure, statesmen differ from one another in a host of other qualities and attributes. Some are ruthless, others compassionate; some, by the standards of most great ethical systems, are distinctly moral, others are amoral or immoral; some are calculating and rigorously rational, others are logically negligent and emotional; some are professional careerists in international affairs, others are amateurs; some are superior in training and native intelligence, others are incredibly lacking in both. Moreover, while some countries take rightful pride in long and successful traditions in international affairs marked by outstanding statesmen, no state has been able to monopolize international political wisdom. Neither has any state fully avoided mediocrity at the helm.

A great deal is going to be said in this book about statesmen and their behavior. Implicitly, and sometimes explicitly, judgments are going to be offered about particular statesmen and their actions at critical junctures in history. Most of these evaluations will follow, *post hoc,* from strictly pragmatic criteria. In a fascinating discussion of statesmanship in his *Peace and War,* Raymond Aron suggests that *prudence* must be the criteria for evaluating diplomatic-military performance.[23] So it must, for any statesman in any situation controls limited resources, and receives limited information of limited accuracy. He generally depends heavily upon a great many other men to relay and execute his decisions. Furthermore, he is always confronting the political wills of other statesmen in other states—and they may well be both more powerful and more obstinate than he. In short, no statesman can really control more than a segment of an international episode or sequence of events, and the segment may be a small one. Therefore, we must judge a statesman's performance by asking how well he fared *under the circumstances in which he was acting, with the resources at his disposal.* The prudent statesman optimizes because

23. *Ibid.,* pp. 609–610.

reality prevents maximization.[24] Success in international interaction amounts, in effect, to either reaping the greatest possible rewards, or reducing penalties to the greatest extent possible *under existing circumstances.* In some history books, personal greatness in international politics appears to follow most often from winning spectacular triumphs on the battlefield or around the bargaining table. However, a critical observer of international politics might suggest that the outstanding among statesmen are not necessarily those who win the most for their states, but rather those who lose the least. By the same token, the truly great among statesmen are not necessarily those who win impressively but intermittently, but rather those who never lose.

24. Herbert A. Simon, *Models of Man* (New York: John Wiley, 1957), pp. 170–182.

CHAPTER THREE
PUBLIC OPINION
AND FOREIGN POLICY

IF THIS book were being written in the eighteenth or even the nineteenth rather than the twentieth century, no chapter would be devoted to discussing public opinion and foreign policy. In those earlier eras, international politics remained an elitist game by and large. Mass populations were minimally aware of statesmen's maneuverings and their import, and, except in wartime, mass populations were minimally affected by international political developments. Consequently, public opinion, at home and abroad, was seldom a major factor in statesmen's international political considerations. The man-in-the-street was in no sense an actor in international politics.

It would, however, be an exaggeration to say that international politics has been democratized in the twentieth century to the extent that public opinion now directly influences foreign policy. International politics remains largely an elitist game. Nevertheless, understanding public opinion and foreign policy is essential for understanding present-day international politics for a number of important reasons:

First, mass awareness of international political developments and mass concern about international politics have heightened considerably during the past half century, due mainly to the worldwide increase in literacy and education and to revolutionary developments in printed and electronic mass communications. Men the world over now perceive themselves as citizens or subjects residing within political units that interact competitively or cooperatively, hostilely or amicably with other political units. Continual media exposure shapes and maintains the salience of these perceptions. While it is not wholly accurate to say that *most* people are aware of and concerned about international affairs, or that the man-in-the-street understands international events in a very sophisticated way, it can be said that more people understand more about international politics today than ever before.

The idealisms and myths of populist legitimacy and democratic participation in government born and nurtured in the great revolutions of the late eighteenth and mid-nineteenth centuries, have become facts of political life in the twentieth century. Even modern totalitarian regimes find it necessary to pay lip service to symbols of democracy, popular will, and people's government. One result of the pervasiveness of the democratic ideology has been a widespread heightening of expectations of obligation and efficacy in mass political participation. Sizable segments of the mass population in many countries today feel obligated to participate in national politics, and these groups tend to expect that their participation will affect public policy, including foreign policy. In countries where a democratic electoral system meaningfully functions as a leadership recruitment mechanism, popular influence over foreign policy can be considerable, especially when foreign policy issues separate candidates at election time. Even in states where there are no meaningful elections—or no elections at all—utter nonresponsiveness seems a tactic that no modern government can employ successfully for any great length of time. Public opinion has become a political force in the twentieth century.

While developments in communications, progressive mass enlightenment, and spreading democratic ideology have contributed to heightened popular political awareness and participation in our time, modern warfare and military technology have forced direct mass involvement in international politics. In contrast to the chess game-like maneuvers of small professional armies, the limited victories and defeats, the exchanges of border districts, and the minimal involvements of national populations in most of the wars of past centuries, major wars in the twentieth century have caught up total populations in life and death struggles. Military mobilization for twentieth-century wars has meant (1) the massing of multi-million-man citizen armies through pervasive conscription, (2) the complete retooling of national economies for military hardware production, and (3) the psychological conditioning of populations to promote collective valor, hostility, defiance, and willingness to sacrifice. Airpower and strategic bombardment in

modern warfare have discriminated poorly between military and civilian targets, even when such discrimination was intended. Moreover,
in World War II both Axis and Allied attacks were deliberately directed against civilian populations in efforts to break national morales.

The impact of modern warfare on public opinion, therefore, has been
to greatly heighten the salience of international politics for the man-in-
the-street by aggravating his anxieties. The development of nuclear
weapons and missile delivery systems in the second half of this century
has injected still more apprehension into men's lives. Whether future
wars will assume the tragic patterns of total warfare laid down in the
two world wars of the first half of our century, whether wars will again
be fought by professional armies with limited popular involvement for
limited objectives, or whether warfare will eventually be abandoned as
an international political instrument are questions that no one can
answer. What is certain, however, is that the image of total war and the
relationship between total war and international politics have both
been forced into men's minds in our century. Hence the twentieth
century man-in-the-street not only knows a good deal more about
international politics than his counterpart in past centuries, he also
cares a good deal more about international politics.

Finally, largely as a result of the observed or expected influence of
public opinion in foreign policy, manipulating public opinion in other
countries has become an important instrument in twentieth-century
statecraft. Whether one terms the practice of manipulating foreign
public opinion "overseas information programs," or "propaganda," or
whether a state employs such tactics to better its own image, defame
an opponent's image, buttress a foreign regime, or foment a revolution,
assumptions about the efficacy of public opinion in target countries are
similar. Propagandists assume that some of their states' international
political goals can be attained, or can be made attainable, by bypassing
the governments of other countries and focusing directly upon the
peoples of these countries. While the history of propaganda as an instrument of foreign policy dates at least from the period of the Pelo-
ponnesian Wars of ancient Greece, and probably even earlier than
that, large-scale attempts at government-to-people communications
are products of our own century. One reason is that modern radio
communications readily expose national populations to direct messages from foreign governments. More important, in the twentieth

century—especially since World War II—the minds, attitudes, identifications, and loyalties of mass populations have become the most valued prizes in international political competition. The largely territorial goals of traditional international politics have been replaced in our century by ideological goals. Therefore, public opinion and foreign policy become important topics for discussion not only because public opinion and foreign policy are more closely linked in the twentieth century than in the past, but also, and significantly, because public opinion in the twentieth century has become a prime target of foreign policy.

Three broad areas of discussion can be mapped under the heading "Public Opinion and Foreign Policy." First, understanding links between public opinion and foreign policy requires special probing into the nature of mass feelings about and reactions to international issues, episodes, and events. Second, exploring public attitudes toward international affairs requires an elaboration on the sources and bases of such attitudes. In short, how does the man-in-the-street form his opinions about international politics? Where do his opinions come from? Finally, and most related to the general theme of actors in international politics, investigating relationships between public opinion and foreign policy means examining ways in which public opinion may influence foreign policy and conditions under which such influence is either maximized or minimized.

THE NATURE OF PUBLIC OPINION ABOUT INTERNATIONAL AFFAIRS

Three characteristics of public opinion about international affairs are worth underlining. First, the mass populations of countries are typically poorly informed about international issues. Second, mass opinion tends to oversimplify international issues and events, often to the extent of reducing international politics to "good guys" and "bad guys." Third, public opinion about international affairs is characteristically unstable and may shift greatly or fluctuate erratically over relatively short time spans. Each of these characteristics of public opinion requires elaboration.

Public Information About International Affairs. While the average mid-twentieth century man-in-the-street tends to know a good deal more about international affairs than his eighteenth or nineteenth century counterparts, levels of public information about international developments should not be exaggerated. Since average citizens generally devote most of their time and efforts to the demands of their occupations, their roles as parents, their recreational pursuits, and to myriads of personal problems, large and small, it is not very surprising that their functioning as "citizens" in the political sense is generally constricted and intermittent. Moreover, except when major questions of war and peace flood media and raise anxieties, the political information most relevant to citizens' daily lives tends to be news about local and national domestic matters. Local mass media typically allot limited and superficial coverage to international developments, and public educational institutions in most countries provide meager instruction in international affairs. Typically then, the world of international politics is an unfamiliar one for the average citizen.

Public Opinion Simplifies the World of International Politics. The complexities and ambiguities of international politics, often elusive and frustrating even to seasoned statesmen, are frequently beyond the intellectual grasp of the average citizen. As a result, the subtleties of international affairs are seldom reflected in public opinion. Instead, mass interpretations of international actors, states, and statesmen, tend to be reduced to stereotypes, or simple, value-laden, thought-pictures. Moreover, international actions tend most often to be perceived and understood in terms of value and attribute dichotomies—e.g., "friendly/hostile," "aggressive/pacific," "favorable/unfavorable," "we/they," and the like.[1] What is noteworthy is that popular images of world politics are never very sophisticated, and, furthermore, they are often biased, distorted, or otherwise inaccurate. Such simplifications however permit the average citizen both to interpret international developments in a rudimentary way and to "have opinions" about international affairs.

The stereotypes displayed in Table 3.1 have little contemporary substantive relevance since the poll data from which the stereotypes were reconstructed were gathered in 1948. However, Table 3.1 is offered here mainly to show some of the generalized images of foreign countries and peoples harbored by national populations. The listings of

1. Donald J. Puchala, "Factor Analysis in International Survey Research," in *Western European Perspectives on International Affairs*, Richard L. Merritt and Donald J. Puchala, eds. (New York: Praeger, 1968), pp. 142–172.

TABLE 3.1. INTERNATIONAL STEREOTYPES AMONG
FIVE POPULATIONS (1948)

I. Adjectives Most Frequently Used to Describe *Russians* by:

British	French	Germans	Norwegians	Americans
Hardworking	Backward	Cruel	Hardworking	Cruel
Domineering	Hardworking	Backward	Domineering	Hardworking
Cruel	Domineering	Hardworking	Backward	Domineering
Brave	Brave	Domineering	Brave	Backward
Practical	Cruel	Brave	Cruel	Conceited
Progressive	Progressive	Practical	Practical	Brave

II. Adjectives Most Frequently Used to Describe *Americans* by:

British	French	Germans	Norwegians
Progressive	Practical	Progressive	Hardworking
Conceited	Progressive	Generous	Practical
Generous	Domineering	Practical	Progressive
Peace-Loving	Hardworking	Intelligent	Generous
Intelligent	Intelligent	Peace-Loving	Peace-Loving
Practical	Generous	Hardworking	Intelligent

III. Adjectives Most Frequently Used to Describe *Fellow Countrymen* by:

British	French	Germans	Norwegians	Americans
Peace-Loving	Intelligent	Hardworking	Peace-Loving	Peace-Loving
Brave	Peace-Loving	Intelligent	Hardworking	Generous
Hardworking	Generous	Brave	Brave	Intelligent
Intelligent	Brave	Practical	Intelligent	Progressive
Generous	Hardworking	Progressive	Generous	Hardworking
Practical	Progressive	Peace-Loving	Progressive	Brave

SOURCE: Derived from William Buchanan and Hadley Cantril, *How Nations See Each Other* (Urbana, Ill.: University of Illinois Press, 1953), pp. 51–52.

attributes shown in the table represent consensus observed among representative samples of five national populations. In light of the stereotypes of Russians and Americans respectively harbored by the various populations shown in Table 3.1, it is not surprising that most American international moves during the period in question were welcomed with favor by many of the peoples of the world, while Russian moves were viewed with suspicion and apprehension.

Instabilities in Public Opinion About International Affairs. The short-run instability of public opinion about international affairs has two aspects: intensity and direction. On the one hand, mass opinion goes through cycles of excitement with international developments. Periods of relative indifference to international affairs alternate, depending upon events, with periods of almost feverish international attentiveness, apprehension, and concern. While routine international occurrences or problems in distant lands seldom attract the man-in-the-street from his personal concerns, threats or insults to his country quickly attract his attention to the international scene. Public apprehension about international politics holds until crises taper in intensity and threats diminish. Attention wavers as brinkmanship gives way to conciliation and international politics returns to routine.

Gabriel A. Almond, in pioneering work on public opinion and foreign affairs, mapped "intensity of involvement" cycles by recording American responses to the poll question: "Do you consider foreign policy issues as the most important problems facing the American people?"[2] Notice in Figure 3.1 how peaks in the arousal of public opinion tend to coincide with threats to national security and how public interest in international affairs rapidly subsides as threats pass.

In addition to shifting according to intensity of concern about international affairs, as noted, public opinion also tends frequently to shift *direction* in its reactions to issues and events. This shifting Almond attributed to a "moodiness" characteristic of public opinion in most countries. Given typically low levels of public information, mass responses to international issues tend to be more in the nature of emotional reactions rather than reasoned positions. These reactions fluctuate with events, the duration of events, official governmental stimuli, and sometimes foreign states' propaganda. Events, moreover, tend to be perceived as unconnected occurrences rather than as phases of continuing interaction patterns. Hence, public optimism or pessimism, or approval or disapproval of a war effort may shift radically with the outcomes of battles. Or public enchantment or disenchantment with an international organization may shift radically as the organization acts

2. Gabriel A. Almond, *The American People and Foreign Policy* (New York: Harcourt, Brace, 1950), p. 73.

on different issues. There is, moreover, a prevailing tendency toward overreaction in public mood changes due again primarily to low information levels, which make most international events appear rather abrupt, surprising, and probably more dramatic for the man-in-the-street than for the specialist who monitors the world daily. Hence, when opinion shifts direction, the shift is likely to be extreme—as be-

FIGURE 3.1. CYCLES OF AMERICAN PUBLIC INVOLVEMENT IN FOREIGN AFFAIRS (NOVEMBER, 1935–OCTOBER, 1949)

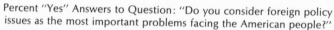
Percent "Yes" Answers to Question: "Do you consider foreign policy issues as the most important problems facing the American people?"

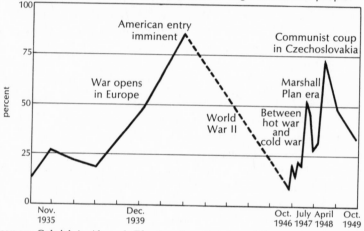

SOURCE: Gabriel A. Almond, *The American People and Foreign Policy,* p. 73.

tween bellicosity and meekness, idealism and cynicism, patience and impatience, optimism and pessimism, and the like.

One of the most interesting, and best researched "mood cycles" in public opinion about international affairs is the "pacifism, war-fever, war-weariness, pacifism" cycle. This cycle was initially uncovered by Lewis Richardson, who attributed both latent and manifest attitudes about international affairs to public opinion and reasoned that as international crises intensify, manifest mass desires to avoid war give way to latent hostility aroused by antagonists' insults and provocations; manifest hostility later gives way to latent war-weariness as combat continues and casualties multiply; manifest war-weariness finally gives way to latent desires for peace.[3] In other words, before the war, few people want it. But as provocative incidents accumulate, the public begins to react with anger, though, still, few actually want war. As the situation deteriorates, however, hostility begins to dominate and the public begins to react with a "let's get in there and get this thing over with" attitude. War-fever mounts; the war begins; the antagonist turns out to be stronger than anticipated; casualties mount; the home front begins to feel the strains of war. War-weariness sets in and a negotiated settlement—initially unthinkable—becomes increasingly attractive to public opinion.

Joel Campbell and Leila Cain have empirically documented this war-fever/war-weariness cycle with public opinion poll data collected in the United States and Great Britain before and during World War II.[4] Notice in Figure 3.2 how pacifism shifted to war-fever (abruptly in the United States and more gradually in Great Britain) and then how war-weariness began to set in among both Americans and Britishers as the war dragged on.

SOURCES AND ROOTS OF MASS ATTITUDES ABOUT INTERNATIONAL AFFAIRS

Knowing that the average citizen responds to international political developments largely from stereotypes and moods carries us only part of the way toward the sources of mass attitudes. What remains to be explained is where the stereotypes, images, and emotional propensities that determine opinion originate. While it would be beyond the scope of this book to probe deeply into the psychology and social-psychology of mass opinion, even a cursory examination of opinion formation, however, must take account of three determinants—media exposure, group identification and socialization, and basic personality.

Direct and Indirect Media Exposure in Opinion Formation. It should be obvious that an individual can have opinions only about events, issues, problems, and policies that he is aware of. Therefore, the mass

3. Lewis Richardson, *Arms and Insecurity* (Pittsburgh: Boxwood Press, 1960). See also Kenneth E. Boulding, *Conflict and Defense* (New York: Harper Torchbooks, 1962), pp. 19–40.

4. Joel T. Campbell and Leila S. Cain, "Public Opinion and the Outbreak of War," *Journal of Conflict Resolution*, IX, No. 3 (September, 1965), 318–329.

FIGURE 3.2 PACIFISM, WAR–FEVER, WAR–WEARINESS CYCLES (UNITED STATES AND GREAT BRITAIN, 1937–1946)

I. Proportion of People in the United States Overtly in Favor of World War II According to the Polls

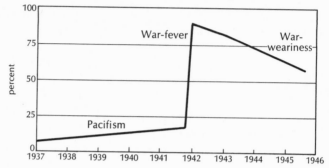

II. Proportion of People in Great Britain Overtly in Favor of World War II According to the Polls

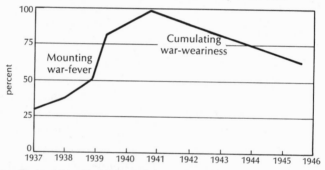

SOURCE: Derived from Joel Campbell and Leila Cain, "Public Opinion and the Outbreak of War," IX, *Journal of Conflict Resolution,* 321, 326.

media and those with control over the mass media are "opinion-makers." They display before the public the range of social and political issues that men form opinions about. The media in their editorializing, and the men whose statements and activities get reported in the media of course frequently accomplish a good deal more by way of "opinion-making" than merely introducing issues to the public. They also present their interpretations of issues, their prescriptions for policy, and their suggestions about the kinds of opinions that the public ought to have about social and political issues. In effect, those with control over the content of the mass media not only introduce issues, they also set out the ranges of alternative positions to be taken on issues. In an open society, these ranges may be broad enough to include diametrically opposing positions; in a closed society with tightly controlled media, issues and problems may be either introduced to the public with a single "party line" interpretation or suppressed from public awareness. The mass media, then, are starting points in the opinion-formation process.

But the mass media are starting points only. Communications analysts discovered a number of years ago that mass media influence in opinion formation can actually be minimal unless exposure to the media is supplemented by interpersonal, word-of-mouth communications.[5] Media messages have been observed to have the greatest impact in opinion formation when they are transmitted in two steps: first from the mass media to "opinion leaders" at the local level, and then from "opinion leaders" to their local audiences. Hence, the local "opinion leader"—a figure of authority, status, prestige, or expertise within a local interpersonal communications network—plays a pivotal role in mass opinion formation. He functions as the link between the mass media and the mass public by adding credibility and prominence to media reports and interpretations, by contributing persuasiveness difficult to attain through impersonal channels, and, most important, by pointing out the local relevance and implications of general issues raised in the media. In short, the local opinion leader, whether he is a ward boss in an American city, the priest in a Brazilian parish, the party agitator in a Russian factory, or the man who owns the radio in an Egyptian village, personalizes general and abstract issues for local audiences and in this way contributes directly and effectively to opinion formation. Though little empirical research has been conducted concerning opinion leaders' influence in forming opinions about international affairs, it is likely that their functioning is crucial in this area— since international issues tend to be so distant from the average citizen's experience and understanding. In sum, mass media messages generally influence public opinion only when these messages are made noticeably personally salient to media audiences. The second step in the two-step communications flow—from opinion leader to the individual citizen—contributes this personal salience.

5. James N. Rosenau, *Public Opinion and Foreign Policy* (New York: Random House, 1965), pp. 74–96.

Group Identification and Affiliation and Opinion Formation. Media exposure, both direct and indirect, helps to explain opinion formation by underlining the fact that awareness of issues and alternative positions must be a starting point in the opinion-formation process. However, relationships between media exposure and awareness do not satisfactorily explain why different individuals pay attention to different media sources and different opinion leaders. Why does a particular editorial delight one individual and anger another? Why, when several alternative positions on an issue are voiced, do different individuals accept different positions?

Alternative public positions on various issues are likely to become an individual's personal positions (i.e., his opinions) when such positions are consonant with his values and aspirations. Values and aspirations are largely the products of socialization experiences—that is, those life experiences that contribute to making the individual *who* he is. Except for a very few intractable individualists, most people tend to identify or affiliate with various social, occupational, political, religious, and other kinds of formal groups or associations. Moreover, all people are also members of different socio-demographic subpopulations defined by commonalities in various kinds of social, economic, or cultural attributes. Social class, educational accomplishment, age, and ethnic background, for example, are common attributes distinguishing among such subpopulations.

One link between formal group affiliation and opinion formation lies in the fact that individuals tend to internalize the values, myths, and goals of the groups with which they most intensely identify. They relate their personal fortunes and accomplishments to group fortunes and accomplishments, and they react to national and international social and political issues in terms of the implications these issues may have for their groups. Hence, the individual's "personal opinion" on a political issue often turns out to be the widely held opinion of a group with which he identifies, and, frequently also, the official position of the group's formal leadership, who function as opinion leaders for group members.

Socio-demographic subpopulation membership may also be a determinant of opinion because of group consciousness and formal leadership cues, as in the case of social classes or ethnic minorities. But, more often, people sharing socio-demographic attributes share opinions simply because they share similar life experiences. For example, "generation gaps," or differences in attitude and opinion according to age, usually reflect differential exposure to life experiences rather than any kind of group consciousness or formal position. In the same way, differences between the generally observable cosmopolitanism among university educated people, and the similarly observable provincialism among lower-educated subpopulations reflect differential capabilities for empathy—a product of differential educational experience—rather than group consciousness. In the United States the traditional isolationism of Midwesterners and the internationalism of Northeasterners reflect continuing differences in access to international information and contact with foreigners rather than regional group consciousness.

Basic Personality and Opinion Formation. No discussion of opinion formation can be complete without a probing into the relationship between opinion and personality. While an individual may take a position on an issue because such a position is consonant with his socialization experiences and group identifications, he may also hold an opinion because it satisfies basic, inborn human drives tailored by expressive or suppressive mechanisms fashioned in early childhood.

In a summary work on attitude theory, Daniel Katz and Ezra Stotland distinguish among four psychic links between personality and attitude (or "opinion" as the concept is used here): [6]

1. OPINIONS MAY SERVE A "PROXIMAL" PERSONALITY FUNCTION when they represent evaluations of objects (people, places, events, ideas, etc.) that serve individuals' psychic needs directly. In general "individuals put high value on objects which satisfy their needs and low values on objects which frustrate them." [7] For example, a man driven by a craving for power (or by fears of impotence) may hail symbols of national might, extol military demonstration, and favor forceful international stances. This same individual may respond contemptuously to acts or other indicators of weakness from his own government or foreign ones. By the same token, a man motivated by needs for affection (or driven by fears of persecution) may hold favorable opinions about movements toward international détente. This same individual might also favor policies of international appeasement, and

6. Daniel Katz and Ezra Stotland, "A Preliminary Statement to a Theory of Attitude Structure and Change," in *Psychology: A Study of a Science,* Sigmund Koch, ed., III (New York, London, Toronto: McGraw-Hill, 1959), 436–442.

7. *Ibid.,* p. 437.

he might overreact in near panic to harbingers of war. Then too, an individual may find himself compelled by a driving need to "understand" his world, in which case "having opinions" on international issues might eliminate uncertainties and ambiguities he fears.

2. OPINIONS MAY SERVE AN "OBJECT-INSTRUMENTAL" PERSONALITY FUNCTION when holding and displaying them contribute indirectly to the satisfaction of psychic needs. That is, men may hold opinions because holding these opinions opens pathways to motivational satisfaction. Many individuals' attitudes towards international affairs are of the "object-instrumental" variety. For example, a man driven by needs for achievement and advancement may adopt opinions about politics, current events, and foreign affairs similar to those of his occupational superiors in the hope that his demonstrated "sound thinking" will win him favorable attention. Ivy League political "liberals" may hence become Wall Street "conservatives" if advancement in the financial community seems enhanced by political conservatism. More generally, David Riesman's "other-directed" personality type tends to adopt and display any opinions—about politics, economics, international affairs, or any of a host of objects—that will win him social acceptance or otherwise diminish his isolation in "The Lonely Crowd." [8]

3. OPINIONS MAY SERVE AN "EGO-INSTRUMENTAL" PERSONALITY FUNCTION when they serve to maintain an individual's conception of himself as a certain kind of person. Here opinions become tools of self-assurance. The man who fancies himself a "Leftist," for example, may strengthen his self-image by digesting and voicing politically radical interpretations and slogans. Concurrently he may reject any of a wide range of opinions and positions that threaten his self-image. What is noteworthy about the "ego-instrumental" function here is that opinions follow and reinforce, rather than precede and generate, the self-image. Much the same, of course, might be said of "ego-instrumental" functionings for people who fancy themselves "internationalists," "pacifists," "patriots," "isolationists," and the like. None of this is to argue against the sincerity of truly committed individuals. By contrast, the man who chooses opinions to match a particular self-image tends to be the "bandwagon rider" or the faddist rather than a committed individual.

8. David Riesman, *The Lonely Crowd,* abridged ed. (New Haven: Yale University Press, 1961).

4. Finally, OPINIONS MAY SERVE AN "EGO-DEFENSIVE" FUNCTION when an individual uses them to protect his self-image from a recognition of undesirable qualities. We all recognize qualities in ourselves that are not particularly wholesome, or at least are not completely compatible with our ideal self-images. Moreover, we all possess elaborate psychological defense mechanisms that permit us to "live with ourselves" in relative psychic equilibrium. Extensive personality research conducted over several decades has cumulatively revealed that evaluating external objects—i.e., having opinions—can become an ego-defense mechanism by distorting objective reality in such a way as to mask psychic shortcomings. In the now classic study of *The Authoritarian Personality*, T. W. Adorno and his colleagues showed that individuals driven by pent-up aggressiveness, feelings of inadequacy, and fears of authority tend to defend themselves against recognizing these qualities by projecting the undesirable traits onto others.[9] Of particular relevance to opinions about international affairs is the fact that individuals with "authoritarian" tendencies project undesirable qualities onto "foreigners"—alien nationalities, ethnic groups, and governments. At the same time, the "authoritarian" reinforces his own ideal self-image by perceptually investing his personal reference groups with highly desirable qualities. Hence, the "authoritarian" tends to live in a dichotomized perceptual world of "good guys" and "bad guys," "we" and "they." "We" are powerful, yet virtuous and unaggressive; "they" are deceitful and aggressive, yet imperfect, inferior, and weak. In opinion about international affairs, authoritarianism gets reflected in a combination of intense ethnocentrism, distrust of foreigners, defensiveness and *weltschmerz,* mixed with deference toward power and sadistic intolerance for weakness. Projecting all of his unsavory motives unto "them" out there in the external world helps the "authoritarian" to hide from himself.

EMPIRICAL AND THEORETICAL LINKS BETWEEN PUBLIC OPINION AND FOREIGN POLICY

After all has been said concerning the characteristics of public opinion about international affairs and factors in opinion formation, a central question remains: How does public opinion influence foreign

9. T. W. Adorno, *et al., The Authoritarian Personality* (New York: Harper, 1950), *passim.*

policy? Attempting to answer this question calls for a survey of some of the intensive research on the topic currently being carried on by social scientists. But since the question has not been completely answered as yet, approaching it here also involves presenting a number of hypotheses which, if empirically validated, may further enhance our understanding of the links between public opinion and foreign policy. Therefore, in this last section of Chapter 3 discussion will proceed from what we know about mass influence over foreign policy to what we suspect about mass influence over foreign policy.

The conventional, and most general, answer to the question "what are the links between public opinion and foreign policy?" is that public opinion—the moods and whims of men-in-the-street—sets limits on governmental policy-making prerogative. "Limits" here mean *political costs*. Public moods may be perceived by governing elites as indices that signal generally desired as well as unacceptable policy alternatives. While public opinion can actually *compel* governmental action only in extraordinary situations, the opinion "barometer" nevertheless continually displays levels of mass political consensus, acquiescence, and apathy—or restiveness and opposition—which all ultimately influence the security and tenure of governors and governments. Repeatedly contradicting public opinion generally paves the way for a government's downfall. In pluralistic democratic systems this can mean an eroding of electoral support; in authoritarian systems it might mean the mobilization of revolutionary zeal.

However, before the impression is lent that public opinion actually guides foreign policy, or that statesmen are domestic politicians first and foremost and perhaps only, a number of qualifying points must be introduced. First, the influence of public opinion in foreign policy is more generally negative rather than positive. Public moods offer cues to governments concerning untenable policy choices, but such moods are poor guides to actual policy choices within the range of the tenable. The only times that public opinion may offer direct positive guidance concerning policy choice are at election times in some democratic countries, where electing a government may amount to selecting a policy program. Second, and more important, when theorists speak of "limits" over policy prerogative imposed by public opinion, it must be understood that such "limits" are in no sense absolute. In some countries elite and government efforts are directly aimed at molding and controlling public opinion. Here it is nonsense to talk about mass opinion "limiting" policy range, flexibility, or prerogative. Moreover, in all countries elite and government efforts are aimed at educating public opinion—i.e., overcoming mass resistance by information and persuasion. Initially untenable policy choices are in effect made tenable through deliberate efforts to change public resistance into public support. When one allows for persuasion and acknowledges that it more often succeeds than fails, the influence of public opinion over foreign policy dwindles from a limiting factor to a postponing factor at most.

Third, and very important also, it must be noted that public opinion in most countries supports most government policies, most of the time. This is especially true with regard to foreign policy. Because of emotional nationalism, basic allegiance to regimes, and basic legitimacy accorded governments, public opinion most often gives the reigning government the "benefit of the doubt" and supports official foreign policies. For example, Alexander Inkeles, Raymond Bauer, and Clyde Kluckhohn's *How the Soviet System Works* shows, to the surprise of many in the West, that most Soviet citizens support their nation's foreign policies—not because these people have been "brainwashed" but because they see the Soviet Government's policies as *their government's policies* and they lend approval to the extent that they lend the Soviet regime legitimacy (and this is to a considerable extent).[10]

Fourth, facts challenge the notion that the statesman is first and foremost a domestic politician bending always to the will, whims, and moods of public opinion. Many diplomatic histories could be written around the "profiles in political courage" theme, and many episodes could be described where statesmen moved against the grain of domestic public opinion toward what they perceived as a national interest that superseded both partisan politics and their own political careers. West Germany's Konrad Adenauer, for example, moved in face of overwhelmingly negative domestic opinion in the early 1950's to initiate German rearmament as a step toward regaining full sovereignty for West Germany in international politics.

10. Raymond A. Bauer, Alex Inkeles, and Clyde Kluckhohn, *How the Soviet System Works* (New York: Vintage Books, 1960), pp. 168–180.

CONDITIONS CONDUCIVE AND PROHIBITIVE TO PUBLIC OPINION INFLUENCE IN FOREIGN POLICY

While a good deal can be said about the influence of public opinion in foreign policy in terms of general limitations and restraints as discussed above, social scientists would like to be much more definite and specific about the "hows," "whens," and "whys" of mass influence. The first variety of questions that we would like to have better answers to concerns the predominant directions of flows of influence among masses, elites, and governments in particular countries and in all countries generally. At a high level of theoretical abstraction one can think of influence as indexed by attitude change induced by communications transmitted from one social/political sector (mass, elite, government) to another over time. Figure 3.3 depicts three alternative patterns of induced attitude change over time: (A) mass attitudes in one time period induce changes in elite attitudes in the second time period, and changes in elite attitudes in turn induce changes in governmental attitudes and policies in the third time period; (B) governmental attitudes and policies in the first time period induce changes in elite attitudes in the second period, and these in turn induce changes in mass attitudes in the third time period; (C) elite attitudes in the first time period induce changes in governmental attitudes and policies in the next period, and these policy changes induce changes in mass attitudes in the third time period.

Each of the patterns sketched in Figure 3.3 matches recountable historical situations and episodes. Pattern A, for example, is typical of "war-fever" such as one finds particularly in American history during years preceding the War of 1812, and, later, preceding the Spanish-American War in 1898.[11] Pattern B on the other hand is a typical "opinion mobilization" pattern with historical analogues in the Roosevelt Administration's attempt to educate American opinion away from isolationism during the period 1937–41, or in the West German Government's attempt to induce German masses and elites to accept rearmament during the period 1950–54. Pattern C, in which prerogative rests with elites or elite factions, has found realization in recent years in the movement toward international integration in Western Europe,

11. Julius W. Pratt, *Expansionists of 1812* (New York: Peter Smith, 1949), *passim;* Pratt, *Expansionists of 1898* (New York: Peter Smith, 1951), *passim.*

FIGURE 3.3. MODEL INFLUENCE PATTERNS LINKING PUBLIC OPINION AND GOVERNMENTAL POLICY

PATTERN A — MASS-INDUCED POLICY CHANGE

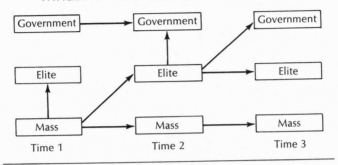

PATTERN B — GOVERNMENT-PRODUCED OPINION CHANGE

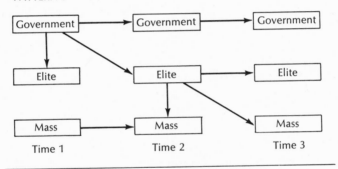

PATTERN C — ELITE-INITIATED POLICY CHANGE

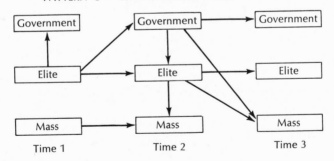

where initial elite inspiration was later officially endorsed, espoused and promoted, and still later, mass approved.

Since various patterns of initiation and influence are reflected in different historical situations, one central question for further research must concern conditions under which we may expect one or another of these influence patterns to occur, prevail, or predominate. Under what conditions does mass opinion move governments? When do governments educate mass opinion? Under what conditions do elite inspirations foment government policies and policy changes?

Though no firm answers to these questions are yet available, it is possible to point to a number of factors or variables that tend to influence patterns of induced attitude change. First, of course, it makes a difference within which country one is trying to chart flows of influence. This is for two reasons: (1) basic political/cultural patterns of initiative and compliance differ from country to country and these differences persist over time, and (2) the political/institutional structures of countries differ and such differences facilitate or prohibit certain patterns of communications, accessibility, and responsiveness. We would expect, for example, that influence would flow more readily from the masses to the government in a country with a strong democratic tradition, an effective and responsive legislature, a free press, and a system of organized interest articulation, than in a system without these characteristics. Similarly, we would expect a predominant flow of influence from the government to the masses in a country with an imbedded authoritarian tradition, a strong central administration, a controlled press, and an underdeveloped system of interest articulation. These points are obvious, but the obvious is easily overlooked. Less obvious, but still very important, we would also expect the direction of flows of influence to vary with the salience of issues and with the differential salience of issues to governments, elites, and masses respectively. In addition, the predominant direction of influence will vary according to the degree of mass, elite, or government consensus on an issue. Here it might be hypothesized that one sector's relative ability to induce attitude change in other sectors could be enhanced to the extent that it is united and the other sectors are divided, and diminished to the extent that it is divided and the other sectors are united. Therefore, political tradition, political structure, differential salience, and varying degrees of consensus are certainly among the variables that determine directions of influence in political systems. There are likely several additional variables that will ultimately have to be taken into account. The task for social science at the present time, however, is to isolate these additional relevant variables and to discover the nature of variable combinations that produce different patterns of induced attitude change. Success in this theory-building venture would carry our understanding of relationships between public opinion and foreign policy a major step forward.

PART TWO
GOALS AND MOTIVATIONS IN INTERNATIONAL BEHAVIOR

CHAPTER FOUR
GOALS IN INTERNATIONAL
POLITICS

TWO major themes pervade the several chapters in Part II: goals and motivations. In Chapter 4 analysis focuses first upon the goals that states and statesmen pursue in international politics. The chapter consequently takes inventory of the objects of international action, the values that states seek to preserve and promote, and the conditions they strive to realize. Then, at a less abstract level, analytical attention turns to the reasons why states and statesmen pursue particular goals at certain times. Chapters 5, 6, and 7 focus upon motivations for international behavior. There, in successive examinations of different international phenomena, attempts are made to discern why statesmen act to either realize or frustrate particular international outcomes. Overall, Part II moves from the general to the particular, from the abstract to the more concrete, in a broad effort to accumulate facts and findings concerning purpose in international politics.

INTERNATIONAL GOAL-SEEKING TO PRESERVE AND PROMOTE VALUES

In Chapter 1, international politics was depicted as a process of cooperation and competition among actors pursuing values or rewards. In that chapter, however, analysis was conducted at a very high level of theoretical abstraction, and, consequently, little was said about particular values or rewards actually pursued. Now we descend somewhat from the realm of high abstraction to discuss goal-seeking in international politics more comprehensively.

At least five pursuits must be included in any basic inventory of in-

73

ternational political goals: (1) self-preservation, (2) security, (3) prosperity, (4) prestige, and (5) peace. These aims are very general to be sure. But they are invariant historically and geographically, and hence serve well as foundation stones for a theory of international political goals. More than this, they translate readily into specific pursuits and policies for specific states at specific times. All foreign policies embody one or more of these general aims; and the pursuit of each of them tends to be fraught with implications, complexities, and ambiguities. Exploring the pursuit of these goals, therefore, carries one well beyond the simple checklist above and into an enriched understanding of some of the dynamics of international politics.

Some Ambiguities of Self-Preservation. Self-preservation is certainly a primary goal in international politics. In one sense, this goal is so basic that it is obvious, and therefore hardly worth discussing in great detail. Put simply, political units seek to survive. Complexity, however, begins to gather as soon as one steps beyond simple assertions. For one thing, what precisely does it mean to "survive" in the international arena? What survives? What is the "self" in self-preservation? Then too, what are the implications of states and statesmen pursuing self-preservation in a world arena where one government can deny the legitimacy or reject the existence of another? What are the implications of pursuing self-preservation in a world arena where the survival of one unit can become incompatible with the survival of another? In short, why have so many wars been fought under the banner of self-preservation?

Normally, preserving the state is prerequisite to pursuing all other goals in international politics, so that self-preservation must rank first in any hierarchical ordering of international political ends. "Preserving the state," however, means a number of things. First, it generally means preserving the sovereignty of the political unit, its external autonomy, and its government's authority and control over internal affairs. In addition, preserving the state means acting to guard the territory of the political unit and acting to protect the lives, well-being, and cultural values of populations residing on that territory. Then too, during revolutionary eras in world politics such as the present, acting toward self-preservation also comes to mean acting to preserve particular kinds of political, economic, and social traditions, institutions and practices characteristic of particular states. It is only under very special circumstances that a statesman would and could deliberately pursue policies that abnegate a state's survival in any of the senses listed here.[1]

There are, however, ambiguities in the goal of self-preservation. Many of these stem from inconsistencies in different states' political maps of the world. Through time, philosophers, scholars, and statesmen have argued, quite rightly, that expansionism and interventionism are among the major causes of war among states. They have also pointed out, quite reasonably, that one of the steps along the way to world peace should involve all states adopting a "live and let live" ethic embodied in policies of respect for neighbors' territories and populations and restraint from meddling in others' internal affairs.[2] Granted, such policies would contribute to world stability, *if international political reality permitted a realization of the "live and let live" ethic.*

Unfortunately, the political world is not parceled out into the kinds of neatly defined and universally recognized territorial and population units that the "live and let live" theorists postulate. Instead, in the world arena it is not always clear exactly where one state's territory ends, and where another's territory begins. Presently, for example, it is not exactly clear where India ends and China begins in the Himalayan region, or where the U.S.S.R. ends and China begins in Central Asia and in the Manchurian region. Nor, relatedly, is it always clear where one population ends and another begins, as in Nationalist and Communist China's conflicting claims to jurisdiction over the populations of both mainland China and the island of Formosa; North Vietnam's claims to jurisdiction over the population of South Vietnam; and Hitler's claims in the late 1930's to responsibility for Germans wherever they happened to reside. In extreme cases of ambiguity about the "self" in self-preservation, states have defined entire neighboring states as parts of themselves. Intermittently through the centuries both Japan and China have defined Korea as parts of themselves. Today, both Vietnams define each other out of existence. Not surprisingly, the two Germanys do likewise. The point here is that as long as political boundaries remain indefinite—and they will as long as it

1. Arnold Wolfers, *Discord and Collaboration* (Baltimore: The Johns Hopkins Press, 1962), p. 93 ff.
2. Raymond Aron, *Peace and War* (Garden City: Doubleday, 1966), pp. 749–752.

remains in some actors' interests that they should—states will tend to define neighbors' territories and populations as their own. Hence, we have probably not seen the last of "border" wars fought under the banner of self-preservation.

The Pursuit of Security and the Security Dilemma. While self-preservation and security are popularly used interchangeably, this usage, however, blurs some of the richness of meaning in the idea of security as applied to international politics. Seeking *security* for the state means seeking self-preservation, but it also means seeking an international environment wherein the question of survival is unlikely ever to be raised. More simply put, most states and most people desire a world where threats to their values and interests are minimal. Seeking security then means working to build the kind of world one would most like to live in—i.e., a threat-free environment.

Pursuing security can mean acting to preserve a particular state of affairs, or status quo, in international politics, if preserving such minimizes threats and maximizes comforts. More often though, seeking security means attempting to alter characteristics of the international environment that are perceived as militarily, politically, or economically discomforting or threatening. Consequently, while the pursuit of self-preservation is ideally defensive and should not lead to expansionism, or external meddling, the pursuit of security, as some statesmen see it, may well lead to assaults on international stability. The point here is not to justify aggression by calling it "acting in the pursuit of security." Rather, we simply note as a matter of empirical fact that acts of aggression frequently have been, and will continue to be, committed by states acting in the name of security. None of this is to say that security in altered international environments is not also pursued through international conciliation and cooperation.

Irony and foreboding surrounding the pursuit of security follow from the fact that different governments' definitions of "security" may be different to the point of incompatibility. The "tragic flaw" in international politics, lamented by philosophers over the years, is that different states' international political utopias tend often to be mutually exclusive, with the result that one state's *security* comes to be defined as another state's *insecurity*.

Problems in security-seeking can be illustrated with a few easily

3. Herbert Butterfield, *History and Human Relations* (London: Collins Clear-Type Press, 1951), pp. 9–36.

concretized theoretical models. Extending a line of analysis introduced in Chapter 1, the international environment at any point in time can be characterized in terms of distributions of attributes. In Figure 4.1, for example, the three graphs roughly illustrate what the contemporary international environment "looks like" according to prevailing distributions of military capabilities, per capita wealth, and ideological predispositions along an anti-Communist to Communist continuum. Each of the distributions is greatly skewed: (1) Figure 4.1A reflects a world where a very few states possess phenomenally great military might, and where most states cluster at moderately low levels of capability; (2) Figure 4.1B depicts an environment where a very few states control extremely high per capita wealth, a few too are extremely poor, and most cluster at moderately low GNP/capita levels; (3) Figure 4.1C shows a world where more states are committed to anti-Communist policies than to Communist policies, but where the greatest number of states cluster just "west" of the "uncommitted" center of the ideological continuum. Needless to say, these figures are impressionistic since only the wealth distribution is actually measurable. Still, they serve their descriptive purpose.

The first inference we might draw from Figure 4.1 is that some governments may feel secure with these prevailing distributions of military capability, wealth, and ideological predisposition. Many are nevertheless likely to feel anxious about one or all of them. Hence, some governments will define their security (i.e., stipulate the kind of world they want to live in) in terms of preserving some or all of the properties of the distributions pictured in Figure 4.1. But other governments will define their security in terms of changing some or all of the distributions (or, alternatively, changing their own positions within the prevailing distributions). We might guess, for example, that the United States would be relatively content in maintaining the present distribution of military capabilities in the world, since this preserves its positions of predominance at the extreme "superpower" end of the distribution. Therefore, Americans would define their security in terms of maintaining the world military status quo and they would act against others' attempts to alter this distribution. On the other hand, we might speculate that Communist China would probably define its security in terms of altering the world distribution of military capabilities, or at least altering its own position in this distribution. This being the case, if both the United States and Communist China actually define

FIGURE 4.1. APPROXIMATE GLOBAL DISTRIBUTIONS OF MILITARY CAPABILITY, PER CAPITA WEALTH, AND IDEO-LOGICAL PREDISPOSITION IN THE 1960'S

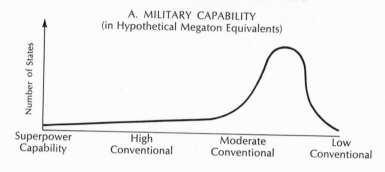

A. MILITARY CAPABILITY
(in Hypothetical Megaton Equivalents)

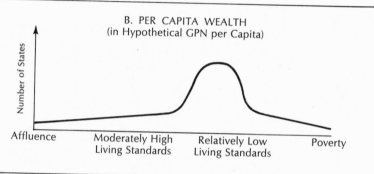

B. PER CAPITA WEALTH
(in Hypothetical GPN per Capita)

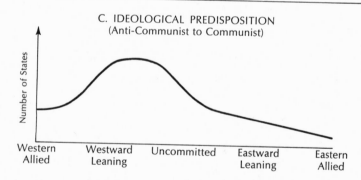

C. IDEOLOGICAL PREDISPOSITION
(Anti-Communist to Communist)

military security as we speculated, the two definitions would be incompatible and security for one state would mean insecurity for the other.

In the case of distribution of ideological predispositions, we might hypothesize that neither the United States nor the Soviet Union (nor certainly Communist China) is very satisfied in the contemporary environment. Each ideological leader views the other, as well as those who lean toward him, with apprehension. Hence, each would define his own security in terms of shifting the distribution of ideological adherence radically in his own favor. Therefore, if we speculate about the American definition of security in terms of world distribution of ideological predispositions we might picture an environment as depicted in Figure 4.2A, where the Communist and Communist-leaning portions of the distribution have all but disappeared as a result of a marked shift toward the anti-Communist end. From the Russian side, of course, the preferred environment would be exactly the opposite, and perhaps even a bit more extreme, as shown in Figure 4.2B. Here, in the "world" most comforting for the Soviet Union, the anti-Communist portion of the distribution has completely disappeared and even the "uncommitted" range is nearly depopulated. Most states have swung into Communist alignment.

Finally, concerning the distribution of wealth in the world, we can hypothesize a situation where no state in the present-day system is content with the international environment as depicted, and where all states would like to live in a world where the distribution of wealth has been altered in the direction of more equality at higher economic levels. If we accept the industrialized states' affirmations of interest in aiding economic development in the poorer countries, and recognize these poorer countries' interests in betterment, then we can hypothesize a possible "future" that approximates Figure 4.2C, where everyone is economically "better off." This example was introduced to point to the possible, rather than to predict the probable. That is, one state's security need not necessarily be defined in terms of others' insecurity. Security can be pursued through cooperation as well as competition, and a key to peaceful evolution in the world environment lies in the ability of states to find more mutually compatible definitions of security.

Prosperity: The Economic Ends of International Politics. The quest after wealth takes many forms in the history of international politics—some noble and some ignoble. This quest, embodied in the foreign policies of states, both in remote and more recent times, has been carried on by open plunder, by direct and indirect exploitation, by

FIGURE 4.2. ACTUAL DISTRIBUTIONS OF IDEOLOGICAL PREDISPOSITION AND PER CAPITA WEALTH COMPARED WITH HYPOTHETICALLY PREFERRED DISTRIBUTIONS

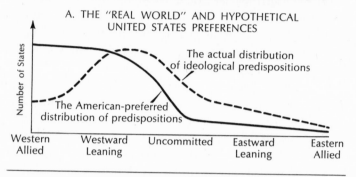

A. THE "REAL WORLD" AND HYPOTHETICAL UNITED STATES PREFERENCES

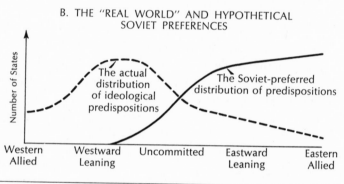

B. THE "REAL WORLD" AND HYPOTHETICAL SOVIET PREFERENCES

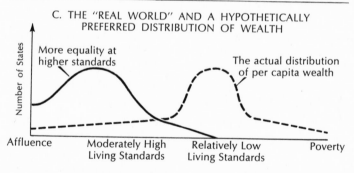

C. THE "REAL WORLD" AND A HYPOTHETICALLY PREFERRED DISTRIBUTION OF WEALTH

trade and barter, by cooperation in resource development, and by agreements to international schemes for economic integration.

Need and greed are the motivations for wealth-seeking via international politics. States and statesmen enter the international political arena to procure resources essential to national economic well-being but unavailable (or available only at great cost) domestically. Procurement sometimes takes the form of reasonably equitable exchanges among states. But countless examples of disguised or outright seizure can also be offered. Moreover, while mutual efforts to promote economic well-being have both fostered and nurtured amicable bonds among peoples, drives toward economic imperialism have also been at the roots of countless international wars. The paradox in wealth-seeking as an international political goal is that it can be a source of international conflict, but it does not have to be. Conversely, wealth-seeking can be a foundation for international cooperation, but it frequently is not.

Some of the dilemmas and varied outcomes from wealth-seeking in international politics stem from inconsistencies between assumptions of international economic theory and the realities of politics. According to the economic theory of "comparative advantage," all states should gain from international exchanges.[4] In theory, lowest costs in the production of any given commodity are incurred by producers whose mastery over technology, proximity to basic resources, climatic environment, established marketing facilities, and the like result in highest efficiency. Moreover, because of differences in the distribution of resources, "know-how," and other efficiency-generating factors around the world, almost every country has the opportunity to be a "most efficient producer" of some group of commodities. Hence, in theory, the whole world would stand to gain if each country produced only those commodities it could produce most efficiently and traded these for other commodities "most efficiently" produced in other countries. Adherence to the dictates of comparative advantage would certainly result in an economically interdependent world. Some have argued that community built through economic interdependence might provide the foundation for lasting international peace.

Well it might, but the world of free trade is not the world we live in, and for a number of strong *political* reasons equitable exchanges among most efficient producers are not the most characteristic forms of international wealth-seeking. Basically, a world economic system built from the logic of comparative advantage and free trade must be a

4. Gottfried Haberler, *A Survey of International Trade Theory* (Princeton: Princeton University, Department of Economics, 1961).

system wherein the rationale of economic efficiency, *and this rationale alone,* determines international wealth-seeking behavior and accounts for flows of goods, capital, and labor from point to point in the international system. But, in the "real world" political considerations tend often to be more important than economic ones in determining wealth-seeking behavior:

1. Free trade considerations discriminate among potential economic partners on the basis of relative efficiency in production and comparative advantage only. However, world political lines of amity and enmity encourage economic flows in some directions and discourage them in others, so that political patterns influence economic patterns regardless of where comparative advantage might lie.

2. The economic rationale of free trade and comparative advantage implies states' acquiescence in universal economic development and heightened well-being around the world. Because of the strong perceived relationship between economic development and military prowess, though, the economic logic of universal growth is often contradicted by the political logic of military superiority. Retarding an enemy's economic development is often sought (or at least welcomed), and international economic policies may be specifically formulated to enhance the accumulation of wealth at home while hindering such accumulation in a hostile state.

3. Relatedly, under the tenets of comparative advantage and free trade, states should, by economic logic, refrain from producing raw materials and finished products that might be more efficiently produced elsewhere. This might make sense when one is talking about tropical- and temperate-zone foodstuffs; but most governments would argue that it becomes political nonsense once one begins talking about coal, petroleum, steel, guns, tanks, and airplanes. States choose to produce strategic raw materials and finished products, often at very great cost, rather than to leave themselves dependent upon other states and upon shifting patterns of international unity and enmity. Hence, quite contrary to the economic good sense of comparative advantage, which calls for specialization, political good sense in a tenuous world seems to call for economic autarky. This same kind of political reasoning has also prompted aggressive drives designed to gain control over resources deemed essential for autarky.

4. There are reasons stemming from domestic politics why statesmen may be prohibited from engaging in cooperative forms of wealth-seeking in the international arena. First, to the extent that a state is not the most efficient producer of a given commodity but produces it anyway, movement toward free trade in that particular commodity would undermine a domestic industry and result in bankruptcy and unemployment. Very often, and in many countries, the threat of domestic disruption from foreign competition unleashes powerful local political forces that demand tariffs and other protective measures designed to offset the comparative advantages of "foreigners." As often as not, though, unilateral protectionist actions are met by international retaliations, with the result that reciprocal rounds of "tariff raisings" reap significant gains for scattered local industries, but mark overall losses for the world economy. In addition, of course, economic warfare fosters immediate and sometimes long-lasting international political animosities.

5. Finally, a system of free trade based upon comparative advantage must be a system where all states are economically developed to the point where their full economic potentials are realized. When this is not the case, comparative economic advantages become artificial and reflect differential levels of economic development rather than differentials in productive efficiency. It might be argued, for example, that the United States enjoys a comparative advantage over India in producing automobiles not because the United States is nearer to raw materials, and not because Americans are more technologically inclined or inventive than Indians, but rather because the United States has an automobile industry and India does not. Were India to develop such an industry, it is conceivable that that country might gain the comparative advantage and a slice of the international automobile market. It is clear that such a situation of artificial comparative advantage based upon differential economic development has critical political implications in a world where economic underdevelopment is prevalent. In effect, remaining within the contemporary international economic system, and abiding by the tenets of comparative advantage, real and artificial, dictated by this system, would demand that many states forego industrialization and continue in perpetuity as producers of foodstuffs and raw materials. Understandably, governments in most

underdeveloped countries reject these tenets and seek industrialization not so much to gain access to a cooperative world economy as to gain exit from an economy which they perceive as biased against them.

Summing up, the quest after wealth through interactions and exchanges among states is prevalent, but its forms and outcomes are varied. The wealth of one state need not be increased at another's expense. But it often is. Economic cooperation can be a pathway to widespread increases in well-being. But economic competition, nevertheless, tends to be the pathway most frequently chosen. The divergences between the many "oughts" and "ises" raised here can be explained in terms of contradictions between the kind of political world necessary for cooperative economic interactions, and the kind of political world that exists. Economic rationality leaves no place for political animosities, national military security considerations, domestic political footballs, and national inferiority complexes. But political reality includes all of these, with the result that the pursuit of wealth via international politics most frequently comes to mean the pursuit of one state's wealth at another's expense.

Prestige: Attributes, Symbols, and Impacts of International Status. Attempting to define exactly what "prestige" means in the context of international politics can be somewhat involved, since "prestige" is both an *attribute* and an *attribution*. Prestige in international politics means "attention, deference, and respect accorded to one state by others." But this definition implies, of course, that the prestigious state possesses attributes commanding of attention, demanding of deference, and worthy of respect. It is hardly worth a long elaboration here to show that prestige is sought in international politics. It most certainly is. But more significant and more interesting questions have to do with why states seek prestige, how they seek it, and when and why they gain it or lose it.

High positions in the international status ordering are sought primarily for two reasons. First, for some states and statesmen, under particular conditions, gaining or escalating prestige may become international political ends in themselves. Various statesmen throughout history have consciously and deliberately set their states on paths of glory for glory's sake alone. More often, however, statesmen seek prestige for their states because heightened prestige tends to facilitate the attainment of other more fundamental international political goals.

Prestige buys security, and it buys influence. Furthermore, it implies responsibility, but it sometimes permits irresponsibility.

For some nations, as for some men, accomplishment is hollow without recognition. Gaining recognition therefore becomes an integral part of accomplishment. At a pathological extreme, gaining recognition can become the sole definition of accomplishment, and ego-satisfaction can become the paramount motive for action. Few states enter international politics solely, or even primarily, to improve their positions in the international status hierarchy, and fewer lapse toward the pathological extreme of obsession with status. Nevertheless, some elements of action in pursuit of ego-satisfaction can be detected in the behavior of many statesmen and in most states' foreign policies. How else, for example, are we to explain glamorous international airlines operated and subsidized by the governments of poverty-stricken countries, or heavy naval vessels moored in the inland lakes of land-locked states, or "races" into outer space, except by noting that statesmen and their constituent populations gain satisfaction from possessing and displaying symbols of international status?

More seriously, international status-seeking as an end in itself is closely linked to *revanchism* in international politics. For states defeated in wars, especially major wars or encounters with traditional rivals, for states duped in diplomacy or otherwise outdistanced by competitors, and generally for states descended from the pinnacle of former world power, psychological frustrations from undermined status can become prime determinants of foreign policy. In fact, the drive to regain lost status may become an obsession. Witness, for example, Hitler's passion to overturn the Versailles settlement, Adenauer's drive to rebuild German status after World War II, De Gaulle's obsessions with recapturing France's former grandeur, and American reactions to the first Soviet Sputnik.

Relatedly, much of what can be said about older states in search of lost status, may also be noted of newer states in quest of recognition. Here again, felt needs for status may become prime determinants of foreign policy. This is especially the case, for example, with revolutionary regimes whose postrevolutionary priority must be to gain recognition and legitimacy for the new government. The drive for status can be acute when a new revolutionary elite suffers from an "inferiority complex" fostered by years of alien rule, and the new government feels it must prove to the world that it is capable of self-government and hence deserving of status in the international system. Then, too, a revolutionary regime may also strive vigorously for international political status when its ascent to power represents the first institutionalization of a new political ideology. In such cases gaining international status is linked to bringing recognition and deference for the new political credo.

It is difficult to say exactly when a state seeks international prestige as an end in itself, and when the state seeks prestige in order to promote other ends. The two are closely linked. What is clear, however, is that gaining international prestige often opens the way to attaining other ends. For example, states may project images of powerful military capability and determination and thereby contribute to their security by discouraging external threats. Here the projected image may or may not follow from actual military might. What is significant is that the *image* brings deference and cautions would-be aggressors. Furthermore, reputations for military prowess tend often to carry through time so that a state's projected image of power may continue to discourage external threats long after the material bases for power have deteriorated. The bases for French power, for example, were irreparably destroyed during World War I, but French prestige, flowing from former power, served France's security for nearly twenty years after Versailles. In the same sense, it took nearly twenty years after World War II for diplomats, analysts, and Britons to recognize British descent from major-power rank.

Projected images of greatness and positions near the top of the international status hierarchy are springboards to international political influence. Prestige in international politics can impute to the possessor a "right to be interested," a "right to be informed," and a "right to be involved" in most political episodes and interactions about the globe. These "rights" tend to be both expected by prestigious states and, tacitly, though not always enthusiastically, accepted by less prestigious ones. But, while prestige paves a way for influence, it also tends to permit a certain arrogance that may be destructive both to states' interests and to world stability. Arrogance is the product of self-satisfaction and self-confidence generated by the attainment of major-power status. It is expressed in self-righteousness, rigidity of policy, preaching, and refusals to accept counsel from allies or compromise from enemies. Projecting arrogance may be functional to preserving a state's security in the short run. But arrogance embodied as the predominant attitude of foreign policy may well signal an ossification of that policy, fleeting capabilities for adjustment to world political change, and the beginning of descent from major-power status.

Prestige in international politics follows from possessing, or at least appearing to possess, a number of status-endowing attributes. Generally speaking, reputation follows first, and perhaps foremost, from past performance. Attention and deference attach almost automatically to a state that embodies, symbolizes, or "carries along" a tradition of international political involvement and a record of challenges met and mastered. In international politics, as in many political cultures around the world, status adheres to longevity, deference goes to experience, and continuing action and accomplishment attract attention. One of the most effective ways to preserve status in international politics is to have had it for a long time. Relatedly, optimum means for gaining status seem to involve either surviving in the international system for a long time, or remaining continually active in the system, or, most effectively, both surviving for a long time and making a good deal of "noise" while doing so. Moreover, as noted earlier, since status follows from past performance, it very often persists for some time after the forces and factors that generated it disappear. For example, among the many suggestive findings in J. David Singer and Melvin Small's research into international status is the observation that Spain still holds residual prestige carried over from its "golden age" in the fifteenth and sixteenth centuries.[5]

Beyond the relationship between past performance and international prestige, status tends also to follow from states' possession or control over more tangible attributes. These tend to vary in prestige value from era to era in international political history. Among attributes almost universally recognized as contributors to international prestige one could list territorial immensity, large population, affluence, formidable military capability or potential, and other "bigness" factors that gain attention, respect, and deference by inspiring awe or invoking dread. Whereas large states can build prestige by projecting ominous-

5. J. David Singer and Melvin Small, "The Composition and Status Ordering of International Systems: 1815–1940," *World Politics*, XVIII, No. 2 (January, 1966), 236–282.

ness, smaller ones must seek status by projecting images of enlightened statesmanship, effectiveness at international mediation and conciliation, stubborn and persistent neutrality, and initiative in drives toward international peace and stability.

Regarding variance in international prestige symbols over time, one may note that during the sixteenth and seventeenth centuries prestige accrued from the affluence and grandeur of princely courts; in the eighteenth and nineteenth centuries prestige was measured by the expansiveness and wealth of overseas empires; and in the early twentieth century naval power became the prime attribute of status. At present a dubious kind of prestige accompanies membership in the "nuclear club." Industrialization, rapidly rising rates of economic growth and development, scientific and technological sophistication, and spectacular space achievement also contribute positively to international status in our era. Moreover, with the revolution in world communications, and the consequent "exposure" of one society to others, projected images of internal tranquillity, harmonious relations among domestic minorities, and democratic government are also becoming international prestige symbols. Among Communist states, deference flows to those who can demonstrate ideological leadership by convincingly arguing the soundness of their particular Marxist interpretations. In the Western world prestige was for a time linked to anti-Communist zeal displayed. The governments of some of the newer nations have boosted their international prestige in recent years, at least among their peers, through persistence and articulateness in voicing anti-colonial and anti-imperialist themes. Others in this group have gained high status by their steadfast noncommitment in the Cold War.

The Pursuit of Peace in International Politics. Examining peace as a goal in international politics can be productive only if one avoids cynicism. To be sure, if peace is a fundamental goal of states and statesmen, it is seldom attained in an historical era, and never attained lastingly. But to show that peace is elusive is not to argue that it is unsought or insincerely sought. Neither does the history of peace efforts shattered necessarily demonstrate that all of those who pursue peace are utopians.

Professing peace is by far more common in diplomatic practice than actually pursuing it. But both cold logic and moral sensitivity motivate statesmen to eschew war. The political "realist" in world affairs, who bases his international behavior on a strict calculus of values gained and lost in political-military encounter, may well try to avoid violence because of the costs involved. War has always been highly wasteful of human and material resources, and each advance in weaponry over the centuries has exponentially escalated the price of warfare to both vanquished and victor. In terms of men, money, and constructive investments foregone, all sides lose in every war. At present, the prospect of thermonuclear conflict makes any "gains versus costs" calculus almost farcical, for, even if there may once have been some dubious kind of rationale for warfare based on relative losses among contestants, nuclear exchange must add up to utter senselessness. Hence, if "peace" is taken to mean "the avoidance of violent conflict," even the most Machiavellian of statesmen may pursue peace as the less expensive alternative to war.

After all is said about the calculus of war and peace (and a great deal more will be offered on the subject here when the theme is confronted directly in Chapter 7), it would be shortsighted to conclude that statesmen pursue peace only because this tends to make good sense in preserving and promoting rather narrowly defined national self-interests. Philosophers since classical times have passionately, and among their students at least, convincingly, argued for the justice, virtue, and desirability of universal peace. Peace, they have proclaimed, should be the primary goal of statecraft because it is right, noble, humanly elevating, and humanly enlightening. War, by the same arguments, is morally wrong and humanly degrading. Foundations for philosophies of peace range from religious mysticisms, to secular metaphysics of natural law, to humanist premises for civilization, to utilitarian assumptions about popular will and reason, to Marxist postulates about universal community.[6] While recoiling from the utopianism of most philosophers' designs, statesmen have not been able, nor have they generally wanted, to ignore the wisdom and promise of the philosophers' ends. Scrutiny of diaries, autobiographies, biographies, and state and private papers of many world leaders has convinced analysts that efforts to avoid war as well as initiatives to institutionalize peace have often followed from deeply rooted personal

6. F. H. Hinsley, *Power and the Pursuit of Peace* (Cambridge: The University Press, 1967), pp. 13–152.

abhorrence of war and consequent conviction about the moral imperatives of world peace.

As elaborated in Chapter 7, most designs and proposed instrumentalities for world peace follow from assumptions about the primary causes of war. Those, for example, who see the roots of war in man's primordial aggressive instincts, offer peace designs that embody plans for reforming human nature and remodeling human character. Alternatively, those who lament the anarchy that customarily prevails in the international system, and see the prime cause of war in this, offer peace plans that call for world order through world government.[7] Still others see the roots of violent conflict in "communications gaps" among peoples and hope, optimistically, that international harmony will be a product of a world made "smaller" through communications technology and heightened intercultural contact. Those essentially pessimistic about human reform and international institutionalization suggest that peace might be preserved in two possible ways: either all states might deny themselves war-making capabilities through disarmament, or each state might arm to the teeth and participate in a system of globally balanced power.[8] Finally, the idea that world peace through world empire is conceptually and technologically possible has never been entirely lacking in advocates. Neither, for that matter, have the ideas of peace through appeasement and peace through unilateral capitulation gone without theorists and practitioners.

SOME AMBIGUITIES IN INTERNATIONAL GOAL-SEEKING

For the sake of clarity in presentation, a number of simplifying conventions were followed in this chapter's discussion of goals in international politics. First, descriptions of goals were cast in abstract categorical terms—self-preservation, security, prosperity, prestige, and peace. These terms perhaps are more meaningful to the theorist and observer of international politics than to the practitioner. Second, goals were separated analytically and separately defined and discussed. Isolating goals and tracing their pursuits as discrete patterns

7. Kenneth N. Waltz, *Man, the State, and War* (New York: Columbia University Press, 1959), *passim*.

8. Hans J. Morgenthau, *Politics Among Nations*, 4th ed. (New York: Alfred A. Knopf, 1967), pp. 161–171.

of international behavior were useful measures for general understanding. But, they again were a substantial step away from international political reality, in which states simultaneously pursue multiple goals, and in which single acts may have manifold ends. Third, much of the discussion of international goal-seeking in this chapter followed from necessary, but somewhat artificial, assumptions about congruences between objective and subjective reality. It was implied, for instance, that statesmen consciously and deliberately pursue certain goals, and that they are always able to recognize the goals they are pursuing. Relatedly, it was also postulated that statesmen have relatively little difficulty in identifying the goals that their allies and adversaries are pursuing. While these assumptions, again, are formally useful, they distort reality to a considerable extent. Hence, since the formal treatment of goal-seeking in this chapter in fact circumvented many of the ambiguities of actual international behavior, it is appropriate and important, now that the rudimentary concepts have been introduced, to underline some of the complexities.

Generality and Specificity in Goal-Seeking. We, as analysts, might order our understanding of international politics by conceiving of international goal-seeking in terms of abstract values pursued. But, for the typical statesman, goal-seeking usually means pursuing a desired *specific* outcome using a specific set of instrumentalities. Self-preservation, security, prosperity, prestige, and even peace mean different specific things to particular statesmen acting in particular situations. In practice, the abstract goals are concretized into tangible and immediate policy ends—e.g., winning a boundary dispute, deterring a would-be aggressor, signing a trade agreement, buttressing an international organization, and many, many more. Hence, when we say, theoretically, that we can "observe" a state pursuing self-preservation, what we are saying operationally is that we can observe statesmen engaged in particular patterns of action that we interpret as contributing to their states' preservation. The point here need not be labored. Goal-seeking in the day-to-day interplay of international politics is seldom immediately conceived by statesmen as a quest after abstract values. Values, however, certainly underlie and condition choice of specific ends and means in specific situations.

Multiple Goal-Seeking. It is conceptually possible to link single motivations to single patterns of behavior executed to produce single outcomes. But such conceptualization is neither very satisfying nor very realistic. Most individuals in personal endeavors, most groups in social endeavors, and most states in international politics continually mix—simultaneously—multiple motivations to pursue multiple ends by multiple means. Furthermore, men in action seldom pause to unravel their mixed motivations and jumbled ends. Hence, while it is theoretically possible, and—for developing rudimentary understanding, desirable—to talk about discrete goals in international politics, in actuality it is nearly impossible to identify acts taken in pursuit of one and only one goal. Practically speaking, statesmen generally act either to change a situation "for the better," or to keep it from "changing for the worst"; and such action almost always involves the simultaneous pursuit of several goals. Consider a border dispute, for example. In strict territorial terms we could say that the participants in the dispute are acting in pursuit of self-preservation. However, if the disputed territory holds mineral deposits or forms a military staging area, we might also argue that the contestants are acting for prosperity or security. Then too, if settlement means an end to a long-festering, unpleasant episode, we might say that the participants are pursuing peace. Finally, if victory or settlement raises the international stature of one or both parties, we could say that heightened prestige might be one sought outcome. The mixture of goals sought in any situation depends, of course, upon the situation. But in almost every situation, states' actions will follow from multiple goals. Careful analysis must take this complexity into account.

Actual Goals and Attributed Goals. It goes almost without saying that information about the goals and intentions of other states is an essential input into every state's foreign policy system. Moreover, *having information* about other states' goals means a good deal more than assuming that they are pursuing self-preservation, security, prosperity, prestige, and peace. It means knowing how other states define these abstract values in concrete terms, and it means knowing what kinds of specific outcomes they will prefer and act toward in specific situations. Needless to say, any state's policies can succeed or fail in the light of accurate or inaccurate assessments of others' goals.

In a theoretical world of perfect information, identifying and assessing states' goals poses no problems. But in the real world of international politics—where geographic, technical, ideological, and cultural barriers hinder the rapid effective flow of information, where states deliberately distort information, and where men's predispositions and suspicions work to prevent the accurate interpretation of otherwise valid information—identifying and assessing international political goals becomes a practical problem of major magnitude. So much is this the case that *the uncertainty and ambiguity of goals is a basic fact of international political life.* No statesman ever knows *for sure* what goals his adversaries, or even his allies, are pursuing.

To take an example, the effectiveness of much of American foreign policy at present depends to a considerable extent upon an accurate assessment of the international political goals of the Soviet Union. Yet, no one knows *for sure* whether the U.S.S.R. remains a revolutionary state bent upon overturning the international system and reforming it in a Marxist-Leninist mold, or whether the Russians have abandoned, or never really espoused, the goal of world revolution. American goals, of course, must be equally perplexing for Kremlin analysts.

The statesman's response to the ambiguity of international goals generally takes the form of more or less "educated" guessing. Since it is practically impossible to frame one's foreign policies without considering other's goals, such consideration sometimes amounts, for want of any alternative, to cautiously taking others' stated goals at face value. Then, too, goal assessment may amount to assuming that the adversary or ally is basically rational and attributing to him goals that a "rational man" would pursue.[9] Beyond this, goals are oftentimes attributed on the basis of historical analogy, with the reasoning that states pursue "traditional" goals over spans of decades or even centuries, or that when a particular situation arises, a state will pursue the same goals it pursued the last time that kind of situation arose.[10] Often too, and perhaps too often, goals are attributed on the basis of ideologically tinged assumptions and predispositions. To Communist statesmen, states with capitalist economic systems are believed to be internationally imperialistic *by definition.* Similarly, to some Western statesmen, Communist states are taken to be conspiratorial and revolutionary by implication, since Communists are seen as conspiratorial and revolutionary.

9. Thomas C. Schelling, *The Strategy of Conflict* (Cambridge: Harvard University Press, 1960), pp. 3–20.

10. Roy C. Macridis, ed., *Foreign Policy in World Politics,* 2nd ed. (Englewood Cliffs, N.J.: Prentice-Hall, 1967), *passim.*

While attributing goals to other states is necessary when these goals remain unknown, and while attribution is sometimes accurate, the probability of error is high for obvious reasons. Furthermore, the implications of error are sometimes disastrous. Neville Chamberlain, for example, took Hitler's goals at face value in the 1930's, and Franklin Roosevelt read moderation into Stalin's goals in the 1940's. Historians now agree that Roosevelt inadvertently handed Stalin the "keys" to Eastern Europe. Chamberlain nearly lost all of Europe.

CONCLUSION

To provide descriptive breadth rather than analytical depth has been the plan of this chapter. The main focus has been on international political goals, their definitions, and some general characteristics of their pursuit. Only tangential attention has been paid, however, to the motivations that underlie various goal-pursuits—the drives, if you will, that egg men and nations onto paths of glory, paths of peace, or paths of destruction. As noted in the introduction to the chapter, we will now select three very different international political phenomena—imperialism, regional integration, and peace—and ask "what," "how," and "why" of each. In this way it will be possible both to observe the abstract goals discussed in this chapter in more concrete forms, and to expose some of the motivational dynamics behind international goal-seeking.

CHAPTER FIVE
IMPERIALISM:
WHAT AND WHY?

AGGRANDIZEMENT is an elemental and recurrent pattern of political behavior. Indeed, the more somber among international political analysts encapsulate the entire history of international politics into a continuing story of different states' successful and unsuccessful attempts at territorial, economic, political, and cultural aggrandizement. Those who take a broader view of the spectrum of international political behavior suggest that while cooperative behavior should not be minimized in international history, the record of international domination, exploitation, and subjugation cannot be ignored. All would agree that attempted aggrandizement, or imperialism, met by provoked resistance is a basic causal sequence leading to international war.

Understanding why statesmen set their states on courses of aggrandizement means explaining the motivations beneath and behind international imperialism. Why, for example, do some states find it desirable to control or dominate other states and to exploit or subjugate alien peoples? Is an act of imperialism a predetermined historical necessity, a playing out of some grand teleological design? Or is it rather a willful and calculated statesman's choice? Is imperialism a manifestation of some inherent human aggressive drive? Or is it a phenomenon that follows logically and empirically from certain forms of social, economic, and political organization? Does imperialism follow from capitalism? Are imperialism and imperialist wars predictably recurrent for all time? Or can we envisage a future relatively free from economic, political, and cultural exploitation, subjugation, and domination? These are some of the questions that this chapter is addressed to answering. Working towards answers involves first a search for a satisfactory operational definition of "imperialism," next an analysis of manifestations of imperialism, and finally a linking of the defined phenomenon and its manifestations with theories concerned with underlying causes.

IMPERIALISM AS PROCESS AND SITUATION

There are almost as many definitions of "imperialism" as there are theorists, political analysts, and historians who have tried to define it. However, the different definitions are by and large complementary, since each clarifies a particular aspect of the phenomenon. William Langer, one of the most eminent historians of imperialism, defines "imperialism" both as a socio-economic-political condition and as a motivational drive. Imperialism, says Langer, is rule or control by one people over another or the urge to establish such control.[1] By Langer's definition, one acts imperialistically by exercising control over alien peoples, but one becomes an imperialist by feeling the urge to dominate. Hans J. Morgenthau, arguing on a more abstract level and addressing himself more directly to political forms of imperialism, suggests that:

A nation whose foreign policy aims at acquiring more power than it actually has through a reversal of existing power relations—whose foreign policy in other words seeks a favorable change in power status—pursues a policy of imperialism.[2]

For Morgenthau, imperialism is a process of acquiring power—i.e., by implication beyond the cited passage, a process of taking resources that constitute the bases of state power away from other states in the international system. Though "rule" or "control" by one people over another is not explicit or even essential in Morgenthau's definition of "imperialism," his later descriptions of means for acquiring power include the imposition of direct controls.[3]

Whereas Morgenthau's frame of reference for defining "imperial-

1. William L. Langer, *The Diplomacy of Imperialism, 1890–1902,* 2nd ed. (New York: Alfred A. Knopf, 1956), p. 67.
2. Hans J. Morgenthau, *Politics Among Nations,* 4th ed. (New York: Alfred A. Knopf, 1967), pp. 36–37.
3. *Ibid.,* p. 55ff.

ism" is primarily political, Vladimir Lenin's classic approach is economic. For Lenin, imperialism is both a process and a situation—a *process* of political subjugation that follows from needs for economic exploitation, and a *situation* wherein the world becomes territorially subdivided into politically controlled economic spheres of influence. According to Lenin then, imperialism:

> . . . is the highest stage of capitalism characterized by: (1) monopolies and the concentration of production capital, (2) financial oligarchy in control, (3) the export of capital, not commodities, (4) the sharing of the world among internationalist capitalist monopolies, (5) the complete territorial sub-division of the earth.[4]

Finally, on a somewhat different tack, Joseph Schumpeter in his essay *The Sociology of Imperialism* lays primary emphasis on the social-psychological dimension in imperialist behavior. For Schumpeter, the social-psychology of imperialism amounts to a pathology, an activity without rational meaning or material reward, an "objectless disposition on the part of a state for unlimited forcible expansion."[5] Imperialism here becomes an expansionist drive motivated by sinister mechanisms inherent in group psychology.

The various theories of causation behind imperialist behavior mentioned here certainly deserve to be explored more elaborately, as they will be later in this chapter. For the moment, however, let us attempt to piece together a working definition of "imperialism" from the collection of themes given in the partial definitions offered so far. Upon analysis it is clear that there are at least two major themes running through the various definitions. First, imperialism may be thought of as a *condition* or *situation* wherein one state or people politically, economically or culturally dominates or subjugates another state or people. While there is a good deal of controversy concerning why the imperialist situation prevails, there is nonetheless agreement in the observation that imperialism is characteristically a superordination-subordination situation. Second, the theme of *process* or *policy* also runs through the different conceptions of imperialism. That is, imperialism is not only domination but also the act of dominating or

4. Vladimir Lenin, *Imperialism the Highest Stage of Capitalism* (New York: International Publishers, 1939), p. 89.
5. Joseph Schumpeter, "Imperialism," in *Two Essays by Joseph Schumpeter*, Heinz Norden, tr. (Cleveland: The World Publishing Company, 1955), p. 6.

attempting to dominate. Langer also implies that the process of imperialism actually begins with wanting to subjugate: hence, an imperialist may be either a ruler over dominated peoples or an aspirant to such a role. Combining both themes into a single definition then, let us say that *imperialism is the actual or attempted political, economic, or cultural domination of one state or people by another.*

Deriving the definition of imperialism as I have done here amounts to a kind of semantic hairsplitting, but such hairsplitting here is not a mere intellectual game. The term "imperialism" has highly controversial and often inflammatory connotations in contemporary international politics, and it tends to be used extremely loosely by most polemicists. The term represents, for example, a key concept in Communist propaganda directed against the West; a fundamental rallying cry in "third world" denunciations of broad ranges of Western policy; a concept in dispute between Maoist and Russian Communists; a major lament of New Left opponents of American foreign policy here in the United States; and, ironically, a Western description of Communist rule in Eastern Europe and elsewhere. It is also a descriptive term applied to a particular and recurrent pattern of international behavior characterized by the actual or attempted political, economic, or cultural domination of one state or people by another; and this latter sense is the only sense in which "imperialism" is used in this book. *Regardless of what the polemicists argue, the test for imperialism in any state's policies rests in the weight of empirical evidence showing actual or intended political, economic, or cultural domination.*

VARIETIES OF IMPERIALISM

When one thinks about imperialism in practice, or pictures to oneself what the phenomenon "looks like" as it occurs, one tends to think most often about a particular variety of political-military imperialism wherein one state achieves and exercises its domination by directly controlling the government of another state, or else, more simply, by destroying the government of another state and subjugating its people. Political-military imperialism, especially when implemented violently, is indeed the most conspicuous form of the phenomenon. Historically it has probably been the most common form. Great conquests—Rome over the Mediterranean world, Spain over the New World, Napoleon over Europe, Britain over India, Russia over central Asia, and the like—mark historical eras. Nevertheless, it should be borne in mind that imperialism also assumes other, more subtle forms: [6]

1. ONE STATE MAY DOMINATE ANOTHER ECONOMICALLY WITHOUT MANIFESTLY CONTROLLING IT POLITICALLY. The economy of an economically underdeveloped state may be externally controlled, for example, by virtue of an economically advanced state's ability to manipulate the weaker state's foreign trade markets and foreign exchange reserves. For many underdeveloped nations, foreign trade markets are the only available sources of wide ranges of manufactured goods, and sales on foreign markets are the only sources of foreign exchange with which manufactured goods may be purchased. Moreover, a great many economically underdeveloped nations, either by tradition or by necessity, do the bulk of their trading with a single economically advanced nation. This kind of economic dependence may reach a point where decisions made in the advanced nation can spell economic disaster for the weaker one. Moreover, when such is the case, economic control may also be fostered by the direct investment of capital from advanced states in the economies of weaker states: when a high proportion of a state's industry is foreign owned and operated, employment comes under control of foreign entrepeneurs, government revenue comes in large part from taxes paid by foreign-owned firms, the managerial strata in the country are made up largely of foreigners, and the course of economic development is often predicated upon the needs and suggestions of foreign economic interests. Again, in such situations, prosperity or depression in the weaker state come to rest upon decisions made by foreign economic interests, whose first interest often must be self-interest.

The severe North-South split in the contemporary world—i.e., the gap between the economically advanced and the underdeveloped states—holds great potential for economic penetration and domination. Many underdeveloped countries, for example, are currently highly dependent upon commodity and exchange markets in economically advanced countries. Forty-six percent of Panamanian foreign trade was trade with the United States in 1965, and earnings from this trade accounted for nearly one-fifth of Panamanian national income. Similarly, transactions with Great Britain accounted for 79 percent of

6. Hans J. Morgenthau, *Politics Among Nations*, pp. 55–60.

Nigeria's trade and earned 17 percent of that country's national income in 1965.[7] In addition, major industrial sectors in a number of underdeveloped countries are foreign owned and operated—as, for example, in Liberia, where the rubber extraction and processing industry is American controlled, or in the Congo, where Belgian interests continue to direct the metals mining industry. Thus, potentials for foreign economic manipulation are certainly present in relationships between foreign interests and local economic well-being.

Even with the prevailing world economic bifurcation into "have" and "have not" states, it would be rash to jump automatically and inferentially from seeing the potential for foreign economic manipulation to seeing foreign economic domination in fact. Economic dependence is not equivalent to economic domination; it only opens opportunities to the would-be imperialist. Moreover, it is similarly, and even more illogically, rash to jump automatically and inferentially from the potential for economic manipulation to *political* domination in fact. Certainly, economic dependence opens a way for economic domination, and economic domination does open a path to political control. But these are only options open to economically stronger states, and not necessarily empirical descriptions of the behavior of these states *vis-à-vis* economically weaker ones. Economic influence does not mean economic domination and even strong economic influence does not necessarily mean political control. *The empirical test for imperialism in such cases must lie in evidence showing actual or intended economic domination and political control stemming from economic dependence.*

Historically, there is a good deal of evidence of economic domination and consequent political penetration in, for example, Western relations with China during the nineteenth century, in Nazi relations with some Eastern European countries during the 1930's, in United States relations with Cuba particularly and Latin American countries generally, in Russian relations with Eastern Europe, in Belgian relations with Katanga, in French relations with Algeria, and in Western European relations with other African states. This historical evidence, however, neither shows that economic imperialism is currently or

7. International Monetary Fund and International Bank for Reconstruction and Development, *Direction of Trade: A Supplement to International Financial Statistics, Annual 1961–1965.*

necessarily a cornerstone of any economically advanced state's policies toward the underdeveloped world, nor does it document the bogey of world capitalist conspiracy feared by certain leaders in the "third world." Nor finally, does the blatant economic imperialism of the past show that such behavior persists today in subtler neo-imperialistic forms. Clearer understanding of the nature and impacts of contemporary relations between developed and underdeveloped countries can emerge only in separating expediently circulated myths of neo-imperialism from the realities of advanced states' economic policies and political intentions concerning the third world.

2. ONE STATE MAY DOMINATE ANOTHER STATE POLITICALLY, YET INDIRECTLY, BY EXTERNALLY CONTROLLING PROCESSES OF POLITICAL RECRUITMENT, POLITICAL EXPRESSION, AND POLICY FORMATION IN THE DOMINATED STATE. The experiences of the contemporary world are so vivid in this area that little documentation needs to be offered here. When adherence to a universalist ideology is an absolute criterion for leadership status in a country and when such an ideology provides the wellspring for domestic and foreign policy, the center of ideological orthodoxy becomes the center of political control. Whatever trappings of sovereignty the Eastern European Communist states may have had during the late 1940's and 1950's, Communist party membership, adherence to the Communist ideology, and approval (or appointment) from Moscow were required of all national leaders. National policies, domestic and foreign, were either dictated in detail from Moscow or at least strictly controlled by the CPSU party line. For all intents and purposes the Eastern European countries, though formally independent, were rigidly politically controlled from Moscow. Moreover, though external control through ideology is now becoming increasingly difficult in Eastern Europe because of a combination of factors, including polycentric tendencies in ideological orthodoxy and nationalist revival, strong elements of ideological imperialism persist in the Soviet sphere and will likely continue to persist for some years to come.

Stepping back a few years into the history of twentieth century international politics, one finds a similar pattern of external political control by enforced ideological orthodoxy in relations between Hitler's Germany and Nazi regimes established in Hungary, Bulgaria, and other Axis satellites. In addition, one cannot, with objectivity, ignore evidence of United States penetration into the political processes in

Guatemala, Cuba, Colombia, West Germany, and certainly South Vietnam. To a greater or lesser extent in each of these cases, the political tenure of indigenous regimes rested largely on American military and economic aid and political support, and aid and support flowed in proportion to the displayed anti-communist zeal of the indigenous leaders. Moreover, and more subtly—in West Germany notably, and to limited extents in other countries—military and political dependence upon the United States have had the effect of partially muting political expression and partially stigmatizing political leaders at the far left of the political spectrum. Hence, while direct political imperialism by takeover has faded from contemporary international politics, indirect external political penetration and control persist to a notable extent in the form of the superpowers' insistence upon ideological orthodoxy in client states.

3. ONE STATE MAY ATTEMPT TO DOMINATE ANOTHER STATE INDIRECTLY BY DIFFUSING ITS CULTURE AMONG THE POPULATION OF THE CLIENT STATE. While the record of cultural imperialism dates at least as far back as the Ancient Chinese Empire, the impacts of this phenomenon were most notable in the relations between metropolitan and colonial states during the nineteenth and early twentieth centuries. France especially, and other metropolitan powers to a lesser extent, promoted acculturation in colonial areas through control over indigenous education and through attempts to "export" political institutions, economic systems, religions, and secular social-political philosophies. As a result, impacts of past cultural imperialism are clearly visible today. Western languages have replaced native dialects in many former colonial states; French- and British-styled assemblies represent the constitutional centers of governments in these states; European codes have replaced indigenous legal systems; Christianity has largely overcome paganism and made inroads against Eastern religions; and indigenous elites, by and large educated in the West, share life styles often centuries divorced from traditional customs and mores. The political reasoning behind cultural imperialism is simple: people acculturated to share one's own perceptions, thinking, behavior, and institutions will, largely of their own accord, share one's interests and recognize the wisdom of policies designed to promote that interest.

However, attempts at cultural imperialism promoted by the major metropolitan powers were not, obviously, entirely successful. While cultural affinities between the former metropolitan powers and their former colonial peoples persist today, the political assumptions beneath acculturation policies have proven invalid. Acculturation does not necessarily contribute to loyalty and allegiance. In fact, rather than facilitating control, exposure to new and alien ideas about political organization and economic modernization tends to contribute to protest and upheaval in colonial areas. This seems especially the case when extending the material attributes of modernity lags behind the implantation of modern political, social, and economic institutions, and when the philosophies of democratic government that have been introduced contradict the realities of political subjugation. Moreover, it would seem that attempts at injecting alien cultures tend to produce new hybrid cultures wherein traditional life patterns are mixed with alien patterns rather than replaced by them. Political aspirations and styles generated in the hybrid cultures tend to be as unpredictable to the acculturators as they are novel to the traditional societies.

Despite the ambiguous history of European attempts to export culture for the purpose of political control during the colonial era, attempts at cultural imperialism have not disappeared along with the disappearance of the great colonial empires. The diffusion of Western technology to all parts of the globe continues, for instance, and will continue for some time to come. While this diffusion of technology is not cultural imperialism, strictly speaking, since Western technology is more often sought than injected, it is now widely realized that the diffusion and incorporation of this technology often carries with it unforeseen, unintended, and sometimes disturbing social and political consequences. In the context of the Cold War, too, one discerns deliberate superpower attempts to inject values and philosophies into the thinking of the leaders and peoples of uncommitted states and to present these peoples with "models" for political, economic, and social organization and with formulas for modernization and development. While we should certainly recognize some altruistic concern for improving qualities of life and standards of living in this East-West competition, we cannot ignore the world political context of the competition. Both the East and the West are exporting values and designs in attempts to sway minds, influence foreign policies, and strengthen respective alignments in the Cold War.

Describing varieties of imperialism is useful in that such examination exposes the more subtle instruments which states have used, and continue to use, to control or dominate weaker states. It must be borne in mind that in practice one often encounters difficulty in separating varieties of imperialism since the instruments of control or domination are most effectively used in combination. European colonization in Africa and the Near and Far East during the nineteenth century, for example, embodied in theory and in practice a combination of instruments for domination that included direct political-military control, economic manipulation, and attempted acculturation. When, for example, the French moved militarily into Algeria in 1830 they worked simultaneously to make the inhabitants of Algeria political subjects of France, to develop the Algerian economy for the benefit of France, to inextricably intertwine Algerian well-being with French prosperity, and culturally to make over the indigenous Algerian elite into Frenchmen. Here, as in many other colonial ventures, different varieties of imperialism were woven into a program of control.

After all is said, however, about varieties of imperialism and instruments of external control, one is left with the question "why?" That is, what motivates statesmen toward imperialist policies? Why do men seek to dominate one another? There seems no single definite answer to these questions. But a variety of answers have been suggested.

MOTIVATIONS FOR IMPERIALISM

Motivations for imperialism may be grouped and discussed under two broad headings. First, there are those theorists, with Joseph Schumpeter most prominent among them, who find imperialistic behavior stemming from deep, and basically irrational, drives born or conditioned into men. Following as they do from elemental drives, imperialistic acts may have no acquisitive purpose, no measurable value in terms of material rewards, not even a reasoned course or direction. They may be self-destructive to their perpetrators. In a contemporary mode, one could say that men are "programmed" to act aggressively, and the program runs from generation to generation. Second, there are those theorists who, in contradistinction to the psychological and social-psychological motives emphasized by the Schumpeter school, place primary emphasis for imperialism upon political and economic motives. For these writers imperialistic behavior has definite acquisitive purposes. Deliberate and reasoned, it is directed toward acquiring power, territory, wealth, status, or human souls. However, despite their agreement on the purposefulness of imperialism, theorists in this second group differ considerably among themselves about the social, economic, and political conditions that prompt acquisitive behavior. The themes and variations on imperialism presented by both schools of thought are worth exploring in some detail.

Schumpeter's Imperialism. Joseph Schumpeter's classic essays *Imperialism* and *Social Classes* were first published in sections in the German journal *Archiv für Sozialwissenschaft und Sozialpolitik* in 1919 and 1927. Despite the term "social classes" in the title, Schumpeter's thesis does not amount to a Marxist interpretation. In fact, the Schumpeterian interpretation of imperialism is almost a direct contradiction of the Marxist argument, for Schumpeter denies any basic economic motivation for imperialism. His thesis is simple yet elegant. *Imperialism, manifested in external aggrandizement, expansionism, and conquest, stems from warlike habits or predispositions conditioned into men over time and reinforced and perpetuated by certain forms of social structure.*[8]

Not all men are predisposed toward warlike behavior, nor do all social structures reinforce warlike habits. But, Schumpeter points out, there are men—"warrior classes"—for whom fighting is a vocation, and there have been societies—"warrior societies"—for which fighting was a way of life. For the most part, warrior classes were called into being and warrior societies evolved during historical eras of great danger and direct threats to survival—i.e., during times when fighting skills were directly functional to societal continuity. As these threats passed, however, they left in their wake either military classes for whom fighting was their sole skill and social function, or whole societies so accustomed to continual warfare that adjustment to peaceful endeavors became impossible. For such groups war had become a habit, even though violent self-defense had ceased to be a continuing necessity.

For warrior classes, prowess at arms, heroism in battle, and victory in the field are keys to social mobility, status, and deference. More than this, Schumpeter argues, the continuation of warfare and the perpetuation of the threat of war are the only justifications for the

8. Joseph Schumpeter, "Imperialism," pp. 23–64.

continuing existence of warrior classes. From this point, Schumpeter reasons that warrior classes must seek combat or maintain the salience of the threat of combat in the interest of their own self-preservation as social classes. After examining the behavior of military castes in the ancient and medieval world, he concisely observes that in all cases explored the warrior class was "created by the wars that required it" and then later this class "created the wars it required." [9]

Schumpeter's argument is similar, but broader, in cases of whole societies structured for fighting as a way of life. In such cases, again drawn largely from the ancient world, skills of combat and military command were virtually the only skills mastered by the adult male populations of whole societies. The women, the young, and the aged functioned economically and socially to service and support never-ending war efforts. Every social role in the warrior society had meaning only in terms of its functionality for warfare. Without continuing war, Schumpeter observes, warrior societies would have passed into extinction. After enforced pacification, many did.

The major thrust and documentation of Schumpeter's arguments lead to the conclusion that imperialism need not have, and often does not have, any external acquisitive or defensive purpose—political, economic, or otherwise. Of course, acts of imperialism are usually rationalized or justified in a rhetoric of acquisitive or defensive purpose. But, Schumpeter finds beneath and behind all the rhetoric a social-psychological dynamic that makes war, expansion, and conquest ends in and of themselves. To the warrior class and the warrior society acting in the interest of internal stability and tenure, reasons why a war should be fought, or anticipations of material gains in conquest, are largely irrelevant. *Fighting the war* is the act of central importance, because fighting or preparing to fight are the only actions functional to the continued existence and status of the warrior. The need to fight is the motivation behind imperialism!

The tendency of critics of Schumpeter's thesis is to either accept his interpretation *prima facie,* or else to reject it completely. As this tendency indicates, acceptance or rejection of the thesis, unfortunately, often depends more upon the ideological predispositions and personal emotions that the critic brings to the analysis than upon a careful and complete examination of Schumpeter's work. For example, Schum-

9. *Ibid.,* p. 25.

peter appeals to the New Left in the West because he appears to justify condemnations of perceived "military-industrial complexes." On the other hand, Schumpeter draws caustic barbs from Marxist and Communist critics because he dissociates imperialism from capitalism. He pleases democratic critics because some of his "warrior societies" look a good deal like modern totalitarian states. He enrages military men because "warriors" turn out, in *Imperialism* and *Social Classes,* to be not only aggressive, but also somewhat irrational. Finally, Schumpeter disappointed a generation because he predicted an end to imperialism less than a decade before Hitler unleashed the Nazi rampage of the 1930's and World War II. In sum, most evaluation of Schumpeter's theories has followed from the extent to which he has either pleased or irritated ideologues. A meaningful critique, however, can emerge only in setting Schumpeter's work against that of other theorists of imperialism, and in considering all theories in the light of empirical evidence. This task has been undertaken later in this chapter after a number of other theories have been outlined and discussed.

Lenin: Imperialism and Economics. Far from arguing that imperialism is externally objectless, as Schumpeter does, Vladimir Lenin in his *Imperialism the Highest Stage of Capitalism* argues that acquiring wealth by exploiting subjugated peoples is the sole object in imperialism.[10] For Lenin, imperialism is essentially an economic phenomenon. Military conquest, political subjugation, and social castigation are the imperialist's instruments. But these all facilitate the goal of economic exploitation. This goal follows from two underlying motives: (1) basic greed and (2) exploiting classes' needs to alleviate social and economic pressures threatening their domestic positions and tenures. Then too, for Lenin, imperialism is a historically determined phenomenon in the Marxist scheme, a phase of the capitalist era of historical evolution, indeed a stage of capitalism itself. The economic exploitation of the economically weaker by the economically stronger is a willful and deliberate act, but it is also an act of necessity foisted upon capitalist classes by history's closing of all other options.

Lenin's theory of imperialism evolved from his reactions to two trends of developments that took place after the Russian Revolution of 1917. First, the revolution did not spread from Russia to become a general European working class revolt as Marxist theoreticians had

10. Vladimir Lenin, *Imperialism,* p. 99ff.

anticipated and predicted. Second, neither did a progressive impoverishment of the working classes in capitalist countries come about after 1917. In fact, wage levels rose all over Europe. Here again, empirical reality contradicted Marxist anticipations and predictions. For Lenin, the problem amounted to one of explaining these apparent contradictions in Marxist theory without at the same time destroying the theory. His solution emerged from extensive scrutiny of the financial and foreign trade statistics of the leading capitalist countries of his day and from interpreting these figures in the context of trends in international politics.

What Lenin saw in the economic statistics and in the international political world around him were: (1) astronomically high returns on capital invested in underdeveloped areas outside of Western Europe; (2) rampant European colonization, which amounted to a parceling out of the world into exclusive spheres of influence for the leading world powers; (3) rising working class standards of living in the capitalist countries which amounted to making middle-classes of former proletariats; and (4) imposed bare subsistence living standards among subjugated peoples in colonial areas. From these observations, Lenin reasoned that capitalist classes controlling government and economics in the major states of Europe had managed to stave off the predicted working class revolutions in their countries by making foreign peoples in primitive societies new victims for economic exploitation. In effect, Lenin suggests, the capitalist classes circumvented the dilemma posed by the necessity to exploit the working class, in the interest of accumulating wealth on the one hand and avoiding the threat of revolution which followed from exploiting the working class on the other. By forcing subjects in the colonies rather than workers at home to bear the pains of subsistence wages, profits remained high (indeed, they mounted, since subsistence levels in the colonies were lower than subsistence levels in the home countries) and wealth accumulated. At the same time, working class standards of living could be raised at home, thereby obviating revolutionary zeal and prolonging capitalist class ascendancy without affecting the accumulation of capital.

The end product of Lenin's observations and interpretations was a refinement of Marxist theory which amounted, in effect, to broadening the theory in order to make room for the contradictions he was trying to account for. Lenin theorized that before its final downfall in the face of forces of proletarian revolution, capitalism moves into its highest and last phase. This is the *international imperialist phase,* wherein distinctions between the capitalist class and the working class fade within capitalist countries, wherein the population of the whole underdeveloped world becomes a mass proletariat for capitalist exploiters, and where the inevitable working class revolution will take the form of a revolt of the underdeveloped world against the capitalist world. During the imperialist stage of capitalism, the whole world divides into capitalist countries and proletarian dependencies, into exploiters and exploited. This becomes the case, Lenin argues, because history decrees that it must be the case.

Several themes in Lenin's theory of imperialism should be underlined. First, it should be clear that in the Marxist rhetoric, the terms "imperialism" and "capitalism" are used interchangeably. Imperialism *is* capitalism and vice versa in Marxist terms. Therefore, for the Marxist, a capitalist state becomes an imperialist state *by definition,* and, by the same definition, for the Marxist a noncapitalist state cannot act imperialistically. It is of little use, for example, to address a Marxist concerning Soviet imperialism in Eastern Europe, because by his frame of reference, the Soviet Union cannot be imperialistic since the U.S.S.R. is not a capitalist country. By the same token, the Marxist dubs the United States and other Western countries "imperialist" not by objective assessment of their international actions, but rather because their economies are essentially capitalistic. This is one reason why a strong point was made of definitions earlier in this chapter. Rather than demanding the empirical evidence of actual or intended domination as proof of imperialism, as we demanded earlier, the Marxist will infer imperialism directly from evidence of capitalism.

Second, and perhaps more important for this exposition, it should be underlined again that Lenin saw the motivations for imperialism first in the lust for wealth that he saw driving the capitalist to exploitation. This, the Marxist would argue, is the basic motivation underlying capitalist behavior in general. But in addition, behavior in the specifically imperialist phase of capitalism is motivated by the need to stave off impending working class revolution. That is, in the Leninist interpretation, the capitalist is driven to turn outward to the underdeveloped world, to conquest, to colonization, and to the subjugation and economic exploitation of weaker peoples, because he fears that revolution will result from continued exploitation of the working class at home. Therefore, a desire for continued social, economic, and political stability in the home capitalist country motivates external imperialistic behavior.

Finally, and critically important in our contemporary world, Lenin maintains, and indeed amplifies, the Marxist belief in the inevitability of proletarian revolution. Capitalism in its highest stage of imperialism, Lenin says, sets the scene for its own demise by setting the stage for a world proletarian revolution, the imminence of that revolution becoming pronounced as the world becomes thoroughly divided into economic "exploiters" and "exploited." As will be pointed out in more detail later, it makes little difference whether the world ever was, is, or will be divided into exploiters and exploited as Lenin argues. What does make a difference, however, is whether people perceive the world as divided in this way. The "North-South" image, salient in the contemporary international political dialogue, for example, is hung with Leninist trappings. Such perceptions, wrapped in Leninist interpretations, could well affect the course of world history by affecting peoples' receptivity to the Communist Chinese affirmation that time is ripening for the "world countryside" to rise in revolt against the "world cities." [11]

Aberrations and Devils: Economic Perversions and Imperialism. Theorists of imperialism in the liberal tradition attack the Leninists on their assumption that imperialism and capitalism are inextricably interrelated. In the two major liberal alternatives to the theory of imperialism —the *theory of capitalist aberration* and the "devil theory"—spokesmen preserve the insistence that imperialism is economically motivated, but they deny that imperialism must follow from capitalist economics. John A. Hobson, in his early twentieth century work *Imperialism,* observes that overseas expansion, conquest, and colonization during the nineteenth and early twentieth centuries were motivated by pressures to dispose of surplus goods and capital that were clogging markets and slowing growth in capitalist countries.[12] Imperialism, then, was the result of a search for new, exclusive, protected markets, and new commodity and capital outlets to replace glutted home economies.

11. "Red China Urges a 'Peoples War,'" *New York Times,* September 4, 1965, pp. 1–2.
12. John A. Hobson, *Imperialism* (London: Allen & Unwin, 1938).

However, in Hobson's interpretation, the capitalists' turn to overseas areas reflected an aberration of their economic system rather than an historically determined phase of its development. Where Lenin argues that the capitalist has no alternative but to find new victims for exploitation in foreign lands, Hobson sees this as nonsense, and points out that the alternative to imperialism is in domestic economic reform. By increasing purchasing power among domestic consumers through increased wages, income redistribution, and the like, commodity surpluses could be turned into commodity shortages; and capital surpluses could then be channeled into expanding domestic economies to meet newly generated consumer demands. Imperialism is an aberration of capitalism, Hobson argues, because in seeking external outlets, capitalist producers show themselves blind to the logic and necessity of domestic reform. They show themselves insensitive to their own interests in raising wages and expanding the domestic economy. In short, as far as Hobson is concerned, imperialism does empirically follow from capitalism. But it does not have to.

The "devil" theorists, with Charles A. Beard their most ardent spokesman, challenge even the empirical link between capitalism as an economic system and imperialism. In two books, *The Devil Theory of War* and *The Idea of National Interest,* Beard dramatizes his thesis that imperialism is neither a product nor an aberration of capitalism, but rather is the result of individual economic self-interest narrowly pursued.[13] Overseas expansion, conquest, and aggressive war, Beard argues, are promoted by those who stand to gain economically from war. The motive is profit; the drive is greed. The "devil theorists" of the 1930's singled out munitions makers as prime "devils" and linked them to instigating World War I for their own profit. Keeping Beard's tradition alive, contemporary "devil hunters" in the United States and elsewhere interpret intermittent outbreaks of limited wars, continuing tension at the nuclear level, and military aid programs as the products of successful lobbying tactics on the part of self-interested defense industries. Some allege sinister alliances among armaments producers, financial institutions and agencies, and individuals in government. While it is true that certain industries profit by imperialism, especially when it takes the form of military conquest (who would deny this?),

13. Charles A. Beard. *The Devil Theory of War* (New York: Vanguard Press, 1936), also, Beard, *The Idea of National Interest* (New York: Macmillan. 1934).

it must be remembered the "devil theorists" assume that those who would profit from war and other imperialistic adventures both deliberately instigate such action and have sufficient control over states' foreign policies to effect such action. Little documentation exists to validate these latter assumptions.[14]

Variations on Social Darwinist Themes. Just as Lenin argued that imperialism is predetermined economic necessity, writers before and after Lenin have as fervently argued that imperialism is a predetermined political and social imperative. Sinking their intellectual roots into Charles Darwin's theories of biological evolution and natural selection, and drawing also from Spenglerian and Hegelian metaphysics, author-statesmen such as Rudyard Kipling, Cecil Rhodes, and years later, Benito Mussolini and Adolf Hitler, produced variations on the conclusion that the international political world, like the biological world, is a continuing struggle wherein the fittest and strongest survive and the weaker succumb. To these theorists, imperialism is but a reflection of the primal struggle. Every state must by necessity compete for survival in international politics. The only alternative to subjugating is being subjugated. The motivation toward imperialistic behavior then is the imperative to survive.

Social Darwinist themes all have similar rings—the stronger must dominate the weaker—but those motivated to act out their social Darwinist beliefs have tended to attach various forms of quasi-moral justification to their actions. One line of reasoning prominent near the end of the nineteenth century in both European and American practice was the "white man's burden" or "manifest destiny" argument. According to this argument, imperialism was glorified as an *obligation* imposed by history upon the economically and militarily more advanced states of the world. According to this reasoning the stronger are obligated to raise the weaker from backwardness to "civilization," from poverty to well-being, from ignorance to sophistication, and the like. The obligation is unimpeachable; the backward must be "civilized" whether they wish to be or not. Julius Pratt presents a classic item of documentation on the "white man's burden" theme in his description of the American President William McKinley's decision in 1898 to annex the Philippine Islands:

14. Eugene Staley, *War and the Private Investor* (New York: Doubleday, Doran, 1935), *passim.*

McKinley's own account of the religious experience which led to his decision to keep the Philippines is well known. He had, he said, sought counsel from all sides and got little help. He had paced the floor of the White House till midnight night after night. Finally, he had prayed for guidance, and the answer had come that "there was nothing left for us to do but to take them all, and to educate the Filipinos, and uplift and civilize and Christianize them, and by God's grace do the very best we could by them as our fellow-men for whom Christ also died." [15]

By a slight twist of reasoning the Social Darwinist theme can be transposed from one that pictures history imposing obligations upon powerful states, to one that pictures history granting *rights* to such states. This variation, argued with particular force by circles of German nationalists during the nineteenth century, was adopted and turned into action by German Nazis and Italian Fascists in the twentieth century. The theme, blatantly stated, boils down to the proposition that "superior" peoples have the right to rule over "inferior" peoples. In the words of Adolf Hitler:

History itself is the presentation of the course of a people's struggle for existence. . . .

This earth is not alloted to anyone, nor is it presented to anyone as a gift. It is awarded by Providence to peoples, who in their hearts possess the courage to conquer it, the strength to preserve it, and the industry to put it to the plough. Hence every healthy, vigorous people sees nothing sinful in territorial acquisition, but something quite in keeping with nature. The modern pacifist who denies this holy right must first be reproached for the fact that he himself is being nourished on the injustice of former times.[16]

In contradistinction to the "white man's burden" theme, in which imperialism is morally justified by its practitioners because it contributes to an "uplifting" of backward peoples, imperialism justified by a perceived right to rule implies no obligation for beneficence. Pushed to its extreme this latter argument becomes a grotesque rationale for racial and ethnic genocide. Hitler pushed the rationale to its extreme in both theory and practice:

Since our point of departure is that one people is not equal to another, the value of a people is also not equal to the value of another people. . . .

15. Julius W. Pratt, *Expansionists of 1898* (New York: Peter Smith, 1951), p. 316.
16. Adolf Hitler, *Hitler's Secret Book,* Salvator Attanasio, tr. (New York: Grove Press, 1961), pp. 5 and 15.

If a man appears to have cancer and is unconditionally doomed to die, it would be senseless to refuse an operation. It would be still more senseless were the surgeon to perform the operation with only limited or partial energy.[17]

Some observers of contemporary international politics would argue that Social Darwinist rationales for imperialism are now defunct. Such rationales are at least discredited, and their extreme manifestations in international practice have disappeared. Nevertheless, one wonders at the imperatives for ideological expansion that are apparently felt at ideological centers in the East and also in the West. One wonders at the oftentimes smug paternalism that leading industrial states both East and West display in dealing with economically underdeveloped states, and in explaining penetration into these states. One wonders too about the public fervor of Arab Nationalism and perceptions of superiority and inferiority oftentimes reflected in statements of Arab goals vis-à-vis Israel. Finally, when one turns from international politics to politics within certain states today one finds relationships between racial and ethnic groups characterized by superordination and subordination and unabashedly justified in the Social Darwinist rhetoric of "obligation to rule" and "right to rule."

Imperialism and the Individual: Social Mobilization and Diversion. One of the facts of the history of imperialism is that public enthusiasm in dominating societies often goes hand in hand with adventurous and expansionist statesmanship.[18] Such mass enthusiasm for overseas expansion and domination can be partly explained by diffusion and internalization of beliefs in economic determinism, Social Darwinism, and the like—i.e., by populations' sharing in the motivations of their statesmen. In addition, it has been observed that imperialism wins public approval because it complements individuals' motivations, aspirations, and psychic needs in a number of ways.

First, it is clear that social and economic mobility in the dominating society is frequently a direct result of imperialist expansion. As was pointed out in Chapter 2, the elite stratum of any society is necessarily narrow. Room at the top is limited. Imperialism overseas accomplishes the task of making more room at the top of dominating societies and generally opening more channels of social, economic, and political ad-

17. *Ibid.,* pp. 27 and 41.
18. William L. Langer, *The Diplomacy of Imperialism, 1890–1902,* 2nd ed. (New York: Alfred A. Knopf, 1956), pp. 81–96.

vancement in these societies by superimposing dominating societies atop the dominated ones. Political domination, for example, requires political administrators, and this opens opportunities for advancement to administrators whose careers might otherwise have come to rest at intermediate bureaucratic levels. It opens opportunities for entrance to individuals who might otherwise have never been admitted to government service. Similarly, overseas military expansion and occupation require military officers, and this need opens channels for promotion to officers who might otherwise have remained at intermediate levels of the military hierarchy, as well as creates commissions for individuals who might otherwise never have become officers. Moreover, where imperialism takes the form of colonization or of economic domination, channels of economic mobility and status are opened to individuals who might otherwise never have made it economically in the home country. The enterprising farmer restricted at home to small holdings has the opportunity to carve out a plantation on virgin or expropriated colonial lands. The skilled worker who is one of many in the home country becomes a manager in a colonial area, where his skill is a rare and needed commodity. One can infer from the results in social and economic mobility that follow from overseas expansion that a people's motivation toward imperialistic behavior amounts, in part, to a sum total of personal aspirations toward higher social status, greater economic accomplishment, and elite roles.

In addition, even individuals who may not see imperialism as complementing their material aspirations, may nevertheless find psychological ego-satisfaction in imperialist adventures. Perception of his society's domination over other societies and intense identification with his society may give a sense of power, satisfaction, and fulfillment to the man who can experience these in no other way. The man at the bottom of a country's social and economic hierarchy, whose life is one of informal subjugation and frustration, may well find psychic exhilaration in the realization that he is a part of a society that is dominating other societies. He sees himself as no longer at the social, economic, political, and psychological bottom of the world. He fulfills his need to dominate by vicarious participation in his state's imperialism. The same kind of individual, and a great many others whose lives are characterized by envelopment in monotonous routine, identify with their state's foreign adventures also in efforts to escape boredom.

These individuals find excitement in imperialism just as they find entertainment in a tabloid press that glorifies imperialism, or in a mass media that generally extol adventure and violence. Hence, while statesmen embark upon imperialist courses out of the perceived economic interests of their state or out of a sense of historical obligation or right, individual citizens support their statesmen, approve their acts, and indeed egg them onward, out of motivations toward personal advancement, needs for ego-satisfaction, and desires to experience the sense of excitement that empire-building evokes.

IMPERIALISM: SUMMARY AND CRITIQUE

The purpose of this chapter, as part of a broader survey of goals and motivations in international politics, has been to explore motivations that prompt imperialistic behavior. The search for imperialist motives here has taken the form of examining classic theories of imperialism, their variations, and adaptations. While these theories contain a wide range of explanations concerning motivations for imperialism, it must be recognized that such explanations are accurate only to the extent that the theories are valid.

When evaluated in terms of their correspondence to empirical reality, most of the theories offered in this chapter could be brought into question. The Leninist theory, for example, and the several variations on Social Darwinism leave the social scientist skeptical because they require him to accept metaphysical, and essentially unprovable, first premises concerning laws of nature, or history, or dictates of Providence. Moreover, these same theories follow from assumed determinisms which wholly eject human voluntarism from the course of history. Any such implied determinism tends to disturb many political scientists who, in observing records of centuries of human events with close scrutiny, find no political decisions determined without alternatives, and no episodes initiated without definite (though not always wise) choice. Then too, each theory discussed—Schumpeter's, Lenin's, Hobson's, Beard's, and the Social Darwinists'—implies essentially unidimensional causation. Each theorist claims that there is one primary cause for imperialism and one primary motive behind imperialistic behavior. Such affirmations are again difficult to accept for social scientists and students of history, who view and understand human events as the results of multiple and complex causes and motivations. It is too simple to say that innate militarism motivates imperialism, or that capitalist desires for continued ascendancy motivate imperialism, or that the struggle to survive motivates imperialism. Rather, it is more likely that all of these have motivated imperialism at different times, in different places, and in different combinations. The more difficult questions concern times, places, and combinations, or the conditions under which imperialistic behavior is likely to be generated.

Moreover, the universality of all of the formal theories of imperialism suffers at the level of empirical fact. In contradiction to Schumpeter's assertion that military classes (warriors) seek combat and perpetual tension, for example, modern political and social-psychological analysis reveals a prevailing caution and conservatism among professional soldiers, a prevailing sense of responsibility to the social order above and beyond their own class, and a professional bowing to civilian control.[19] With regard to the Leninist argument, careful analyses of the behavior of business communities (i.e., capitalist classes) prior to and during wars dubbed "imperialist wars," reveal mixtures of pacifism on the assertion that "war is bad for business," and indifference on the assertion that business and politics are separate spheres of activity.[20] Moreover, the economic balance sheet of nineteenth century colonization shows as many examples of colonies as economic liabilities, as cases of colonies yielding high economic returns.[21] As for the Social Darwinist image of the struggle for survival and the rights and obligations which follow from it, how, in viewing the world in this image, can we account for international cooperation, and if the image does not account for this phenomena, what becomes of the Social Darwinist insistence upon the imperative to "dominate or be dominated"?

After all has been said in qualification of the different explanations for imperialism, what remains of the theorists' suggested answers to the question: "What motivates imperialism?"

1. While the theorists' abstract interpretations and universal generalizations should be called into question, their reporting on what they

19. Morris Janowitz, *The Professional Soldier* (Glencoe: The Free Press, 1960), pp. 215–282.
20. Julius W. Pratt, *The Expansionists of 1898*, ppl 230–278.
21. Bernard B. Fall, *The Two Viet-Nams*, rev. ed. (New York: Praeger, 1964), p. 27ff.

saw in the world they observed is probably accurate. Schumpeter did observe military classes agitating for war; Lenin did see financiers and industrialists advocating overseas expansion; Hobson did see businessmen calling for protected overseas markets to relieve pressures on glutted home markets; Beard did observe "devils" profiting from war; the Social Darwinists did see a fierce competition for colonial empires; and men did believe in "civilizing missions" and racist creeds. Each of these observations, however, pertained to particular times, places, and conditions. The theorists' shortcoming was that they generalized their particular observations into universal propositions.

What all the varied observations on imperialism suggest is that imperialistic behavior indeed has multiple causes and follows from multiple motivations. Different forces, and different combinations of forces, produce imperialism at different times and places. Therefore, in assessing a state's *propensity to engage in imperialist activities,* the analyst must remain continually sensitive to a range of considerations which should at a minimum include: (1) militarism within society; (2) perceptions of economic profit from overseas expansion harbored by groups within the society; (3) the appeals of expansionist ideologies such as "manifest destiny," "communist internationalism," and "saving the world for democracy," among elites and masses within the society; (4) levels of mass boredom and routinization in the society; and (5) general social, political, and economic pressures within the society that might be alleviated by external expansion. In addition, such an assessment would have to be made within the context of a broader evaluation of countervailing isolationist appeals and solutions, the availability of "victims" for imperialism, and the world distribution of power. *The propensity to imperialism is strongest when several motives shared by several different groups bring pressures on governments from several directions.*

2. Despite recommended caution against generalization, one cannot help but note that several of the explanations for imperialism examined in this chapter have focused wholly or partly upon relationships between internal social, economic, and political pressures and external expansionism. Only among Social Darwinist theorists do we find any great emphasis on the idea that the characteristics of the potential victims prompt or invite imperialism. The other explanations by and large emphasize the idea that the characteristics of the potential pred-

ator prompt imperialism. For the Schumpeterians imperialism follows from class efforts to preserve status and from societal efforts to preserve stability—motives generated exclusively by internal problems and strains. Similarly, for the Leninists, imperialism follows from capitalist class efforts to alleviate revolutionary pressures and maintain ascendancy. Again, the imperialist drive is generated by internal pressures rather than invited by external opportunities. Moreover, in explanations for the mass support that imperialism generates, emphasis falls upon individual and group social and economic aspirations within societies, and upon psychic needs to escape the monotonies of mass society. Again, imperialism serves internal purposes and alleviates internal pressures. *All this suggests that a society under internal strain is more prone to embark upon imperialistic courses than one in which internal strain is minimal.* These observations also suggest that several varieties of internal strain are possible catalysts for imperialism. Among these one should note threats to the tenure of elites or ascendant classes, threats to social stability arising from gaps between aspirations and opportunities for mobility, threats to economic stability arising from limited marketing areas or lagging growth, and threats to societal vigor arising from routinization and boredom.

3. Finally, even though much of the discussion in this chapter was phrased in the past tense, the reader must realize that much of what has been said has essential contemporary relevance. Phrasing the question "what motivates imperialism?" rather than "what motivated imperialism?" was deliberate. Certainly the age of great colonial empires has passed. But, as early sections of this chapter hopefully have made clear, actual or attempted political, economic, and social domination is still very much with us, and will remain with us as long as the world remains divided between powerful and weak states, developed and underdeveloped economies, and assertive and passive societies. Therefore, we will continue to confront imperialism; we will continue to hear the justificatory rhetoric of dominators and the renunciating rebuttals of potential victims; and we will continue to find motivations for imperialism rooted in perceptions of external profit, visions of external obligation and privilege, and concerns for internal tenure and stability.

CHAPTER SIX
MOTIVATIONS AND DYNAMICS
IN REGIONAL INTEGRATION

AS indicated earlier, the several chapters in Part II are intended as a survey of goals and motivations connected with a variety of international political phenomena. For this reason, the shift of focus from the discussion of imperialism in the last chapter, to this chapter's examination of regional integration is necessarily and intendedly abrupt. Regional integration, in peaceful form, is a very different kind of phenomenon from imperialism; and because peaceful integration is so different from imperialism, understanding it gives one the opportunity to broaden his understanding of the variety of goals and motives that underlie international political behavior.

Explaining the motivations that underlie regional integration is best done in three steps. First, some time and space must necessarily be allotted to explaining the phenomenon, because, explaining what regional integration is becomes a starting point for explaining why statesmen choose to promote it. Second, an attempt must also be made to examine its external and internal implications. These become directly relevant to understanding motivations, because, as will be shown, statesmen promote regional integration in pursuit of particular rewards that follow from it. Third, with the groundwork laid in examination of the phenomenon and its implications, the question of motivations can be approached directly, as it will be in the third section of this chapter.

REGIONAL INTEGRATION IN INTERNATIONAL POLITICAL HISTORY

"Regional integration" may be defined as "the merger of two or more states to form a new and larger state." The phrase "merger of two or more states" in this definition is used in the broadest sense to imply:

1. THE MERGER OF TERRITORIES—symbolized and accomplished by the obliteration or de-emphasis of international frontiers within the integrated region. After regional integration, former state boundaries either disappear or become provincial demarcation lines.

2. THE MERGER OF GOVERNMENTS—symbolized and accomplished by the establishment of new institutions of government at the regional (i.e., supranational) level. The regional government either overarches, or wholly replaces, the governments of the formerly separate and independent states by operating, with preeminent competence, in jurisdictions formerly reserved for national authorities. Newly formed amalgamated regional government becomes responsible for policies and strategies of regional defense, for regional foreign and commercial policies *vis-à-vis* the external world, and for policies regulating intraregional social and economic intercourse.

3. THE MERGER OF POLITICAL SYSTEMS—symbolized and accomplished by the emergence of political groups and processes at the regional level. Political parties, economic interest groups, and other formal and informal political organizations become supranational in character and membership; and political competition and interaction shift during regional integration from separate national arenas to a regional arena. Regional political interaction comes to focus on attempts to influence the functioning of the regional government and the regional allocation of political rewards.

4. THE MERGER OF ECONOMIES—symbolized and accomplished by the removal of intraregional barriers to economic intercourse; the restructuring of production, consumption, and distribution patterns to reflect maximum regional economic efficiency; the growth of regional economic planning, regulation, and administration; and the emergence of a regional commercial policy toward the outside world.

5. THE MERGER OF SOCIETIES AND PEOPLES—symbolized and accomplished by the emergence of regional class and social structures, and the growth of common identifications, allegiances, and other at-

tributes of assimilation among the regional population. In effect, in the course of regional integration, but usually in the long run, separate nationalities merge to become a new nationality.

It is hardly necessary to point out to anyone familiar with the history of international relations that peaceful regional integration is a relatively rare phenomenon. This is especially the case when we discount the numerous historical episodes during which large regional areas were consolidated into modern states. Consolidation of the region we now call France, for example, was accomplished during the fifteenth through the eighteenth centuries by a combination of military conquest and dynastic intermarriage, which welded diverse feudal sovereignties into a single state. Similarly, the present-day United Kingdom of England, Scotland, Wales, and Northern Ireland was united largely by force. The German principalities were amalgamated into the German Empire during the nineteenth century under Bismarck's policies of "blood and iron," which amounted to political persuasion backed and supplemented by the might of the Prussian army. In addition, the now defunct Austro-Hungarian Empire and the present-day state of Italy were also welded largely by force. More cases could be cited, but the point is clear. The bulk of historical cases of "national unification" are most appropriately labeled and studied as cases of amalgamation by imperialism rather than as examples of peaceful regional integration.[1]

We do, nevertheless, have a number of historical cases of regional integration to observe, and we currently have a number of incipient cases to monitor. The amalgamation of the thirteen British North American colonies into the United States of America during the latter part of the eighteenth century was by and large accomplished voluntarily rather than imposed by force.[2] Similarly, the welding of the Swiss cantons into the Swiss Confederation was peacefully accomplished during the eighteenth century, and the now-dissolved union of Norway and Sweden was peacefully concluded during the nineteenth century.[3] Recent times have witnessed the establishment and subsequent dissolution of the United Arab Republic, the Mali Federation, the East

1. Crane Brinton, *From Many One* (Cambridge: Harvard University Press, 1948), p. 23.

2. Richard L. Merritt, *Symbols of American Community, 1735–1775* (New Haven: Yale University Press, 1966); Edmund S. Morgan, *The Birth of the Republic, 1763–1789* (Chicago: The University of Chicago Press, 1959).

3. Raymond E. Lindgren, *Norway-Sweden* (Princeton: Princeton University Press, 1959).

African Federation, and the West Indian Federation. The Federation of Malaysia represents a more successful recent case of regional integration. Among incipient cases of regional integration we have the most impressive, and by far most important, case of Western European integration—the emergence of "Europeanism," the establishment of the Common Market, and official commitments and widespread enthusiasm for ultimate political federation among France, West Germany, Italy, and the Benelux countries. Similarly, though less spectacularly, we observe common markets in operation in Central America and East Africa, and in both of these areas we hear murmurings about ultimate political unity.[4] Finally, if propaganda outpourings from Communist Eastern Europe have any validity at all, we can surmise that even the COMECON countries have been somewhat inspired by the idea of regional integration. In sum, peaceful regional integration has been a relatively rare phenomenon; lasting amalgamation accomplished peacefully has been even more rare; but the idea of regional integration is currently "in the air" and we may well witness impressive movements toward regional integration over the next several decades.

EXTERNAL AND INTERNAL POLITICAL IMPLICATIONS OF REGIONAL INTEGRATION

Political implications follow from regional integration mainly in two areas: (1) in the international political system generally, where the world is forced to adjust to and cope with a new actor on the international political scene; and (2) in the domestic politics of the states involved in international merger, where political processes and tactics must alter in order to adjust to changing centers of governmental authority. In short, regional integration involves the formation of a new state, and it implies widespread adjustment to this formation. As will be shown, adjustment may take the form of acclamation, encouragement, and support; or it may take the form of intense, and sometimes violent, resistance.

The External Implications of Regional Integration. The external impacts of regional integration can be world-shaking in an almost literal sense, since the entrance of a new, large state into the international political system can bring major changes in the world distribution of

4. Joseph S. Nye, "Central American Regional Integration," *International Conciliation,* No. 562 (March, 1967); Nye, *Pan-Africanism and East African Integration* (Cambridge: Harvard University Press, 1965).

military power, wealth, and prestige. It is generally (though not always) the case that a new state created through regional integration will have more military capability or at least more military potential than any of the component smaller states possessed before regional integration. Similarly, it is generally the case that the new, larger state formed during regional integration will have more wealth, more resources, or at least more economic potential than any of the component smaller states possessed before integration. Then, too, since international status tends to flow from territorial extensiveness, populousness, military might, wealth, and various other attributes customarily associated with "bigness," a new state created through regional integration is likely to be a more prestigious political actor than any of the smaller component states before integration. Therefore, regional integration, may, and most often does, alter the world rank orderings of states in conspicuous and critical ways.

1. DEFENSIVE RESPONSES TO REGIONAL INTEGRATION. Adjustments to the alterations in world power, wealth, and prestige effected by regional integration assume notable variety. First, as might be expected, some states will invariably interpret the creation of a new power center by regional integration as a threat to their own security, prosperity, or prestige. They will react defensively. Such defensive adjustment may take the form of efforts to block a proposed international merger—i.e., a "nipping in the bud" tactic to ward off anticipated threats. This, for example, was the Soviet response to Western European efforts to create an integrated European Defense Community (EDC) between 1950 and 1954, in which the Russians combined threats with positive enticements in attempts to persuade, pressure, and frighten governments and peoples in Western Europe into abandoning the EDC design.[5] An attempt to block integration and to ward off anticipated economic threat was apparent also in British responses to the proposal for a European Common Market between 1955 and 1958. By suggesting alternative schemes the British hoped to entice prospective Common Market members away from the idea of an integrated closed economic community, which the British felt constituted a serious threat to their own foreign trade and economic stability.[6]

5. Daniel Lerner and Raymond Aron, ed., *France Defeats EDC* (New York: Praeger, 1957), *passim*.
6. Miriam Camps, *Britain and the European Community* (Princeton: Princeton University Press, 1964), pp. 93–172.

A second variety of defensive adjustment to regional integration accepts the international merger as a *fait accompli* and, in response, bolsters forces to stand against the new threat. This was the Soviet Union's response to the creation of the Western European Union—the integrated European arm of NATO—in 1955. This too, was the initial Indonesian response to Malaysia's entrance into the international system in 1963. Again, in the economic sphere, the British response to the opening of the European Common Market in 1958 took the form of a British attempt to bolster their own European trade by sponsoring the European Free Trade Association (EFTA). Mustering forces and resources in adjustment to regional integration may be a preparation for a more or less permanent standoff, as was likely the case in Russia's responses to Western military integration. Or such moves may be a preparation for a subsequent attempt to crush the integration movement and dissolve its products, as was explicitly the case in Indonesia's initial reactions to Malaysia.

Finally, a third common defensive adjustment to regional integration takes the form of minimizing threats by joining the integration movement—i.e., "if you can't beat them, join them." Any threats that regional integration may pose to outsiders are mitigated if one can successfully opt to become an insider. This, of course, was the ultimate British response to the perceived economic threat posed by the European Common Market. Britain opted for membership in the EEC in 1960, again in 1966, and again in 1969. Similarly, one can discern somewhat the same kind of thinking among American statesmen who framed the Trade Expansion Act of 1962 and favored its projected scheme for a North Atlantic common market for industrial goods. In another area, currently, Panama, after initial resistance, is leaning toward opting for membership in the Central American Common Market.

4. ACCLAMATORY RESPONSES TO REGIONAL INTEGRATION. While some "outside" states invariably manifest apprehension in response to the new centers of military, economic, and political might created by regional integration, others welcome regional integration and the alterations of the international system it effects. Positive reactions to regional integration are likely when an outside state expects that the newly amalgamated state will become a new military ally, or a new economic or political partner, or all of these. When such expectations prevail, regional integration tends to be viewed as offering opportunities rather

than imposing threats. Under such conditions, outsiders' tactics include offering verbal encouragement to instigate integration; material inducements to support its momentum; military aid and guarantees to protect its progress; and proposals of political, economic, and military partnership to share its culmination.[7] France, for example, encouraged and materially supported the amalgamation of the thirteen American colonies during the American Revolution, and subsequently welcomed the newly formed United States as an ally and political partner. The French saw in the United States a source of new support in their continuing rivalry with Great Britain.

Much more recently, the United States has played an important role in support of the Western European efforts toward regional integration. Perceiving opportunities for a reinforced military and political bulwark against the world Communist threat, for trade expansion in European markets, and for Atlantic Community approaches and aid directed to underdeveloped countries, the American government worked actively to encourage, entice, and even pressure Western Europeans toward regional unity. Indeed, American contributions under the Marshall Plan materially initiated the movement toward economic integration in Western Europe. American loans carried the integrated European Coal and Steel Community (ECSC) over early hurdles. Furthermore, American diplomatic pressures pushed the European Defense Community, diplomatic encouragement greeted the EEC (Common Market), diplomatic endorsement backed Britain's efforts to join the Common Market, and American strategic initiatives set the stage for the dialogue concerning the MLF (Multi-Lateral Nuclear Force) and other plans for integrated nuclear weaponry. Although the wisdom of United States support of regional integration in Western Europe has been called into question because many anticipated rewards from European unity have not materialized, nevertheless there is no doubt but that the United States initially viewed European unity as offering opportunities and consequently adjusted to regional integration on the Continent by encouraging and supporting it.

Some Internal Political Implications of Regional Integration. While regional integration generally provokes widespread alterations and

7. Amitai Etzioni, *Political Unification* (New York: Holt, Rinehart and Winston, 1965), pp. 70–71.

adjustments in the international political system, these may sometimes be minimal when compared to the fundamental realignments that regional integration inflicts upon political processes within amalgamating states. These realignments follow directly from the fact that state sovereignty, state governmental decision-making, state governmental authority, and state administrative prerogative are all partially or completely undermined as states merge into larger regional political units. During amalgamation, sovereignty comes to reside in regional government; political decision-making becomes the prerogative of regional organs and councils; authority shifts to the new regional decision-making centers; and administration comes under central regional direction. In short, during regional integration, political allocation, regulation, and administration shift from separate national control to unified regional control.

Moreover, as the center of political authority shifts during regional integration, the focus of political attention for parties and interest groups shifts accordingly. Thus, as regional government grows in power and stature, political competition among groups for influence over government shifts in focus from the smaller national arenas to the larger regional arena. After all, national governments denuded of ultimate authority in important policy realms understandably cease to be targets for groups seeking influence in these areas. Then, too, not only are parties and interest groups forced to redirect their pressures toward regional targets, but they are also forced to adjust their tactics to suit effective competition in the larger regional arena.

Analysts monitoring Western European integration have observed two evolutions in political tactics employed by lobbying forces in their attempts to influence regional decision-making. First, there has been a proliferation of cross-national amalgamations, coalitions, and alliances among predispositionally similar political groups in different countries. That is, for bargaining and competitive effectiveness, national parties are merging to form regional parties; national interest groups are linking in regional associations; and national social, economic, and political issues are being regionalized. The exigencies of a new regional politics effectively create new *regional* political groups.[8]

Second, during regional integration, nationally based political groups

8. Ernst B. Haas, *The Uniting of Europe* (Stanford: Stanford University Press, 1958), pp. 283–528.

may continue to approach and pressure national governments in the expectation that those governments will lobby for their particular interests in regional councils. In the autumn of 1964, for example, German agricultural interests displeased with impending Common Market regulations in grain pricing, confronted the Bonn Government in the hope that their government would lobby for German agriculture in EEC councils. While such tactics may have the appearance of traditional national politics, they are really marked deviations from traditional styles primarily because the supranational bodies and not the national governments are the actual targets of political pressure, and because national governments here function as political lobbies rather than sovereign authorities.

Regional integration's impacts upon domestic politics in merging states will, of course, vary with the extent of shared authority between regional and national governments, with the policy-making sectors regionalized, and with the gradualness or abruptness of transition from separate national to regionally amalgamated government. Nevertheless, even relatively minimal and very gradual dilutions of national sovereignty may foster major realignments and tactical adjustments in internal political processes.

One central point is blurred in the mechanistic description offered here of shifting authority, political attention, and political tactics during regional integration. This is that not everyone involved in these domestic political adjustments to regional integration can be completely happy with the processes he finds himself caught up in. Certainly, some individuals and groups gain in power and influence during regional integration as they rise from positions of national to positions of regional stature. But a moment's reflection about sovereignty undermined, and about political authority lost and transferred, exposes the fact that many individuals and many groups generally stand to lose a great deal by regional integration.

First, regional integration usually implies a contraction of political elites since all of those who hold offices or positions of high influence nationally do not automatically move into such roles at the regional level. The functioning of six independent states, for example, requires six prime ministers, six foreign ministers, six defense ministers, and the like. But the functioning of a state amalgamated from the six requires only one minister in each of these offices. The disappearance of offices and officers implies the disappearance of political influence for particular national elite members who formerly operated in channels of access to the defunct positions. Then, too, regional integration generally implies a contraction in governmental bureaucracies, or at least an impediment to upward mobility for bureaucrats. Administrative efficiency would demand some regional centralization in administration and elimination of redundant offices, bureaus, and agencies. At the same time, competition for bureaucratic advancement would be regionalized and stiffened, because the number of high-level posts available after regional integration would contract more drastically than the number of lower-level posts. What can be said for the bureaucracy can also be said for the military—where national commands, generalships, and channels for promotion can be integrated out of existence. Regional integration can also be highly frustrating to political party and interest group leaders who find themselves unable to adjust to political maneuvering in the regional arena. Successful lobbyists, for example, typically spend the best part of their careers carefully cultivating interpersonal channels of access to national government decision-making. When regional integration undermines the authority of national governments, it may close these carefully nurtured channels of influence, and, consequently, dash twenty or thirty years of invested effort on the part of pressure group leaders. All of this is really to say that the domestic political impacts of regional integration can generate bitter resistance among individuals and groups who are politically penalized by international amalgamation. It should certainly be noted that domestic opposition to regional integration is founded to some extent upon people's emotional attachments to state sovereignty and their suspicions of one another. Nevertheless, the more salient sources of domestic opposition to regional integration are the penalties to particular individuals and groups who lose power and influence.

SOME ECONOMIC IMPLICATIONS OF REGIONAL INTEGRATION

Economic integration, or the merger of economies, is one of the most thoroughly researched and best understood aspects of regional integration. The theory of international economic integration builds directly from classical theories of free trade.[9] Regional economic integration is initiated by the formal creation of a common market, which in practice means the removal of all formal restrictions on interstate flows of goods, capital, and labor within the amalgamated region. The purpose in removing barriers to interstate economic intercourse is regionally to maximize comparative advantage in production and consumption, and consequently to raise levels of economic efficiency throughout the region. Greater productivity (i.e., more output for less input) for producers, lower prices and therefore higher living standards for consumers, and heightened regional competitiveness on external markets are anticipated to follow from the increased efficiency stimulated by economic integration.

Certain efficiency-producing mechanisms implicit in regional economic integration deserve elaboration. When intraregional tariffs, trade quotas, trade subsidies, frontier taxes, and other instruments and practices designed to protect national industries are abolished, economic competition is regionalized. Under the pressure of regional competition production expands at centers where goods can be produced at lowest cost and sold for lowest prices; production declines or ceases at less efficient centers, where higher costs compel higher prices. What results from this development is a regional restructuring of production and consumption activities in which the most efficient producers become the primary regional producers regardless of nationality, and in which consumers buy from those producers who offer the lowest prices, again regardless of nationality. (Economists call this restructuring of production and consumption in the interest of greater efficiency a *rationalization* of the economic system.) With the opening of a broad regional common market, opportunities for mass production are opened to efficient producers, who thereby become even more efficient as a result of economies in large-scale production. Similarly, as part of the regional rationalization of production, labor gravitates toward, and capital pours into, expanding industries, where the former can be the most productive, and hence the highest paid, and where the latter can yield the highest returns. Hence, theoretically, an entire region can be raised through economic integration to a higher level of economic efficiency, with the result that production expands, profit

9. Bela A. Balassa, *The Theory of Economic Integration* (Homewood, Ill.: Richard D. Irwin, 1961).

margins increase, wages rise, prices lower, capital yields higher returns, and the whole region becomes more externally competitive.

After examining the strong positive case that can be made for regional economic integration in terms of efficiency, production and consumption, lower prices, higher wages, increased returns to capital, and the like, one may wonder why economic integration schemes are often strongly resisted and haltingly implemented. As was the case in the earlier discussion of political integration, economic integration tends to benefit certain groups and individuals (even though in theory its benefits are fairly universal), but tends to penalize other groups and individuals. For example, bankruptcy, dislocation, and unemployment are all implicit in the regional rationalization of production. After the abolition of tariffs, quotas, subsidies, and other protective practices, less efficient national firms that cannot meet regional competition naturally pass into bankruptcy. Executives are displaced and workers are left jobless. While in theory these dislocated groups should move to expanding industries elsewhere, such movement turns out to be extremely difficult in practice, especially when it involves traveling to another country. Therefore, anticipated dislocation foments strong resistance to economic integration among groups who expect to suffer under free regional competition. Furthermore, the more cynical—and sometimes the most realistic—among labor leaders in countries about to establish common markets point out that while economic integration may indeed produce higher profits and returns on capital, whether these benefits will be passed on to workers in the form of higher wages and lower prices hinges upon producers' willingness to redistribute profits and financiers' willingness to redistribute returns. Theoretically, working classes' standards of living should be raised by economic integration. But escalation in living standards is by no means automatic. International cartels, monopolies, and price-fixing practices, for example, can siphon off all potential improvements in working class living standards. Therefore, strong resistance to economic integration emanates from working classes, especially in states with traditions of class antagonism.

Another reason why economic integration schemes are resisted is that while economic integration may heighten the competitiveness of an entire region on world markets, there are conditions under which this result will not follow. If, for example, an external center of production is more efficient than even the most efficient intraregional center, economic rationality could call for import from outside the region rather than expanded production within the region. Such a condition would imply either opening the regional common market to imports from the outside in the interest of maximizing efficiency in consumption, or else closing the region to imports from the outside and sacrificing maximum efficiency to protect regional industry. When such a choice arises, consumers interested in the lowest possible prices might strongly oppose regional economic integration, especially when it is promoted by producers interested in the greatest expansion in production and therefore in regional tariffs to protect internal industry.

Finally, the theory of the integration sometimes deviates from social-cultural reality in its assumptions concerning regional economic rationalization and consequent mass production for a broad regional market. A regional common market in theory becomes a common market in actuality only when consumers throughout the formally integrated region constitute a community of economic tastes and preferences. The potentials of economic integration might never be realized if consumers persist in their provincial tastes, in their suspicions concerning "foreign-made" goods, and in their reluctance to change consuming habits in favor of the new regional instead of their old national market. Some skeptics about regional economic integration tend to withhold endorsement pending evidence showing that regional consumers constitute a truly "common market."

MOTIVATIONS TOWARD REGIONAL INTEGRATION

It becomes clear in examining some of the implications of regional integration, both political and economic, that a policy directed toward amalgamating a region and creating a new state is likely to encounter a great deal of resistance. Opposition to regional integration tends to be both external and internal, and such opposition follows from penalties that international merger invariably imposes. Except for the brief discussion above of anticipated positive impacts from economic merger, little has thus far been said about rewards from regional integration. In fact, so little has been said about rewards that the reader must by now wonder why any statesman would choose to pursue a policy directed toward international merger. Examination of rewards from regional integration has been purposely postponed until now because questions about rewards are directly linked to questions about motivations. That is, despite inevitable and sometimes intense opposition, statesmen pursue policies of regional integration because these policies can yield dramatic rewards. Aspirations toward these rewards motivate the drive for regional integration. Anticipated rewards from regional integration and, relatedly, motivations for seeking regional integration may be grouped into three categories: (1) regional integration yields rewards in enhanced security; (2) when carefully engineered it yields rewards in heightened prosperity; and (3) it may also yield rewards in enhanced governmental and personal prestige. *Simply stated, statesmen are motivated to seek regional integration out of needs or desires for enhanced security, prosperity, and prestige.*

Regional Integration and Increased Security. It has already been pointed out that the amalgamation of two or more states generally results in a new state that possesses more military capability or potential than any of its component units possessed before integration. Historically, desires for improved military capability in the face of external threats have typically prompted the formation of military coalitions. However, military coalitions rarely turn into amalgamated political units since they typically dissolve as external threats fade. For this reason, analysts generally put little stock in the argument that perceptions of and reactions to external threats are prime factors motivating regional integration.[10]

Nevertheless, under certain conditions statesmen may find it desirable to perpetuate military coalitions by building them into politically amalgamated units. First, regional integration may follow from military coalition when common external threats remain salient and constant over long periods of time. Under such conditions, the exigencies of military preparedness and planning may demand integration of military commands and supranational centralization of defense policy-making. Pluralistic decision-making, in which coalition members separately control national forces, separately formulate defense policies, and then seek coordination, can become overly cumbersome under the pressure of constant and intense external threat. Officers may then advocate amalgamated decision-making in the defense sector, and, in response,

10. Karl W. Deutsch, *et al., Political Community and the North Atlantic Area* (Princeton: Princeton University Press, 1957), pp. 44–46.

wary political leaders may approve with the stipulation that the integrated military organization must be subject to an integrated civilian directorate. The aggregate reaction to continuing external threat consequently takes the form of a perceived need for regional military and political amalgamation.

It is true that intense external threats have seldom been so prolonged as to stimulate drives toward regional integration. However, something of this nature was almost realized in Western Europe between 1950 and 1954, when the need for closely coordinated military planning in the face of the Soviet threat prompted plans for an integrated European Defense Community (EDC). The proposed EDC subsequently generated calls for a civilian directorate in the form of an integrated European Political Community (EPC). Though the EDC–EPC scheme died in the French National Assembly in August, 1954, demands for an integrated Western European political confederation persist at present and will likely continue to persist as long as the structure of the international system remains bipolarized.

Regional integration may follow from military coalition also when initial military collaboration creates or exposes broader ranges of common interests among partners. Coalition experiences may generate habits of political cooperation and either generate or expose common foreign policy aims among coalition members. In interacting, therefore, coalition partners may find that they share (or may come to share) common aims concerning preservations and changes in the international environment or—in the broadest sense—common definitions of "security." Recognition of such common aims raises interests in international merger and stimulates political movements in that direction. Under such conditions, perpetuating the military coalition becomes tantamount to maintaining capabilities to support common security aims. Historically, this seems to have been the case with the amalgamation of the Swiss cantons into the Swiss Confederation. Habits of cooperation fostered in military coalitions of the cantons exposed and created common aims in broader policy areas. Recognition of these broader common interests—combined with trust, confidence, and predictability born of military collaboration—then stimulated the Swiss drive toward amalgamation.

While cases in which regional integration has followed from military coalitions prompted by external threats are rare, cases in which regional integration has been pursued for the purpose of enhancing military capabilities are somewhat more common. The twist of reasoning here is important. On one hand we have regional integration prompted by previous favorable experiences in military coalition. On the other, we have regional integration prompted *because it produces a military coalition.* Along this second path, military strength is perceived to be necessary for political bargaining purposes; and regional integration is deemed desirable because, by aggregating forces, it produces politically requisite military strength. For example, French President De Gaulle and many others who shared his views, desired a Western European Confederation to generally heighten Europe's impact upon international politics and to specifically enhance Europe's bargaining position in superpower politics. One reason why the Gaullists (French and otherwise) have seen European unity enhancing European political influence is that they see in such unity greatly increased military potential to buttress political bargaining.

It must not be forgotten that regional integration may be, and indeed has been, pursued out of motivations linked to fairly narrowly defined national interest. In the realm of relationships between regional integration and rewards in terms of security, for example, it is clear that regional integration may be pursued solely to enhance national security. A state may entice or politically coerce a neighbor into international merger for the purpose of eliminating that neighbor as a possible source of threat militarily. The French in the early 1950's made no attempt to hide the fact that economic integration appealed to them because it served to harness West German economic war-making potential by placing the German economy under supranational control. During the same period, similarly, the EDC plan was publicized in France as a supranational device designed to prevent the emergence of an independent West German national army. More broadly, prime motivations behind early efforts at Western European unity shared by all interested governments, were the desire to create a state of perpetual peace in a region plagued by centuries of intra-regional warfare, and the desire to create a zone of economic cooperation in a region plagued by centuries of intense, universally disastrous economic competition. Here the drive toward regional integration stemmed much more from convergent national security interests than from any common regional security interest.

Regional Integration and Enhanced Prosperity. Through this chapter's probe into the theoretical foundations of economic integration, it should have become clear that regional economic integration can produce economic rewards in the form of expanded and rationalized production and consumption, higher living standards, and enhanced international competitiveness. Integration can also produce economic penalties in the form of bankruptcy, unemployment, and cartelization (or it may produce no economic change at all if provincial economic habits bar the realization of a regional common market). The advocate of regional economic integration is naturally likely to publicize potential rewards while ignoring potential penalties, and the critic of economic integration, of course, is likely to do just the opposite. However, the statesman pursuing regional integration is likely to steer a middle course—attempting to devise policies that realize the positive impacts of regional economic integration, while they control or eliminate the negative ones. He seeks economic integration because he sees the economic gains in it, and because he feels that he can minimize economic penalties.

The ministers and technocrats of the European Economic Community have shown that maximizing rewards from regional economic integration involves—actually necessitates—comprehensive central monitoring of the developing regional economy. First, while they see the ultimate goal in regional economic rationalization through free trade and open competition, they also realize that abrupt movement from a system of protected national industries to a system of completely free trade would have disastrous repercussions in some industries in all countries. For this reason intraregional tariffs are being eased downward very slowly in order to give weak industries ample time to prepare for competitive activities on the regional common market. Combined with the gradual liberalization of commerce are numerous programs designed to offset the destructive impacts of dislocation. Centrally allocated subsidies, for example, are provided to marginal industries to help in modernization and thereby improve competitiveness. At the same time, retraining programs are open to workers displaced from noncompetitive industries, and an international relocation program for workers has also been instituted. Plans are being discussed for enhancing the convertibility of national currencies and later instituting a common regional currency to permit unfettered movements of capital throughout the common market area. Efforts are being made to combat international cartelization. Finally, regional tariffs will be levied with an eye to maximizing gains on external markets while prohibiting deluges of imports that might destroy promising regional industries. Prosperity therefore is sought through regional integration, and it is reaped through farsighted economic planning and regulation at the supranational level.

Just as it was earlier noteworthy to point out that increased military capabilities resulting from regional integration are often sought for international political purposes, it is worth pointing out here that regional economic integration is often promoted by statesmen pursuing other than economic goals. Economic power may be sought for political purposes, for instance. Wealth enhances political bargaining positions by contributing to one's image of power. Wealth is related positively to military potential, therefore this relationship tends to amplify one's political voice. Furthermore, control over a large bloc of the world's trade may in itself become a useful political lever. Statesmen seeking heightened influence in world politics, therefore, may well promote regional economic integration as a means toward building a political power base.

Moreover, and more notably with respect to contemporary Western Europe, numerous statesmen inspired by the writings and speeches of Jean Paul Monnet see economic integration as a first stepping-stone toward political federation. While the reasons why Europeans want political unity vary from desires for an independent "third force" in world politics to desires for a strengthened "second force" in the West, many agree that the way to get the political unity they desire is to start in the economic sphere and to work outward from there. Functionalists such as Monnet have argued that the dynamic leading toward full amalgamation runs almost automatically once the integration process is set into motion in the economic sector.[11] Others have pointed out that integration does not automatically spill over from one policy sector to the next, but that there is nevertheless a great deal of wisdom in promoting regional integration through gradualist schemes in which participating states are gently prodded toward relinquishing greater amounts of sovereignty. Such approaches tend to minimize some of the earlier discussed domestic political disruptions wrought

11. John Pinder, *Europe Against De Gaulle* (New York: Praeger, 1963), pp. 5–30.

by regional integration. The point here however is not to question the wisdom of functionalist designs, but rather to note that they do have adherents among those who promote economic integration because they ultimately hope to attain full political amalgamation.

Regional Integration and Heightened Political Influence. A great deal has already been said in this section about desires for heightened political influence and prestige that prompt drives toward regional integration. As noted, prestige and influence flow from "bigness." The actions of an extensive, populous, wealthy, and militarily powerful state can have dramatic impacts upon stability and instability in the international system. Such a state can hardly be ignored in world councils. Regional integration tends to create such states. Statesmen who seek "bigness" and its economic and military correlates through regional integration are therefore often motivated by the desire to have impact upon the international system, to establish political platforms from which they can be heard in world politics, and to accumulate capabilities with which they can alter the course of world politics. Promoting regional integration and capitalizing upon its results thus are tactics in international politics.

Heightened political influence from regional integration is to be found also in the considerable amount of personal prestige that tends to accrue to the statesman or groups of statesmen who have managed an international merger successfully. Personal motivations and ambitions are seldom underlined in discussions of regional integration. But they should be. Reflection on the past reveals that the "great unifiers" are among history's most heralded heroes. Special chapters in history are reserved for the Alexanders, the Caesars, the Charlemagnes, the Washingtons, Lincolns, Bismarcks, Mazzinis, and Churchills, who all made their marks by either carving out sprawling empires, unifying or holding together great states, or first voicing great themes of unity. To the statesman with a slightly better than average sensitivity to his place in history, and with a real opportunity to act, the motivation to become a "unifier" can be irresistible. The drive toward regional integration, then, may—and we would suspect often does—in part, stem from statesmen's personal desires for esteem and historical celebrity.

SUMMARY AND CONCLUSION

As was the case in previous chapters in Part II, there is no possible simple summing up here. The motivations behind regional integration are as complex as the phenomenon itself. Several essential points, however, do stand out:

First, regional integration is a multidimensional phenomenon. It has a dynamic dimension and can be analyzed as a set of social, political, and economic processes leading toward international merger; it also has a static dimension and can be analyzed as a political unit formed by international merger. Moreover, the processes and products of international merger are themselves multidimensional. Accordingly, understanding regional integration requires tracing and explaining territorial merger, institutional amalgamation, political integration, economic integration, and social-cultural assimilation. This last dimension—social-cultural assimilation—was simply mentioned in this chapter, and then passed over, the analysis omitted because research has not yet produced a satisfactory explanation of processes by which and through which peoples alter their identifications and political allegiances. Promising work now in progress, however, indicates that this threshold in our knowledge about regional integration may soon be crossed.[12]

Second, the fact that regional integration has disruptive as well as constructive implications was underlined several times in this chapter. Regional integration alters the international system; it alters domestic politics within merging states; and it alters patterns of economic production, consumption, and exchange. While states, subnational groups, and individuals surely benefit by regional integration, this by no means implies the absence of penalties. Indeed, it is only by observing and reflecting upon the costs of regional integration that we begin to understand why most movements toward international merger arouse intense opposition, why many such movements are either internally undermined or externally squelched, and why successful regional integration turns out to be such a rare phenomenon in international political history. In the contemporary era—in which the idea of regional inte-

12. Harold Guetzkow, *Multiple Loyalties: Theoretical Approach to a Problem in International Organization* (Princeton: Center for Research on World Political Institutions, Publication No. 4, 1955).

gration, and especially economic integration, is so widely voiced and praised—it is essential that the analyst recognize the wide gap between the articulation of the "unity" theme, and the actual consummation of regional mergers.

Third, and central to this chapter, has been the point that regional integration is more often pursued as a means rather than as an end in itself. Statesmen are motivated to promote regional integration because a variety of political military, economic, and even personal rewards follow from it. Achieving successful international merger is a step that can turn statesmen's ambitions—as well as aspirations for greater security, enhanced world political status and influence, higher living standards and economic dynamism, and personal stature—into actualities. The numerous causal paths from motivation to reward through regional integration sketched in this chapter all underline the basic point that regional integration is pursued, despite opposition, *because its payoffs can be extremely high.*

Fourth and finally, most of the arguments concerning regional integration presented in this chapter were documented with references to developments in Western Europe over the last two decades. This was partly because the author is most familiar with the Western European case, and partly too because the Western European model is the prototype for regional integration experiments currently in progress in other parts of the world. Seldom do we have a case of a phenomenon so close at hand and so amenable to analysis. What happens to Western European integration during coming decades will certainly enhance our understanding of regional integration generally. It will also provide clues to developments in Central America, Africa, and elsewhere in the more distant future. Therefore, the interested student is urged to continue monitoring Western European developments for the insights concerning regional integration that they will invariably provide.

CHAPTER SEVEN
THE INTERNATIONAL POLITICS
OF PEACE

THE study of peace in international relations is a study of paradox. "Peace" is undoubtedly one of the most frequently used words in the vocabulary of statesmanship. Yet, it is also one of the most ambiguous and least communicable terms in diplomatic rhetoric. Ironically, those who profess peace with the most sincerity are frequently those whose professions are greeted with the most suspicion. Furthermore, when the record of diplomatic dialogue is set against the record of international events, it appears that peace is at the same time the most desired and the most elusive state of international affairs. Historic eras welcomed by contemporaries as new departures in lasting peace have turned out actually to be periods of prelude to new wars. Then, too, even a cursory examination of the historical record reveals a bitter contrast between the nobility of peace as an international goal, and the ignobility of means men sometimes employ in its pursuit. Numerous wars have been fought under the banner "building a peaceful world," and these have been among history's bloodiest wars.

Understanding the significance and implications of peace as a goal in international politics follows from explaining and unraveling the paradoxes associated with its profession and pursuit. Accordingly, the analysis of peace as a political goal is developed in this chapter in four parts. First, ambiguities in meaning surrounding the term "international peace" are examined, and different meanings and shades of meaning are distinguished and separated. Second, since the central paradox in the study of peace lies in the contrast between the continuing appeal for lasting peace and the actuality of continuing war, this contrast is documented in the second section of this chapter and then analyzed in the third. Questions concerning the sincerity of statesmen in their pursuit of peace, and concerning the position of peace in the value hierarchies of both statesmen and peoples are of central relevance in these sections; relevant also is the inventory of related questions asking why motivations toward peace are repeatedly frustrated in and by international politics. Finally, after asking and answering questions concerned for the most part with conditions that foment the breakdown of peace, it is appropriate to ask about conditions conducive to the perpetuation of peace. While continuing tranquility among neighboring states is rare in international politics, it is not unknown. Therefore, analysis of cases of long-prevailing harmony among certain pairs and groups of states provides insight into preconditions for peace. This analysis is the subject of the last section of this chapter.

THE MANY MEANINGS OF PEACE

Technically, the world has been at peace since 1945. But few would accept a description of the contemporary era in international politics as fulfilling a definition of "peace." It is true that no state has formally declared war on another state since the end of World War II. Yet it is clear even to the most casual observer of the international scene that the post-World War II era has been a period of peace "on paper" only. There have in fact been more than twenty armed conflicts in various parts of the world since 1945 that qualify as "international wars" since forces of more than one state were involved. Though the wars of the contemporary era have been tactically limited and geographically confined, they nevertheless have been highly costly in human lives and property. In the light of this post-World War II record of informal, intermittent, small-scale conflict, we may hardly call our era a period of peace.

Although fortunately there have been no wars between nuclear superpowers since the beginning of the Atomic Age, the Soviet Union and the United States (and most recently Communist China) have been engaged in intense political-ideological competition throughout the past two decades. Politically, the East-West Cold War has been characterized by verbal harangues, exchanged warnings and threats, and attempts to align sympathetic states and intimidate unsympathetic ones. Militarily, the competition has taken the form of a spiraling arms race, periodic acute crises that escalate to the brink of nuclear war, and material support of client states actually engaged in violent conflict. Again, regardless of sloganized "peaceful coexistence," we can hardly call this period of Cold War a period of peace.

In yet another dimension, our international system remains a system of separate and independent states despite bipolarity, bloc structures, and international organizations such as the United Nations. In this system each state remains the final arbiter of its interests; and each remains ultimately responsible for deciding whether, when, and how to introduce force into international politics. Conflict in our system remains ultimately controlled by unilateral state decisions. No other effective structure or mechanism for conflict control currently exists. That no major war has occurred since 1945 can be largely attributed to the sensitivity, rationality, clear-headedness, and farsightedness of individual statesmen. Yet, can we call an era where the avoidance of armed conflict rests solely on individuals' good judgment an era of peace? Or, in light of the long historical record of lapses of good judgment, might we more pessimistically label our era a period of prelude to war? In short, the question asked here is: Is it possible to offer a definition of peace that excludes references to effective structures and mechanisms for conflict control?

Not only is our era characterized by intermittent small-scale wars, intense political-ideological competition, and missing mechanisms of conflict control. It is also marked, as all eras have been, by continuing tensions that follow from international suspicion, distrust, and unpredictability. Certainly, much of the tension in our system stems from the Cold War, but much of it is also simply endemic in international politics and would doubtless remain even after an East-West conciliation. No government or people are fully confident in the intentions of others, and no government or people ever feel fully secure in their predictions and expectations concerning the behavior of others. Whether dealing with allies or antagonists each state hopes for the best, but prepares for the worst. There is, in brief, no basis for absolute security in the international system because there is no real foundation for it in international understanding and confidence, and no apparent mechanism for building these. Continuing tension generated by a continuing "security dilemma" is not compatible with international peace.

Thus, a definition of peace should not exclude reference to international community and understanding, and mechanisms for promoting these.

Peace in Four Dimensions. While it is instructive to examine a nominally "peaceful" era in international history and to find it lacking in attributes implicit in normal understandings of "peace," such an analysis leaves one short of any really satisfactory definition of a state of affairs that could be termed "international peace." The definitional problem, however, can be approached more directly. "Peace" meaning different things to different people, it would simply be toying with words to present any composite definition. There is some worth, though, in showing exactly what peace does mean to different people. As might be gleaned from the above discussion of the contemporary system, different conceptions of "peace" embody one or more of four basic themes:

1. For some, peace is simply the absence of violent conflict, or sometimes merely the absence of large-scale conflict. Under this minimalist definition, peace becomes synonymous with relative military stability (i.e., the absence of major military disturbances in the international system).

2. Some analysts would call the minimalist definition much too minimal, and would suggest that peace should be conceptualized in political-ideological as well as military terms. Here, international peace becomes the absence of both violent conflict *and* intense political-ideological antagonisms that might generate such conflicts. In other words, peace and stability remain synonymous, but stability takes on broader meaning and implies the relative absence of both major military and major political disturbances.

3. Defining peace simply in terms of the *absence* of disturbances does not satisfy more positive-minded analysts and advocates, however. Some of these note that to define peace as the absence of major military and political disturbances is really to define peace as a prelude to war, since such absences tend to be temporary. Peace, these analysts insist, must be a state of affairs wherein intense political and military disturbances cannot arise to unbalance international stability. Peace to them, therefore, is stability guaranteed by international institutions and practices by which and through which conflicts are controlled and settled short of unilateral resorts to violence by antagonists. By this definition, peace and stability become synonymous with *enforced*

international order. All of these who emphasize peace through order are not necessarily advocates of nonviolence, however. Some point to the intermittent necessity for coercion exercised under international institutional auspices in the interest of maintaining order. Others see peace in single-power world hegemony. Most advocates of peace through order are, however, advocates of world government in one form or another, and most find a basic incompatibility between a system of sovereign states and an ordered peaceful world. For these people, achieving peace means taking a major step beyond traditional relations among sovereign states.

4. A step beyond the advocates of positive conflict control and international institutionalization, one finds advocates of peace through international community. Peace, for these spokesmen, means absolute security through international trust, understanding, common identification, and harmonious interaction in a global system. Peace here is a social-psychological rather than a military, political, or institutional state of affairs. In a global community of peoples, the conflicting interests of separate states would fade as the separateness of states disappears. Peoples' differing points of view would be greeted with tolerance and integrated and compromised in a continuing and candid world dialogue. War would become an unthinkable crime against the world community and an intolerable detriment to global progress and well-being. For this last group of thinkers (let us call them Utopians, while respecting their views), peace is tantamount to productive tranquility, and this tranquility would stem from world community or cultural assimilation on a global scale.

Allocating the different themes and definitions of peace into four categories hardly does justice to the many shades of meaning and expression one finds in the thoughts and ideas that are here lumped together. Since time and space considerations compelled abbreviated presentation, Table 7.1 was prepared as a guide to the many meanings of peace. In working through the "characteristics" and "comments" describing various military, political, structural, and social-psychological states of peace, the reader will find it possible to analytically locate most of the nominally "peaceful" periods in international history. The most sobering observation that comes in comparing Table 7.1 with a survey of history is that, empirically, "peace" has seldom been more than temporary relative military stability.

TABLE 7.1. SYSTEMIC CHARACTERISTICS OF STATES OF PEACE

Dimension	Characteristics	Comments
I. Military	1. Absence of all violent conflict	1. Utopia to some peace designers. Has characterized only scattered and short-lived periods in history.
	2. Absence of large-scale violent conflict	2. Small-scale conflict, however, may be intermittent or continuous. Characteristic of last half of the 19th century and the contemporary era.
	3. Intermittent large-scale violent conflict	3. "Peace" is but a period of prelude before and preparation for the next war. Characteristic of the first half of the 20th century.
II. Political/ Ideological	1. Political/Ideological harmony	1. Most or all states' interests common or compatible; wide-ranging international cooperation possible and likely. Condition sometimes realized in bilateral and regional relations; never, to this point in history, at the global level.
	2. Mixed Political/Ideological harmony and discord	2. Conflict control and even cooperation possible out of convergent self-interest; basic incompatibilities, however, limit range of cooperation and capabilities for conflict control; characteristic of contemporary system.

Dimension	Characteristics	Comments
III. Structural/ Institutional	1. World government	1. Central authoritative control over interactions among states. Central coercive mechanism to guarantee order. Implies either world federation or empire, e.g., Pax Romana.
	2. Separate sovereign states/imposed system control	2. Collective security or peacekeeping under auspices of international organization, e.g., United Nations peacekeeping or U.N. Collective Security Action in Korea.
	3. Separate sovereign states/adherence to explicit norms or tacit "rules" for conflict avoidance and control	3. Respect for international law, or for tacit "rules of the game" concerning "spheres of influence," "peaceful coexistence," etc. Somewhat characteristic of contemporary system. Characteristic of classic European "balance of power" system.
	4. Separate sovereign states/no external control	4. Self-interest ultimate guide to policy and behavior; self-defense ultimate means of survival. Tenuous peace maintained through balanced power, mutual deterrence, and astute statesmanship.
IV. Social/ Psychological	1. Community among peoples	1. Mutual identification among a global community; high degrees of cultural assimilation, high fidelity and effectiveness in intra- and

TABLE 7.1. Continued

Dimension	Characteristics	Comments
		intercultural communications; high mutual predictability; trust and confidence. Characteristic of relations among some pairs of states historically and presently. Never achieved at global level.

THE RHETORIC OF PEACE AND THE REALITY OF WAR

While international politics remains unpredictable in many ways, one variety of international political behavior is highly predictable. When one knows that a statesman or other public official is about to make a public address concerning foreign policy, one can reasonably predict that he is going to embrace the cause of international peace, identify his policies with the pursuit of peace, and assure his audience of his vigorous efforts in the direction of peace. There are, of course, some exceptions to this rule of rhetoric; but the exceptions, such as certain Arab leaders' repeated proclamations of "holy war" against Israel, are also by and large predictable.

As one moves back through history, again and again one finds the appeal for peace framed and voiced in solemn, impressive, and grandiose forms. In 1920, for example, twenty-four countries of the world signed the *Covenant to the League of Nations,* in which they agreed "to promote international cooperation and to achieve international peace and security, by the acceptance of obligations not to resort to war." [1] A short time later, in 1928, sixty-three countries signed the Pact of Paris (Kellogg-Briand Pact), wherein they affirmed the illegitimacy of aggressive war, renounced war as an instrument of foreign policy, and agreed to pacific settlements of international disputes. In the words of the document:

Article I: The High Contracting Parties solemnly declare in the names of their respective peoples that they condemn recourse to war for

1. Joel Larus, ed., *From Collective Security to Preventive Diplomacy* (New York: John Wiley, 1965), Appendix I, p. 519.

the solution of international controversies, and renounce it as an instrument of national policy in their relations with one another.

Article II: The High Contracting Parties agree that the settlement or solution of all disputes or conflicts of whatever nature or of whatever origin they may be, which arise among them, shall never be sought except by pacific means.[2]

More recently, in 1945, fifty-one countries signed the *Charter of the United Nations,* and since that time over seventy more states have affirmed this document, which opens: "We the peoples of the United Nations determined to save succeeding generations from the scourge of war, which twice in our lifetime has brought untold sorrow to mankind."[3] Later in the same document, the signatories promise to "practice tolerance and live together with one another as good neighbors." With these principles affirmed, states signatory to the UN Charter agreed to establish an organization, the first purpose of which is, "to maintain international peace and security, and to that end: to make effective collective measures for the prevention and removal of threats to the peace."

It would be possible to amass and display countless other solemn oaths denouncing war and affirming peace. Such documents are scattered through international political history in great profusion. However, further documentation on the profession of peace is unnecessary. The point has been made: the rhetoric of peace has been, and continues to be, a major part of the public dialogue of diplomacy.

Contradiction comes to the fore when the record of peace appeals, peace professions, and solemn oaths is set against the record of international behavior. Despite the volume of peace appeals, despite the recurrent commitments to nonaggression, despite the international organizations, and despite the hopes of peoples, war can safely be called the *normal* state of affairs in international politics. Documentation on this point is vivid. According to Quincy Wright, in his study *The Causes of War and the Conditions of Peace:*

The data are inadequate to estimate this in early times, but there is not much doubt but that Greece and Rome were at war a larger proportion of the time than are modern nations, even allowing for the Pax Romana under the Antonine Caesars which, however, was not an unalloyed peace. In the middle

2. Samuel Flagg Bemis, *A Diplomatic History of the United States,* 4th ed. (New York: Holt, Rinehart and Winston, 1955), p. 719.
3. Joel Larus, ed., *From Collective Security to Preventive Diplomacy,* p. 531.

ages, Europe was broken up into many fighting groups and small wars were continuous. Important wars occupied a larger proportion of these centuries than during the Roman Empire, but probably less than in Greece or the Roman Republic. Coming to modern times, we have more accurate statistics. In the Seventeenth Century, the Great European states were formally at war about 75% of the time. In the Eighteenth Century about 50% of the time, and in the Nineteenth Century about 25% of the time. This refers only to legal war. If we counted the expeditions into America, Asia, and Africa against people with inferior war techniques, then most of the Great Powers have been fighting a larger proportion of the time even in the last century.[4]

Since Wright's work was written during the 1930's, he did not have the opportunity to take a statistical tally of fighting during the twentieth century. Updating Wright's work is not difficult. There were thirteen formal wars fought between 1900 and 1945 that involved at least one major power (Great Britain, France, Germany, Italy, China, Japan, the United States, and Russia). If for each major power we compute the ratio of years at war to total years between 1900 and 1945, we arrive at the following:[5]

TABLE 7.2. WAR INVOLVEMENT FOR MAJOR POWERS, 1900–1945

State	Years at War 1900–1945	Percentage of Time at War
Great Britain	16	36
France	13	29
Germany [a]	14	31
Italy	13	29
China	15	33
Japan	22	47
United States	9	18
Russia [b]	13	29
Great power average	14	32

[a] Empire and Third Reich
[b] Empire and U.S.S.R.

Interpreting the figures in Table 7.2 one way, we see that during the first half of the twentieth century the average major power was at war about one-third of the time. The range around the average varies from

4. Quincy Wright, *The Causes of War and the Conditions of Peace* (London, New York: Longmans, Green, 1935), p. 32.
5. Data here were gathered from Lewis F. Richardson, *Statistics of Deadly Quarrels* (Pittsburgh: Boxwood Press, 1960), pp. 32–127.

the United States' low of war involvement during only 9 of the 45 years, to the Japanese high of involvement during 22 of the 45 years. If we look at these figures another way, however, and ask how many years out of the 45 was there a war going on that involved one or more of the major powers, we find that the number turns out to be 27. That is, there were major-power wars in progress during about 60 percent of the time between 1900 and 1945. Again these figures, with one or two exceptions, represent only formal wars, explicitly declared and legally ended, and they represent only major-power wars. When one adds all of the informal military operations and wars fought among minor states, the only conclusion that one can infer is that there was a war going on most of the time during the first half of the twentieth century. For any particular state, periods of peace tended to be somewhat more frequent and longer lasting than periods of war; but for the world at large, war seemed almost the normal state of affairs. Except for the virtual disappearance of formally declared war in our era, and the relative decline in major-power involvement, the post-World War II record of continuing warfare deviates little from patterns established in the first half of this century.

The contradiction then comes into full light. Men talk about peace, obviously cherish it, and solemnly promise to promote it. But they profess peace while preparing for, fighting, and recovering from wars. Verbal and physical behavior here seem thoroughly at variance. It would appear that if the pursuit of peace is a motivation for international behavior, it is either a weak and subordinate motivation, or if a strong one, it is frequently frustrated.

PEACE AS A MOTIVATION FOR INTERNATIONAL BEHAVIOR

Why should it be that war is the dominant pattern in international politics when most men profess to hold world peace as a primary goal? Reflection on this problem, which, after all, is a central one in the study of international politics, generates two hypotheses concerning the sincerity and integrity of statesmen. First, it might be assumed that those who profess to pursue peace are hypocrites. Their statements are simply propaganda designed to disarm their enemies and impress their friends. Thus, they say that they want world peace, but they really do not want it at all; or—put less strongly—they really do not care much about peace in one way or the other. In direct contrast to this first hypothesis, it might be proposed that most statesmen do truly desire peace, and work for and towards it whenever they can. Their motivations are sincere, but for various reasons beyond the control of individual statesmen, the goal of peace is most often frustrated or sidetracked.

Animosity and Indifference to Peace. If we choose to accept the first hypothesis, which denies the sincerity of statesmen's peaceful professions, then the contradiction of peaceful words and warlike actions dissolves. We no longer have a case of men wanting peace and getting war. Instead, we have a situation in which since nobody really cares very much about peace, no one is very surprised when war erupts. Or, alternatively, we have a situation in which men profess peace and provoke war.

It cannot be denied that there have been, and still are, statesmen who fancy themselves "political realists," viewing international politics as an arena of continuing and inevitable conflict where peace is unattainable, but where themes of peace can be used to good advantage. Machiavelli was certainly not the first, but he was probably one of the most articulate advocates of "realism" in international politics. At one point in *The Prince*—Machiavelli's handbook for statesmen—the Italian writer astutely observes that:

A certain Prince of the present time, whom it is well not to name, never does anything by preach peace and good faith, but he is really a great enemy to both, and either of them, had he observed them, would have lost him state or reputation on many occasions.[6]

Machiavelli was looking out upon the world of Renaissance politics, where grandiloquent expressions of the lofty principles of peace masked and facilitated a vicious politics of continuing tests of strength. He consequently advised those of his readers in ruling positions to master the art of deception in the interest of survival.

Not surprisingly, Benito Mussolini turned out to be one of Machiavelli's most serious twentieth-century students. Before his public audiences, foreign and domestic, Mussolini embraced the cause of world peace; before his Fascist disciples, he glorified war and ridi-

6. Niccolo Machiavelli, "The Prince," in *Introduction to Contemporary Civilization in the West*, 2nd ed., I (New York: Columbia University Press, 1954), 383.

culed the weakness of those who worked to avoid it. "And above all," Mussolini wrote in the Italian *Encyclopedia* in 1932,

Fascism, the more it considers and observes the future and the development of humanity quite apart from political considerations of the moment, believes neither in the possibility nor the utility of perpetual peace.[7]

The theme of peace has clearly been employed for purposes of deception by those preparing for aggressive adventures, or by those otherwise convinced that peace is actually impossible. Furthermore, one tragic legacy of men's past duplicities in proclaiming peace while provoking war is that now most peace appeals are taken as suspect. The common and widespread response to a man who proposes a plan for peace is that he must be either a self-seeking statesman practicing deception, or a whimsical dreamer who cannot be taken seriously. International antagonists almost automatically assume false motives behind one another's proposals for peace and reconciliation. Similarly, New Left critics of existing regimes in the United States and Western Europe find it inconceivable that contemporary statesmen could be sincere in their appeals for peace, since they perceive these statesmen knit into "establishments" that profit from war. Ironically, the very philosophers and political theorists who through the years have formulated classic "grand designs" for peace have been the most suspicious of all of statesmen's sincerity. The main lament of the peace philosophers is that governments do not really want lasting peace.[8]

Sincere Motives but Elusive Ends in the Pursuit of Peace. While it is well to note and remember that peace is not always a goal sincerely pursued, and that paying lip service to peace may in certain instances be a way of psychologically disarming potential enemies or victims, it would be rash to jump immediately into cynicism. It is difficult, for example, to question the sincerity of the peace appeals of statesmen such as Woodrow Wilson, Neville Chamberlain, Jawaharlal Nehru, and Dag Hammarskjold. Moreover, it is equally difficult to completely write off the proclaimed peaceful intentions of Cold War statesmen such as Dwight Eisenhower, John Kennedy, Adlai Stevenson, Winston Churchill, and even Nikita Khrushchev—all of whom shouldered the

7. Benito Mussolini, "The Political and Social Doctrine of Fascism," in *Introduction to Contemporary Civilization in the West*, II, *ibid.*, p. 1151.

8. F. H. Hinsley, *Power and the Pursuit of Peace* (Cambridge: The University Press, 1967), p. 84 ff.

awesome responsibility of avoiding superpower confrontation and who unquestionably shared the desire to spare the globe from nuclear holocaust.

Then too, it can and should be pointed out that avoiding war is actually a "realist" policy, with appeal to even the coldest calculator among statesmen. Wars, after all, are costly to defeated and victors alike, and more than this, they are terribly unpredictable in their outcome. The cautious realist avoids war or resorts to violence only as a last resort. One might question his sincerity in promoting peace, but this is not the same as questioning his seriousness in wanting to avoid war.

The point here is that there is value in exploring the second assumption advanced earlier—i.e., that statesmen do sincerely desire peace but that their lofty motives tend to be frustrated as their efforts are sidetracked. This hypothesis should be examined not necessarily because it is completely true (and not because we wish it were true) but because examining it opens the way to understanding more thoroughly why the goal of international peace has been traditionally so elusive. In effect, a broader analysis carries us away from the implicit "devil theory" advanced to this point, which, in this author's estimation, is just too simple to be completely valid. If, for the moment, we accept the sincerity of statesmen, can we find the reasons why the goal of peace escapes even those who want it and work towards it? The answer here is "yes."

Reasons for the elusiveness of international peace fall under four headings. The first one has to do with the position of peace in statesmen's and people's hierarchies of values. Second, and relatedly, desires for peace and perceptions of rewards from it cannot blur the fact that war has always had, and continues to have, a certain utility in international politics. Third, the pursuit of peace frequently falls victim to many of the perceptual and definitional dilemmas examined earlier in this chapter. As it turns out, the most difficult task in pursuing peace is to convince antagonists and even partners of one's sincerity, and to compromise incompatibilities in definitions of peace. Fourth, the pursuit of peace has continually fallen victim to the predicament which might be labeled "good intentions/faulty methods." Ironically it seems that almost every method that men have devised for promoting peace has in fact helped to directly or indirectly instigate war.

1. Peace is but one among the many goals that states pursue in international politics. Under conditions immediately threatening survival, security, or sometimes even prosperity, the pursuit of peace falls to a subordinate position in statesmen's and people's value hierarchies. It is not that the goal of peace is abandoned. Rather, other goals demand priority. "No statesman wants peace at any price" Vernon Van Dyke notes,

There are always some things which they want more than they want peace. It may be the protection and promotion of commercial interests or ideological principles; it may be survival or security; it may be freedom and justice. The very fact that wars occur demonstrates that peace is not the paramount value.[9]

Regardless of the sanctity they attribute to the goal of peace, men always affirm that there are certain values worth fighting for, and when these values are threatened they feel obligated to fight. Few but extreme pacifists value peace at any price.

One begins to get a feeling for value hierarchies and the place for peace in these hierarchies by examining the responses to the set of public opinion poll questions asked of Western Europeans in 1955 and shown here in Table 7.3.

Notice first in Table 7.3 that with very few exceptions pluralities in each of the three countries were willing to fight to preserve all of the basic values listed. The British were especially committed to preserving Western values even at the cost of war, the Italians somewhat less so, and the Germans usually only by bare plurality. Nevertheless, each of the peoples polled clearly held some values above peace.

Another source of interesting documentation on the place of peace in people's value hierarchies is in the texts of reservations that various countries attached to their accessions to the *Pact of Paris* in 1928. Reservations to the "no war" pact amounted to statements of the conditions under which the various countries refused to abide in obligations for pacific settlement—i.e., the situations they valued more highly than peace.[10] For example, the British Government stipulated that they would not tolerate interference with British sovereignty in outlying areas of the British Empire. Hence, the security of the empire was more highly valued than peace. Similarly, the United States Gov-

9. Vernon Van Dyke, *International Politics*, 2nd ed. (New York: Appleton-Century-Crofts, 1966), p. 178.
10. Robert H. Ferrell, *Peace in Their Time: The Origins of the Kellogg-Briand Pact* (New Haven: Yale University Press, 1952).

TABLE 7.3. PEACE AND THE HIERARCHY OF VALUES

QUESTION: "Of course, almost everyone wants peace. But there are some things that people say are worth fighting for. What about a threat to [given value]? Which would you choose—stay at peace or fight for it?"

	Stay at Peace	Fight	Don't Know
A. *National Independence of Respondent's Country?*			
West Germans	30%	45%	25%
Italians	21	63	16
British	10	64	6
B. *Individual Liberty of People in Survey Country?*			
West Germans	24	53	23
Italians	22	57	21
British	10	82	8
C. *Human Dignity and Respect for the Individual?*			
West Germans	24	53	23
Italians	21	53	26
British	14	69	17
D. *Democratic Way of Life?*			
West Germans	44	35	21
Italians	25	51	24
British	20	69	11

SOURCE: From survey made in 1955 and recorded in R. L. Merritt and D. J. Puchala, eds., *Western European Perspectives on International Affairs* (Frederick A. Praeger: New York, 1968).

ernment insisted upon the inviolability of the Monroe Doctrine and the special position of the United States in the Western Hemisphere. Here again the preservation of peace was subordinated to the preservation of a certain more highly valued state of affairs. The point here is not difficult to grasp. Certainly, statesmen pursue and value peace. But they also pursue and value other conditions, and gaining and preserving these often takes priority over achieving and keeping peace.

2. Adding to the predicament of the peacemaker is the fact that war traditionally has been, and nonnuclear war remains, an effective instrument for accomplishing certain international goals.[11] That is, the reason that men choose to fight to protect valued objects is because fighting very often accomplishes the protective task, and the reason men choose to fight to acquire valued objects, too, is because fighting very often accomplishes the acquisitive end. Warfare may be morally despicable, especially to those reared in a humanist tradition; it may be costly in human lives and property; it may be a barbaric instrument of conflict resolution; and its outcomes may be unpredictable. Nevertheless, it has certain pragmatic utility—it works. To compel men to abandon war is to undermine a traditionally effective instrument of foreign policy—and men seem fundamentally unwilling to wholly relinquish this instrument no matter how sincerely they abhor using it.

George Kennan, in his *Realities of American Foreign Policy,* vividly underscores the traditional utility of war as an instrument of policy:

There is hardly a national state in this world community, including our own, whose ultimate origins did not lie in sets of violence. The source of every governmental claim to legitimacy will be found to rest in some situation created by arbitrary assertion of armed might. There is hardly a constitution that does not trace its origins to some set which was formally one of insurrection or of usurption.[12]

Similarly, James T. Shotwell, in his classic *War as an Instrument of National Policy,* makes an even broader case for the utility of war:

War, then, has been the instrument by which most of the great facts of political national history have been established and maintained. . . . The map of the world today has been largely determined upon the battlefield. The maintenance of civilization itself has been, and still continues to be, underwritten by the insurance of army and navy ready to strike at any time where danger threatens. Thus, even in peace, the war system has to a large degree determined not only international relationships but the character and history of the nations themselves.[13]

11. Vernon Van Dyke, *International Politics,* pp. 354–379.
12. George F. Kennan, *Realities of American Foreign Policy* (Princeton: Princeton University Press, 1954), p. 37.
13. James T. Shotwell, *War as an Instrument of National Policy* (New York: Harcourt, Brace & World, 1929), p. 15.

To these citations we could add many more from works in the currently proliferating literature of guerrilla, irregular, and limited warfare.[14] Here, all strategists and tacticians begin from the basic assumption that military confrontations and acts of terrorism should be perpetrated—indeed must be perpetrated in the authors' views—because they are effective in accomplishing ends. Violent revolutionists embrace the doctrine of guerrilla warfare because they are convinced that it works. And it often does!

There tends to be as much utility, furthermore, in threatening acts of violence as there is in actually committing such acts. States that have threatened war frequently have gained objects or values from others by intimidation. They have also frequently preserved objects and values that they might have lost had they not demonstrated ultimate conviction and commitment. Hitler gained as much by intimidation and threatening war during the late 1930's as he later gained (and then lost) on the battlefield. Implicit American threats to go to war favorably ended the Cuban Missile Crisis in 1962, too, and well-articulated American threats to go to war have helped to preserve the tenuous security of West Berlin for two decades. In the same sense, the deterrent value of the NATO Alliance stems directly from the fact that signatory nations are pledged to a joint threat to go to war in response to any armed incursion into NATO territories. The point here is that threatening war has a certain diplomatic utility, and as long as it does, statesmen, no matter how desirous of peace they might be, are unlikely to relinquish the violent threat as an instrument of foreign policy.

Nowadays we hear a great many references to the obsolescence of war as an instrument of national policy, and a corresponding number of predictions about the dawning of a new peaceful era in international politics, where war has outlived its usefulness. If this were actually the case, if war truly has lost its utility, then all that has been said above would of course be without contemporary relevance. Statesmen would no longer be faced with the problem of pursuing peace at the cost of abandoning an effective instrument of policy. However—and unfortunately—neither war nor the threat of war have lost their utility

14. Mao Tse-Tung, *Mao Tse-Tung on Guerrilla Warfare*, Brigadier General S. B. Griffith, tr. (New York: Praeger, 1961); Ernesto Guevara, *Che Guevara on Guerrilla Warfare*, Major H. Peterson, tr. (New York: Praeger, 1961).

in contemporary international politics. While certainly a nuclear war of mutual annihilation has little utility, threatening such a war reaps political gains. Moreover, conventional wars, guerrilla wars, and terrorist activities have as much utility as ever. As long as warfare continues to promise rewards that appear to some as greater rewards than peace might provide, the pursuit of peace is likely to continue assuming lower priority.

3. Ironically, even if the pursuit of peace were allotted top priority universally, the realization of a world without war would likely remain distant. The reason for this is that the pursuit of peace is deterred by centuries-old feelings of international suspicion and animosity. Even when a statesman is sincere and positive in his convictions concerning the desirability of peace, he may have strong doubts about the sincerity and conviction of his traditional enemies, and they may well feel the same way about him. Mutual suspicion generates a security dilemma wherein actual peaceful intentions are blurred by perceived aggressive intentions, and this dilemma thwarts all cooperative efforts toward conciliation and peace.[15]

The security dilemma as it relates to the thwarting of peace has two major themes. On the one hand we frequently hear the defense, "I want peace, but I cannot let my guard down because my antagonist will interpret this as a sign of weakness and jump at the opportunity to attack me. I am peaceminded, but he is out to destroy me." The press in both the East and West carries this theme almost daily, and has done so for the last twenty years. Mutual suspicions may be well founded in objective reality or they may be ill-founded in paranoiac illusion. However, the accuracy of such perceptions is seldom questioned in the Communist East, where governments and peoples cannot seem to conceive of capitalism except in the context of international conspiracy.

This perceptual "security dilemma" is not peculiar to East-West relations in our time. The leaders of new states consistently attribute aggressive motives to the governments of the more developed countries, and Arabs and Jews consistently find sinister plots underlying each other's every move. In his dispute with Dag Hammarskjold in 1960, Soviet Premier Khrushchev went so far as to insist that no

15. Raymond A. Bauer, Alex Inkeles, Clyde Kluckhohn, *How the Soviet System Works* (New York: Vintage Books, 1960), pp. 144–156.

statesman is capable of acting from universalistic motivation, and that any man who claims to do so must be suspect. Interestingly, we find that Adolf Hitler too was plagued by the perceptual "security dilemma." Addressing a German audience on the opening of World War II in 1939, Hitler noted:

I have seen this coming for years. What did I ask of the other world? . . . nothing which would have meant a loss to other nations . . . I had not the slightest wish to rearm. . . . When I saw that the same old warmongers were mobilizing once more . . . I realized that this struggle would have to be fought once more. . . . the other side did not want peace.[16]

On the other hand, we frequently hear another theme associated with the perceptual "security dilemma." In voicing this theme, statesmen admit to one another's sincerity in pursuing peace, but they see ignoble motives behind one another's definitions of peace: "Of course, he wants peace, but he wants peace on his terms, which I cannot accept. I want peace too, but I feel that his definition of peace is really not peace at all but rather a more favorable position for him." Governments in both the East and the West at the present time appear convinced that their adversaries are defining peace in terms of world hegemony for themselves. Therefore, proposals for peace emanating from either side are almost automatically unacceptable to the other. The point here is clear: different statesmen may pursue peace most sincerely, but perceptual narrowness convinces each that he is really the only one pursuing peace while all rivals are pursuing self-interest defined as peace.

4. Finally, one of the major impediments to the realization of peace in international politics is the lack of any effective mechanisms for preventing and controlling violent conflict, and for institutionalizing and perpetuating pacific settlements. Various conflict control and peacekeeping mechanisms have been devised, and many of these have actually been tried over the years. Each was greeted with enthusiasm; each partly or wholly failed in attempted practice; many subsequently passed into disrepute.

In the heyday of the League of Nations during the late 1920's and early 1930's, great emphasis was placed upon voluntary compliance with international law, internationally arbitrated juridical settlement

16. Adolf Hitler, "To the German Workers," in *Introduction to Contemporary Civilization in the West* (above, n. 6), II, 1181.

and universal sanction against aggressors by political ostracism, and economic boycott. Peacekeeping hopes in the League were dampened and later dashed when it turned out that compliance with international law depended upon coincidence between national interests and legal practices; and sanctions against aggressors fell short of effectiveness due both to ambiguities in defining the term "aggressor" and to states' unwillingness to support policies of ostracism and boycott when it appeared against their narrowly defined national interests to do so.

Later, in the 1930's, British and French statesmen revived the classical idea and policy of appeasement.[17] Reasoning that no aggressor could be insatiable, the proponents of appeasement advocated small concessions in the interest of preventing war. Historical hindsight now reveals that appeasers' commitments to their new policies open the way for "salami" tactics (i.e., one small slice at a time) on the part of expansionist statemen, whose territorial lusts *can* be more or less insatiable. If the historical record of the 1930's is any guide, one must conclude that appeasement may postpone war, but it does not prevent it.

The post-World War II era has seen the introduction of the multi-faceted United Nations peacekeeping system. This system includes: (1) a concert of major powers to control conflicts among minor states; (2) a forum for continuing open dialogue and debate to improve international communication and to generate "world public opinion" pressures for pacific settlement; (3) a plan for collective security, in the form of obligations to universal political, economic, and military sanctions against aggressors; (4) a mechanism for preventive diplomacy, in the form of an injected United Nations presence designed to physically separate disputing states and parties; and (5) a provision for third-party arbitration and conciliation through the World Court and the impartial offices of the Secretary General and his staff.

Without belittling the peacekeeping accomplishments of the United Nations, one must, in objectivity, conclude that the UN system has operated with minimal effectiveness, due largely to the ideologically heterogeneous world in which the UN is compelled to operate.[18] The concepts of major-power concert and collective security fell early victims to incompatible ideological differences among the major

17. A. L. Rowse, *Appeasement* (New York: W. W. Norton, 1961).
18. See Chapter 14 of the present text.

powers. It became apparent that as long as its members could not agree among themselves, the Security Council could not control conflicts; and collective security arrangements have only resulted in arranging one-half the world against the other since no state will cross the ideological lines to join in collective security actions against a state in its own fraternity. Furthermore, the intended dialogue of the General Assembly more frequently has taken the form of provocative diatribe, with the intended pressure from "world opinion" resulting in resentment on the part of the castigated but proud.

In spite of all these difficulties, preventive diplomacy has in fact prevented some armed conflicts and halted others. UN forces have been used in Palestine, the Congo, Cyprus, and elsewhere; and these areas have been isolated from the Cold War. But the dilemma of preventive diplomacy is that the injection of UN forces does little more than separate feuding parties. It does not settle underlying disputes. Consequently, when UN forces enter an area, they cannot be withdrawn without risking renewed fighting between the separated parties. The UN forces either stay indefinitely, or else withdraw in the face of budgetary or political pressure only to see their efforts dashed in new wars.

Finally, in the area of third-party arbitration and conciliation, juridical settlement under the World Court has been no more successful under the United Nations system than it was under the League, and for the same reasons. However, quiet diplomacy by the United Nations Secretary General and his staff has contributed to settling a number of smaller international political disputes since 1946, and there is reason to believe that United Nations Secretary General U Thant played an important role in easing the Cuban Missile Crisis away from the nuclear threshold in 1962. While there is promise in the continuing mediatory efforts of the Secretary General, there is also a real danger that his office and role could be undermined by any step that would identify him with one or another of the ideological camps. This danger stems from the necessity to hold appeal and approval from ideologically incompatible constituencies. To act at all, the Secretary General must appear impartial so that in a world of intense ideological antagonism, impartial action can come to mean no action at all.

What is left in the inventory of peacekeeping mechanisms after all international legal and institutional schemes prove ineffective, either because they cannot be adapted to competitive state politics or because competitive state politics cannot be adapted to them? What is left, certainly, are unilaterally engineered balances of power and systems of mutual military deterrence, the former accounting for the tenuous peace in Europe through the last half of the nineteenth century, and the latter largely explaining the absence of major-power wars in our era.[19] The peace of balanced power and nuclear deterrence is a peace built on mutual fear, but it seems to be the dominant mode of peace in the history of international politics. We might perhaps feel gratified that presently we have a tenuous peace at all, even if this state of affairs is based on fears of mutual annihilation. But, if we take history as our guide, we have little reason to be optimistic. Past periods of peace built from balanced power or mutual deterrence have proven short-lived. They have always broken down largely because their continuity depended upon the caution, wisdom, and rationality of statesmen and—as all men—statesmen are fallible.

Periods of peace built on balance and deterrence are typically preserved and prolonged by universal commitments to the existing status quo, by acceptance of tacit norms of international behavior, and by mutual recognitions of major-power "spheres of influence." During these periods international competition can proceed with gusto, but always within tacitly accepted limits. Peace is typically broken by the entrance of a new and revolutionary power unwilling to accept the existing status quo, untutored in the prevailing tacit norms of international behavior, and unaware of the acceptable outward limits of competition. Hence, to be optimistic about the perpetuation of a peace system such as ours built on mutual deterrence, relative major-power commitment to the status quo, and tacit limitations on competition, is to predict a future unmarred by the rise of a new revolutionary power. Such a prediction is questionable in light of the line of aspirants for superpower status now assembling.

In sum, the crux of the problem of peace in the international system is that world peace has to be something more than a goal, no matter how universally and how sincerely this goal is pursued. Peace must be a system—a set of universally accepted practices and institutions for conflict control. Such a plan must be designed, adapted, and

19. Richard Rosecrance, *Action and Reaction in World Politics* (Boston: Little, Brown and Company, 1963), pp. 220–278.

adopted; or peace will continue to rest on the fickleness of statesmen's competence and intentions, and on balanced power and mutual fear. The tragedy of international politics is that no universally acceptable system of conflict control has yet been effective.

PEACE IN INTERNATIONAL SECURITY COMMUNITIES

Though this chapter has been by and large an inventory of blind alleys, some more positive notes can be offered in conclusion. If one looks over the map of the world, one can discern certain clusters of neighboring countries that have not warred or even seriously feuded for generations. One even finds neighboring countries, such as the United States and Canada, that have maintained peaceful relations for more than a century. Such countries typically make no preparations for possible wars between them, and their governments and military planners conceive of no contingencies that would suggest military preparations. Furthermore, when one interviews people in such neighboring countries, one finds that the very idea of violent conflict tends to be alien to their thinking. Confidence in the pacific settlement of disputes seems endemic, and expectations of productive interaction are widespread. Lasting peaceful relations among states and peoples are certainly atypical in international politics. But they are worth serious study. Consequently, the origins and the sources of continuity of pacific relations among certain intensely interacting states and peoples such as Americans and Canadians; Americans and Britons; and Swedes, Danes, and Norwegians have recently become focuses of attention for social scientists seeking insights into international peace.[20]

To date, the most impressive research into preconditions for peaceful relations among states has taken the form of inquiries into the nature and origins of international security communities. The concept "security community" was initially proposed by Richard Van Wagenen and later developed and empirically explored by Karl W. Deutsch and his associates in their basic work, *Political Community and the North Atlantic Area*.[21] As alluded to above, a security community is an ag-

20. Karl W. Deutsch, "Security Communities," in *International Politics and Foreign Policy*, James N. Rosenau, ed., 1st ed. (Cambridge: Harvard University Press, 1960), pp. 98–105.

21. Richard N. Van Wagenen, *Research in the International Organization Field: Some Notes on a Possible Focus* (Princeton: Center for Research on World Political

gregation of interacting states and peoples among whom preparations for war have ceased and stable expectations of peace prevail. While most security communities take the form of constituent units amalgamated under central governments which monitor and regulate their interrelationships, several do exist in pluralistic form, in which separate sovereignty and continuing pacific interaction have proven wholly compatible. Understanding the pluralistic security community is really most relevant to the problem of international peace at hand.

Though no complete or wholly satisfactory explanation is yet available to account for security community relationships among some countries and the absence of such relationships among others, several important findings have been made. First, the stability of the security community is directly related both to high levels of and increasing rates of *assimilation* among its separate peoples. The community is, or over time comes to be, characterized by similar life styles, cultural norms, political and economic institutions, and value hierarchies. Most notable and significant among the impacts of international assimilation are, first, the emergence of mutual identifications or "we feelings"; and, second, increased capabilities for mutual empathy among individuals and groups within the international community. Why and how international assimilation takes place and how it might be promoted are not yet clearly understood. It is clear, however, that international transaction and communication, learning, and emulation all play a part.

Second, and pivotally important, security communities tend to be characterized by continuing high levels of mutual responsiveness among governments. In Deutsch's words, governments of component states within security communities,

... have acquired the political habits, practices, and institutions necessary to perceive one another's sensitive spots and ... "vital interests" and to make prompt and adequate responses to each other's critical needs.[22]

There is within security communities a prevailing air of mutual predictability among statesmen, a predictability which lends each the confidence that his counterparts are aware of, interested in, and willing

Institutions, 1952); Karl W. Deutsch, *et al., Political Community and the North Atlantic Area* (Princeton: Princeton University Press, 1957).

22. Karl W. Deutsch, *Political Community at the International Level* (Garden City: Doubleday, 1954), p. 37.

to support his critical preferences and vital needs. Mutual responsiveness sometimes takes the form of anticipating partners' needs and preferences, and acting to accommodate these before they are even articulated. Again, the bases of mutual responsiveness are not clearly understood as yet. But it is assumed that they are related to levels of assimilation among peoples, and to the familiarity which such assimilation fosters. Moreover, it is also likely that high levels of assimilation and mutual identification sustain security communities during lapses in intergovernmental responsiveness.

Third, security communities tend to be characterized by relatively high levels of political, economic, and military interdependence among component states and peoples. The foreign policies of the separate community member-states often depend upon the backing and material support of partner states; economic interactions tend to be complementary and relatively high in volume; community members tend further to be formally or informally pledged to mutual defense, or alternatively, weaker community members look to stronger ones for protection.

Finally, the continuing stability of a security community appears to depend heavily upon component governments' and peoples' abilities to adjust to the increasing volumes and rates of international interaction that follow from community formation. Assimilation, responsiveness, and interdependence all demand heightened levels of international attentiveness, and broadened physical and intellectual facilities for keeping abreast of, and dealing with, community concerns. Community formation and participation can therefore strain national capabilities for international attention, perception, and response. Stability in the security community depends upon minimizing such strains by expanding capabilities. If formal and informal channels of intracommunity communications fail to expand to keep pace with increasing loads, if adequate personnel are not assigned to rapidly and effectively handle community problems, and if provincial self-interestedness impedes community empathy, international frictions quickly develop and security communities ultimately dissolve.[23]

Though research into security communities remains inconclusive, the early results of such study as that discussed above suggest that the

---

23. Bruce M. Russett, *Community and Contention: Britain and America in the Twentieth Century* (Cambridge: The M.I.T. Press, 1963), pp. 26–33.

traditional difficulties involved in the pursuit of peace are neither imponderable nor inevitable. If international assimilation, responsiveness, interdependence, and successful adjustment to communications loads have been among conditions that account for generations of peaceful interaction among some states, it is possible that these conditions, if fostered and nurtured, might contribute to reduced friction in interactions among larger groups of states, or perhaps among all states. Peace research founded on the security community design could well move in two directions—toward isolating additional preconditions for security community and better explaining those preconditions already identified, as well as toward mapping policies that would build security communities.

PART THREE
CAPABILITIES FOR ACTION
IN INTERNATIONAL POLITICS

CHAPTER EIGHT
POWER AS THE CAPACITY TO ACT

UP to this point, this book's discussion has been primarily concerned with the question, *who* wants *what* and *why* in international politics. However, answering this question, as has been done in Chapters 2–7, only begins to account for international political behavior because most of the answers offered have left an important assumption unexplained. In short, when motivations and goals were discussed, the question of *capabilities* was not raised. Throughout the discussion of actors and goals it was implicitly assumed that an actor motivated toward the pursuit of a certain goal was in fact *able* to pursue the desired end.

The chapters in Part III are offered to display and weld the link between aims and actions in international politics. This link has to do with states' capabilities for action—termed *power* in the aggregate—with the sources of these capabilities, and with relationships between capabilities and goals. The *power* of states determines their abilities to pursue goals, and endowments of power help to determine the variety and ambitiousness of the goals that states pursue.

Chapter 8 keynotes Part III by introducing and examining the threefold proposition that the relationship between international political goals and action in their pursuit tends to be contingent upon: (1) the *price* or *cost* of the object sought or goal pursued, (2) actors' abilities to pay this price or cost, and (3) actors' willingness to pay. Elaboration on the concepts of cost and payment carries discussion in Chapter 8 directly into the concept of international political power. Discussing power abstractly raises a number of practical questions about the bases of actual world power distributions; reflecting on such distributions raises further questions about restraints and limitations on states' power, and especially about the present-day paradox in the gap between material power and political influence. All of these questions and themes are approached and elaborated also in Chapter 8.

Chapters 9 and 10 deal with special, and somewhat unconventional, considerations relating to states' capabilities to act in international politics. Chapter 9, for example, focuses upon the origins and dynamics of nationalism. As will be explained further, nationalism is treated in the section concerned with capabilities for international action because of strong and intriguing relationships between nationalistic emotions and national power. Chapter 10 takes up the problem of communications and information in international politics. Again, this topic is treated in the section on capabilities because the power of states is related to their abilities to accurately receive and effectively process information about the external world. The chapters in Part III by no means represent an exhaustive survey of the basic factors of state power. They are intended rather to introduce and underline the essential link between states' capabilities and their international behavior.

ACTION AND RESOURCE DEMANDS

As noted above, whether an international actor will actually act to pursue his goals in the international arena depends fundamentally upon three factors—the price of the object sought, his ability to pay, and his willingness to pay. Every international objective carries a price tag marked "cost in terms of national resources." In a very rough sense, one could say that in international politics governments spend national resources in attempts to buy foreign policy objectives. "Resources" are very broadly defined in this context and may range, as will be elaborated later, from taxpayer's renditions, to states' endowments of natural wealth, to allies' support, to statesmen's time and physical and intellectual energies, or even to citizens' lives. The essential point, and one that must be grasped, is that any action, no matter how grandiose or insignificant, *requires* the allocation and expenditure of resources. Fighting a war, for example, requires and drains huge quantities of all varieties of resources. But even checking an alien's passport requires the time and energy of a government officer and a certain small allotment of taxpayers' money. *All action requires the expenditure of resources.*

The Ability to Pay and the Politics of Resource Allocation. How many resources a government is able to spend in the pursuit of a particular foreign policy objective depends, first, upon the total resources under government control; and, second, upon the government's ability to allocate its resources to the pursuit of the particular objective. As common sense tells us, governments controlling larger resource bases typically and traditionally either pursue their foreign policy aims more successfully, or else pursue more numerous and grandiose aims than governments that operate from smaller resource bases. One must have resources before one can invest them in action. However, in addition to simply having resources, a government must also be able to allocate them to the pursuit of particular objectives. Since governments pursue multiple goals, and since different groups and individuals influential in government decision-making attach different preferences and priorities to different goals, resource allocation typically becomes a focus of internal political competition. The ability to allocate resources to a particular desired policy pursuit, therefore, becomes a function of successful political persuasion, consensus formation, or, sometimes, coercion.

A contemporary example lends some insight into the politics of resource allocation. During the years 1966 to 1968 the United States government faced particularly difficult problems in resource allocation. Strains on the resource allocation process came from at least four sides: (1) prosecuting the war in Vietnam demanded huge investments of government resources, (2) maintaining other American overseas commitments to foreign aid, NATO support, UN support, and the like demanded similarly large outlays of resources, (3) maintaining strategic security and nuclear superiority required continuing massive expenditure on defense and weapons research and development, and (4) acute social and economic problems on the domestic scene also demanded large resource allocations. The government, therefore, was faced with a number of dilemmas in resource allocation, all exacerbated by the fact that powerful political groups and forces, within the government and without, were aligned in support of different courses in resource allocation. Moreover, the electorate at large tended to resist increasing expenditure in any of the problem areas when such increases implied higher taxes. Hence, if the government chose to increase the allocation of resources to the war effort in Vietnam, other foreign policy objectives may have suffered. Similarly, if the government chose both to increase outlays to Vietnam and to maintain other overseas commitments, then strategic defense programs may have suffered. And if the government chose to increase outlays in Vietnam, maintain other overseas commitments, and preserve maximum strategic capabilities, then domestic programs would have suffered. Finally, if the government chose to continue or increase outlays in all crucial foreign and domestic program areas, then the American taxpayer would have suffered.

In actual practice the allocation problems were a good deal more complex than outlined here, and the solutions were a series of compromises, rather than a set of choices among dichotomous alternatives. Nevertheless, the oversimplified example underlines the central point: the ability to pursue a particular objective depends upon the ability to allocate resources to its pursuit, and this latter ability amounts to the ability to overcome or placate political opposition that demands alternative allocations. In general, and in most simple form, competition for resources is always three-cornered. Foreign policy objectives compete with domestic policy objectives; and government objectives generally compete with taxpayers' personal objectives.

Willingness to Pay and the Question of Costs and Priorities. It is sometimes, or, indeed, we might say often, the case that a government controls and is able to allocate resources requisite to the pursuit of a particular goal, but yet refrains from initiating action. Several instances from American foreign policy come immediately to mind. For example, during the later 1940's and early 1950's, the United States could have executed a policy aimed at freeing Eastern Europe from Communist control. Similarly, the United States could have intervened to aid Hungarian insurrectionists during the uprising of 1956, and, again, could have acted to tear down the Berlin Wall in 1961. Restraint in these cases was not due to limited resources, or to any inability to allocate adequate resources because of internal political pressures. In all three instances the United States possessed more than adequate military capabilities to pursue the objective to successful fruition. Military experts point out that even had the Berlin situation in 1961 resulted in a Soviet-American nuclear exchange, the United States would have come out considerably less damaged than the Soviet Union. Moreover, in all three cases, an American political consensus supporting the goal could have been readily mustered. Therefore, restraint in these instances and other similar ones rested not in'the problem of resource limitations, but on the question of *willingness* to pay the expected costs. In no instance was the United States government willing to invest the requisite resources in the pursuit of the goal. Lack of willingness stemmed from the enormity of the expected costs and the relatively low priority of the goals involved. Freeing Eastern Europe, taking advantage of disorders in Communist countries, and removing the Berlin Wall certainly were, and still are, goals of American foreign policy, but they have low priority in comparison to the goals of avoiding nuclear war, preserving Western Europe, containing Communist expansionism in Asia, and other goals in which the United States has clearly been willing to pay out enormous costs in resources. Generalizing, we can conclude that the probability that a government will pursue a particular objective with a particular expected cost in resources, is a function of the government's control over adequate resources, its ability to allocate resources to the objective, and its willingness to pay the expected costs.

POWER AS THE CAPACITY TO ACT

The concept of power as used in the analysis of international politics has given rise to endless, and in this author's estimation, often meaningless, definitional debate. In some writers' definitions, the term is equated with "influence" and is defined as "the ability to affect the behavior of others." Alternatively, it has been defined as "the ability not to be influenced by others." For some, power is an absolute concept or the sum total of "power factors" possessed. For others, power is a relative concept seen in terms of differential shares of total "power factors" available in the international system. For a good many writers, power becomes an almost metaphysical concept, a largely intangible quality characteristic of some international actors and denied to others. In addition, some see the acquisition of power as the end of international behavior, others see it as one end among many, and still others view it as a means to other ends. Some authors have determined to quantitatively measure power. Others lament that it cannot be measured. Some insist that it should not be measured.

Defining the term "power" could be left an inconclusive semantic game if it were not for the fact that understanding the concept behind it is central to the study and understanding of international politics. Despite the continuing debate about its meaning and measurability, though, power is not really a very difficult concept to grasp. If one understands and accepts the relationships between resources and actions discussed in the preceding section, one can see that the definition of power can follow directly. Having power means having the wherewithal or *capacity* to act. Since the capacity to act stems from possessing, controlling, and directing resources requisite for action, power becomes synonymous with resource control. Resources are the means to action; power, too, is the means to action. In an excellent analysis in *A Theory of Foreign Policy,* George Modelski expresses the definition of "power" in several different ways as, broadly, "the capacity to act." At one point in Modelski's analysis we find "power" defined as "the state's present means, as its ability to act on the international scene." Somewhat later Modelski points out that "all actions have means, or power, as one of their minimum elements," and later still, he notes that "basically, all power consists of capacity for organized action in the service of foreign policy." [1] Hence, having power is tantamount to having control over the requisite means or resources for action. Specifically with reference to international politics, having power means having control over requisite means for international action. *Power then is the capacity to act in international politics.*

Gross National Power and Externally Projectable Power. Despite the relative simplicity of this explanation of the concept of power, a number of refinements and distinctions must be made before the concept becomes useful for international political analysis. First, two varieties of power should be distinguished. *Gross National Power* is the absolute total of resources available in a given state or society— i.e., simply put, the sum total of men, money, and materials available in the political unit. *Externally Projectable Power,* on the other hand, is the total of resources available to the government for the pursuit of foreign policy objectives. The significance of this distinction is manifold. [2]

1. Gross National Power and Externally Projectable Power are

1. George Modelski, *A Theory of Foreign Policy* (New York: Praeger, 1962), p. 59.
2. *Ibid.,* pp. 21–23. The terms "Gross National Power" and "Externally Projectable Power" are roughly synonymous with Modelski's "national power" and "governmental power."

seldom equivalent. Only near the end of a prolonged, intense, and ultimate struggle for survival does a state mobilize and channel its total
resources into foreign policy (i.e., the war effort). This was the case,
for example, in the Soviet Union in 1940 and 1941, when almost all
human and material resources remaining after the Nazi invasion and
plunder were mobilized in the war effort. It was the case too in Germany and Japan in 1945.

Normally, however, resources allocated to foreign policy objectives
represent only a very small fraction of a state's Gross National Power,
since the bulk of resources generally go either into domestic government programs or into the individual pursuits of citizens. For example,
in the year 1964 the American Gross National Product (GNP) was
approximately 500 billion dollars. The federal government budget
for that year was roughly 98 billion dollars, and 55 billions from this
budget were allocated to the pursuit of foreign policy including defense. Therefore approximately 10.5 percent of the American GNP,
or total wealth, generated in 1964 was converted to Externally Projectable Power. Looking at human resources, again in 1964 there were
approximately 250,000 people employed in the foreign affairs agencies
of the United States government, and about 2.5 million personnel in
the armed forces, to make about two and three-quarters million people
working in the pursuit of American foreign policy. This was about 1.5
percent of the nation's population. If one adds people employed in full-
time defense industries, the proportion of total human resources allocated to foreign policy pursuits rises to perhaps 5 or 6 percent, but even
this percentage is relatively low. The point here is that in 1964 the
vast proportions of American economic and human resources were
allocated to domestic and individual pursuits. Externally Projectable
Power, measured in terms of resources allocated to the service of
foreign policy, was only a small fraction of Gross National Power.
Moreover, it must be noted that by comparison with other countries,
the United States devotes phenomenally large quantities of resources
to foreign policy pursuits. Though no figures are available it is safe
to estimate that the world average for total national resources allocated
to foreign policy is less than one percent.

Small resource allocations to foreign policy are in some countries a
matter of choice, and in others a matter of necessity. Governments
and peoples in many countries—such as Sweden, Switzerland, Canada,

Mexico, and contemporary Japan—deliberately opt for a passive role in international politics, and consequently channel few resources toward creating Externally Projectable Power. Such countries are for the most part content with what they deem adequate defense establishments, diplomatic establishments, and essential commitments—none of which normally demand very large resource allocations. Hence, their capacities to act are kept limited because their desires to act in international politics are similarly limited. On the other hand, some countries and leaders that may have aspirations for greater action in international politics are restrained by inabilities to muster resources requisite for Externally Projectable Power. In countries such as Egypt, Indonesia under Sukarno, Ghana under Nkrumah, and even Communist China, domestic pressures stemming from economic development programs and overpopulation drain resources to the extent that few are left for allocation to more active foreign policies. Leaders in such countries may want to enter more actively into international politics, but their capacity to act is undermined by limitations on Externally Projectable Power. Regimes that place foreign policy objectives above domestic social and economic well-being and allocate scarce resources accordingly, moreover, are typically short-lived.

2. Relatedly, the distinction between Gross National Power and Externally Projectable Power underlines the fact that one cannot always directly associate a state's "bigness" with its capacity to act in international politics. Textbook writers concerned with ranking states according to power sometimes fall into the error of listing states in descending order according to territorial size, population size, size of Gross National Product, and related characteristics. Their assumption is, of course, that "bigness" implies "power" or "capacity to act." This is only qualifiedly true, as will be explained under point 4 below, and is true only in a long-run sense. While territorial expansiveness, large populations, and high gross national incomes are indices of Gross National Power (or long-run power potential, or ultimate viability in life or death struggles), they are not always indicative of immediately available Externally Projectable Power. As noted, what counts most in a state's capacity to act in international politics is the immediate availability of resources for the service of foreign policy. In this sense, small, industrialized states, with skilled and highly educated populations, relatively high levels of domestic social and economic satis-

faction, and efficient systems of revenue collection may well possess greater capacities to act in international politics than large, economically underdeveloped states with semiliterate populations and diffuse or confused administrative systems. British control over a sprawling empire during the nineteenth century is testimony to a small state's capacities for international political action. Similarly, comparison of the foreign policies of Japan and China during the first half of the twentieth century places the differences between sheer size and power into sharp perspective. Size may indicate potential in the form of Gross National Power, but it does not always indicate capacity to act in the form of Externally Projectable Power.

Figure 8.1 provides some interesting examples of the incongruence between "bigness" and capacity to act in international politics. In observing and reflecting on the map shown in Figure 8.1 we are asked to imagine what the world would look like if the sizes of countries were proportional to their populations. What is worthy of note on this distorted map is not the coincidences of large populations with political-military power centers, but the numerous deviations. That is, if capacity to act in international politics were independently measured in terms of the size and equipment of military forces, the size of budgets for foreign affairs agencies, the numbers of personnel serving abroad, or simply the range of states' international involvements, we would likely find some positive relationships with large population, as in the cases of the United States and the Soviet Union; but the overall correlation between capacity to act and large population would be low. If Figure 8.1 were adjusted to reflect capacity to act in international politics, India, Pakistan, Indonesia, Sub-Saharan Africa, and even Communist China would have to be drawn much smaller than shown; and on the other hand, several Western European countries, and a number of tiny countries in terms of population such as Taiwan, Israel, and South Korea, would have to be drawn considerably larger than shown. The reason for the deviations between large population and capacity to act in international politics is in the difference between Gross National Power, of which population or total human resources is a measure, and Externally Projectable Power, in which population counts only to the extent that human resources are mobilized in the service of foreign policy.

Similar graphic analyses of relations and deviations between Gross

FIGURE 8.1. THE WORLD WITH TERRITORY DRAWN EQUIVALENT TO POPULATION

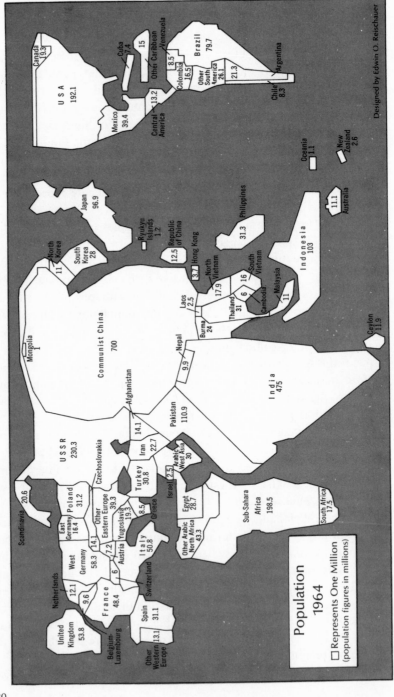

Designed by Edwin O. Reischauer

Population
1964

☐ Represents One Million
(population figures in millions)

National Power and Externally Projectable Power could be carried out using maps distorted according to the sizes of states' Gross National Products (GNP) and their reserves of natural wealth, or even using an undistorted map of countries according to territorial size. *In the short run, then, power differentials among states in the international system stem much more from differential abilities to allocate resources to foreign policy pursuits than from differential endowments in basic resources.*

3. The transformation of Gross National Power into Externally Projectable Power is often indicative of preparations for more active participation in international politics. Such transformations, of course, are intended to enhance states' capacities to act in the international arena. Traditional military mobilizations on the eve of wars or in anticipation of attack were, in effect, transformations of Gross National Power into Externally Projectable Power. Human and economic resources were drawn away from domestic and individual pursuits and pressed into the service of foreign policy. Though the introduction of nuclear weaponry has made traditional prewar mobilization obsolete, one still finds various kinds of resource mobilizations indicative of preparations for more active international involvement. For example, aspiration toward membership in the "nuclear club" generally coincides with desires for more active involvement in international politics, and this requires a huge channeling of human and economic resources into nuclear development programs. More subtly, government-sponsored or -supported language and foreign area training programs often precede, and are indicative of, government interest and anticipated expanded involvement in certain areas of the world. For example, one can trace the beginnings of American, Soviet, and Chinese expanded involvement in underdeveloped countries to mobilizations of human resources in government-supported area studies programs. The point here is that action requires resources, and expanded actions require expanded resources. Expanding resources for international action requires converting Gross National Power into Externally Projectable Power. The ability to accurately monitor and interpret such conversions, incidentally, is a cornerstone of the intelligence officer's profession.

4. Gross National Power combined with capabilities for conversion to Externally Projectable Power is the measure of a state's future

power potential or its capacity to act in the future. When one asks about a state's capacities to act over the long run, one must inquire first into the nature of the state's Gross National Power, and then into the state's long-run capabilities for converting increasing increments of its Gross National Power into Externally Projectable Power.

The first conclusion to come clearly from such an inquiry is that certain states will probably never greatly enhance their capacities to act in international politics since the sum total of their resources is meager. It is true that on occasion some small states poorly endowed with human and material resources have climbed to world ascendance by gradually absorbing neighboring small states and thereby enlarging their resource bases. The tiny ancient city-state of Rome is perhaps the most outstanding example here. But by and large, small, poorly endowed states remain perpetually limited in their capacities to act in international politics.

But what of large, weak states that nevertheless contain sizable reserves in human and material resources? Are such states destined for greatness over the long run? The contemporary observer is tempted to answer "yes" almost automatically. However, a moment's reflection might reveal that the basis for this answer is founded in worries about Communist China, hopes for India or Brazil, or visions of a United Europe, rather than in any reasoned assessment of forces and processes that convert power potential into actually enhanced capacities to act in international politics. Answering the question about destinies in greatness positively, means not only pointing to Gross National Power reserves but also explaining whether, why, how, and how fast, these resources can be converted to Externally Projectable Power. It would be pretentious here to offer any formula for greatness since the process involved in the long-run conversion of Gross National Power into Externally Projectable Power is highly complex and only minimally understood. Nevertheless, certain elements in this process are apparent.

First, "conversion" here must be taken to mean "liberation," in the sense that converting Gross National Power to Externally Projectable Power means freeing resources for external uses, or, in other words, increasing resources available to governments for foreign policy pursuits. This implies among other things that domestic resource needs must be accommodated, and that resource surpluses must exist after domestic accommodation. In the typical large underdeveloped country—the candidate for possible greatness under discussion—domestic resource needs are barely accommodated at minimal living standards, and very little surplus in resources exists to enhance foreign policy capabilities.

Surpluses can be achieved, however, by making more efficient use of basic human and material resources through industrialization and general economic development. The industrialization of large, populous states has been, and remains, the pathway to great power status in the modern era. Rapid industrialization after 1865 forecasted the American debut as a world power; rigorous industrialization under Stalin transformed a weak and backward Russia into the powerful Soviet Union; Japan rose to ascendance in Asia as a result of industrialization launched after the Meiji Restoration; and industrialization lifted Germany to major power status during the last decades of the nineteenth century.

In power analyses, industrialization is customarily linked to enhanced capacity to act in international politics by virtue of the relationship between industry, technology, and war-making capabilities. This is true, certainly, but to argue simply that industrialization builds factories, factories produce arms, and large, sophisticated arsenals enhance capacities to act in international politics, is really to miss the pivotal relationship between industrialization and Externally Projectable Power. The result of increased efficiency in the use of resources that follows from industrialization and general economic development is to raise the population of the state above bare subsistence standards, and, in so doing, to provide an assessment base for increased government revenues. While these revenues can be used to buy arms, they can also be used to pay soldiers and to train them; to finance, support, and expand diplomatic activities; to entice allies with loans and grants; and to provide for simultaneous involvement in multiple overseas ventures. The most important link, then, between industrialization and enhanced capacity to act in international politics is the link between higher living standards resulting from industrialization and increased government revenue.

While industrialization and economic development are certainly the keys to converting Gross National Power to Externally Projectable Power, one must recognize the naiveté in saying that all a country has to do to enhance its capacity to act in international politics is to industrialize. Industrialization and general economic development are certainly no mean accomplishments. They do not happen overnight; they do not happen painlessly; and sometimes, they do not even happen at all. Since economic development is a central focus in Chapter 13, there is no need to go into detail here. Suffice it to say, however, that industrialization and economic development imply basic social and economic revolutions in developing countries. They can foment political drives for institutional reform. Sometimes they result in coups, rebellions, and revolutions; and they often drain scarce government resources into maintaining domestic order. They require huge initial inputs of capital which are seldom available domestically; they require wide-ranging improvements in human resources through education and training; and they can be completely thwarted and their benefits wiped out by uncontrolled population explosion.

Therefore, in replying to the initial question, "what of the large weak states that nevertheless contain sizable reserves in human and material resources?" the cautious analyst can only offer another set of questions. What is the potential for economic development in these states? Is it likely that industrialization efforts will succeed? Can resources come to be used so efficiently that surpluses will result to be channeled into external pursuits? Will population pressures be quelled, or will exploding population perpetuate the cycle of domestic subsistence and international impotence? Present Gross National Power alone is not a sufficient basis for estimating Externally Projectable Power in the future. The probability of converting Gross National Power to Externally Projectable Power through the vehicle of economic development must also be estimated. With these stipulations in mind, one might want to take a closer look at Communist China, India, Brazil, and Western Europe.

GOAL–RESOURCE BALANCES AND INTERNATIONAL ACTION

The discussion of capacity to act in international politics has thus far underlined the point that pursuing international political objectives requires the mustering of requisite resources. It has been implied, in short, that goals determine resources requirements. There is, however, another important dimension to the relationship between goals and resources. This is that *resource availability may influence or even determine a state's choice of international political goals.* Not only are government demands for resources adjusted to match goals, but goals too are often adjusted to match resources available to governments. The full nature of the relationship between goals and resources shows clearly in the simulated goal-resource system shown in Figure 8.2.

In the diagram, the decision-sequence 1,2,4,7,8 summarizes much of the discussion in this chapter so far: Goals are set (1); their pri-

FIGURE 8.2. SIMULATED GOAL–RESOURCE BALANCING

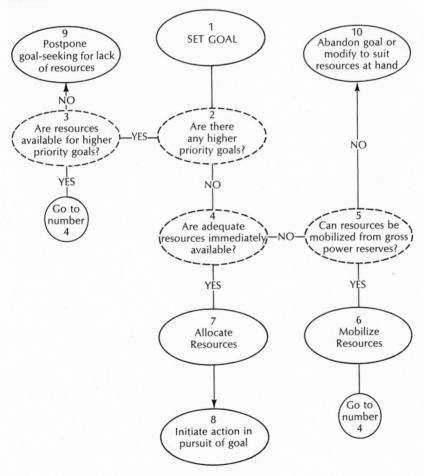

orities are determined (2); resource availabilities are investigated (4); resources are allocated (7); and action is initiated (8). Relatedly, de-cision-sequence 1,2,3,4,7,8 adds a check on priorities, and sequence 1,2,4,5,6,4,7,8 adds a successful search for new resources in the state's Gross Power reserves. In each of these sequences, goals remain con-stant and resources are mustered to initiate action in their pursuit. It must be emphasized, however, that to move through each of these se-quences is to assume that resources required for action are either available or mobilizable. When this is not the case, the availability of resources begins to affect the articulation of goals, and the direction of the relationship between objectives and resources reverses. For ex-ample, in sequence 1,2,4,5,10, a lack of immediately available re-sources (4,NO) and a subsequent inability to mobilize additional resources from Gross Power reserves (5,NO) results either in the modification of the goal in the direction of decreasing ambitiousness, or in a complete abandonment of the goal. Similarly, the sequence 1,2,3,9 suggests that as long as higher priority goals drain resources, those with lower priority remain wishes rather than active pursuits.

Goal-resource balancing is an integral part of the foreign policy process, and numerous empirical examples show that statesmen re-peatedly ask and answer sequences of questions similar to those built into the model in Figure 8.2. After World War II, for example, states-men in Great Britain, the Netherlands, and France found that they could no longer muster the resources necessary to preserve and pro-tect their far-flung colonial empires. Nationalist agitation in the colonies greatly raised the costs of preserving internal order—enor-mously, in cases where agitation exploded into armed rebellion—at the same time that the costs of reconstruction after World War II were draining resources into domestic channels. Moreover, the revolution in weaponry after World War II rendered remaining European military forces obsolete and inadequate to protect even the metropolitan coun-tries, let alone the colonies. Resources to build imperial defense in the Atomic Age were simply not available to the old colonial powers. The result of these new pressures on scarce resources was a gradual, and sometimes painful, adjustment of imperial objectives. The British acceded to colonial demands for independence, modified the concept of empire to the concept of commonwealth of nations, and incremen-tally abandoned most of their global defense commitments. Similarly, the French, after two highly costly colonial wars in Indochina and Algeria, followed suit and modified the concept of empire to the concept of community of nations. The Dutch and later the Belgians simply dissolved the greatest part of their overseas empires.

At present, there is some concern in Washington, and especially in the Senate Foreign Relations Committee, about overextended American involvement in foreign policy pursuits. The concern comes in the wake of the resource drain caused by the war in Vietnam and what some have described as the "bottomless pit" of military and economic foreign aid. Certain critics of American foreign policy who point to the immense costs of the war in Vietnam, and to broad-ranging American commitments that might obligate the American government to further "Vietnams" or several simultaneous "Vietnams" are rhetorically asking whether American resources are really adequate for this "free world policeman's" role. As J. William Fulbright notes in *The Arrogance of Power,*

Despite its dangerous and unproductive consequences, the idea of being responsible for the whole world seems to be flattering to Americans and I am afraid it is turning our heads, just as the sense of universal responsibility turned the heads of ancient Romans and nineteenth-century British. . . .

An excessive preoccupation with foreign relations over a long period of time is more than a manifestation of arrogance; it is a drain on the power that gave rise to it, because it diverts a nation from sources of its strength, which are in its domestic life. . . . I would doubt that any nation has achieved a durable greatness by conducting a "strong" foreign policy, but many have been ruined by expending their energies in foreign adventures while allowing their domestic bases to deteriorate. The United States emerged as a world power in the twentieth century, not because of what it has done in foreign relations but because it had spent the nineteenth century developing the North American continent; by contrast, the Austrian and Turkish empires collapsed in the twentieth century in large part because they had so long neglected their internal development and organization.[3]

With concerns about resource availabilities, and a perceived imbalance between resources and objectives in mind, Senator Fulbright and many others have suggested a general reassessment of American objectives and a realignment of goals and resources.

Few states have managed to operate beyond their foreign policy

3. J. William Fulbright, *The Arrogance of Power* (New York: Vintage Books, 1966), pp. 19 and 20.

means for very long, and several that have attempted this have brought disaster upon themselves. Overextension cost Napoleon an empire in 1815. France's collapse before Hitler in 1940 showed that the French had steered through the 1920's and 1930's largely on their reputation of past power rather than from a base of actual power. Ambitious Gaullist-like foreign policies today ring somewhat hollow to one who stops to assess the actual state of French resources. Moreover, lack of adequate resources for protracted conflict sealed the fate of the German Empire in the First World War, and the fates of Germany, Japan, and Italy in World War II. Similarly, inability to efficiently mobilize resources has contributed to Arab defeats at Israeli hands on three occasions since 1949, and mutual inability to mobilize resources for decisive action has perpetuated the Indian-Pakistan stalemate over Kashmir for the past twenty years. In these cases, now part of history, ambitious goals, obstinately pursued, demanded more resources than could be mustered; and disasters and disappointments were the results. The analogous contemporary cases may well end similarly.

POWER RESOURCES: AN INVENTORY

The meaning of "resources" has been left rather indefinite throughout this chapter largely because there is no concise way to sum up all that the term connotes. Broadly speaking, a resource may be anything that facilitates action in the pursuit of an objective. As such, state power resources include the men, money, and materials mentioned earlier; but these resources may also include such factors as time and talent, traditions, attitudes and emotions, seacoasts, mountains, pleasant or hostile climates, fertile soils and fertile women. Furthermore, the inventory of state power resources is ever changing. Thirty years ago uranium ore was a waste by-product in mining industries; today it is among the most highly valued minerals and is a basis of international political power. Fifty years ago men knowledgeable in the Chinese language, or even the Russian language, were of minimal use in the American foreign policy establishment; today men with such talents are begged, borrowed, and stolen from universities and pressed into government service, and thousands more are trained yearly by the State Department and the Armed Forces. Finally, since resources are convertible from one form to another, resource inventories are often misleading. For example, iron ore is a power resource, but so are the iron and steel made from it, as well as the guns and ships, typewriters and computers made from them. Then too, as noted earlier, a flourishing, industrialized economy is a power resource, but so is the government revenue that such an economy makes possible.

No attempt will be made here at taking a comprehensive inventory of all factors that can be called power resources. Available works in political economy provide much more thorough discussions of power factors than could be offered in the limited space allotted here, and most standard textbooks provide bibliographical guides to these works. More in accord with the abstract nature of this chapter's discussion would be the development of a model that both categorizes varieties of resources and links resource input and output in the foreign policy process. Such a model was developed by George Modelski and presented in *A Theory of Foreign Policy*. Figure 8.3 shows this model, with some slight modifications, in diagrammatic form.[4]

Most of the entries in Figure 8.3 are self-explanatory, and the dynamics of resource utilization, as indicated by the arrows are also clear. Resources that contribute to a state's power may be grouped under three broad headings—Internal:Human; Internal:Nonhuman; and External.

1. Under *Internal:Human* resources we may include the services of all personnel in the employ of a state's government and working in the pursuit of foreign policy—civilians and soldiers working at home and abroad, and government contract holders and members of their organizations—and we may also include all of those individuals and organizations that can be pressed into the service of foreign policy if and when resource needs develop. Furthermore, and significantly, human resources include not only the physical and intellectual capacities of a state's populace, but also peoples' emotional identifications with the state, their allegiances to the government, and their willingness to work—and, if need be, to sacrifice—for the state. Nationalism is intangible and basically immeasurable; but, as Chapter 9 makes clear, its presence within a population enhances a state's capacities to act in international politics, and its absence sometimes saps state power. In addition, it must be recognized that human resources (and

4. George Modelski, *A Theory of Foreign Policy,* pp. 23–57.

FIGURE 8.3. POWER RESOURCES AND RESOURCE UTILIZATION

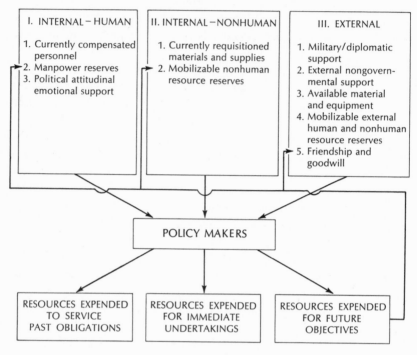

POWER INPUTS

I. INTERNAL – HUMAN	II. INTERNAL – NONHUMAN	III. EXTERNAL
1. Currently compensated personnel 2. Manpower reserves 3. Political attitudinal emotional support	1. Currently requisitioned materials and supplies 2. Mobilizable nonhuman resource reserves	1. Military/diplomatic support 2. External nongovernmental support 3. Available material and equipment 4. Mobilizable external human and nonhuman resource reserves 5. Friendship and goodwill

POLICY MAKERS

RESOURCES EXPENDED TO SERVICE PAST OBLIGATIONS	RESOURCES EXPENDED FOR IMMEDIATE UNDERTAKINGS	RESOURCES EXPENDED FOR FUTURE OBJECTIVES

POWER OUTPUTS

for that matter nonhuman resources too) have a qualitative as well as a quantitative dimension. As noted earlier, large, educated, productive, and politically loyal populations enhance states' power. But large, illiterate, relatively unproductive, and rebellious populations may undermine power. In the same sense a small number of perceptive, highly competent statesmen may carry a state safely and successfully over obstacles and through challenges that no sprawling bureaucracy could cope with.

2. Under *Internal:Nonhuman* resources we may include all natural and manufactured materials, structures, and items used in the service of foreign policy, as well as all such resources that may be mobilized for foreign policy purposes if and when needs arise. A list in this category would go on to infinity and might include everything from paper

clips to hydrogen bombs, and from advantageous terrestial geography to reconnaissance satellites orbiting in space. The availability of non-human resources for the service of foreign policy depends largely upon a government's abilities to purchase, borrow, or expropriate from private individuals or organizations; and these abilities depend respectively upon the government's revenue, credibility, or effectiveness at internal coercion. Then too, the availability of nonhuman resources used for foreign policy purposes follows to some extent from a state's geographic location, its topology, and sometimes even its climate. Seacoasts and natural harbors are prerequisites for powerful navies; mountainous frontiers facilitate defense; harsh climates may frustrate would-be invaders. The availability of nonhuman resource reserves depends upon such factors as natural resource endowments, industrial capacities, and levels of technological sophistication. But it must be emphasized again that such reserves can contribute to capacities to act in international politics only to the extent that they can be mobilized for foreign policy purposes. In this sense, therefore, the capacity of a society to bear the economic, social, and political strains of extensive mobilization must in itself be considered a power resource.

3. Under *External* resources we may include all the supplements to a state's human and nonhuman resources and reserves that may be acquired from other states. Herein, for example, lies the value of alliances and mutual commitments. Each state in an alliance receives the opportunity to supplement its own resources by drawing upon those of its partners. Under the mutual commitments of the South-East Asia Treaty Organization (SEATO), the tiny state of Thailand may under stipulated contingencies multiply its power resources several hundredfold by calling upon the American power base. Moreover, under NATO, where commitments are even more specific, small states such as the Netherlands, Belgium, and Denmark have their defense backed and guaranteed by American, British, French, and West German resources. In addition to resource sharing in alliance partnerships, external resources may also be mustered through successful applications for foreign economic and military aid channeled either to other states or through international organizations. Nor must it be forgotten that external resources may be, and often have been, acquired by conquest, by pillage, and by forced reparations. Japan's industrial capacities were significantly enhanced during the 1930's by the seizure of

Manchuria; French reconstruction after World War I proceeded to a substantial extent on reparations extracted from Germany; and Soviet reconstruction after World War II was greatly stimulated by wholesale removals of industrial plants, natural resources, and even technical personnel from Germany, Austria, Hungary, and other occupied former Axis countries. Finally, and interestingly, support from nongovernmental groups in other states may become an important asset in a given state's inventory of power resources. At one end, pressures from "friendship lobbies" may foster receptiveness and cooperation from other states at a minimum cost to one's own resources. More potently, subversive organizations or "fifth columns" in other countries have often been effectively used by states pursuing aggressive objectives vis-à-vis those other countries.

While a good deal is generally to be gained in searching out and exploiting external resources, there are certain pitfalls involved in overdependence upon other states. For one thing, to depend upon the continuing availability of external resources is to depend upon decision-making in systems over which relatively little control can be exercised. Alliances can be, and often have been, unilaterally abrogated; foreign aid can be cut off at the whim of a budget-minded parliament, or it can peter out in an impoverished international organization; and attempts at conquest can backfire to become others' demands for reparations. Moreover, depending and calling upon external resources generally implies some sort of reciprocity, so that credits in the form of others' resources are always to some extent liabilities upon one's own resources. Accepting foreign aid, for example, most often implies accepting either political, military, or economic obligations toward the donor; and entering into alliance partnership at least formally links one's own survival to that of one's ally.

The "output" side of the resource utilization model is uncomplicated. On the one hand, resources are used to facilitate action in immediate undertakings. These may include normal day-to-day diplomatic activities and normal peacetime maintenance of military forces. Or they may include the prosecution of wars, emergency allocations to allies, or extraordinary political/diplomatic ventures. On the other hand, resources may also be demanded and used to service obligations incurred in the past. Most broadly, this category includes the allocation of resources for the continuation of all currently active foreign policy programs initiated in the past—i.e., support for alliance participation, assessments for international organization membership, funding for contracted aid agreements, and the like. The category may also however include obligations imposed by past military defeats, such as reparations demands, as well as obligations imposed by past military victories, such as occupation costs. Also included here would be the repayment of past borrowings, the maintenance of veterans' programs, and upkeep costs on physical facilities. Finally, a part of expended resources generally also goes into investment toward foreign policy objectives in the future. As the arrows in Figure 8.3 indicate, such investment takes the form of developing internal and enticing external power reserves. For many of the currently underdeveloped countries with power potential, past obligations and immediate undertakings tend to be minimal, and the bulk of resources are invested for the pursuit of foreign policy objectives in the future.

POWER AND INFLUENCE: A CONTEMPORARY DILEMMA

All that has been said in this chapter about relations between resources and capacities to act in international politics leads to a rather ironic conclusion in the context of contemporary international politics. Resources certainly do enhance states' capacities to act. There is no question about this. *But in contemporary international politics there is no direct relationship between the capacity to act and the probability of exercising influence.* It is not that there is no relationship at all between power and influence. Certainly, the superpowers have gained and maintain a good deal of influence (i.e., positive responsiveness to their wills and desires) among their respective allies. Certainly too, resources poured into foreign military and economic aid have in fact *bought* influence for the superpowers in many weaker countries. On balance, however, the exercise of influence through persuasion backed by power, by threatened coercion, or even by actual coercion is minimal in the contemporary system. The superpowers do not influence one another greatly, and they do not greatly influence one another's allies. Moreover, the relatively low correlations between the receipt of foreign aid and diplomatic support for donors, the alternative and oftentimes fickle anti-Western or anti-Communist leanings of weaker uncommitted states, and their obstinate insistence upon autonomy even under considerable superpower pressure suggest that the superpowers do not really have a great deal of influence over many weaker countries. Then, to further underline the superpower predicament, we find that adeptness at international political persuasion and relative diplomatic success are as characteristic of several of the weaker states as they are of the superpowers. States such as India, Egypt, Israel, Cambodia, and Canada generally do no worse in their attempts at exercising influence than do the United States and the Soviet Union; and they sometimes do a good deal better. India, for example, has been able to gain favorable responsiveness from both the U.S. and U.S.S.R., and her initiatives at the same time have gained the deference of many of the weaker countries.

The ineffectiveness of the superpowers in the contemporary period confuses only those who insist upon equating power with influence. The capacity to act neither implies that action will be taken, nor, more importantly, does it guarantee that actions taken will succeed. This has always been true, but it is most blatantly true today. What might be called the "impotence of contemporary power" rests in the fact that persuasion within a system of autonomous, sovereign states is optimally effective only when the persuader can offer substantial rewards for positive responsiveness or credibly threaten substantial penalties for nonresponsiveness. For several reasons the superpowers today can meet neither of these preconditions either *vis-à-vis* one another or toward the uncommitted countries.

First, due to parity in countervailing military power neither the United States nor the Soviet Union can coerce the other without largely destroying itself, and neither can even threaten coercion without taking grave risks. Mutual threats articulated frequently during the early years of the Cold War resulted in more embarrassment than influence for the threateners. Threats exchanged during the Cuban Missile Crisis in 1962 seem to have convinced both the U.S. and U.S.S.R. of the suicidal implications of nuclear "saber rattling," and the East/West military dialogue since that time has been a good deal more cautious. Hence, there is really no coercive backing for American and Soviet attempts to exert political influence upon each other. The only credible coercive threat recognized on either side is the other side's promise to launch a devastating second-strike if attacked, and confidence in second-strike potential supports obstinance much more than responsiveness. If one cannot be hurt, there is little reason to bargain or compromise with anyone.

In addition while each side's coercive "stick" remains neutralized, neither side has a very impressive "carrot" to hold before its rival. True enough, each side can offer the other some security by promising military restraint. But beyond this, due to the real, or at least perceived, incompatibility of most American and Soviet political goals, neither side can offer the other any acceptable plan for political settlement of the many long-standing and festering East/West issues. As long as both sides perceive as unfavorable any movement away from the status quo proposed by the other side, the status quo remains intact and all attempts to exert influence from either side continue frustrated in obstinacy and suspicion. Ironically, the greatest concentrations of power in history have become virtually useless in crucial areas of international politics.

Moreover, while power is neutralized in superpower relations, it is also greatly undermined in relations between superpowers and weaker states. Again, coercion and the coercive threat lose their value as "persuaders" because superpowers are unable to act coercively to their full capacities. A superpower nuclear threat leveled at a smaller state brings an almost immediate guarantee to the smaller state from the other nuclear power, and therefore such threats almost always carry the risk of all-out nuclear war. If a superpower statesman then threatens or employs conventional military power, he restrains his capacity to coerce and often finds that even a weaker state—or a weaker state supplied by his Cold War rival—can match him in conventional capacity. The United States faced this dilemma in Korea, where North Koreans and Chinese were able to fight United Nations forces to a conventional stalemate, and again in Vietnam, where externally supplied North Vietnamese and Viet Cong forces fought American forces to a similar conventional statemate. Hence, neither the nuclear threat nor the conventional threat turns out to be very effective in superpower relations with a weaker state. Attempts at persuasion have no really credible coercive backing.

Finally, the superpowers, despite their vast resource bases, actually have few rewards to offer that might be traded for political influence in the weaker nonaligned states. Certainly, the superpowers, and especially the United States, expend sizable quantities of resources on foreign aid, and it is also quite true that the superpowers are willing to offer their military might to guarantee the security of small states. However, neither aid nor protection are offered altruistically. They are intended to "buy" political influence in the form of Cold War alignment. But here again, the "carrots" are not always impressive enough to overcome incompatibilities in political goals. The nonaligned states see more penalties from Cold War involvement than they see rewards from aid and protection, and they remain determined not to lean politically. Moreover, leaders in several nonaligned nations have found that aid can be gotten from both the United States and the Soviet Union simultaneously, and under such conditions any move toward closer alignment might carry stiff economic penalties. Hence, the superpowers expend their resources in search of influence; the underdeveloped countries accept aid but at the same time cut the political strings attached and remain determined in their autonomy. Strangely, power and influence remain worlds apart.

It may be suggested in conclusion that despite the awesome nature of modern power, the resource requirements for effective action (i.e., that which might yield influence) in contemporary international politics are in fact lower than they were in past eras. With traditional styles of persuasion by coercion or threatened coercion substantially undermined in contemporary international politics, the older "iron-steam-steel" pathway that led England, Germany, and other powers to political influence in past eras is becoming a dead-end. The mass armies and navies, the wielding of huge explosive might, most of the factors that once permitted only the big and the industrialized to be great, are no longer directly related to political influence. On the contrary, essential international political resources today are such factors as highly astute, highly competent, and highly sensitive and perceptive statesmanship; capacities for world awareness, both physical and intellectual; and reputations for sincerity and world-mindedness rather than narrow national-mindedness. If it is true that mind rather than muscle is the key to contemporary international political influence, then even very small states may have potential for greatness.

CHAPTER NINE

NATIONALISM AND THE MOBILIZATION OF HUMAN RESOURCES

TO insert this discussion of nationalism into the section of this book concerned with resources and capabilities for action in international politics, is to step away from conventional textbook format. Nationalism is generally, and quite appropriately, treated near the beginning of most textbooks on this subject; tracing the relationship between "nation" and "state" then becomes part of the traditional discussion of actors in international politics. And it is true, certainly, that no analysis of international politics can be complete without an examination of nationalism and the nation-state.

Here this examination has been postponed until now for two reasons. First, in all discussion up to this point the concepts "state" and "nation-state" could easily have been used interchangeably. Differentiating between these concepts would have added little to the analyses of international structure and behavior in Parts I and II. Second, and more important, understanding the relationship between nation and state contributes most to one's understanding of international politics when the examination of this relationship focuses upon the *impacts* of nationalism on world politics. One of nationalism's greatest impacts has been to psychologically and physically mobilize mass populations in the service of foreign policy. Men's intense emotional identifications with "fatherland," "motherland," and regime, and their sometimes unquestioning and oftentimes heroic willingness to sacrifice in the name of patriotism, national glory, and national honor contribute directly to states' power. Therefore, a discussion of nationalism that explains men's willingness to sacrifice for their countries, fits well into a broader discussion of the bases of national power.

FROM STATE TO NATION-STATE

Earlier in this book, a "state" was defined as "a politically sovereign territorial unit." The international political system is an aggregation of such units. Conceived in one way, the political map of the world could be likened to a patchwork quilt on which each separate state is represented by an irregularly shaped, different-sized piece of material. Looked at in a slightly different way, a map of the international system could be thought of as a pattern of political discontinuities—i.e., a network of boundary lines indicating the perimeters of different governments' effective jurisdictions and sovereign responsibilities.[1]

The images of patchworks and discontinuities provide convenient stepping-stones to a description of the nation-state. While political frontiers are the most apparent, and often the most dramatic, boundary lines separating men, their affairs, and their concerns, other important lines also subdivide the globe.

For example, the world population is also a patchwork of *linguistic communities* within which men communicate in mutually intelligible words and between which exchanged utterings mean nothing. Points at which languages become mutually unintelligible mark the boundaries of linguistic communities and set the world pattern of linguistic discontinuity.

In broader terms the world is also subdivided into *communications areas* defined by other than linguistic boundaries. Geography and topology are traditionally responsible for linking some men into close communications relationships and also for isolating them from others. Areas of intense communication have emerged around river basins, along ancient caravan routes, and parallel to harbored coastlines. But natural barriers such as deserts, mountains, oceans, and seas have at times prevented peoples from even becoming aware of one another. Though modern technology has closed some natural communications gaps, world society remains a patchwork of areas of intense communication separated by communications gaps.

More than this, the economic world is an aggregation of *natural marketing areas* characterized by producing centers and consuming hinterlands and bounded at the limits of profitability in exchange.

1. Karl W. Deutsch, *Nationalism and Social Communication* (Cambridge–New York: M.I.T. Press–John Wiley, 1953), p. 20 ff.

Economic discontinuities are marked along the lines at which transportation costs make goods produced at one center noncompetitive with similar goods produced at a nearer center.

Human society is also marked by cultural discontinuities. The world is subdivided into *communities of custom, habit, and tradition* within which men share ways of life. Between cultural communities, ways of life are mutually alien and men understand one another, if at all, only by study and familiarity.

Reflecting on these different patterns of discontinuity in human society leads to an interesting observation: the perimeters of linguistic communities, natural communications networks, natural marketing areas, and cultural communities tend often to be more or less congruent, with the result that populations living within the congruent perimeters form *multidimensional communities.* That is, these populations are at the same time communities of language or dialect; communities of intense information exchange; communities of economic exchange; and communities of custom, values, and general life style. These people communicate a great deal more with one another than with populations outside of their communications area; trade a great deal more with one another than with populations outside of their marketing area; and dress more as one another, more often marry one another, and generally behave and think more as one another than as populations outside of their cultural area. When we add to these shared characteristics the stipulation that the populations of the multidimensional communities are aware of their commonalities and conscious of their distinctiveness; and when we grant that they have lived together long enough to have developed common memories of shared experiences, we need no longer refer to them with the cumbersome phrase "multidimensional communities." We can call them nationalities and we can refer to their communities as nations.

Reflecting again on the global patchwork of discontinuities, it is apparent that in the contemporary era, and especially in certain areas of the world, the political perimeters of states are congruent with the ethnic perimeters of nations. For example, Frenchmen, speaking French, communicating most intensely with one another, trading most intensely among themselves, and consciously sharing a peculiarly French way of life, today inhabit the politically defined state of France. The same, of course, could be said for Americans, Italians, Swedes,

Danes, Hungarians, Rumanians, Japanese, and a great many other peoples in political units. When the political perimeters of the state and the ethnic perimeters of the nation coincide (or at least substantially overlap) the resulting political-cultural entity is the *nation-state*.

Though the conceptual step from "nation" and "state" to "nation-state" is a small and uncomplicated one, the historical step was complex and spanned several centuries. Furthermore, in many areas of the world this step has not yet been taken. Ancient and medieval states, with very few exceptions, were not nation-states. The Ancient Egyptian Empire, the Empire of Alexander, the Roman Empire, the Turkish Empire, and medieval France, Spain and Austria, for example, were all *multinational* states, whose political frontiers stretched far beyond the ethnic perimeters of single nationalities and frequently enclosed several nationalities. Concerning medieval states, the noted historian Joseph R. Strayer points out:

It is clear that such a *regnum* (medieval state) could not be a cultural unit any more than it was an ethnic unit—there were always many dialects, frequently many languages, always different customs, and usually different laws for each of the constituent groups. Even geography does not help much, for a *regnum* was only roughly a geographical unit. It might have had a core, but it would be hard to define its boundaries—there were, everywhere, contested districts and loosely attached, more or less autonomous dependencies . . . .[2]

On the other hand, the city-states of ancient Greece and Renaissance Italy, and the tiny, but formally sovereign principalities of post-Renaissance Germany, were *subnational* states, whose political frontiers subdivided nations.

Sometime between the period of the late Renaissance, when the idea of the nation-state was already in the air, and the late nineteenth and early twentieth centuries, when nation-states emerged in great profusion, the processes that produced this new form of political-cultural organization were set into motion. In some areas, they were processes of fragmentation that transformed expansive multinational empires into smaller nation-states. In other areas, they were processes of unification and consolidation that welded tiny, culturally similar princi-

2. Joseph R. Strayer, "The Historical Experience of Nation-Building in Europe," in *Nation-Building,* Karl W. Deutsch and William J. Foltz, eds. (New York: Atherton Press, 1963), pp. 17–18.

palities into larger states. In discussing the emergence of nation-states, we can shift our time perspective from past to present, as well as shifting our geographic perspective. Processes similar to those that produced nation-states in Europe during the last two centuries, are producing new nation-states in Africa and Asia today. The "hows" and "whys" of national consolidation are therefore of great contemporary interest and relevance.

NATIONAL CONSCIOUSNESS, STATE–BUILDING, AND NATION–BUILDING

Perhaps nothing is more frustrating to the political theorist than his attempts to generalize about the formation of nation-states. Understanding this phenomenon demands abstraction and synthesis, but observing it empirically reveals such diversity that meaningful abstraction becomes almost impossible. To demonstrate, France was a political unit long before it became a cultural unit. Except for the territory of Lorraine, added in 1766, France as we know it existed as a political unit as early as the mid-seventeenth century.[3] However, the inhabitants of many of the regions in France were not recognizably "French" until the turn of the nineteenth century. By the mid-nineteenth century, nation and state were integrally interwoven on French territory. By adjusting dates somewhat, we find similar patterns of "state first, nation later" in the cases of Great Britain, Turkey, India, the United States, and several other present-day nation-states. Moreover, as will be elaborated in a moment, "state first, nation later" appears the incipient pattern in many of new states born out of the twentieth-century decolonizations.

Very much to the contrary, however, the Irish nation existed as a cultural and linguistic unit, and as a people bound in common traditions, experiences, and emotions, long before the Irish Free State came formally into being in 1921; and this same "nation first, state later" pattern can be noted with regard to present-day Poland, Greece, Norway, Bulgaria, and Iceland.

For more contrasts, several nation-states were consciously and deliberately built by governments who pushed political boundaries to

3. Crane Brinton, *From Many One* (Cambridge: Harvard University Press, 1948), pp. 49–64.

congruence with cultural frontiers or encouraged assimilation of diverse populations within their political domains. This was certainly the case with Germany, where Bismarck, after adopting a *klein-deutsch* (little Germany) definition of the German nation-state which excluded German-speaking populations in Austria, pushed Prussian frontiers to coincide with his definition. In the case of Italy, political boundaries were also pushed to perceived ethnic frontiers, and, after unification, efforts were made to assimilate populations who were not yet fully aware that they were supposed to be Italians. As René Albrecht-Carrié notes,

The wish of the Italian people to constitute themselves into a single state we may . . . take as simple fact, . . . though the qualification is important that the consciousness of unity, hence the desire to use it as a basis for action, did not deeply affect the mass of the Italian people; it was largely confined to the politically conscious, the literate minority, and especially among those to whom cultural matters, the memory of Rome, were a reality. The phrase was wholly apt, uttered after unification, was accomplished: "We have made Italy, all that remains to do is to make Italians." [4]

But while some nation-states were built by governments, others formed in opposition to governments. Governments that became targets of nationalist coups and revolutions, it should be noted, were for the most part controlled by elites that came to be viewed as nationally alien. *"Came to be viewed as nationally alien"* must be emphasized here because throughout most of history the fact that governing elites differed ethnically, culturally, and even linguistically from mass populations neither stirred nor bothered very many people very much. However, as the ideal of the nation-state gained increasing respect and legitimacy during the nineteenth century, peoples such as the Greeks, Poles, Romanians, Czechs, Irish, Magyars, Ukrainians, and many others, grew increasingly aware of their national distinctiveness, and increasingly restive under what they perceived as culturally alien and sometimes culturally stifling rule. Simultaneously, these nationalities grew ardently desirous of self-government in autonomous nation-states, with the result that the early twentieth century became an explosive era of national upheavals and successful, as well as unsuccessful, secessionist movements. By the mid-twentieth century, this pat-

4. René Albrecht-Carrié, *A Diplomatic History of Europe Since the Congress of Vienna* (New York: Harper & Row, 1958), p. 95.

tern of initial recognition of cultural distinctiveness, followed by restiveness under alien rule, nationalist agitation, and explosion became a
worldwide phenomenon, and a death knell for European colonialism.[5]

Nation-Building and Human Volition. Certainly no abstract discussion of the formation of nation-states can do justice to the diversity of
processes involved, or capture their many variations in specific cases.
Only thorough reading of history and astute monitoring of the present
can accomplish this. Nevertheless, a number of gross similarities do
prevail among most cases of nation-building past and present.

1. Contrary to beliefs put forth in French and German circles during the nineteenth century, and later adapted by Fascist movements in
our century, national consciousness and membership in national communities are not biological, instinctively "natural," or divinely ordained
phenomena. Nor are there "natural" frontiers for nation-states in a
geographic sense, or any divinely mapped "missions" for nations. National consciousness, the political significance of cultural distinctiveness, and the desirability of political-cultural unity and autonomy are
taught and learned (and *with a purpose,* as will be shown below).
In the same way, notions of "natural frontiers"; national "living
space"; and messianic schemes such as "manifest destiny," "pan-
slavism," and "pan-Africanism" are concocted (again, with a purpose).
Nations and nation-states are products of human volition: they follow from men's aspirations, and grow from men's plans, policies,
and efforts.

This denial of "naturalness" in the formation of nations and nation-
states may appear to contradict what was said earlier about the nation
as a multidimensional community. But this is not the case, since "national consciousness" is a stipulated part of this chapter's working
definition of *nation.* The infusion, diffusion, awakening or reawakening
of a sense of distinctiveness, and fraternity (a sense of "belonging togetherness," if you will) among inhabitants of a multidimensional community is prerequisite for nationhood. At some point in the history of
every nation these senses were deliberately infused, diffused, awakened
or reawakened by men's efforts.

2. Nation and nation-state are products of the efforts of *nationalist
elites.* National consciousness traditionally develops first among small,

5. Rupert Emerson, *From Empire to Nation* (Boston: Beacon Press, 1960), pp.
37–88.

educated, culturally sensitive, historically aware groups—scholars and teachers, theologians, writers and artists, political leaders and soldiers who are intellectually equipped to recall the history of the peoples, recognize the distinctiveness of their language and customs, and rationalize the legitimacy of political-cultural unity and autonomy. Members of these nationalist elites become the carriers of nationality, the publicists, propagandists, prophets and politicians who diffuse national consciousness among mass populations and lead political drives toward national political autonomy in the identity of nation and state. In short, nations initially exist because small activist groups think they exist, or should exist; and nation-states develop because these same groups work to build them.[6]

The nationalist elite may be identical with or overlap a state's governing political elite, in which case the government becomes the prime diffuser of national consciousness and the most vigorous nation-builder. Such was the case, for example, in postrevolutionary France and in Italy after unification. But, more typically, nationalist elites form as nongovernmental groups with anti-governmental aims. Such nationalist counter-elites tend to emerge among populations living under alien rule—e.g., in Austria-Hungary and in the Ottoman Empire prior to 1914, in nineteenth-century Ireland and Poland, in twentieth-century colonial Africa and Asia. Here, the leaders of the nationalist counter-elites become the polemicists, agitators, and revolutionary generals in highly emotional and sometimes violent drives toward national "liberation" and "self-determination." For these leaders, the first step in building a nation-state is taken in destroying the legitimacy and effectiveness of alien rule.[7]

In most cases, the role of the nationalist elite evolves in phases during the passage from alien rule to national autonomy. Early phases in nationalist movements are characterized by counter-elite activities in which the nationalist leadership works to recruit adherents to its cause by diffusing national consciousness. At the same time the nationalists begin agitation against the alien government. Later, with their position among the mass population and their material resource base strengthened, the nationalist elite meets the alien government in direct political or military confrontation. If the confrontation succeeds, the nationalist

6. Karl W. Deutsch, *Nationalism and Social Communication,* pp. 18–20.
7. Rupert Emerson, *From Empire to Nation,* pp. 37–59.

elite becomes the state political elite in a new state, and its role becomes one of using the instruments of government to diffuse national consciousness among the mass population more thoroughly. Typically, the bulk of the mass population remains indifferent during nationalist struggles and develops little national consciousness until after nationalist elites gain control over government and launch vigorous nation-building programs.

3. Diffusing national consciousness through mass populations and thereby finally linking nation and state are facilitated by a variety of persuasive, manipulative, and coercive instruments and techniques available to nationalist elites. Most of these become available, however, only after nationalist elites assume control over state government operations, *so that most nation-building actually occurs after formal national independence.*

First, the nationalist elite may take measures to insure and enforce the coterminousness of the state and the economic, linguistic, and communications unit that is the nation. Various man-made contrivances which serve to create unity and intense interaction within and isolation between political units can be used to underline the distinctiveness and separateness of nation-states. For example, artificial tariff barriers, frontier taxes, and the like can effectively focus most of a state's economic intercourse inward, thereby making the political unit also an economic unit and its population a community of intense economic exchange. State-controlled education similarly may serve to make the political unit into a common linguistic unit, while government direction in the construction of physical communications networks can stimulate internal communication and effectively enforce external isolation. Notice in Figure 9.1, for example, how French, German, and Italian railroad construction during the nineteenth century both enhanced internal communications and frustrated international communications. Major railroad lines paralleled rather than transversed international frontiers (note the French and German rail lines paralleling the western and eastern banks of the Rhine, the Turin-Milan-Venice line paralleling the Italian northern border, and the Munich-Leipzig-Dresden line winding in alignment with the German-Austrian border). Moreover, as the figure clearly shows, railroads focused national communications generally inward and specifically toward national political-cultural centers. The French pattern,

**FIGURE 9.1. MAJOR EUROPEAN RAILROADS IN
THE NINETEENTH CENTURY**

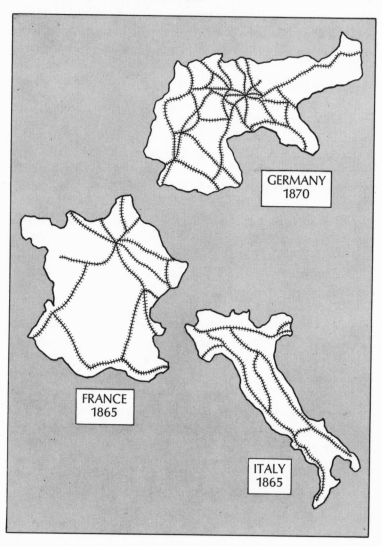

for example, is radial, with all lines leading to Paris; while the German
pattern is more gridlike, mutually interlinking all major cities. When
one complements Figure 9.1 with related highway and telecommunica-
tions networks, it becomes quite clear that physical communications

were deliberately designed to cement national unity, and indeed also to mutually isolate nation-states. Where national "togetherness" was not felt, it was engineered.

In addition to fostering internal information flows and external isolation through appropriately designed physical communications networks, a nationalist elite may mold a population into intense intranational communications by sponsoring the formation and activities of nationally based social, economic, and political groups. The purpose in creating such groups with national memberships is to establish interpersonal communications channels which cut across regional, ethnic, religious, and other diversities within the state's population so that such diversities might lose some of their divisive significance. National political parties; national labor unions; national professional, fraternal, and youth organizations; national armies; and even national women's associations contributed in the past, and are contributing in Africa and Asia today, to national political unity and identification.[8] Such organizations are at once symbols of the national collectivity, amalgams of diverse segments of the national population, and communications channels that foster information exchange in a national network.

To insure the congruence of political unit and cultural community, national elites may use their control over education to socialize succeeding generations in national customs, mores, values, and political allegiance. But even before common education begins to have nation-building impact, the national elite can encourage national cultural assimilation (i.e., the adoption of cultural standards and values upheld by the elite) by offering rewards to those willing to assimilate and by inflicting penalties upon those who remain reluctant. A national elite in control of the instruments of government can link opportunities for social and economic mobility—as well as political participation, influence, and office—to willingness to adopt national cultural standards, willingness to pay allegiance to national political symbols, and willingness to identify with the nation-state. The elite can, of course, also deny such opportunities to nonassimilators or even go further toward actual persecution. In short, the nationalist elite can make national consciousness rewarding for those willing to cherish it and painful for those who reject it.

8. Thomas Hodgkin, *Nationalism in Colonial Africa* (New York: New York University Press, 1957), pp. 84–92, 139–168.

Despite instruments available to nation-building elites, the habitual kind of national consciousness—unquestioned identification, spontaneous patriotism, corporate personality—that we observe among the peoples of the older nation-states, develops slowly in mass populations. Political units can be made to look like nation-states long before common people feel profound political identifications. Because of the time lag between national elite ascendance and the emergence of mass nationalism, theorists list "aging in the wood" as an essential part of the nation-building process.[9] Mass populations within political units must mutually interact, and must constantly and positively interact with nationalist elites over extended periods of time, before national consciousness begins to diffuse effectively. The nation-building tasks of the nationalist elite during these periods of "aging in the wood" are to maintain the integrity of the political unit, the arena for interaction, and to provide common political symbols and a common history of political experiences for the mass population. In addition, during these periods the elite acts to suppress movements, groups, and ideas which could dilute developing national consciousness or divide the developing nation. External wars, unsuccessful civil wars, great national efforts at social or economic uplifting or reform, widespread popular political participation, political martyrs, charismatic national leaders, and periods of commonly shared national suffering, have all acted—in various nation-states—as catalysts to speed the national "aging in the wood" process. Nation-building is never completed in months or years. It initially takes generations or centuries, and it starts anew as each new generation is born into a national population.

Nationalism and Loyalty to the Nation-State. No more concise or better worded definition of nationalism has been offered than that which appears as the opening sentence of Hans Kohn's *Nationalism; Its Meaning and History:* "Nationalism is a state of mind, in which the supreme loyalty of the individual is felt due to the nation-state." [10] Nationalism is subjective; it is emotional; it consists in bonds of loyalty that psychologically link the individual to his people and the people collectively to the national political unit they inhabit, or aspire to in-

9. Rupert Emerson, *From Empire to Nation,* p. 113.
10. Hans Kohn, *Nationalism: Its Meaning and History* (New York: D. Van Nostrand, 1955), p. 9.

habit. Nationalism is the "state of mind" that nationalist elites seek to diffuse through mass populations.

Though the bases and dynamics of national loyalty are rather poorly explored in social science, several facts are clear. First, national loyalty and emotional identification with the nation-state are learned and reinforced habits rather than "natural" instincts. If loyalty to the nation-state were instinctive, disloyalty would be almost unknown. Loyalty itself, or the need to be loyal, is deeply imbedded in the human psyche. But setting the nation-state up as the object of loyalty is a product of nation-builders' efforts.

If one could venture a hypothesis, it might be proposed that loyalty to the nation-state is initially instrumental in character. In the course of the nation-building process, the individual trades his loyalty—in the form of willingness to comply with the social, cultural, and political norms of the nationalist elite; willingness to cooperate in preserving and protecting these norms; and willingness to identify as a part of a community engaged in upholding these norms—for rewards that follow from loyal behavior or in avoidance of penalties that may follow from disloyal behavior. Rewards may be in the nature of opportunities for social, economic, and political advancement, as mentioned earlier. But probably more important rewards are such satisfactions of conformity as in-group acceptance and respect, camaraderie, and meaningful self-identification. Similarly, penalties for disloyalty could take the form of official sanctions. But ostracism, pressures for conformity, and failure to achieve self-identification, hurt even more deeply. Therefore, initially at least, an individual demonstrates loyalty to nation, state, and nation-state because such demonstration at least keeps his body, home, and psyche intact. Moreover, as nationalism diffuses ever more widely from nationalist elite to mass population, self-reinforcing social pressures for conformity in allegiance intensify, and rewards and penalties in loyalty and disloyalty increase respectively.

Few of us, however, consciously calculate the potential rewards and penalties from accepting or rejecting the nation-state as an object of loyalty. Still, most of us consider ourselves loyal citizens of a nation-state; most of us offer our national identities first when asked who we are; and most of us would probably make substantial sacrifices for our country. For most people in the older nation-states, loyalty has become a habit—much in the same way that any repeated behavioral response becomes a habit. Space limitations here do not permit the long digression into the psychology of learning that would be required for a thorough explanation of habit formation. Very generally though, any repeated pattern of behavior that continually yields rewards or avoids penalties is reinforced in performance to the point where the behaving individual ceases to consider alternative patterns. At the point where a pattern· of behavior gets enacted automatically, without thinking, that pattern becomes a habit.[11]

Our national ancestors learned habits of loyalty by trial and error. Early Americans, for instance, learned by experience that rewards flowed and penalties were avoided when loyalties focused inward upon the United States instead of outward toward Great Britain. Similarly, nineteenth-century Bavarians learned that rewards flowed and penalties were avoided when loyalties focused on Berlin rather than Munich. Most of us, however, have not had to learn loyalty by experience. Political socialization in our countries has acquainted and equipped us with appropriately loyal and rewarding response patterns. Our social-political habits are passed to us from previous generations, but the learning experiences that produced these habits have faded into obscurity. Therefore, when we "instinctively" feel nationalist emotions, we are actually acting out behavior patterns learned in past generations and passed to us via education and other processes of political socialization.

In several important senses, the nation-state is the most powerful object of political loyalty that history has yet produced. First, the nation-state is real and concrete: it can be pictured on a map; its territory can be traversed; its population can be identified by shared national characteristics; its government can be visualized in operation. Because it is real and concrete, the nation-state fares far better as an object of loyalty among the intellectually unsophisticated than do abstract political ideas and designs such as world federation or even the communist "classless society." The nation-state also offers the internal political-social orderability and external defensibility offered by the traditional state, and it gains loyalty in exchange for protection very much in the way that similar loyalty was gained by traditional

11. Neal E. Miller and John Dollard, *Social Learning and Imitation* (New Haven: Yale University Press, 1941), pp. 1–68.

states. But even more than this, the nation-state embodies the nation; and its government comes to stand—in the eyes of its people—for the protection, preservation, and promotion of all cultural values and norms associated with the nation and cherished in national tradition. Because the state embodies the nation, it can be seen as standing for everything political and nonpolitical that nationalities deem sacred. Relatedly, the nation-state aggregates many mutually reinforcing loyalties at a single focal point. Where state, church, economy, language, literature, art, and music are all distinctively national—combined deference to, and pride in each and all of them, adds to loyalty to the nation-state. Once the inseparability of state and nation become internalized in citizens' thinking, disloyalty to the nation-state becomes tantamount to self-betrayal and psychological self-destruction. The traditional state could capture subjects' political loyalties, but the nation-state is uniquely suited to capture citizens' total loyalties.

NATIONALISM AND STATE POWER

Originally, the ideal of the nation-state and the goals of nation-building were noble. Eighteenth and nineteenth-century liberal nationalists such as Thomas Paine in America, Jean Jacques Rousseau in Geneva, and Giuseppe Mazzini in Italy equated the achievement of the nation-state with the realization of political liberty and the heightening of human well-being. During the same era writers such as Jules Michelet in France and Adam Mickiewicz in Poland expressed the notion and hope that a world of nation-states would be a world of liberated and contented peoples, and consequently a world of peace. History, however, has been cruel to these early idealistic nation-builders, for instead of generating liberty and peace as expected and predicted, extreme nationalism in the twentieth century produced heinous totalitarian despotisms under Fascism and Nazism; it produced emotional exclusionism, intolerance, and hatred among peoples; it produced innumerable passionate wars. Yet, despite nationalism's shamed history, nation-building continues apace in many areas of the world today.

The reasons for continued nation-building are peculiar to particular states and nationalist elites. Leaders in some newly emerging nations remain adherent to the ideals of liberal nationalism and interpret the colonial liberations of the mid-twentieth century as new opportunities to rebuild the relationship between nation-state and human liberty and well-being. Men such as Mohandas Gandhi, or Jawaharlal Nehru were unquestionably liberal nationalists in the nineteenth-century vein. Indeed, nationalist elites in many new states rode to political power on impassioned nationalist oratory and on utopian promises and commitments to nation-building. For many of these elites, tenure in political office depends upon continued nation-building efforts and evidence of movement toward realizing their earlier promises and forecasts. Still, over and above the different reasons why particular nationalist elites engage in nation-building, one outcome in nation-building is almost universally sought: *nationalist passions among populations enhance the power of states by mobilizing human resources for political service.* Creating a nation from a mass population and relatedly a nation-state from a state tends to supplement state power resources in almost exponential proportions.

Nationalism and War-Making Potential. When political loyalty and allegiance reach points at which entire populations willingly turn their full efforts to protecting the state and pursuing its international goals, when men can be so inflamed with dedication to community and hatred for outsiders that they would rather die than capitulate or retreat in the face of threats from outsiders, and when men so adore their distinctive ways of life that they would attempt to foist such ways upon others whom they consider culturally inferior, war becomes an impassioned crusade rather than a calculated political instrument. Wars injected with nationalist passions are confrontations between secular religions. They explode with the emotional fury of contests between believers and infidels, and terminate only after one state's forces are decimated into nonresistance, after one government's institutional edifice is dismantled, and after one national creed has been ripped from the minds of its adherents. While political wars between traditional states were most often strategically limited and tactically restrained, secular-religious wars between nation-states are total, unconditional, and barbaric.

Hans J. Morgenthau vividly captures the contrast between warfare involving traditional states and modern national wars in a brilliant chapter on "Total War" in his *Politics Among Nations.*[12] Comparing

12. Hans J. Morgenthau, *Politics Among Nations,* 4th ed. (New York: Alfred A. Knopf, 1967), pp. 350–370.

the limited warfare of fourteenth- and fifteenth-century Italy with the total warfare of our century, Morgenthau notes first that

Italian wars of the fourteenth and fifteenth centuries . . . were fought primarily by mercenaries who, their interests being in the main financial, were not eager to die in battle or to invite that risk by killing too many of their enemies. . . . The *condotteri* (leaders of mercenary armies) were not interested in decisive battles and wars of annihilation, for without a war and without an enemy there was no job. In consequence, these Italian wars consisted in good measure in skilled maneuvers and tactical artifices to compel the enemy to give up his positions and retreat, losing prisoners rather than wounded and dead.[13]

Contrasting this with twentieth-century nationalist wars, Morgenthau reports that

In the twentieth century the character of war . . . changes. . . . Now not only are able bodied men conscripted, but in totalitarian countries, women and children as well. . . . Everywhere, however, all the productive forces of the nation are harnessed to the purposes of war.[14]

Then,

. . . Nationalistic universalism in the two world wars of the twentieth century [has] supplied that principle of justice and with it, that passion and enthusiasm which have restored to masses of fighting men the willingness to conquer and die for an idea.[15]

Clearly, what nationalism has given to warfare is emotional zeal. By the same token, among the contributions of nationalism to states' war potential is enhanced capacity to endure long siege, momentous sacrifice, and continued setback. To attack and defeat a nation-state requires not only the ability to destroy the opponent's material capacity to resist, but also the ability to destroy his will to live as a nation. Then too, nationalism has also added to states' war potential the ability to unleash full destructive capability without moral restraint. When nationalist zeal and related convictions of political-cultural superiority and "mission" inflame a people, and when vainglorious pride leads them to believe that they are "right" and "just" and their enemies are contemptible, only material limitations can constrain their fury. Moral

13. *Ibid.,* p. 350.
14. *Ibid.,* p. 355.
15. *Ibid.,* p. 353.

qualms and humanitarian considerations can be all but lost in "holy" crusades. Hence, cultivating nationalism means building war potential, and nation-building therefore remains the interest of defense-minded or expansionist elites. As Kohn notes, "what . . . peoples . . . did not learn from the French Revolution . . . they learned from Napoleon: nationalism, not as a vehicle of individual liberty but as adoration of collective power." [16]

It has been argued that nuclear weaponry militates against further "total" wars in the pattern of World Wars I and II, since total nuclear war is tantamount to the total annihilation of contenders. There is reason in this argument, but its rationality may also be its weakness. By rational standards of costs and gains, objectives and tactics, offenses and penalties, World Wars I and II were not "reasonable" wars. They were ideologically interpreted, emotionally charged, spasmodic fights, in which many of the contenders were driven by perceived national missions, and in which national hatreds fired political-military objectives and condoned inhumanities. Indeed, two nuclear bombs were dropped on civilian populations during World War II! Although total nuclear war is irrational, and therefore appears "unthinkable," the kinds of political-military disputes that could escalate to nuclear war remain bound in intense nationalist emotions. Any international contest that can become an emotional nationalist crusade, can also become a total war.

Nationalism and Economic Development. While relationships between nationalism and war potential were certainly on the minds of Hitler and Mussolini, Bismarck, Napoleon, and other leaders of history, and doubtlessly remain salient in the thinking of some adventuristic national leaders today, a more salient reason for cultivating nationalism in many of the newer states is found in the relationship between nation-building and economic development. Rising from poverty and technological backwardness to economic modernity is a painful ascent. Making this ascent requires great human endurance, patience, and the ability to withstand short-run hardship. More than anything else perhaps, economic development requires the full efforts of total populations and a "faith to live by" while these efforts are invested for the future. Nationalism, in its extolling of collective personality, its imbuing of willingness to sacrifice for community, and its generation of

16. Hans Kohn, *Nationalism: Its Meaning and History*, p. 29.

pride in collective accomplishment, mobilizes human resources, builds collective endurance, and provides an exhilarating secular "faith."

As noted in an earlier chapter, initial stages of economic development are periods of high input and low output. Consumption is often severely curtailed during these early stages so that resources can be invested in economic infrastructure facilities such as transportation and communication networks, and energy-generating plants, or in agricultural and industrial machinery, or educational and training programs, and the like. Moreover, consumption during early stages of development is often also curtailed so that domestically produced commodities can be sold on foreign markets to earn the foreign exchange necessary to procure machinery and other prerequisites for launching into industrialization. What this means is that for the sake of economic development, populations living at or near subsistence are asked to fall temporarily into deeper misery. Moreover, "temporarily" can mean several generations, so that many of those who are asked to sacrifice for economic development can expect never to enjoy the fruits of their sacrifice. In such situations the national elite interested in economic development can opt either to force sacrifice by coercion—as was largely the case in Soviet development between 1920 and 1940—or they can opt to encourage sacrifice by generating enthusiasm and dedication for the goals of development. Such enthusiasm and dedication are fostered by arousing identification with the nation, linking the nation and the state, and then linking the state to the goal of economic development. In this way, the collective future of the nation-state can come to supersede each individual's personal future. Sacrifice can come to be understood as martyrdom to a great national cause. Contentment can be sustained by creative satisfactions in building instead of material satisfactions in consuming. What this suggests is that if an elite is unwilling or unable to coerce its population, then it must engage in arousing national passion for collective goals and sacrifices. Nationalist zeal mobilizes human resources for economic development.

Nationalism and Internal Control. It must be kept in mind here that the relationship between nationalism and economic development enters the discussion of state power because, as noted in Chapter 8, economic development liberates resources that may be used to enhance capacities to act in international politics. In the same way, when a population accepts the authority and bends to the will of a governing elite by compliance rather than by threat of coercion, resources that might otherwise be allocated to internal policing can be invested in other programs and objectives, including foreign policy objectives. It can be argued therefore that nationalism, in the form of identification with the nation-state and allegiance to its government and official policies, enhances national power because it minimizes resource allocations for internal control and frees resources for external purposes.

Nation-building to alleviate the costs of internal control turns out to be almost essential in many of the new states of Africa and Asia, where tribal, religious, and other separatisms and provincial "nationalisms" constantly threaten political unity and stability. Where no sense of collective national unity pervades a population, and especially a population under the strains of adjustment to self-government and the pain of economic development, preventing and quelling secessionist upheavals can consume great proportions of a state's limited resources. In fact, where resources have to be poured into arming military forces for domestic use, into pursuing omnipresent guerrillas, and into fighting recurrent civil wars, few resources may be left for economic development and none for foreign policy programs. Nation-building again, therefore, is in the governing elite's interest. Fostering loyalty and allegiance, encouraging identification with national symbols while condemning allegiance to symbols of divisiveness, sometimes even creating "external threats" to weld national unity—all contribute to lower cost internal control, consequent resource surpluses, and state power.

THE CONTINUING PREVALENCE OF NATIONALISM: A CONCLUDING NOTE

In view of nationalism's history of ethnocentrism, human intolerance, and impassioned barbarous war, it might be satisfying if in conclusion we could say that intense nationalism was a nineteenth- and early twentieth-century phenomenon, that it has outlived any usefulness it may have had, and that it is rapidly being replaced by world regionalism and tolerant internationalism. Some students of regionalism and international organization are in fact already tolling a death knoll for nationalism, without regret.[17] Evidence, however, contradicts

17. A. H. Robertson, *European Institutions* (New York: Praeger, 1958), p. 5.

this conclusion. In almost every area of the world, save perhaps in a few Western European countries, nationalism seems as intense as ever. Nation-building elites in the new nations are working, for reasons cited earlier, to strengthen nationalism in their states. Moreover, East-West cold warfare and its tactics of subversion and informal penetration in weaker states, are placing premiums on national loyalty and identification. In many nonaligned states, fears of superpower subversion are stimulating governments to more vigorous nation-building efforts. Moreover, though once officially discouraged, nationalism is reemerging in some of the Communist states and even being stimulated by Communist governments. In many of the older nation-states of the West, lip service to internationalism still rings hollow beside nationalist oratory and patriotic appeals. Hence, anyone who stops to gather and assemble nationalist "straws in the wind" may well conclude that the era of intense nationalism is far from passed. Indeed, nationalism has grown from a nineteenth-century European phenomenon to a twentieth-century divisive world creed.

CHAPTER TEN
THE ABILITY TO PAY ATTENTION
AS A POWER RESOURCE

INFORMATION is one of the most important, indeed perhaps *the* most important, among resources consumed in international political activity. No action can be taken in international politics unless and until actors are informed about situations requiring action. No decisions can be made without exchanges of information among decision-makers. No decisions can be executed unless and until information is transmitted, and no policies can be evaluated unless and until information about their impacts is reported back to decision-makers. The quantity of information available to statesmen, and even more important, the quality of information available, contribute greatly to determining the variety of a state's international behavior and the effectiveness of its policies.[1]

Singling out information and information flows for special consideration in the discussion of international political resources is a relatively new departure in international political analysis. Heretofore, the information ingredient in international behavior had been more often implicitly assumed rather than explicitly analyzed. Recently, however, revolutionary developments in the science of cybernetics have equipped social scientists with a set of specialized concepts and tools that open information flows to enlightening analysis. Latter sections of this chapter therefore draw heavily upon the pioneering cybernetic

1. Roger Hilsman, Jr., "Intelligence and Policy-Making in Foreign Affairs," in *International Politics and Foreign Policy,* James N. Rosenau, ed., 1st ed. (Glencoe: The Free Press, 1961), pp. 209–219; Charlton Ogburn, Jr., "The Flow of Policy-Making in the State Department," in Rosenau, pp. 229–233.

efforts of Norbert Wiener, and parts of the text closely follow the politically applied cybernetics of Karl W. Deutsch's *The Nerves of Government*.[2]

This chapter's overall analysis is developed in three parts designed to pinpoint and underline the strong relationship between states' capacities to receive, process, and transmit information and their capacities to act in international politics. Attention and discussion focus descriptively first on the tactical manipulation of information in international politics, and on some of the international political impacts of misinformation and missing information. In a second section, the discussion of information processing in foreign policy formulation is theoretically formalized and elaborated. Then, in summary, requirements for the effective development and exploitation of information resources are outlined.

THE INFORMATION INGREDIENT IN INTERNATIONAL POLITICS

Technically, information is the symbolic representation of objects, persons, places, or events.[3] Or, in slightly different words, we could say that information describes or characterizes objects, persons, places, or events through the arrangement of symbols—i.e., words, numbers, ciphers, pictures, or sounds. Such symbols can be transmitted via physical and interpersonal communications facilities, and transmission permits receivers to reconstruct or otherwise share the experiences of senders. For example, when a war correspondent witnesses a battle, his experience can be shared by newspaper readers only after it is transformed into an item of information, or *message* (i.e., a set of symbols that can be transmitted). Hence, what the reader finds in the daily paper is certainly not the battle that the correspondent observed, but rather a more or less intelligible set of symbols describing or characterizing the battle. The point here is that information *is about* objects, people, places, and events, but is distinct from the objects, etc., themselves. Therefore information is immaterial, although generally it symbolizes or refers to something that exists or happens which we may call a *material referent*. It should be noted, however, that in

2. Norbert Wiener, *Cybernetics,* rev. ed. (Cambridge–New York: M.I.T. Press–John Wiley, 1961); Karl W. Deutsch, *The Nerves of Government* (New York: The Free Press, 1963).

3. Karl W. Deutsch, *The Nerves of Government,* p. 146.

cases of utter prevarication, not unknown in international propaganda, information may exist that has no material referents whatsoever.

Underlining the distinction between information and its material referents helps to explain the meaning and international political significance of accurate information on the one hand, and misinformation and missing information on the other. The accuracy of information depends, first, upon the fidelity achieved in transforming material referents into transmittable symbols; second, upon clarity in transmission; and, third, upon effectiveness in reception. Carrying forward the "war correspondent" example, it may be the case that the reporter's verbal talents were such that he could transform his observations exactly into words; that these words were exactly reproduced by the teletype operators; that they were clearly transmitted without mechanical, electrical, or atmospheric interference; that they were exactly reproduced by the printer; and that when read by the reader they had exactly the same meaning as they did for the reporter. If all of these conditions combined, we could assume that newspaper readers were given and received accurate information about the battle, or at least as much of the battle as the reporter witnessed and reported.

On the other hand, if the reporter exaggerated, understated, or lapsed into ambiguity in transforming his observations into words; if human errors or mechanical interference then distorted these words in transmission; and if the words took on meanings for readers that differed from those intended by the reporter, we would have a case of information inaccurately offered and received. The measure of accuracy in information flows then is the degree of identity between the material referent reported by the sender and the image of the material referent reconstructed by the receiver. Inaccuracy or *misinformation* can stem from faulty symbolization, from faulty transmission, or from faulty reception. Distortions that produce misinformation may be either conscious and deliberate, or unconscious and unintended, on the part of human agents sending and receiving; or they may even result from mechanical quirks in transmitting equipment. Complete misinformation results when information is transmitted concerning nonexistent material referents, as would have been the case had our reporter written about a battle that never took place. *Missing information,* on the other hand, results when material referents exist that are not symbolized, transmitted, or received, as would have been the case had our reporter not written his story about the battle, had editors rejected the story, or had readers ignored it. Table 10.1 summarizes the relationships between information and material referents.

TABLE 10.1. RELATIONSHIPS BETWEEN INFORMATION AND MATERIAL REFERENTS

Relationship	Symbolization (Sender)	Possible Causes In: Transmission (Human/Mechanical)	Reception (Receiver)
I. Accurate Information			
Identity between material referent and image transmitted and received.	Exact transformation of material referent into transmittable symbols.	No human error. No mechanical failure or distortion.	All symbols transmitted also received. Symbols interpreted as intended by sender.
II. Misinformation			
Deviation between material referent and image transmitted and received. *Extreme:* No material referent at all.	Deliberate or unintended exaggeration, understatement, omission, or ambiguity in transformation of material referent into transmittable symbols.	Human error in transmission. Mechanical failure or distortion in transmission.	Some symbols transmitted but not received. Symbols received deliberately or unintendedly misinterpreted or misunderstood.
III. Missing Information			
Material referent not completely reconstructed in image transmitted or received.	No symbolization of material referent, or grossly incomplete symbolization.	Human error or omission in transmission. Mechanical failure in transmission or lack of transmitting facilities.	Symbols either not received, or received but ignored.

Misinformation, Missing Information, and International Setbacks. It is difficult empirically to isolate the impact of information on international behavior in episodes where information flows accurately. Successful foreign policy operations are the products of numerous input factors, among which accurate information is surely one. But it is nevertheless hard to single out particular developments and conclude that they are the direct results of accurate information. Accurate information about political and economic conditions in Europe in 1946 and 1947, for example, largely determined the timing and content of the United States Marshall Plan proposal and thereby contributed to the success of the aid program. But accurate information was only one among several factors that helped the program to success. In the same sense, accurate information about weaknesses and subversive opportunities in the Czechoslovakian state and society contributed to the timing and tactics of the Soviet engineered Communist take-over there in 1948. But again, accurate information was one of several factors that contributed to policy success and the exact contribution of this information is difficult to pinpoint. Hence, in cases of policies successfully executed, accurate information is always an ingredient, but it is usually part of a syndrome of ingredients that constitute all-round good judgment.

However, in cases of policy failure or international political setback, the information ingredient sometimes stands out starkly, because mis-information or missing information can occasionally be a single factor producing political setback. Several examples underline the point:

1. On December 7, 1941, Imperial Japanese naval and air forces attacked American military installations in the Hawaiian Islands, the Philippines, and other parts of the Pacific. The United States was taken almost completely by surprise, and consequently suffered a resounding defeat in its opening battle of World War II. Historical controversy exists concerning the amount of warning the United States actually had of the planned and incipient Japanese attack. There is little doubt, however, that the disaster at Pearl Harbor stemmed from a major failure in American acquisition or handling of information.[4]

2. Similarly, on June 25, 1950, a North Korean army of some forty divisions moved south across the 38th parallel dividing North and South Korea. The lightning strike initially routed South Korean de-fenders, and in succeeding weeks North Korean forces nearly pushed a United States army fighting under United Nations auspices into the Yellow Sea. Again, there is some controversy about the amount of information that could and should have been gathered to warn South Korean forces and their American advisers of the impending invasion

4. Roberta Wohlstetter, *Pearl Harbor; Warning and Decision* (Stanford: Stanford University Press, 1962), *passim*.

from the North (someone must have noted and reported the massing North Korean divisions). But there is little doubt that the initial Korean disaster stemmed from a major intelligence failure.[5]

3. While an initial failure in information acquisitions and handling paved the way for the opening of the Korean War, a second intelligence failure later frustrated total United Nations victory:

Under loose . . . mandate the United Nations commander advanced his forces northward toward the Manchurian boundary in a movement to unite all Korea, little believing that Red China would enter the war from that quarter.

Again the unexpected happened. Communist Chinese forces swarmed across the border into Korea in November, 1950. . . . Overpowered by the new forces and great reserves behind them, the UN troops fell back toward the 38th parallel as fast as recently they had advanced beyond it.[6]

It has been established that both North Korean and Chinese sources provided ample warning of probable Chinese intervention in the Korean War to the point of specifying conditions that would definitely prompt intervention.[7] Discounting this information was a major and disastrous case of intelligence failure.

4. In April, 1961, the United States supported an expedition of some four hundred armed Cuban expatriates to the Bay of Pigs region of southern Cuba. It was anticipated that this landing would serve to rally anti-Castro forces in Cuba, provoke a general uprising in the island nation, and bring down the Castro government.[8] However, as most readers will recall, the Cuban people rallied to, rather than re-volted against, their government as word of the invasion spread. Most of the intruding commandos were slaughtered on the beach. Those who survived were captured. Condemnation of American aggressiveness and underhandedness was offered in all parts of the world. Whether a success or a failure, the Bay of Pigs operation would likely have be-come a black mark on the record of American foreign policy. Still, the failure was first and foremost a product of faulty information.

5. One must not get the impression from the above examples that only the United States government suffers periodic foreign setbacks

5. Allen S. Whiting, *China Crosses the Yalu* (New York: Macmillan, 1960), *passim.*
6. Samuel Flagg Bemis, *A Diplomatic History of the United States,* 4th ed. (New York: Holt, Rinehart and Winston, 1955), p. 934. (Italics mine.)
7. Allen S. Whiting, *China Crosses the Yalu,* pp. 92–115.
8. Roger Hilsman, Jr., *To Move a Nation* (Garden City: Doubleday, 1967), pp. 30–33.

as a result of information failures. Surprises that stem from faulty information are endemic to international politics. All countries suffer from them. For example, the British and the French were as surprised as the Americans on December 7, 1941; and the South Koreans were as surprised as the Americans in June and November, 1950. Furthermore, when the British and French in cooperation with Israel launched an invasion of Egypt in October, 1956, the Russians were certainly as surprised as the Americans; and no one perhaps was more surprised than the Egyptians.

Moreover, the classic case in the twentieth century of intelligence failure followed by surprise attack and military disaster is the case of Hitler's invasion of the Soviet Union in June, 1941. Details of the pre-invasion events in the Soviet Union are available in only fragmentary form, but even scant evidence presents a picture of utter surprise and confusion despite ample warning. From recent interviews with Field Marshal Budenny, commander of Soviet Reserve Army defense forces after the Nazi invasion, and Ivan M. Maisky, Soviet Ambassador in London in 1941, Harrison E. Salisbury has been able to piece together the hours in Moscow before Hitler's strike. Salisbury's story is worth quoting at length:

Late on Saturday afternoon, June 21, 1941, Marshal Budenny recalled, Stalin summoned a meeting of the Politburo to which he invited some military leaders. The possibility had arisen Stalin told them, that Hitler might attack Russia either on the night of June 21–22 (which he did) or during the weekend.

The Marshal seemed to be unaware that Stalin had been receiving for months warnings from his intelligence network in Germany, from Richard Sorge, the Soviet spy in the German embassy in Tokyo (naming the date and time of the Nazi attack), from Prime Minister Winston Churchill, from Sumner Welles, Under Secretary of State; from the Soviet Ambassador in London Ivan M. Maisky, from military commanders on the Western Front, from Naval and air patrols in the Baltic, the Arctic, and the Black sea, and had not only ignored warnings but had arrested some of those sending in such reports on charges of treason.

. . . Some troops had been ordered to move Westward but were still far away. Stalin had been so fearful of provoking action by Hitler that he forbade his armies to move up to advanced positions and banned firing at German reconnaissance planes.

. . . When the Germans struck at 3:30 A.M. on June 22, Marshal Budenny was in the People's Commissariat of Defense on Frunze Street in Moscow, working furiously. He had no army, no staff, no equipment, no weapons. The planes were still staked to the ground and 95 percent of them were destroyed in the first German air strikes.

. . . "The tragedy of it," said Ambassador Maisky, . . . "was that Stalin believed in nobody except Hitler. He believed in Hitler. He thought he could outmaneuver Hitler. It was a question of "psychology."

Stalin's "psychology" cost Russia dearly. The disaster made the Japanese surprise of the United States at Pearl Harbor look like a child's game. The Soviet Union won the war. But it remained the disaster of a century.[9]

Certainly, history could be mined for many more examples of missing and misinformation followed by political-military disaster. But the point has been made. Information distorted by senders ("the Cuban people will rise in revolt against Castro"); information misperceived or disbelieved by receivers ("if United Nations forces threaten to destroy the North Korean People's Republic, 'volunteers' from the Chinese People's Republic will enter the Korean War"); information ignored or disregarded ("Hitler will attack at 3:30 A.M. on June 22, 1941"); or information missing or unacquired ("the Government of Imperial Japan intends to launch an air attack on American military installations in the Pacific on December 7, 1941") can mean the difference between deterrence and successful defense, or debacle and defeat. There is a premium on accurate information in international politics.

International Uncertainty, Manipulated Information, and Perceptual Gaps. Statesmanship would be much more a calculating and much less a guessing game if statesmen actually acted in an environment of complete and accurate information. But this is not the case. In the same light, foreign policy formulation and execution would result in goal attainment much more often than they actually do if foreign policymakers and administrators operated in a system of a complete and accurate information. But again, this is not the case. Then too, if international politics operated in a system of complete and accurate information, fewer mistakes would be made, fewer wars perhaps would be fought, fewer at least would be lost, fewer needless antagonisms would arise, and fewer alliances would deteriorate. As noted, this is not the case.

9. Harrison E. Salisbury, "Stalinist Purges Left Wide Mark in Soviet," *New York Times,* October 3, 1967, p. 18.

For several reasons the realm of international politics is a realm of uncertainty created by missing and misinformation. First, to be in possession of complete and accurate information cannot be the case in international politics because concealing, distorting, confusing, and suppressing information are traditional, and still very productive, tactics in the diplomatic game.[10] Second, secrecy and the suppression of information are required for the maintenance of national security. Third, the dissemination of biased information is at the heart of international propaganda programs, and propaganda tactics are assuming even more central and sophisticated roles in states' external activities.[11] Fourth, even an international politics of utter candidness and openness would remain a politics of missing and misinformation, since communications barriers and perceptual incongruences among statesmen and peoples would persist to distort or obliterate international messages.

1. When the satirist notes that "a diplomat is an otherwise honest man who goes abroad to lie for his country," he is actually stating—although in a humorous and exaggerated way—a fact of international politics. Deception and delusion certainly do not describe the full breadth of diplomatic activity. But they are nonetheless parts of the statesman's repertoire. In diplomacy information is a resource that tends to be hoarded by its possessors—shared with or denied to others with great caution and deliberateness. At times, withholding, distorting, or even manufacturing information may work to a state's advantage in international bargaining and negotiations. Relatedly, offering accurate and complete information may at times work to a state's bargaining disadvantage. There are times, too, when the demonstrated possession of accurate information yields diplomatic capital; and there are times when offering accurate information gains favors, concessions, or perhaps more accurate information in exchange.

It is fairly standard procedure at international bargaining sessions, especially between antagonists, for statesmen to open negotiations by deliberately overstating their objectives and then projecting images of inflexibility at extreme positions. Generally, the desired effect of such dealings in exaggeration is either to gain concessions by con-

10. Fred Charles Ikle, *How Nations Negotiate* (New York: Praeger, 1967), pp. 62–68.

11. Robert T. Holt and Robert W. van de Velde, *Strategic Operations and American Foreign Policy* (Chicago: University of Chicago Press, 1960).

vincing other negotiators of one's inflexibility, or to create the appearance of great concessions offered for exchange as positions move away from extremes. In a similarly oft-practiced procedure, diplomats sham restraints on their flexibility in order to fortify their bargaining positions. Western diplomats in Cold War negotiations, for example, have—when it was convenient and tactically appropriate—claimed restraints imposed by domestic public opinion and electoral politics. Relatedly, Communist diplomats have time and again claimed binding and narrow instructions from foreign offices and party leaderships. Whether such claimed restraints are real, is immaterial. What is important is that other negotiators believe they are real and consequently concede the positions they buttress.[12]

Of course, too, outright prevarication for diplomatic advantage is certainly not unknown. False promises and assurances have been widely used by would-be aggressors to "buy time" so that military preparations could be completed. At Munich in September, 1938; at Paris later that year; and in Moscow in 1939, Hitler offered assurances of peace and nonaggression to Great Britain, France, and the Soviet Union respectively. Yet, in the ensuing two years, all three of these states came under Nazi attack. Diplomatic "covers" have been used to enhance the impacts of surprise attacks, as was the case with Japanese-American negotiations that remained in progress right up to the time of the Pearl Harbor attack. Certainly, also, we must include among examples of unscrupulous deceptions the occasions connected with the Polish Question in World War II and the Hungarian Revolt in 1956, when, in both instances, the Soviet Government lured foreign leaders to Russia on pretexts of negotiations and subsequently placed its "guests" under arrest.

2. While diplomatic advantages in manipulating and distorting information contribute to uncertainty in international politics, requirements for secrecy in national security affairs create additional information gaps. States typically classify or attempt to keep secret information bearing on the preparedness, size, armament, and especially the deployment of their military forces, as well as on other elements of their national security apparatuses. The reasons for the suppression of such information are obvious. First, full and accurate information about the status of a state's security establishment could become an invitation

12. Fred Charles Ikle, *How Nations Negotiate*, pp. 123–126.

to attack by an aggressor who concludes his own advantage after coming upon such information. Moreover, the dissemination of information about armaments could destroy a state's technological advantages in this area. Full information about a state's military potential could undermine diplomatic bargaining positions buttressed in claims of military strength, or such information could expose a state to political-military "blackmail," or such information could even facilitate sabotage operations by subversive elements. More subtly, however, concealing accurate information about military might opens the way for disseminating misinformation which can be used to political-military advantage. As long as a state effectively conceals its true military might, it has opportunity to symbolically inflate it (or very rarely deflate it) to suit diplomatic situations. In short, when military secrecy is maintained, bluffing is facilitated.[13]

Until the advent, during the last ten years, of orbiting reconnaissance satellites and other long-range surveillance devices, certain strategic and tactical advantages rested in "closed societies," such as totalitarian dictatorships, where the secrecy of information bearing on military force levels, armaments, and deployments could be strictly maintained. Contrariwise, marked disadvantages rested in "open societies," where perceptive newspaper reading, attention to political oratory and debate, technical acquaintance with scholarly works in strategy and defense, and simple roaming of the countryside, could reveal almost the whole of a state's security posture. Clearly, the "open society" in such situations is more vulnerable to attack than the "closed society." But even more important, statesmen of the "open society" are denied the opportunity to symbolically inflate their military capabilities for diplomatic advantage, while statesmen of the "closed society" can bluff whenever diplomatic conditions invite the tactic. Between 1957 and 1962, for example, the Soviet Union created an image of superiority over the United States in Intercontinental Ballistic Missiles (or, more accurately, the United States created the image and the Russians did nothing to alter American beliefs). The "missile gap" raised Soviet world prestige, caused great consternation in the United States, injected extraordinary caution into American diplomacy, significantly altered the directions of American defense

13. Thomas C. Schelling, *The Strategy of Conflict* (Cambridge: Harvard University Press, 1959), p. 23.

spending, and entered directly into the 1960 presidential election campaign. However, when data on Soviet missile development were finally procured and assessed in the mid-1960's, it turned out that the "missile gap" had been a myth.

The new developments in electronic surveillance have at present significantly reduced the military and related diplomatic advantages to "closed societies." It must be remembered, though, that information about foreign policy-making processes, military-political designs, intra-elite debate, popular dissent or consensus, and the like in other countries is as valuable as information about military forces and deployments. As far as the former are concerned, "open societies" remain very open, "closed societies" remain tightly closed, and secrecy still lends a diplomatic edge.

3. Information distortion and suppression in diplomatic dealings and national security matters are traditional in international politics. However, in twentieth-century international politics these age-old techniques of information control have been supplemented by voluminous disseminations of biased information in the form of propaganda. Currently, all major powers, and a good many lesser states as well, operate overt and covert propaganda agencies, whose dual function it is to advertise and extoll qualities of the propagandizing state while deriding, embarrassing, and condemning that state's rivals and enemies. In contradistinction to traditional flows of international communications through government-to-government channels, propaganda is channeled from governments directly to populations in other states. Its purposes range from attempts to nurture popular affinities and sympathies for foreign causes and policies, to attempts to bring popular domestic pressures on foreign governments, to attempts to foment rebellion to bring down foreign governments.[14]

While international propaganda programs are not wholly unprecedented, twentieth-century initiatives, political circumstances, and technological developments have greatly enhanced the effectiveness of propaganda techniques. First, modern technological breakthroughs in mass communications have rendered all states penetrable to information flowing from the outside. Radio transmissions know no political frontiers (most smaller states cannot afford expensive jamming

14. Andrew M. Scott, *The Revolution in Statecraft* (New York: Random House, 1965), *passim*.

equipment), and printed matter can be reproduced and overtly or clandestinely disseminated in billions of copies. Second, and perhaps more important, peoples are now more exposed to foreign propagandizing attempts than at any other time in history. More people own radios; more people are literate; more people are clustered in more urban areas than during any previous era. But third, and most important, while it would be overstating the point to say that mass populations are accurately informed about political affairs, people are today more politically aware, attentive, and participant; more expectant of government responsiveness; more able to influence governments, and more prepared to exert influence than ever before.

... public opinion is playing an increasingly important role in a great many nations. Even in countries where decision-making has not been democratized, the likes and dislikes, the wants and fears of the public are receiving increasing attention. In an earlier era, when decision-making tended to be the exclusive province of a monarch, a strong man, or a tiny elite, there was little point in trying to achieve access to the population as a whole since it was almost devoid of influence.[15]

Hence, the twentieth-century propagandist has more sophisticated equipment, more assailable audiences, and better prospects for effectiveness than ever before.

Propaganda messages are not always or necessarily items of misinformation. United States Information Agency (USIA) programs designed to acquaint foreign peoples with aspects of American life and with American social, economic, political, and scientific accomplishments, for example, purvey relatively accurate information.[16] The same might be said for Soviet propaganda programs along the same lines. But the accuracies in propaganda are at most half-truths, since it is in no state's interest to display its shortcomings before the world; and it is in no state's interest to advertise the accomplishments of a rival or to emphasize the strong points of an antagonist's policies. But while most propaganda amounts in fact to the dissemination of biased information, propaganda at its worst can amount to manufactured information pure and simple, imaginatively or crudely created for political purposes. Adolf Hitler's propaganda chief Joseph

15. *Ibid.,* p. 11.
16. Oren Stephens, *Facts to a Candid World* (Stanford: Stanford University Press, 1955).

Goebbels once remarked that the most effective lie is one so preposterous that people will take it as truth in the belief that no one could possibly concoct so fantastic a story. Goebbels demonstrated the efficacy of the "big lie" for years in Germany; and his strategies and techniques remain salient in propaganda agencies in Communist China, Egypt, and elsewhere.

One net impact of propaganda dissemination from several different and contradictory sources is to raise levels of world-wide confusion. Since average citizens in countries subjected to propaganda barrages from abroad (and not infrequently from their own governments) are in no position to judge the congruence between the international political information they receive and the material referents this information is purportedly based upon, men tend to believe what is either desirable or profitable to believe, with the result that there are as many images of international actors and events as there are propaganda media. Most people simply accept their own set of images as accurate and rest satisfied. But those who recognize competing myths, and yet have no opportunity to explore material referents, face the frustrating dilemma of never knowing whether what they believe about international actors and events is really true. Therefore, while statesmen and diplomats closer to actual happenings in international affairs live constantly in a world of partial uncertainty that they largely create for themselves, the man-in-the-street, subject to conflicting propaganda messages and unable to observe happenings firsthand, must accept myth or surrender to total confusion.

4. Much that has been said in this section thus far about "information gaps" in international politics has had to do with the transmission of misinformation or the omission of accurate information. There is, however, another dimension to the problem of international uncertainty that has to do with the distinction of information in reception. Accurate information may be transmitted in the form of symbols that exactly describe or characterize given material referents; but, as noted earlier, senders and receivers may attribute different meanings to symbols transmitted. Receivers may not in fact receive all symbols transmitted, or they may even think they have received symbols that were never transmitted.

Relationships between human perception and the distortion of information are explored more formally later in this chapter so that no long elaboration need be presented here. What is directly relevant to this discussion of information gaps, however, is that international political communications are particularly easily distorted in reception for several reasons. Most obvious, in country-to-country information flows, distortions are frequently caused by language differences and translating difficulties. Often even the most skilled translators cannot reproduce identical images in two different languages because exactly appropriate words are not available. For example, the German, *Macht,* and the French, *Pouvoir,* both translate to the English, "Power." But *Macht* to the German means something slightly different from *Pouvoir* used by the Frenchman, and both mean something slightly different from "Power" used by the Englishman or American. But more important, even when words are available, and even when communicators believe they are reaching one another, their similar words evoke very different, and sometimes mutually exclusive, images. When Roosevelt, Churchill, and Stalin left the Tehran Conference in November, 1943, each was satisfied with the agreement that in the postwar era the Soviet Union should have "friendly" states along its Western frontier. Stalin, however, took "friendly" to mean Moscow-controlled, while the two Western statesmen assumed "friendly" to mean nonhostile but free and independent. Similarly, when the British Government promoted the idea of Western European federation in the late 1940's, Frenchmen, Dutchmen, Italians, and others pictured a united Europe *including* Great Britain. But the British pictured a continental federation *plus* an independent Great Britain, and the difference in images was not made immediately clear.

But after all is said about words and connotations, mutual suspicion remains the greatest distorter of international political information. Statesmen from rival powers are predisposed, almost by habit, not to believe information exchanged between them. Suspicions of duplicity lead statesmen constantly to question intentions while exchanging words, and suspicions of sinister or adventuristic intentions discredit any words, no matter how well-intentioned or accurate they might be. As noted in Chapter 8, international rivals cannot communicate effectively about peace since each suspects self-seeking intentions behind the other's peace proposals. In the same sense, statesmen from Western industrial states find difficulty in exchanging information with statesmen from newly emerging nations, since the latter suspect neo-imperialistic intentions behind offers of aid and advice. As transmitted from an industrialized nation, a message in this channel might read: "I want to help." But as received in a new state the message reads: "I want to dominate." Unfortunately, but surely, endemic international suspicions have the marked effect of changing fact transmitted into fantasy received. Duplicity and deception are so much a part of the international political game that accurate information is seldom accepted at face value and almost never accepted until elaborate measures are taken to document credibility.

INFORMATION PROCESSING AND POLICY FORMULATION

Like any basic resource, information must be allocated and processed before it can be used. In recent years, a great deal of theoretical effort in such diverse fields as computer engineering, cybernetics, neurology, public administration, and political science has been poured into isolating and systematizing phases and operations in information processing. Comparing and combining the insights revealed in this wide-ranging literature results in a fascinating theoretical picture of how information is used, and sometimes misused, in foreign policy formulation; and how it is analyzed, synthesized, and transformed in decision-making. Important parts of this picture are presented in this section. While what follows is partly the product of this author's study and reflection, credit for originality must be attributed to Karl W. Deutsch and his pioneering work, *The Nerves of Government.*[17]

Characteristics of Information Processing Systems. Upon reflection, it becomes clear that there are fundamental similarities among such apparently diverse systems as the human brain, human organizations, and electronic computers.

First, all are information-flow networks. In the brain, information flows from cell to cell; in an organization it flows from individual to individual or from office to office; in the computer it flows from linkage to linkage or from unit to unit.

Second, all are goal-seeking and decision-making systems. Human brains produce decisions about individual behavior in pursuit of personal goals; organizations produce decisions about collective goals

17. Karl W. Deutsch, *The Nerves of Government* (New York: The Free Press, 1963), pp. 75–97, 258–261.

and strategies and tactics for their pursuit; computers produce decisions about solutions to problems they are programmed to seek.

Third, all of these systems filter and select information according to set criteria of relevance and usefulness. From all information received by sensory organs, the brain selects only that information useful for the pursuit of behavioral goals; from all information about its environment, the organization selects only that which is relevant to performing its assignments; from all punched columns on data cards, the computer selects only those containing data relevant to solving its programmed problem.

Fourth, all of these systems operate by combining selected new information received with information already held in storage, and all put out ("output") further new information produced by comparing and combining intake ("input") data with stored data. The brain combines new information with information stored in the memory; the organization combines new information with information stored both in members' memories and in filing cabinets; the computer combines input data with data contained in its program.

Fifth, all of these systems are self-monitoring and can "feed" on their own information and behavioral outputs. Connections with the sensory organs permit the brain to receive information concerning the results of decisions made and executed. Organizations use information about the results of past policies to guide future policy formulation. Computers can be programmed to use the solution to an initial problem as input data for solving later problems.

Similarities among information processing systems suggest that it should be possible to model the information-processing operation abstractly. Such a model must depict and interrelate five basic phases in information processing:

I. *Input*—during the initial phase, new information is channeled into the decision-making system via instruments or agencies analogous to human sensory organs, or computer *input* devices.

II. *Selection*—following the initial input phase, information is scrutinized for accuracy, relevance, and priority. That which is deemed valid, useful, or important is channeled on to decision-making centers, while that which is deemed false, useless, or unimportant is destroyed, discarded, or stored.

III. *Decision-making*—this phase consists in assessing selected

FIGURE 10.1 A SIMPLE INFORMATION–PROCESSING SYSTEM

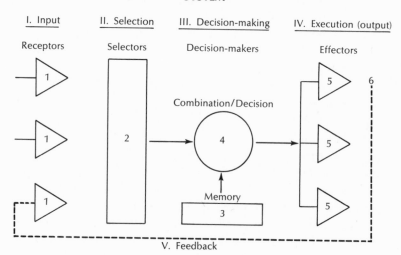

information in the light of previously stored information concerning the programmed goals and past experiences of the system, and in producing new information to direct action toward goal-seeking. In the computer, for example, the machine electronically scans its program to determine what to do with new information, and when appropriate handling is determined, it activates handling processes.

IV. *Execution Output*—once decision-making produces directives for action, these directives must be transmitted to executing agencies, analogous to human muscles, where information is transformed into action.

V. *Feedback*—once action is taken, the result of that action becomes an item of information to be channeled back into the processing system. The "feedback-loop" permits evaluation, adjustment, and re-action, much in the same way that a thermostat operates a temperature control system by adjusting to the results of past directives to turn off or turn on the heating unit to which it is connected.

Figure 10.1 is a modified and greatly simplified reproduction of Karl W. Deutsch's model information-processing system.[18] Arrows

18. *Ibid.*, p. 259.

map the directions of information flow, and numbers and labels indicate the sequential phases of information processing:

Tracing the flow of information through the diagrammed system, we see first that information is taken in by monitoring agencies or *receptors* (1); evaluated for relevance usefulness or priority, or otherwise screened or filtered (2); transmitted to decision-making centers, where it is compared and combined with data already stored (3–4); transmitted to executing agencies or *effectors* and transformed into action (5); and "fed back" in the form of new information about the impacts of the action (6).

Information Processing and Foreign Policy. The model information-processing system is easily concretized in terms of the foreign policy-making process. Foreign policy is, after all, the product of a goal-seeking human organization (or, occasionally the product of a single goal-oriented human mind); and one can easily identify components and phases of policy formulation to match the boxes, circles, and arrows of Figure 10.1's information-flow model. The model's *receptors* become foreign service officers, intelligence officers, ambassadors, liaison officers, unofficial observers of foreign affairs such as news correspondents, or even electronic devices such as orbiting reconnaissance satellites. Similarly, the model's *selectors* become men charged with evaluating incoming information, determining relevance and priorities, and passing items of significance to decision-makers. Among selectors, we could include embassy personnel, country and regional desk officers, military and civilian intelligence analysts, or again unofficial actors such as newspapermen and their editors. *Decision-makers* at area #4 in the model were defined and characterized earlier in this book. As defined, they are those individuals empowered to commit their states to courses of international political action—i.e., heads of state or governments, foreign and defense ministers, ambassadors with plenipotent powers, and the like.

Memory in the model can mean either the personal memories of the decision-makers or of members of their staffs, or it can mean the institutional memory of the foreign policy organization preserved in records, files, background reports, bluebooks, white papers, etc. The memory is the recallable guide to goals and objectives, as well as the record of experience. *Effectors* diagrammed in the model in practice become those men and agencies responsible for the *execution* of foreign policy. Included here traditionally we would have found diplomats and soldiers. But in contemporary international politics we must add such agents as aid officers, propaganda officers, intelligence agents, and—from time to time—private citizens. Finally, *feedback* in the foreign policy system is the reporting back of information about the impacts of policies—the reactions of foreign governments of other target groups, the outcomes of battles, progress made in aid programs, etc. Typically, those who act initially as receptors also act later as feedback agents. In addition, since information about domestic reactions to foreign policy programs can frequently affect the future of such programs, individuals and groups such as domestic politicians, newspaper editors, and political interest and pressure groups intermittently act as feedback agents in the foreign policy process.

Efficiency and Problems in Information Processing. A number of points emerge from the information-flow diagram and its translation into a foreign policy-making system. First, the diagram spells out the requirements for efficient information handling in foreign-policy formulation. These include: accurate, complete, and objective monitoring at the input stage; accurate and relevant selection at the filtering stage; thorough evaluation, relevant recall, and appropriate prescription at the decision-making stage; accurate transmission of directives and exact compliance at the execution stage; and objective monitoring and accurate reporting at the feedback stage. Second, it is also clear that both rapidity in international action and reaction, and success in goal-attainment are directly related to the efficiency of the information-handling process. Other things being equal, statesmen and staffs skilled and experienced in information processing will, with high probability, achieve their international ends more surely, with less cost, and sooner, than those unskilled or inexperienced in information processing. What is more, the flow diagram suggests that whole organizations can *learn* somewhat in the same way that individuals learn. Feedback permits the assessment of organizational behavior and allows decision-makers to judge which patterns of behavior yield rewards in given circumstances, and, alternatively, which patterns yield setbacks and penalties. Recording such experiences in the institutional memory permits later repetition of rewarding patterns and avoidance of penalizing patterns. Finally, just as an organization may learn, so too may an organization *create,* by using its memory and comparison facilities to combine and recombine information in novel ways.[19]

19. *Ibid.,* pp. 133–134.

But what the flow diagram does not, and indeed cannot, show in its boxes, circles, and lines, is that a foreign policy-making organization is an aggregation of human individuals, who, because they are human, are also prone to subjective errors. Because individuals do suffer lapses in objectivity, do make mistakes in judgment, and do sometimes defy organizational regimentation, efficiency in organizational information processing can be noticeably, and sometimes markedly, undermined.

Complete, accurate, and objective monitoring during the input phase in foreign policy information processing, for example, are both physically and intellectually impossible. No statesman or his staff (no matter how large) can pay complete attention to all parts of the world simultaneously. Monitoring, furthermore, becomes increasingly difficult as the international system expands to include new states, and as the new states expand politically to include new groups and parties. Then, to difficulties in complete monitoring, one must add problems in accurate and objective monitoring. Few individuals, no matter how well trained, have the capacity to report exact facts and observations without some bias, exaggeration, or omission prompted by professional zeal, ideological perspective, or personality. Moreover, additional difficulties are foreseeable when it is recognized that *receptors* and *effectors* are very often the same people, so that there is often understandable human temptation to report information in such a way that later policy decisions direct the kind of action that the reporting agent desired in the first place. Finally, after all of this has been said about failings in human objectivity, it must not be forgotten that for reasons explained earlier in this chapter, a good deal of the information a state receives from abroad may be misinformation to begin with.

What has been said of human errors in objectivity and judgment during the input phase of the information handling process, can be easily extended to all other phases. To offer just a few examples, selecting information for transmittal to decision-makers during the filtering process may follow from strict criteria for accuracy and documentation. But it seldom does. More often information is judged accurate or inaccurate, relevant or irrelevant, urgent or unimportant because the reviewer harbors preconceived notions about what is true or false—in which case he believes what he wants to believe and accepts or rejects incoming information accordingly. Sometimes, too, the reviewer reports to the decision-maker only that information which the reviewer knows the decision-maker wants to hear. Moreover, as one moves into the decision-making phase, problems of accuracy and objectivity become compounded under pressures of tensions and "overloads." Several urgent problems all demanding immediate and simultaneous attention and decision can exhaust the capabilities of even the most sophisticated decision-making system and consequently lead to lapses into confusion, irrationality, and generally erratic behavior. During early stages of the Cold War, for example, the Communist powers continually attempted to "overload" the decision-making systems of the Western states by launching simultaneous crises in scattered areas of the world. To move into the execution state, furthermore, is to raise numerous problems of command and control. Here, the history of international politics documents well the difficulties heads of government and foreign ministers have encountered in attempting to direct the behavior of their representatives in foreign countries, who tend often to act as independent agents rather than instructed emissaries. Even the most carefully worded and clearly outlined directive may never get executed if an effector chooses not to carry out his instructions, or if he chooses to carry them out after adding his own interpretations. General Douglas MacArthur's defiance of Washington during the Korean War is one case in point here, but this list could be extended *ad infinitum*.[20]

It has not been the intention here to suggest that humans should be replaced by machines in the interest of greater efficiency in information processing. The point is rather that efficiency in information processing can be extremely difficult to attain—a point, incidentally, well worth remembering by anyone who aspires to the role of foreign policy analyst and critic. A further point is that given the uncertainties and information gaps surrounding the typical statesman and his staff, any increment in the efficiency with which information is gathered, evaluated, and processed is also an increment in a state's capacity to act effectively in international politics. Differential international political power, then, stems not least from differential efficiencies in information processing.

20. Richard Rovere and Arthur Schlesinger, Jr., *The MacArthur Controversy* (New York: Farrar, Straus and Giroux, 1965).

PART FOUR
INTERNATIONAL POLITICS IN THE
MID–TWENTIETH CENTURY
ENVIRONMENT

CHAPTER ELEVEN
CHARACTERISTICS OF THE
CONTEMPORARY INTERNATIONAL
ENVIRONMENT

ACCORDING to the design outlined in Chapter 1, analysis and discussion in Parts I, II, and III of this book were focused successively on actors, goals, and resource requirements in international politics. What remains to be done in this concluding section is to place some of these "whos," "whats," and "hows" of international politics in a dynamic setting. Comprehensive analysis of international political systems in operation should include comparisons of interaction patterns and environmental conditions during a number of eras in international political history. However, time and space considerations limit this section's main discussion to interactions in the contemporary (i.e., post-1945) international political system and environment.

In broad overview, there are marked similarities between international politics in our day and politics in past eras. States remain the predominant international political actors, as they have for several centuries. Goals have varied in emphasis and concrete definition from era to era, but the listing—self-preservation, security, prosperity, prestige, and peace—remains constant. Moreover, the "mixed-motive" nature of the international political game, unequal distributions of power and wealth, patterns of alliance and counter-alliance, the recurrence of imperialism and war, endemic suspicions, time-tested diplomatic styles, and the quest for peace tend to prevail in every era. These are certainly with us today.

In several significant ways, however, the present international system is different from anything that has gone before. Some of these differences are quantitative or differences of degree. For example, philosophical or ideological incompatibilities have always contributed to international tensions and dissensions. But the contemporary world is particularly highly charged ideologically. It is split between East and West, North and South, along major ideological lines, and fragmented too within East, West, North, and South around questions of ideological orthodoxy. Second, international organization and cooperative efforts above the state level have always been themes in international politics, and established organizations have intermittently been parts of the international environment in the past. However, intergovernmental and supranational organizations have proliferated in unprecedented numbers in the contemporary era. It is only since World War II that international organization has gained nearly universal legitimacy, and it is only since the early 1950's that such organizations have begun to dilute state sovereignties and measurably influence the course of international politics. To take a final example, the disarmament theme in international politics has a history dating from the ancient Chinese state system in the sixth century B.C.; and disarmament schemes in one form or another were initiated, or at least seriously proposed, in every major era in international political history. But what is different about disarmament today is the degree of urgency attached to the theme, the degree of persistence with which the objective is pursued, and the cumulative nature of arms control agreements recently concluded.

Over and above the differences in degree that set the contemporary international system apart from past systems, are many completely unprecedented factors that lend contemporary international politics a new, more complex, and unsettled quality. First, the thermonuclear military environment of contemporary international politics is without precedent. Classical elements of military strategy are fading into obsolescence, and new strategies dictate new tactics for using new weapons. Closely related to the nuclear revolution in weaponry is today's unprecedented gap between military power and political influence. Never before have major military powers been able to influence one another so little politically, and never before has the relationship between military weakness and diplomatic strength proven so close. In addition to the unprecedented military characteristics and diplomatic setting of the contemporary system, one must note that the present system is larger, in terms of numbers of states acting, than it has been since the eighteenth century, and it is now global, with sovereignties scattered across all major continents, as it never has been before. Moreover, while the fact of increased numbers has raised the probable volume of international interaction to unprecedented levels, the accomplishments of modern technology have greatly raised the actual volume of such interaction. Not only are more governments today in continual contact with one another, but more people in more countries are more aware of one another than ever before.

Finally, few, perhaps no, systems in the past have been as thoroughly penetrated as our contemporary system by expectations of evolution, revolution, and change. No government today is committed to maintaining the world political, economic, military, or ideological status quo. All embrace philosophies of change (some in a reactionary direction to be sure); all are pursuing policies promoting change; all expect rapid change in the short run (10 years) and momentous change over the long run (25–50 years). There have certainly been transitional eras in international politics before. But has there ever been an era where change was so consciously and universally recognized, so universally accepted as a part of international politics, and so ardently promoted, as in our era?

Themes of change pervade the several chapters in Part IV. Chapter 11 is an attempt to isolate and trace the international developments and trends that produced the most salient characteristics of the contemporary international environment. Relatedly, Chapters 12, 13, and 14 focus on specific features of the contemporary international environment, and on probable evolutions into the future. Chapter 12 introduces the military aspects of the nuclear age in a discussion of nuclear weaponry, strategies, and tactics in nuclear deterrence; and of problems and accomplishments in the diplomacy of arms control. Discussion in Chapter 13 then turns to the expanding international system, the internal and external problems of the new states, the politization of poverty, and the widening North-South gap. Finally, Chapter 14 gives contemporary treatment to contemporary international organization, with special emphasis upon the United Nations. It assesses the role, impacts, and possible future of political organization above the state level.

THE CONTEMPORARY INTERNATIONAL ENVIRONMENT:
POLITICAL ADJUSTMENTS SINCE 1945

At least three basic changes in world politics followed directly from World War II. Each of these had a profound effect in shaping the contemporary international environment. First, after several centuries of ascendance, Western Europe collapsed, in the course of World War II, as the center of world politics, the center of diplomatic influence, and the center of world economic and military might. Second, the collapse of Western Europe, the experiences of World War II, and the "bomb" thrust the United States to world economic and military predominance and Western political leadership after 1945. Third, the chaos that followed in the wake of World War II opened opportunities to Soviet foreign policy. The U.S.S.R. rose to the occasion and made notable political and ideological gains in many areas of the world.

The Collapse of Western Europe and Its Repercussions. For several centuries before our own, international politics was a politics of interaction between and among Western European states. The United States, by its own design, had remained largely irrelevant to world politics through the first 150 years of its history. Similarly, Russia was a part of European politics; but the Czarist Empire was as often as not assigned a secondary role of poor, weak, Eastern cousin. As for the rest of the world, prior to 1945 most of it was a part of one European overseas empire or another; and the few noncolonized states in Asia, Africa, and Latin America played minimal roles in global affairs (with twentieth century Japan the notable exception). Western European ascendance, therefore, was a traditional "given" in international politics.

But this changed after 1945. Different historians trace Western Europe's decline from different causal factors and different points in time. Some, for example, find harbingers of catastrophe in the pathological nationalisms aroused in Western Europe during the nineteenth century. Others see doom forecast in the resource depletions of World War I. Still others lay stress upon the debilitating economic problems of the 1930's. Where most historians concur, however, is in the fact that material and human exhaustion were at the roots of Western European decline. The massive mobilization, expenditure, and subsequent destruction of Western Europe's men and materials during

World War II was the Continent's *coup de grace*. The war left Western Europe physically ruined, bankrupt, significantly depopulated, hungry, and in despair. Almost every major European country that participated in the war lost nearly a generation of its young men, and a large part of its industry and economic infrastructure. Governments lost their capabilities to administer to populations; populations lost their confidence in government. At the war's end, Germany was rubble and had ceased to exist as an independent state. Italy, too, had been a major battlefield and had been consequently reduced to ashes. Frenchmen and French property had fallen victim to German invaders, French partisans, and Allied liberators respectively. Great Britain had mobilized completely during its "finest hour" to emerge from the struggle victorious but drained of power. No Western European country had any functional military establishment remaining at the war's end. In a half-century of internecine warfare, consummated in the battles of World War II, Western Europeans destroyed their capacities to act as major powers in world politics.

The impacts and repercussions of the collapse of Western Europe were revolutionary, both inside Europe and without. Most important, the end of European power signaled the end of European colonialism, and the dissolution of European overseas empires. This dissolution made way for the entrance of scores of new states into the international system. While the most dramatic image of colonial liberation is the picture of violent uprisings and successful revolutionary campaigns against foreign overlords, the more common case histories of passage from colony to independent state after World War II are stories of planned withdrawals and peaceful transfers of sovereignty. Certainly, some colonial peoples snatched their independence by force of arms, and certainly too the early Japanese victories dented the myth of European invincibility and encouraged colonial rebellions. But in most cases colonial independence followed from European realizations that home-country resources were no longer sufficient to provide effective protection and administration for colonial areas. Decolonization was a European concession to European weakness. Lacking the willingness and material ability to expend scarce resources for continued colonial maintenance and control, the European powers— some willingly and some reluctantly—abandoned their empires. Whether colonization perpetuated economic underdevelopment is open to controversy. But there is no question about the fact that decolonization created the "underdeveloped world" as a new international political force. New states, new problems, and new politics emerged as parts of the contemporary international environment.

Another major impact of the collapse and prostration of Western Europe after World War II was the marked dampening of European nationalisms. Immediately, and negatively, this had the effect of undermining popular confidence in European governments, disseminating despair and disgust in old-style statesmanship, and setting populations emotionally adrift toward anarchy. But the rejection of nationalism, the hard-learned lessons of intra-European warfare, and the literal destruction of states also produced the more positive and longer lasting impact of awakening aspirations for Western European unity, cooperation, and integration. In a tragic, though very real, way the destruction of Western Europe as a system of selfishly independent states, and the dampening of peoples' attachments to traditional political authorities and national symbols, was a precondition for the cooperative European unity that is so conspicuously a part of the contemporary international environment. Overstating the point only slightly, one can argue that Europe's destruction in the 1940's unleashed the drive toward regional resurgence that produced the newly powerful Europe of the 1960's.

Power Vacuum and American Ascendance after 1945. As European power evaporated between 1939 and 1945, the United States became the world's political-military center of gravity. It would hardly be accurate to say that the United States *stepped* into the power vacuum created by the destruction of the Axis states and the prostration of the European allies. If anything, the United States *fell* into its world leadership role. Ascendance was gained by default. American policy-makers had harbored no designs for world political preeminence after World War II, framed no plans for world economic centrality, had no desire to maintain the military instrument forged during the war, and nursed no aspirations for a role as guarantor of international stability. Yet, of all combatants in World War II, only the United States emerged physically unscathed. To be sure, the struggle had taken over one-quarter million American lives. But no American cities were destroyed; no internal production, distribution, and consumption facilities were ruined; and no postwar reconstruction costs stifled American economic progress or reduced American military potential.

The United States emerged from World War II unprecedentedly prosperous, far advanced scientifically and technologically, and prepared, as no other state was, to continue acting in international politics. The war, too, had spurred nuclear research in the United States, led to the unleashing of atomic power, and ushered in the nuclear age. Only the United States possessed the facilities to produce atomic weapons in 1945, and this monopoly over "the bomb" became the symbol of American ascendance during the early years of the nuclear era. Hence, the United States was thrust into world leadership after World War II because no other state was able to assume the role. Journalists in 1945 were quick to dub the dawning postwar era "the American century" in world politics.

But just as the United States was unprepared for its sudden rise to preeminent power, so too was this country inexperienced in the responsibilities and involvements that followed from its ascendance. The immediate postwar era, therefore, was a period of radical adjustment in United States foreign policy. Traditional American policies of international aloofness and isolation had to be reversed, not because the United States courted world power, but because the world courted United States power. Americans could not "pack up and go home" after World War II as they had after previous foreign wars. To do so would have left economic chaos and political anarchy throughout Western Europe and much of Eastern Asia. Nor could the United States continue to adhere to its traditional policies of avoiding entangling alliances. To do so would have left Western European and Asian peoples virtually undefended and easy prey to new aggressors. Nor, finally, could the United States abandon the new international organization its statesmen had worked to create during some of the war's darkest hours. Responsible segments of the American government and American public opinion realized that this country's aloofness would have stifled the United Nations just as surely as it had crippled the League of Nations. In sum, after 1945, Americans could no longer sit back and observe world politics from their continental fortress, and dart intermittently into and back out of the international political game. With American ascendance, world politics became American international politics; with foreign dependence upon us, world problems became American problems; and with economic and military predominance, world stability became American responsibility. United

States superpower became a part of the contemporary international environment.

The Communist Challenge and the Cold War. American preeminence after World War II did not go long unchallenged. Hitler's invasion of the Soviet Union in June, 1941, had forged an allied coalition among Russia, Great Britain, and the United States that was from the first an alliance built of necessity. It was a partnership lacking in common goals, however—a negative cohesion *against* Germany and without common positive purposes. Therefore, the early postwar euphoria of international cooperation and East-West goodwill died abruptly when it became clear to Western statesmen that the Soviet Union had taken the opportunities provided by social, economic, and political chaos and Red Army occupation to install Communist governments throughout Eastern Europe, and to weld the East European states into a Soviet empire, military bastion, and possible stepping-stone to the domination of Europe. Historical analysis has not yet clarified whether Soviet moves in Eastern Europe were parts of a prefabricated Stalinist grand design, or whether these were simply opportunistic thrusts through which Stalin moved pragmatically to take advantage of Western short-sightedness and Eastern European prostration. Whichever was the case, the result was the same:

From Stettin in the Baltic to Trieste in the Atlantic an iron curtain . . . descended across the Continent. Behind that line lie all the capitals of the ancient states of Central and Eastern Europe. . . . The Communist Parties, which were very small in all these Eastern States of Europe, have been raised to pre-eminence and power far beyond their numbers, and are seeking every-where to obtain totalitarian control. Police government is prevailing in nearly every case, and so far . . . there is no true democracy.[1]

By the end of 1948, seven Eastern European states had come under Communist control; a Communist regime had been installed in northern Korea; Greece faced an armed Communist rebellion; and France and Italy were in some danger of toppling to strong indigenous Communist movements. The year 1949 saw the defeat of Nationalist forces on the Chinese mainland, Chiang Kai-shek's flight to Formosa, and the consolidation of the Chinese People's Republic under Mao

1. Winston Churchill, "Speech at Westminster College, Fulton, Missouri," March 5, 1946, as quoted in Bruce Bliven, *The World Changers* (New York: John Day Company, 1965), p. 123.

Tse-Tung. That same year, the U.S.S.R. set up the German Democratic Republic, whose territory embraced what had been the Soviet zone of occupation in eastern Germany. Finally, Communist Viet-Minh forces in French Indochina fought French legions to a stalemate in 1954 and the Democratic Republic of Vietnam (North Vietnam) was established shortly thereafter. By 1955, then, a Communist empire, united in common Marxist goals and implacably hostile to liberal democracy and economic capitalism, sprawled across the Eurasian landmass.

As the Soviet Union expanded outward across the weaker states on its periphery and simultaneously forged the Moscow-Peking Axis, the government of the U.S.S.R. set to rebuilding destroyed Russian cities and revitalizing the disrupted Russian economy. Meanwhile, Soviet scientists—with some help from German expatriates and the Russian espionage network in Great Britain, Canada, and the United States—launched into nuclear development. The Russians exploded an atom bomb in September, 1949; a hydrogen bomb in 1952; and then set to work on a ballistics missile program, the results of which amazed the world in 1957 when the Soviet Union placed the first artificial earth satellite—Sputnik I—into orbit. By the mid-1950's then, the U.S.S.R. politically, ideologically, and economically dominated a huge empire stretching from Berlin to Hanoi. In addition, the Soviet Union had become the second most highly industrialized and economically powerful state on earth. The Russians had broken the American nuclear monopoly, mustered massive conventional forces to complement their nuclear capacity, and were racing toward ascendance in the field of guided missiles. Soviet might and their expansionist ideology combined to confront the United States and its allies along the Communist periphery with a new and awesome challenge.

It is unnecessary to go into great detail here in tracing the consolidation of the Western world in the face of Communist challenge. The American alliance system, the Korean War, Western "containment policies," and Western political coordination during countless, and largely fruitless, encounters with the Soviet Union at diplomatic bargaining tables, are all well documented and thoroughly explained in most Cold War histories. What is important to point out in the context of this chapter is that exclusive American ascendance, and absolute military predominance after World War II were short-lived. With the rise of Soviet power and the spread of the Soviet empire, the world political center of gravity bifurcated from one center in Washington to two poles, one in Washington and the other in Moscow. Thus, the hopes for lasting world peace that had been held high in 1945 were dashed by 1949; and between 1949 and 1955 there were real fears of an East-West explosion into World War III. However, the functional parity in American and Soviet nuclear armament and delivery capacity that emerged by 1960 quelled fears of "hot war," as East and West accepted a tense peace founded in mutual nuclear deterrence, or, as some have described it, a "balance of terror." Since the mid-1950's East and West have settled down to a tense "peaceful coexistence" characterized by military caution in direct confrontations (subject to intermittent lapses into "brinkmanship"), a modicum of diplomatic cordiality (subject to intermittent "freezes"), but ceaseless and intense ideological and economic competition designed on both sides to woo and win over the governments and peoples in the uncommitted "third world." The Cold War of the late 1940's and early and middle 1950's, in which imminent danger of world military conflagration lurked just beneath the adverse diplomatic surface, is largely over. But the more subtle Cold War of trade, aid, partisans, and propaganda remains a central feature of the contemporary international environment.

A Bipolar or Post-Bipolar Environment? Had this chapter been written a few years ago, I might have been fully content to leave my readers with a loose bipolar model for the contemporary international system—i.e., an international system composed of two superpowers centered within respective spheres of interest and with various much less powerful uncommitted states distributed between the polar spheres of interest. Though this loose bipolar picture of the world system is still the most accurate picture, several factors have blurred its definiteness during recent years.

First, there have been a number of adjustments in the relationships between superpowers and their allies that add up to modifications in the previously hierarchical structures of the Western and Eastern blocs. On the surface it appears that fragmentation within the Western bloc has been much more marked than in the Eastern bloc. Western European economic independence from the United States has been consolidated and buttressed in the success of the Common Market. Western European assertions of political independence from the United States as reflected in French strivings toward a moderating role between superpowers, in West Germany's new and enthusiastically pursued initiatives toward East Europe, and in Great Britain's movements closer to the Continent and away from the Anglo-American "special relationship," are becoming more common in the Western camp. Furthermore, conflicts within NATO over nuclear sharing, France's withdrawal from integrated NATO commands, the *force de frappe*, American reluctance to maintain force levels in Europe, and the general diminution of the military threat from the East have all contributed to lessening the once strong military interdependence in the American sphere. None of this is to say that the Western alliance is disintegrating or that it will shortly disappear. What has happened, as a result of many factors, is that as the basis of Western cooperation—i.e., the Soviet threat—has weakened, the terms of cooperation have changed. Unity in the West now follows from the assertion, recognition, and accommodation of the separate national interests of all of the major allies and no longer from the imposed congruence of American and European interests. The Western bloc has loosened considerably.

But so has the Soviet bloc loosened. Making such a statement might arouse consternation in light of the August, 1968, invasion of Czechoslovakia by the Soviet Union and four of its Warsaw Pact allies, and in light of the orthodoxy of Moscow's doctrine that has marked most East European policies ever since. It is true that the invasion amounted to a forceful reimposition of hierarchical Soviet control in Eastern Europe; it indicated that Soviet tolerance for deviation from Marxist-Leninist orthodoxy is easily overstepped; it showed that what is left of the Eastern bloc will probably remain intact under strict central control from Moscow for some time to come. But let the Czechoslovakian episode and its after effects not blur the facts that (1) the Sino-Soviet split is probably irreconcilable at least in the short run and the once formidable Moscow-Peking Axis no longer exists; (2) Rumania has broken bloc political unity repeatedly in the United Nations, stepped out of Moscow's economic grip in the COMECON, and become an irritating source of *Communist* criticism for Soviet formulated policies; (3) Albania has followed the path away from Moscow paved by Peking; and (4) if Yugoslavia had any desire to improve relations with Moscow in the late 1960's, such thinking was certainly halted when Russian troops marched on Prague. Thrusts toward national self-assertiveness such as those that have loosened the Western bloc are apparent in the East too. Unity there will persist on the surface for the foreseeable future, but Moscow will likely increasingly be confronted with the choice between prolonging the appearance of unity by threats or acts of coercion, or nurturing actual unity by accommodating the separate national interests of its allies.

The second development that is currently modifying the loose bipolar structure of the international system is the rise of China in the East. For years Western analysts have been alluding to Chinese *potential* for superpower status. That potential is slowly beginning to be realized. Economically, Communist China is industrializing rapidly. Politically, Peking has severed its dependence upon Moscow, and entered into competition with her both within and without the Communist world. The C.P.R. has, moreover, struck out in unabashed attempts to export violent revolution to Asia, Africa, and Latin America; and its leadership has put the United States on warning that Southeast Asia is to be a Chinese sphere of influence. Militarily, China exploded its first nuclear weapon in 1967, and has surpassed all Western predictions in its rapid development of intermediate range and intercontinental missilery. Its already impressive strategic capability supplements the largest and best equipped land army in Eastern Asia. Possible tripolarity is clearly the implication of Chinese power ascendance. Whether and when China will be prepared to bid for superpower status; whether and when Peking will try to enforce its claim for an East Asian sphere of influence; and whether, when, and how the other two superpowers will either resist or accommodate Chinese demands, are all imponderables at present. What is clear is that if and when China reaches superpower capability and is able to enforce its superpower status, the bipolar structure of the international system will be fundamentally altered.

Summing up the course of political adjustments since 1945 means underlining the fact that World War II and its repercussions fomented a fundamental reshuffling in the rank ordering of world powers. The United States and the Soviet Union emerged as superpowers. Traditional European powers faded or disappeared. New states emerged from the demise of the great empires and entered to crowd the world arena. But their weakness has thus far rendered them objects rather than subjects in international politics. The world system in 1970 was a system of superpowers, blocs, and peripheries—a loose bipolar world. Yet a good deal of evidence suggests either that the political adjusting of the postwar era is not yet over, or that a new phase in adjustment has already begun.

REVOLUTIONS IN THE WORLD ENVIRONMENT

If the political adjustments of the postwar era appear revolutionary, the technological, demographic, economic, and social environment in which they have taken place has been even more revolutionary. In a sense, almost every aspect of mid-twentieth century life is revolutionary when compared with modes and trends that characterized living just a few decades ago. Three revolutions, however, are having or will have profound effects on international politics during this last half of our century.

First, there has been a basic revolution in military technology— the nuclear revolution—and a related revolution in military strategy and tactics to accommodate the new weaponry. But the nuclear revolution is only one phase of a more sweeping scientific revolution that has altered both modes of living and life expectancy itself.

Second, and relatedly, the mid-twentieth century faces a demographic revolution, a population explosion, of unprecedented proportions and with unprecedented implications. We stand a good chance of having about seven billion people on this planet by 2000 A.D., and we are already unable to adequately feed a significant proportion of the three billion people with us now. Scarcity therefore will likely become an increasingly significant theme in international politics.

Third, many segments of many populations in many countries today are in the throes of a psychological revolution—a fundamental shifting of perspectives on life, society, and government that comes in the wake of the technological movement toward modernity. We may call this revolution a "revolution of rising expectations," or, more pessimistically, a "revolution of rising frustrations." The attitudinal phenomenon is the same: peoples that have lived for centuries in ignorance, poverty, and subjugation—and expected nothing different—are today recognizing possibilities for better, richer lives. They are demanding change and betterment from their governments, and the political pressures that are created are having far-reaching impacts upon international politics.

The Scientific Revolution. That we live in an intensely scientific age hardly needs documentation. The very word "science" evokes deference whenever it is used; the scientist likewise gains respect almost everywhere he goes. An aura of eminence has surrounded scientific activity since the seventeenth century. But the "explosion" in scientific research, discovery, and technological application is a twentieth-century phenomenon. Ninety percent of all the scientists that have ever lived are living today. Similarly, in 1960 more than 80,000 different scientific journals were published, whereas only about 2,000 such journals existed in 1850, and fewer than 1000 existed in 1800.[2] In the realm of applied science, technological innovations introduced in the industrialized countries during the past fifty years have made each decade a new era in living styles and standards.

What have been the impacts of the scientific revolution on international politics? To answer this question fully would require writing another book. But in an oversimplified way—and speaking only of science, technology, and international politics during the last few decades —it is possible to list impacts under two broad headings: (1) the impacts of science and technology in general, and (2) the impacts of modern military technology in particular.

On the one hand, science and technology have greatly enhanced men's physical capabilities for communication. Today governments based thousands of miles apart may exchange messages in a matter of minutes and emissaries in a few hours. Today, too, citizens in many countries may hear or read about, or even watch events in distant parts of the globe while these events are actually happening. Modern communications technology has stepped up the pace of international politics by facilitating instantaneous reactions among governments; it has revolutionized diplomacy by tying emissaries tightly to their home bases; and it has heightened the salience of international politics within national populations by providing vivid and continuing education in foreign affairs. Some would hope that the continuing high-volume flow of information about world developments reaching citi-

2. Bruce M. Russett, *Trends in World Politics* (New York: Macmillan, 1965), pp. 11–12.

zens via mass communications facilities will someday weld the world population into a single community. We may doubt this prognosis; but still we can note that as a result of mass communications, more mutual awareness and mutual attentiveness exists among the peoples of the world today than ever before.

Science, too—applied in technologies of industry, agriculture, and medicine—has greatly enhanced the power of many states: first, by increasing efficiency in the use of natural and human resources; second, by improving the quality of human resources; and, third, by offering solutions to domestic scarcity problems in some states so that more resources might be allocated to foreign policy pursuits. All of this adds up to increased capacities for action in international politics for some states and a livelier, faster-moving, more involved international politics than ever before.

In another dimension, science and technology have become commodities for international exchange, sought after by the economically underdeveloped states, and readily offered by industrialized states— especially with political "price tags" attached. Procuring external technical assistance, or, if you will, "buying" science and technology, has come to rank high among the foreign policy priorities of many of the new states. But, on the other side of the coin, exporting science and technology has come to rank high as a political instrument by major-power antagonists because technical assistance can be used as a political lever. Science itself has become an international political tool.

Scientific and technical projects are today among the most important bases for international cooperation. The betterment of living standards through technical progress is a point of common interest that even political antagonists can recognize and exploit. Consequently, recent years have seen a proliferation of international organizations and other bilateral and multilateral cooperative schemes built about scientific projects and problems in such areas as nuclear development for peaceful purposes, space exploration, oceanography, international communications and transportation, and weather prediction. Such ventures are usually considerably removed from international politics. But cooperation in common scientific interests does influence the atmosphere of international politics since it hedges against utter estrangement between governments and peoples and helps to blunt the edges of political bitterness. Our era is certainly one of the most conflict-ridden periods in the history of international relations. But it is also an era that surpasses all others in the volume and variety of international cooperation. Man's current preoccupation with scientific progress is a prime reason for the present upswing in international cooperation.

When all is said, however, it must be recognized that the greatest and most direct impact of science and technology upon international politics has been in modern weaponry. Most spectacularly, the power of the atom has exponentially escalated the coercive capabilities of certain states. It is difficult for the layman even to imagine the results of nuclear bombardment. One warhead in the 10-megaton range (appropriate for many missiles in both United States and Soviet arsenals) can produce utter desolation within a 9-mile radius; a 20-megaton bomb annihilates anything within a 20-mile radius from the blast center; the 100-megaton weapon that former Soviet Premier Khrushchev boasted about would probably destroy an area 60 miles across. These figures fall into dramatic perspective when it is noted that the most powerful "blockbusters" of World War II had a blast radius of only one-tenth of one mile—and these spread no lethal radiation and started no all-consuming fires miles from their blast centers. Because of many contingencies concerning attackers' strategies, weather conditions, warning times, and the extent and effectiveness of defense preparations, it is difficult to say anything very definite about the probable loss of life in a nuclear attack. Casualty estimates for different kinds of nuclear attack upon the United States range from 20 million to 160 million dead (even "counter-force" attacks mean tens of millions dead); and economic recuperation estimates, barring irreversible ecological shifts in the balance of nature, range from 10 to 100 years.[3]

Still, the introduction of nuclear weaponry is only one contribution of modern science to military technology. Equally remarkable and awesome have been technological enhancements to speed and accuracy in aerial bombardment. A Polaris missile, for example, can be fired from beneath the surface of the ocean, travel at a speed of several hundred miles per minute, and strike and destroy a small target three thousand miles distant. (And in the arsenals of the nuclear superpowers missiles of the Polaris variety are considered slow and inaccurate!) Modern missile technology has become so sophisticated during the past twenty-

3. Herman Kahn, *On Thermonuclear War* (Princeton: Princeton University Press, 1961), p. 20.

five years that the contemporary stockpiles of the nuclear superpowers include missile weapons that vary in operational range from a few miles to several thousand miles, that vary in delivery mode from missiles launched from terrestrial pads to missiles launched from orbiting satellites, and that vary in warhead size from a few pounds of chemical explosive to the nuclear equivalent of several million tons of TNT. At the time of this writing several smaller states have already deployed their own missile capabilities. The United States and the Soviet Union, meanwhile, are preparing to deploy hard-to-imagine systems of anti-missile missiles and multiple warhead vehicles.

Highlights from the rest of the picture of contemporary military technology include electronic sophistication in military intelligence and reconnaissance undreamed of two decades ago. Strategic deployment and targeting now depend heavily upon data transmitted from orbiting satellites; submarine and anti-submarine warfare amount today to matching of computer against computer; counter-insurgency operations employ such devices as infrared gunsites and photographic equipment, sound amplifiers and odor detectors. Logistical capabilities have developed to the extent where division-sized units can be moved thousands of miles in a few hours and where massive armies can be supplied effectively and continuingly from bases thousands of miles from their fighting front. Finally, in conventional firepower, one soldier can today fire more rounds per minute (and theoretically destroy more enemy soldiers) than could 10 soldiers in 1913 and 2000 soldiers in 1850.[4]

The most obvious impact of modern military technology upon international politics shows in the superpowers' reluctance to use the most sophisticated of their conventional weapons, and in their dread and avoidance of situations that could force the use of nuclear weapons. A tacit agreement among major powers (save for Communist China) that there can and must be no nuclear war currently overrides and conditions the international political game. This consideration influences international political tactics, in which competitors tend to compete indirectly rather than directly, to accommodate rather than deliberately frustrate one another in crisis situations, and to continually postpone or circumvent their problems and incompatibilities in order

4. Hans J. Morgenthau, *Politics Among Nations,* 4th ed. (New York: Alfred A. Knopf, 1967), pp. 358–359.

to avoid risks of military collision. While blunting competition at the superpower level, the awfulness of modern weapons has fostered cooperation also by raising the salience of arms control and disarmament issues to points where common interests in survival override ideological incompatibilities. For all of its dreadfulness, the balance of terror has given us an international politics of caution, and of relative reason and respect at the superpower level.

More than this, the sophistication of modern weapons has provoked —at least in some countries—a revolution in thinking, planning, and acting both in military strategy and in the relationships between war and diplomacy. War is clearly no longer "a continuation of diplomacy by other means," since nuclear war gains no political stakes. Hence, the nuclear threat, the ultimatum, and "gunboat diplomacy" have fallen or are falling from international political discourse both at the superpower level and in relations between superpowers and weaker states. The threat of nuclear coercion at the superpower level gains few political ends since such threats tend to be incredible in proportion to most political ends sought. Similarly, threats of conventional coercion are also low in major-power/minor-power political play-offs—first, because some minor powers may be able to match major powers in conventional capability in localized theaters, and also because strong major-power conventional moves threaten escalation toward nuclear war. The result then has been a deemphasis upon military factors in international persuasion and bargaining—a blunting of the brute force component in international politics—and a reemphasis upon negotiation, mediation, and pacific settlement. If we exaggerate slightly, and at the same time admit some striking exceptions, it can be argued that contemporary international relations— at both the superpower and superpower/minor-power levels—are a good deal more reasonable and "civilized" than was the case fifty years ago.

While modern military technology may have injected a note of civility based on fear into superpower behavior, the same, unfortunately, cannot be said for political-military relations at the minor-power level. In their relations with one another, the smaller states maneuver in a perceived international environment that lacks the enforced cautions imposed by nuclear risks. At the same time, many of these states possess, parade, and use conventional firepower that is several technological generations advanced over World War II qualities. Fervent nationalism, traditional disputes, and technologically sophisticated conventional warfare capabilities combine in small-state relations to produce highly volatile political-military situations and relatively frequent, and unusually bloody, conventional wars. Looking backward from the time of this writing to the end of World War II, the author has counted over fifty small-state wars, most of them internal wars to be sure, but most of them also extremely destructive in lives and property because of the sophistication of weapons used. It would appear then, that while advanced military technology has sobered relations among superpowers, modern weapons capabilities have oppositely encouraged smaller states toward greater willingness to fight in pursuit or defense of their interests.

In summing up other impacts of modern military technology upon contemporary international politics, the obvious fact that modern weapons in and of themselves have heightened tension and dread in international relations should be added. Regardless of how well political issues that might precipitate violence are handled, the spiraling arms race in doomsday weapons adds an unsettling element of impending disaster to our international politics. Second, it cannot be overlooked that modern weapons are extremely expensive and tend to drain resources that might be used for more productive external and internal undertakings. Furthermore, the greatest burdens in defense expenditure naturally fall upon those states which can least afford modern weapons—for example, India, whose economic development has been set back approximately ten years by military necessities in defense against a perceived Chinese threat. Finally, and most disturbingly, concerns with defense against the "lightning" wars dictated by the mobility and high firepower of modern weapons have attracted men's attentions to continual preparedness for war, thus turning the world into a collection of large and small powder kegs. While each state may perhaps feel separately secure in this armed-camp environment, a sober student of the laws of probability may be greatly alarmed.[5]

The Demographic Revolution. Alarmed also must be any student interested enough in world affairs to spend a few contemplative hours paging through the *United Nations Demographic Yearbook.* Almost

5. See, for example, Anatol Rapoport, *Fights, Games and Debates* (Ann Arbor: University of Michigan Press, 1960).

any sampling of the demographic reportings on Asia, Africa, and Latin America exposes the extent of the population explosion:

—If present trends continue, the projected world population for the year 2000 will range between six and seven billion people.

—If present trends continue, the populations of at least ten under-developed countries will double their 1968 levels during the next seven years, and ten more countries will likely follow suit by 1980.

—If present trends continue, well over half of the people in under-developed countries will be under fifteen years of age when this book goes to press; and marriage and conception rates in these countries will be moving toward a level of 60 percent higher than in 1960.

—If present trends continue, populations will be outstripping food production in the underdeveloped countries by 26 percent in 1975.

—At present more than twelve thousand people die of starvation daily.

The blatant picture that the statistics paint is one of increasing pop-ulation and decreasing food supplies; and—as in so many scenarios of human misery—the dark picture is darkest for the underdeveloped countries. Unless some miraculous (and unlikely) breakthroughs in population control or food production are made in the very near future, we must expect that a world environment of acute scarcity will prevail from the early 1970's into the foreseeable and rather distant future. Taking all factors into account, and regardless of whether one chooses to be analytical about the "population problem" or emotional about "impending catastrophe," one is almost forced to draw conclusions about the future in terms of aggravated malnutrition, starvation, and prolonged famine. "Today the people are already here who will cause the famines." [6]

So much has been written on the population crisis in recent years that it is hardly necessary to go into detail here concerning the roots of the problem. In overview the crisis has two dimensions: one con-cerned with reasons for the population increase; the other, with reasons for lagging food production. [7]

Population growth in many non-Western countries has moved out of control since 1946 primarily because public health programs in these countries have reduced death rates rapidly and dramatically.

6. William and Paul Paddock, *Famine 1975!* (Boston: Little, Brown, 1967), p. 20.
7. *Ibid.*, pp. 7–39.

Japan's death rate, for example, dropped 50 percent between 1946 and 1952. Ceylon's death rate fell by a similar proportion between 1946 and 1954. The average death rate for Latin America as a whole decreased by approximately 37 percent between 1950 and 1965.[8] Since the falling death rates for the most part index decreasing infant and child mortality, their impacts have been to greatly increase the size of the younger generation in the underdeveloped countries, and consequently to increase the numbers of childbearing women, the numbers of probable marriages, and hence present and future birth rates.

Furthermore, while rapid population growth may not have been uncontrolled growth ten or fifteen years ago, the latter has become the case through complex combinations of cultural resistance to population control, public indifference to the problem, false hopes, and ineffectual government programs. In the majority of countries under population pressure, population control programs have either not been introduced at all, or they have been introduced in principle only, or they have been introduced too late to do much good. Moreover, even the most farsighted programs have emerged all but defeated from confrontations with traditional cultural values in large families, religious taboos against artificial contraception, and people's very human tendency to love children.

Clearly, exploding population would be a problem of relatively low salience if the growing population could expect a continuing humanly adequate living standard. But as noted, agricultural output projections indicate, grimly, that food supplies presently lag behind population growth in many countries; and this gap is likely to widen in the near future. It is comforting to look toward science for new food production techniques, to hope for large-scale technology of protein synthesis, and to think about farming the seas. Surely, someday science will help to alleviate food shortages. For the present, however, and at least for the next decade of the population explosion, conventional agriculture will have to feed the world—and this task is all but impossible.

The main impediments to expanding agriculture output are the size, topography, and geography of the earth itself. In a very Malthusian sense, there are natural limits on the available arable land on this planet, and several countries have already reached their limits of agri-

8. *Ibid.*, p. 16.

cultural space and arable soil available. Where is Egypt to go, for example, now that the precious fertile strip between the Nile and the desert is under full cultivation, and now that the productivity of new lands opened by the Aswan irrigation system has been cancelled out by expanding population? Experts estimate that the world's arable land may be increased by perhaps 5 percent through irrigation, reclamation, and related conservation practices, and that some marginal lands could possibly be brought under cultivation.[9] But such efforts will hardly produce the 26 percent increase in agricultural output needed to feed the world in 1975! Then, too, intensive farming methods and increased artificial fertilization could significantly increase world food supplies. But in most countries under population pressure, the required fertilizer plants have not yet been built; intensive farming practices have not yet been taught; and where efforts have been made to improve agricultural technologies, peasant resistance to change has dashed optimistic hopes and predictions. Added to this, there has been widespread indifference toward the agricultural sector in many economic development plans. Finally, the entire problem is compounded by the fact that agricultural production in many countries is already well behind population growth, so that stopgap measures for "catching up" drain resources and complicate plans for long-range development.

Social science has not yet produced any very satisfying answers to questions about peoples' political reactions in scarcity situations. Consequently, there arises a certain theoretical cloudiness in thinking about the impacts of acute scarcity on international politics. Can we, for example, expect resignation and a "grimly bear it" attitude as governments and populations experience rationing, inflation, and famines? Or should we rather expect external strikings out in quest of resources? Probably, we might expect both. But when, where, and how remain indeterminate. More definitely, however, we can expect that the scarcity crisis will be felt (indeed it is being felt) politically in two broad theaters: (1) in domestic politics within underdeveloped countries, and (2) in relations between these countries and industrialized nations. Paddock and Paddock predict,

By 1975, civil disorder, anarchy, military dictatorships, runaway inflation, transportation breakdown, and chaotic unrest will be the order of the day in

9. *Ibid.*, p. 38.

many hungry nations—all because hunger will turn inexorably into starvation and starvation will become widespread famine.[10]

The reasoning behind this statement builds from the assumption that people will turn to their governments for solutions to scarcity problems. Governments will be unresponsive because they cannot respond. Demagogism will exploit frustrations, fire emotions, and bring down governments in recurrent cycles. Increasing social-economic stratification, intensified by the ability of the rich to eat despite scarcity and inflation, will doubtlessly lend a class-warfare element to the political volatility; and civil strife will likely take on left-right ideological overtones. In light of what we may expect for the future, there may have been prophetic elements in American reporting on the Indian food riots in 1964:

Storming mobs of angry Indians brought the southern state of Kerala to the brink of anarchy last week. Driven by hunger and prodded by the Communists, crowds looted shops and warehouses in a frantic search for food. . . . Students raced through the streets challenging police to "give us rice or shoot us." [11]

Continuing civil disorder in the underdeveloped countries cannot help but have impacts upon both the substance and the atmosphere of global politics. These impacts are being felt already. First, civil disorder in weaker states invites (and some will argue it necessitates) major-power intervention, especially when such disorder is ideologically charged. When such invitations are acted upon either for ideological reasons, or for the protection of major-power economic or military interests in underdeveloped countries, or sometimes simply out of desire to help, the results are, first, to draw major powers into complex and unpredictable domestic situations; second, to risk major-power confrontation; and, third, to drain major-power resources, usually with little output to show for vast input. More important, even when major powers choose to remain outside of civil strife in weaker states, the very existence of unstable situations and of possibilities for intervention inject strain into major-power relations, again, especially when local disorders take on ideological overtones. Disorder in the international system and the existence of potential Cold War battlegrounds challenge the delicate *modus vivendi* that today defines the

10. *Ibid.*, p. 61.
11. *Ibid.*, pp. 58–59.

tacit rules of East-West peaceful coexistence. Hence, chronic turmoil in any country is inherently destabilizing for the entire international system.

Beyond the Cold War implications of turmoil in the underdeveloped countries, one certain result of the scarcity crisis is a widening of the economic gap between the underdeveloped and the industrialized world. Economic development cannot proceed where consumption outpaces investment, as it must as population races ahead of resources. Moreover, continuing civil strife strangles hopes for economic development. According to figures offered by Bruce M. Russett, per capita income in the United States was roughly thirty times greater than per capita income in India in 1950. By 1975, and barring domestic turmoil in India, projected American income will exceed Indian income more than forty times over.[12]

The most pronounced impact of the North-South split in the international system, however, has been its unsettling effect upon the atmosphere of international relations. Resentment and suspicion stemming from envy and frustration characterize a good many of the smaller states' attitudes toward more prosperous countries, while impatience and lack of confidence mark many of the industrial states' attitudes toward the poorer countries. Ill-feeling could very well escalate in intensity on both sides of the North-South gap as the rich continue to enjoy high standards of living and many of the poor sink toward famine. This forebodes an extremely tense international political atmosphere for the foreseeable future.

The Psychological Revolution. It is ironic after having argued that the underdeveloped world is entering a scarcity crisis, that we must now argue that hunger and poverty are currently far less palatable to Asian, African, and Latin American peoples than they ever were in the past. Our era marks the beginning of the passing of traditional society in the non-Western world. In one aspect, this passing implies a commitment to modernity with all of its material trappings, technological wonders, social structures, and political ideas and institutions. But concomitantly, the passing implies a disavowal of practices and beliefs that accounted for centuries of premodern social, economic, and political stability. Significant segments of Asian, African, and Latin American populations have rejected tradition-bred antipathies

12. Bruce M. Russett, *Trends in World Politics* (above, n. 2), p. 110.

toward change; fatalistic beliefs about the futility of progress; and age-old resignations to poverty, ignorance, subjugation, and exploitation. The overriding attitude in the modernized sectors of underdeveloped societies endorses change, embraces progress, and expects betterment.

The roots of the "revolution of rising expectations" are sunk in four prominent phenomena of change in the underdeveloped world: (1) rapid urbanization, (2) improved education and increased literacy, (3) heightened exposure to mass media, and (4) awakened drives and new opportunities for mass political participation. In all of these areas, the years following World War II marked an historical watershed for the non-Western world that resulted largely from newly independent governments' efforts to foster economic development while improving the quality of people's lives.

Urbanization in the new states has been a spillover effect of several developments, including: (1) colonization, under which Europeans created administrative centers and native economies of tertiary industry grew to service European living; (2) commercialization, under which ancient crossroads and rivers and seaports grew into modern marketing centers as transportation and distribution facilities improved; (3) industrialization, under which new city-based manufacturing industries have been creating new urban labor forces; (4) intellectualization, under which Western education created native intelligentsia equipped with urban skills and urban tastes; and (5) the population explosion, under which public health measures have been so effective in the cities, especially, that natural increase by itself is contributing significantly to rapid urbanization.

More important than the reasons for urbanization, however, are its attitudinal impacts upon society. People drawn from the countryside into the city are drawn, almost literally, from one world into another. They are drawn from the extended families and webs of custom and superstition of the traditional villages into an urban world in which extended families prove economically nonviable, and in which livelihood and survival demand that time-tested rural practices be replaced by modern skills. Migrants from the countryside to the city move from slow-paced, austere environments in which fatalistic beliefs cushion hardship and familial roles guarantee security and identification, to faster-moving milieus in which self-reliance contributes to economic betterment and security and identity rest in membership and participation in new, modern, urban-based groups and organizations. Finally, moving from the countryside to the city transports a man from an environment in which information about his own society and the outside world flows slowly and in trickles, to an environment where information flows rapidly and in high volume—with the result that the new urbanite's societal and world awareness abruptly expand. In all, urbanization contributes toward breaking bonds of custom and belief that buttress acceptance of poverty, ignorance, and exploitation in traditional societies. In so doing, it mobilizes men for social, economic, and political strivings after betterment in modernity.

Literacy, education, and media exposure also serve as agents of expanding awareness. Most profound among disruptions injected into traditional societies via literacy, education, and the mass media are opportunities to compare living among strata within societies and to compare conditions among different societies.[13] Such comparisons serve, first, to make the miserable aware of their misery; second, to make them aware of alternatives to their misery; and, third, to acquaint them with the idea that betterment is possible and with tactics for promoting betterment. Once men grasp the idea that betterment is possible, continued misery becomes mounting frustration. Relatedly, change becomes first a psychological aspiration and then a political demand. Therefore, the heightening of social awareness through literacy, education, and media exposure almost invariably raises men's demands for equality within their own societies and for equality among societies of the world.

Mass political participation is both a cause and a manifestation of the revolution of rising expectations. In many of the new states the propaganda and agitations of campaigns for independence from European rule have injected thoroughly disruptive ideas of populism, democracy, and constitutional government into traditional "ruler-subject" political cultures. The new awareness that political democracy was possible has made popularly chosen and responsive government desirable. At the same time, it has made continuing unresponsive government unpalatable. More than anything else, perhaps, the infusion of Western democratic ideas and myths has raised significant segments of national populations (especially in the cities) out of traditional political apathy. Men educated to the belief that they should influence their govern-

13. Daniel Lerner, *The Passing of Traditional Society* (Glencoe: The Free Press, 1958).

ments increasingly have learned that by participation and organization, and by legal and illegal peaceful and violent tactics they *could* influence their governments. Where elections are meaningful and political organizations are permitted, voting participation and party and group activities are proliferating. Where constitutional popular political activities are suppressed, populations have taken to the streets and to the hills in violent pursuit of the political equality and influence they have come to expect.

The international political implications of the revolution of rising expectations are similar in many ways to those discussed earlier with regard to the population explosion. Rising expectations in the underdeveloped countries are on a collision course with the scarcity crisis. Many expectations for economic betterment, social mobility, and political equality are being dashed by the harsh reality of inadequate resources and little time for development. Regimes are unable or unwilling to provide the social and economic revolutions and the political reforms to accommodate the aspirations of emerging, modern-thinking populations. Ominous figures that show urbanization, education, literacy, media attention, and political organization racing far ahead of general economic development, agricultural output, foreign exchange accumulation, and social mobility, form equations for probable political upheaval in the non-Western world. Internal upheaval in the "third world" tempts superpower intervention and strains superpower relations. The rapid rise and fall of small-state governments injects uncertainty, unpredictability and instability into the international system.

CONCLUSION

Analysis in this chapter has been directed in a broad sweep over highlights of the contemporary international political system and its social, economic, technological, demographic, and psychological setting. Many characteristics of the contemporary world environment, treated quickly here, will be elaborated in succeeding chapters. From what has been said thus far, however, it is possible to compile a condensed checklist of factors and phenomena that deserve particular attention in any more detailed attempt to observe and analyze the contemporary international environment (see Table 11.1).

The horizontal subdivisions in Table 11.1 represent antecedence

TABLE 11.1. THE INTERNATIONAL ENVIRONMENT IN OUTLINE

I. *The Aftermath of World War II*	II. *The World at Present*	III. *Possibilities for the Future*
The collapse of Europe	The economic resurgence of Western Europe	European political federation (?)
The proliferation of new states	Numerous, scattered, politically unstable, economically nonviable states Scattered large and small powder kegs	Recurrent internal upheavals in small states (?) Small-state wars (?) Superpower interventions (?)
United States-Soviet bipolarity	Loosening bipolarity	A fragmentation of blocs (?)
Cold War	Competitive "peaceful coexistence"	East/West détente (?)
Arms racing	Arms racing New initiatives in disarmament	Nuclear war (?) Significant steps toward disarmament (?)
The demographic revolution	The scarcity crisis	Famine in Asia, Africa and Latin America (?)
The psychological revolution	Frustrated, politically conscious populations	An exacerbated North-South split (?) Pathological behavior from prolonged frustration (?)
The scientific revolution	Nuclear parity New initiatives in international technical cooperation	Nuclear proliferation (?) Expanded technical cooperation (?)

and subsequence rather than causality, because the causal pathways from the past to the present and into the future are certainly a good deal more complex than the outline here implies. What is most apparent from the table is that "the world at present" is in transition and that possible courses for this transition are discernible. It is also clear from the table that all of the conditions listed for the possible future cannot evolve concurrently since a good many of these are mutually incompatible (e.g., "nuclear proliferation" and "significant steps toward disarmament," "East-West détente" and "superpower interventions"). Furthermore, while some of the courses into the future, such as "expanded technical international cooperation," "significant steps toward disarmament," and "superpower interventions" can be voluntarily guided and controlled, others, such as "famine in Asia, Africa, and Latin America" and the "exacerbated North-South split" are being generated by demographic and economic forces that are already out of control. There is therefore a great deal of uncertainty even about the near future. The only clear prediction that emerges is that some of the older problems and tensions in the East-West relations may shortly wane. But these are likely to be replaced by new and greater problems in North-South relations. Asia, Africa, and Latin America will emerge as dominant centers of international political attention.

CHAPTER TWELVE
ARMS AND DISARMAMENT IN
CONTEMPORARY INTERNATIONAL
POLITICS

A GENERATION ago, military strategy received scant attention in the general study of international politics. Strategy was regarded as distant from the mainstream of the discipline. It was assumed to concern only the technical and tactical conduct of wars, and it was considered too professionally specialized for civilians to worry about very much. Hence, instructors in international politics noted only vague relationships between governments' military thinking and planning and states' political moves. Some may have assigned Clausewitz, Mahan, and Douhet as optional reading. However, most students of international politics were content to leave military strategy to the professional soldiers and its teaching, study, and development to the military academies and war colleges. But the advent of nuclear weaponry in the late 1940's and the "nuclearization" of military establishments in the late 1950's raised questions about relationships between security policy and foreign policy that the discipline of international relations could not ignore. During the past several years, therefore, problems concerning the use, nonuse, and control of nuclear weapons have become central questions in the very mainstream of international politics.

This chapter traces several nuclear arms and arms control themes as they have evolved through the decade-long (and still continuing) dialogue on appropriate military postures in the nuclear age—a dialogue, incidentally, that is as animated in the Soviet Union and Western Europe as it is here in the United States. The threefold purpose here is to underline the kinds of problems that nuclear capabilities are posing for international politics, to analyze suggested solutions to some of these problems, and in layman's fashion, to anticipate possible arms control developments in the foreseeable future.

THE "NONUSE" VALUE OF NUCLEAR WEAPONS

Paradoxically, a central theme in the development of nuclear strategy concerns the effective *nonuse* rather than the effective use of nuclear weapons. This is not to say that military planners are unconcerned with targeting, delivery, and destruction. Nor, certainly, is it to say that war plans are obsolete. What the "effective nonuse" concept implies, however, is that once nuclear bombardment is initiated, unimaginable and unpredictable destruction falls upon both the attacked and the attackers. Therefore, in both the United States and the Soviet Union, the emphasis in nuclear planning has been upon ways to build, sophisticate, deploy, display, and protect nuclear forces so that these might deter a would-be aggressor from nuclear attack. Hence, while traditional military strategy has emphasized the conduct of war, contemporary nuclear strategy emphasizes the avoidance of war.

Conceptually, deterrence is a condition wherein a potential aggressor refrains from aggressive acts because he assumes—or has been convinced—that his costs in committing aggression would outweigh any rewards he might hope to gain by it. This deterrence concept is at the heart of contemporary nuclear strategy. According to traditional tenets of military thinking, defensive weapons were conceived and designed as barriers to be placed in the paths of aggressors' advancing forces. Nuclear defense, by contrast, rejects the idea of meeting and throwing back an advancing aggressor, and relies instead upon blunting his aspiration to attack. Hence this strategy accepts the fact that an aggressor can and will reap catastrophic destruction should he decide to attack. The main function of a defender's nuclear weapons, therefore, is to persuade the aggressor against attack by promising him unacceptable costs in a nuclear exchange.

Deterrence need not be mutual. But, ironically, the condition seems most stable when antagonists command comparable destructive capabilities. Figure 12.1 illustrates some implications of unilateral and mutual deterrence.

In the unilateral deterrence pattern shown in Section A of Figure

FIGURE 12.1.   UNILATERAL AND MUTUAL DETERRENCE SYSTEMS

A. UNILATERAL DETERRENCE

Actor A	Actor B Fight (Attack or Retaliate)	Don't Fight
Fight (Attack or Retaliate)	A: Slightly damaged B: Defeated; destroyed	A: Unscathed B: Defeated; destroyed
Don't Fight	A: Defeated B: Unscathed	A: Superior in status quo B: Inferior in status quo

B. MUTUAL DETERRENCE

Actor A	Actor B Fight (Attack or Retaliate)	Don't Fight
Fight (Attack or Retaliate)	A: Gravely damaged B: Gravely damaged	A: Unscathed B: Defeated; destroyed
Don't Fight	A: Defeated; destroyed B: Unscathed	A: Unscathed B: Unscathed

12.1, it is assumed that Actor A possesses a decisive margin of military superiority over his antagonist, Actor B. The unilateral deterrence situation is clearly biased against Actor B. His only opportunity for a positive outcome is in a situation where his opponent chooses not to fight or retaliate in response to an attack. Since such restraint on A's part would be highly irrational and therefore highly improbable, the dynamics of the unilateral deterrence system work toward a conclusion at the "Don't Fight—Don't Fight" cell. Here Actor B remains deterred from action against Actor A; and Actor A retains control over the system.

But, despite the probability of a peaceful outcome, the unilateral deterrence system is inherently unstable for two reasons. First, the system includes no logical restraints upon Actor A's behavior and, second, the system leaves a possibility for pathological behavior on

Actor B's part. The system remains a "war avoidance" system only as long as Actor A refrains from militarily exploiting his superiority (what if the Soviet Union rather than the United States had been the first to explode and stockpile nuclear weapons?). Furthermore, the system remains a "war avoidance" system only as long as Actor B refrains from "committing suicide" in desperation over the promise of prolonged inferiority in a world where the will of Actor A predominates.

By contrast, the mutual deterrence pattern shown in Section B of Figure 12.1 is a considerably more stable war avoidance system both because neither Actor A nor Actor B is offered any logical basis for launching an attack, and because neither antagonist is relegated to inferiority or driven to desperation. Pathological behavior is always a possibility (comments on its probability will be offered later in this chapter). But if both the unilateral and mutual deterrence systems could be tested for stability over time, the probability of a "Don't Fight —Don't Fight" conclusion would turn out significantly higher for the mutual deterrence system.

The purpose in introducing deterrence in the abstract at this point is twofold. First, there is a great deal of difference between *deterrence as a theoretical system* such as might be illustrated with cell diagrams and tested with game theoretic reasoning, and *deterrence as a process or behavioral pattern* in international politics. Second, the relative compulsion of the war avoidance outcome from nuclear deterrence illustrated in the second part of Figure 12.1 is currently a point of controversy rather than a point of fact. Therefore, the abstract model of the deterrence system becomes an appropriate point of departure for a more detailed exploration of the deterring process, and a focal point for examining the controversy surrounding the relationship between nuclear deterrence and the avoidance of war.

DETERRING AS A POLICY AND PROCESS

The theoretical solution that nuclear weapons are more effective as deterrents than as defenders raises a number of practical problems. Foremost among these is the question of how a state should actually go about deterring an antagonist from attack. What policies will promote deterrence? What kinds of attack are to be deterred with nuclear weapons? What kind of political behavior complements efforts at nuclear deterrence, and what kind of political behavior contradicts such efforts? Answers to these questions have evolved slowly from intense policy dialogues in the United States and the Soviet Union during the last fifteen years, and these dialogues continue as technology produces ever more sophisticated and versatile weapons systems. The evolution of security policy in the nuclear age is one of the most interesting episodes in the intellectual history of our era.

From Massive Retaliation to Flexible Response. The initial American answer to the problem: "How can we best use nuclear weapons in peacetime so as to reduce the probability that they will have to be used in a war?" was the conclusion that deterrence follows when military deployment is complemented by verbal political behavior. Simply having the weapons is not enough. One must also threaten to use them; and threats must be manifest, explicit, and repeated often. In the "massive retaliation" doctrine first articulated by United States Secretary of State John Foster Dulles in January, 1954, the American Government put forth a blanket threat to retaliate (assumably with nuclear weapons) "in places of our choosing," in response to provocations ranging from a direct attack on the United States to minor Communist thrusts in grey areas.[1] The intent of the threat was clearly to deter would-be aggressors from any hostile moves anywhere by promising the nuclear bombardment of their homelands.

The "massive retaliation" threat was certainly threatening—and it was manifest, quite explicit, and repeated often. The problem was that the threat was incredible. Critics of the Dulles doctrine were quick to point out that the Russians or the Chinese were unlikely to believe that the United States would actually unleash a nuclear world war in response to an aggressive move at the Korean invasion level, or in response to a Communist coup in the Middle East or to Communist guerrilla activity in Asia or Africa. Whether the United States would actually have executed its retaliatory promise had little bearing on the efficiency of the threat. What was important was that the threat was unlikely to deter and therefore unlikely to avoid war because antagonists were unlikely to believe it. The threat became even more incredible by the late 1950's—first, because the United States refrained

1. Morton H. Halperin, *Contemporary Military Strategy* (Boston: Little, Brown, 1967), p. 48.

from its retaliatory promise in a number of "grey area" situations and, second, because Soviet capability reached the point where Russian weapons could be delivered in a strike upon the United States. At this point, with even Washington on the bullseye, NATO allies began to question American willingness to meet Soviet provocations in the critical European theater with massive nuclear retaliation.[2]

The weakness of the "massive retaliation" doctrine, and the criticism directed at it, ultimately enriched strategic thinking and policy.[3] Since credibility was clearly the missing element in the Dulles threat, thought and effort between 1956 and 1959 confronted the problem of how one goes about buttressing the "believableness" of a threat. W. W. Kaufman, writing in 1956, suggested that effective deterrence required a varied deterrent—i.e., a variety of hardware for backing a variety of threats, relevant to a variety of situations.[4] Bernard Brodie, in 1959, pointed out that deterring an attack on one's homeland was a special and specific kind of deterrent situation, and therefore required special hardware and a "second-strike" threat.[5] On another aspect of the deterrent problem, Robert E. Osgood argued in 1957 that the deterrence of conventional thrusts required conventional capabilities and a threat to meet conventional force with overwhelming conventional force.[6] Here, Osgood recognized that conventional warfare situations were again special and specific kinds of situations and deterrence therein required tailored handling. Hence, as the strategic debate evolved, the idea of a flexible response slowly took hold. It became clear that effective deterrence depends upon a credible threat, and that credibility in turn depends upon a matching of capability (i.e., hardware) and threat to different kinds of provocative situations.

Nuclear strategic thinking for the early 1960's was systematized and formalized with the publication of Herman Kahn's monumental work *On Thermonuclear War*.[7] Many of Kahn's principles entered officially

2. André Beaufre, *NATO and Europe* (New York: Vintage Books, 1966), pp. 48–80.

3. Bernard Brodie, *Strategy in the Missile Age* (Princeton: Princeton University Press, 1959), pp. 248–263.

4. W. W. Kaufman, "The Requirements of Deterrence," in *Military Policy and National Security*, Kaufman, ed. (Princeton: Princeton University Press, 1956), pp. 12–38.

5. Bernard Brodie, *Strategy in the Missile Age*, pp. 202–210.

6. Robert E. Osgood, *Limited War: The Challenge to American Strategy* (Chicago: University of Chicago Press, 1957).

7. Herman Kahn, *On Thermonuclear War* (Princeton: Princeton University Press, 1961), pp. 126 ff.

into United States security policy with the Kennedy Administration and the beginning of Robert S. McNamara's tenure as United States Secretary of Defense. Synthesizing a great deal of the strategic dialogue of the late 1950's, Kahn distinguished among three kinds of deterrent situations:

—Type I Deterrence: the deterrence of a direct attack on the homeland;
—Type II Deterrence: the deterrence of extreme provocations short of direct attack on the homeland;
—Type III Deterrence: the deterrence of minor provocations.

Each type of deterrence, Kahn suggested, necessitates the formulation and articulation of a particular kind of deterrent threat. Each kind of deterrence further requires particular weapons and modes of deployment. Table 12.1 summarizes the situation-threat-capability interrelationships for the various types of deterrence.

TABLE 12.1. REQUIREMENTS FOR VARIOUS TYPES OF DETERRENCE

I. *Situation*	II. *Example*	III. *Threat*	IV. *Hardware*
Type I Deterrence: Deterrence of direct attack on homeland.	Soviet first strike on United States, or vice versa.	Threat to retaliate; promise of unacceptable damage to enemy even after he delivers his first strike.	Invulnerable second-strike capability; hardened or mobile facilities able to withstand or evade enemy first strike.
Type II Deterrence: Deterrence of extreme provocation short of attack on homeland.	Soviet attack on Western Europe, or United States attempt to "liberate" Eastern Europe.	Threat to preempt; promise of a first strike even if initial provocation is at conventional level.[a]	First-strike force in constant state of readiness. (May be same hardware as for second-strike force, but invulnerability not prerequisite.)
Type III Deterrence: Deterrence of minor provocations	Small conventional thrusts of Korean War variety; guerrilla activities; externally directed coups and revolutions.	Threat to meet conventional or guerrilla force with overwhelming force at nonnuclear level.	Conventional capability including special forces for counterinsurgency; massive airlift capability.

[a] Nuclear parity and second-strike capability for both the United States and the Soviet Union have made this threat all but obsolete. In current American strategic thinking, extreme provocations will be met by "controlled" or "graduated" responses as discussed below. As also noted below, the result of the introduction of the "controlled response" strategy is to remove the last element of "massive retaliation" from current thinking and to blur the distinction between Type II and Type III deterrence.

During the early 1960's in both the United States and the Soviet Union, expensive efforts were made toward building second-strike capabilities. Both governments apparently recognized that the threat to retaliate (and hence the ability to deter an attack on the homeland) was credible only to the extent forces could survive an enemy first strike. Similarly, both governments also recognized that few of the weapons and delivery vehicles that comprised the arsenals of the 1950's could survive an enemy first strike; and even those that did happen to evade destruction would very probably have been stopped in their retaliatory efforts by the air defense system of a prepared enemy. Consequently, the early 1960's saw notable qualitative and quantitative escalations of the strategic arms race, with emphasis on both sides on hardened missiles, and terrestrial, airborne, seaborne, and submarine mobile launchers, as well as on invulnerable command and control systems. Currently the United States possesses a highly credible second-strike capability and the Pentagon "assures destruction" of the Soviet Union even after a Russian first strike on the United States. But there is every reason to believe that the Soviet second-strike capability is currently also such as to "assure destruction" of the United States.

Nuclear Parity and Controlled Response. In the middle 1960's a number of developments and events combined to provoke a review and revision of American nuclear strategy. First, East-West functional nuclear parity greatly jeopardized the credibility of the American Type II deterrent threat to defend Western Europe. With the Soviet ability to bombard the United States assured, Western Europeans and Americans (and surely the Russians) asked whether the United States would still be willing to retaliate massively to a Communist provocation in Europe. In short, did Washington believe that the defense of Western Europe was worth the devastation of the United States? Second, the escalating Vietnam War raised concern about the limits of escalation, about the sanctity of the conventional-nuclear threshold, and about the implications of possibly crossing this threshold. Many questions were asked about the intensity of the nuclear war that would result from an initial crossing of the conventional-nuclear threshold. Would it be possible to limit a nuclear war? Or would the step over the threshold be a step into oblivion? Third, and relatedly, government-sponsored and private strategic research in the early 1960's was increasingly directed toward the question: "What if nuclear deterrence should fail?"

The result of the strategic dialogue that evolved in response to these new concerns about the defense of Western Europe and the conventional-nuclear threshold, was the Pentagon's conclusion that nuclear war did not necessarily have to be "spasmodic" total war. Nuclear war could be limited by deliberate, planned, and controlled targeting (i.e., counter-force rather than counter-city), by controlled destructive potential, and even by direct communication and negotiation with the enemy during or between nuclear salvos. Herman Kahn was quick to support and elaborate ideas about control, limitation, and variety in nuclear conflict in his study *On Escalation*, published in 1965.[8] Here Kahn argues that there are at least twenty-four conceivable levels or stages of nuclear conflict that lie conceptually between the conventional-nuclear threshold and spasmodic total war. (See Table 12.2)

The "controlled response" doctrine currently espoused by the United States represents the completion of a full circle in strategic thinking. Initial strategic emphasis upon the conduct of war gave way in the 1950's to primary emphasis upon the deterrence of war, and this preoccupation with deterrence has now begun to give way to a renewed emphasis on the conduct of war. The rationale of "controlled response" dashes the myth that nuclear war must be impossible because it is "unthinkable." It suggests rather that nuclear war may break out, and that if such should be the case, efforts should be made to limit damage, to achieve military advantages, and to keep channels of political communication open so that fighting may be terminated short of mutual annihilation. The "controlled response" scheme further postulates that there are ways to limit nuclear war. These include retaliation in kind rather than massive retaliation, selective bombardment for the purpose of communicating resolve rather than for destroying the enemy, and controlled targeting designed to destroy an enemy's military capability rather than his population and civilization. Executing a controlled-response strategy implies that one should continually leave escalatory initiative and decision-making burden up to the enemy, on the assumption that he will choose to terminate rather than

8. Herman Kahn, *On Escalation: Metaphors and Scenarios* (New York: Praeger, 1965).

TABLE 12.2. POSSIBLE VARIETIES OF COERCIVE CONFRONTATION IN THE NUCLEAR AGE

An Escalation Ladder
A Generalized (or Abstract) Scenario

AFTERMATHS

CIVILIAN CENTRAL WARS	44. Spasm or Insensate War
	43. Some Other Kinds of Controlled General War
	42. Civilian Devastation Attack
	41. Augmented Disarming Attack
	40. Countervalue Salvo
	39. Slow-Motion Countercity War

(CITY TARGET THRESHOLD)

MILITARY CENTRAL WARS	38. Unmodified Counterforce Attack
	37. Counterforce-with-Avoidance Attack
	36. Constrained Disarming Attack
	35. Constrained Force-Reduction Salvo
	34. Slow-Motion Counterforce War
	33. Slow-Motion Counter-"Property" War
	32. Formal Declaration of "General" War

(CENTRAL WAR THRESHOLD)

EXEMPLARY CENTRAL ATTACKS	31. Reciprocal Reprisals
	30. Complete Evacuation (approx. 95%)
	29. Exemplary Attacks on Population
	28. Exemplary Attacks on Property
	27. Exemplary Attack on Military
	26. Demonstration Attack on Zone of Interior

(CENTRAL SANCTUARY THRESHOLD)

BIZARRE CRISES	25. Evacuation (approx. 70%)
	24. Unusual, Provocative, and Significant Countermeasures
	23. Local Nuclear War—Military
	22. Declaration of Limited Nuclear War
	21. Local Nuclear War—Exemplary

(NO NUCLEAR USE THRESHOLD)

INTENSE CRISES	20. "Peaceful" World-Wide Embargo or Blockade
	19. "Justifiable" Counterforce Attack

TABLE 12.2. Continued

18. Spectacular Show or Demonstration of Force
17. Limited Evacuation (approx. 20%)
16. Nuclear "Ultimatums"
15. Barely Nuclear War
14. Declaration of Limited Conventional War
13. Large Compound Escalation
12. Large Conventional War (or Actions)
11. Super-Ready Status
10. Provocative Breaking Off of Diplomatic Relations

(NUCLEAR WAR IS UNTHINKABLE THRESHOLD)

TRADITIONAL
CRISES

9. Dramatic Military Confrontations
8. Harassing Acts of Violence
7. "Legal" Harassment—Retortions
6. Significant Mobilization
5. Show of Force
4. Hardening of Positions—Confrontation of Wills

(DON'T ROCK THE BOAT THRESHOLD)

SUBCRISIS
MANEUVERING

3. Solemn and Formal Declarations
2. Political, Economic, and Diplomatic Gestures
1. Ostensible Crises

(DISAGREEMENT—COLD WAR)

Reprinted with publisher's permission from Herman Kahn, *On Escalation: Metaphors and Scenarios,* Fig. 3, p. 39. Praeger Publishers, New York. © 1965 by Hudson Institute.

to take the next mutually penalizing step up the escalation ladder. Hence, in the new "controlled response" strategy for the defense of Western Europe, the initiative is thrown to the Soviet Union wrapped in the Western promise that Eastern military action will be met by appropriate (not necessarily massive) Western counteraction. If the East chooses to cross the nuclear threshold, the West will cross it also; and if the East chooses to escalate so also will the West escalate, until the irrationality of mutual destruction dictates termination and a political settlement.

"Controlled response" appears a rational answer to the danger that someday someone will cross the nuclear threshold. Moreover, it responds to the fact that weapons are now available that would make it feasible to fight a limited nuclear war. Furthermore, it appears a most meaningful strategy in a situation of nuclear parity where there is common interest in damage limitation. Still, there are problems with the "controlled response" doctrine that have left it a controversial rather than a widely accepted policy. First, the doctrine has not been officially espoused by the Soviet Union, whose leaders view the idea of limited nuclear war as contrary to their major strategic interest in deterring all nuclear wars. Russia still clings officially to massive retaliation doctrines. Second, the "controlled response" doctrine has aroused considerable displeasure in Western Europe, where the NATO allies envisage their territories devastated while the superpowers test one another's resolves in limited nuclear strikes. Therefore, Western Europeans also cling to massive retaliation doctrines. Finally, while "controlled response" may be theoretically elegant and highly rational on paper, there remain practical and technical imponderables that work against the probable execution of such a strategy in a real nuclear war situation. Most important among these is the fact that effective and dispassionate civilian control are absolutely essential for the duration of a limited nuclear war. Nuclear bombardment itself jeopardizes facilities for continuing control. Human nature may well prevent dispassioned control in the midst of massive suffering and destruction.

SOME PITFALLS IN NUCLEAR THINKING

While optimism about the avoidance or limitation of nuclear war has been a main theme in the nuclear strategists' arguments during the past fifteen years, the evolving strategic theory has also evoked considerable skepticism. Most of the second thinking about nuclear "war games" seems to build from questions about the compulsions of cold logic. Different strategic critics reach skeptical conclusions about the stability of deterrent systems by reasoning from two very different premises. Some argue that nuclear war can ultimately be neither deterred nor controlled because war avoidance and control demand utterly rational behavior which men cannot be expected to continually display. Others, however, point out that the danger of nuclear war or escalation lies in ambiguities in the military balance that provide compelling rationales for aggressive behavior. In short, one school of critics argues that nuclear deterrence must fail because men cannot be expected to behave rationally forever, while the second school argues that even strictly rational considerations could lead to a breakdown of deterrence.

Nuclear Control and Human Nature. The logic linking second-strike capability to nuclear deterrence and the consequent avoidance of war is compelling. Given a defender's invulnerable second-strike capability, no aggressor's attack, no matter how powerful, can destroy his victim's ability to retaliate massively. Therefore, the most that a first strike can produce is a stalemate in devastation. Hence, logically speaking, there is nothing to be gained by nuclear attack. Similarly, as noted above, the deterrent logic of controlled response is equally compelling. Escalation automatically heightens the escalator's costs. Therefore, again speaking logically, there is nothing to be gained by escalation.

But deterrent reasoning produces restraint only when antagonists bend to the dictates of the logic of nuclear stalemate. *Continuing restraint depends upon the absence of lapses into irrationality,* in which, for example, hostility may spark obliviousness to cost, tension and impatience may induce drives toward action for action's sake, or possibly psychopathology induced or aggravated under strain may affect decision-makers' grasps on reality. Certainly, elaborate precautions are taken in the handling of nuclear weapons to mitigate the possibility and the results of human breakdown—precautions so elaborate that lapses into irrationality and resultant nuclear war are not to be expected. Still, the actual probability of irrationality in the handling of nuclear weapons is not known. ("It has not happened so far.") Moreover, what gives questioners of nuclear logic great concern is the fact that thousands of people ranging from heads of state down to military officers in tactical commands have daily opportunities to order the firing of nuclear weapons; and such opportunities proliferate as weapons systems proliferate. Even more disturbing to those dubious about human stability are the threat of nuclear proliferation beyond the present-day "nuclear club," the consequent emergence of new (and perhaps less responsible?) nuclear powers, and the related manifold increase in the number of men with access to nuclear weapons. Hence, the critics of nuclear thinking are asking whether the bet on human rationality is a wise one, and whether more intellectual emphasis might not have been directed, from the beginning, toward eliminating rather than handling nuclear weapons.[9]

The Logic of the First Strike. While acknowledging that the prophets of "doom through human frailty" have some reason for concern, other critics of nuclear thinking stress that the real cause for concern lies in the fact that men are most often rational, *and that there are conditions under which nuclear war or escalation may become—or at least appear —reasonable.* Beneath this concern is the presupposition that the advantage in a nuclear exchange accrues to the state that strikes first, *if little or no retaliation follows the first strike.* Therefore, the theoretical danger of a first strike increases in proportion to a potential aggressor's expectations of successful attack.[10] Factors that could create such expectations include: (1) difficulties a defender may have in protecting his second-strike forces, (2) difficulties the defender may encounter in launching his second strike after command and control facilities have been partially destroyed, (3) difficulties he may encounter in delivering his second strike upon an enemy who has prepared for it, and (4) difficulties he may encounter in mustering the will for a second strike, knowing that he will receive a third strike in return. In short, conditions —or perceptions of conditions—that would preclude a successful second strike could become invitations to an aggressive first strike. The reasoning here is more likely to be quantitative than qualitative since the potential aggressor will be asking how great a second strike will be forthcoming, and how great a second strike can be endured.[11] The first-strike conclusion would follow from reasoning that the defender's second strike could be endured.

Moreover, the rationality of a first strike could be enhanced by a technological breakthrough in weaponry. It could be enhanced by a "costs-gains" equation that assigns considerably more weight to political factors such as "face" than to human and material factors. Finally, it could be enhanced by ambiguous deterrent threats, "fight or capitulate" political dilemmas, inflated expectations about defensive

9. For a variety of criticisms directed at deterrent thinking see Frederick H. Gareau, ed., *The Balance of Power and Nuclear Deterrence* (Boston: Houghton Mifflin, 1962).

10. Albert Wohlstetter, "The Delicate Balance of Terror," *Foreign Affairs*, XXXVII (January, 1959), 211–234.

11. Morton H. Halperin, *Contemporary Military Strategy* (above, n.1), pp. 33–42.

capabilities, or real or unreal expectations about abilities to survive a retaliatory strike regardless of its magnitude.

Certainly there is a good deal of "devil theory" reasoning implicit in the first-strike argument. Those concerned about the danger of a first strike out of the blue must assume that whenever a potential aggressor is offered an opportunity for success, he will exploit it (and will not act as the United States did during its years of nuclear monopoly). A fairly strong case could be mustered against man's inherent and spontaneous aggressiveness. Still, it is difficult to argue that men and governments do not sometimes become devils in the heat of intense political-military crises. Therefore, while one might put little stock in paranoiac fears about attack out of the blue, the probability that the nuclear threshold will be crossed in the heat of crisis or in the spiral of escalation is not insubstantial.[12] Moreover, any conditions that promise possible success in a first strike will raise this probability.

ARMS CONTROL EFFORTS IN THE POSTWAR ERA

The urgency with which arms control and disarmament problems are approached at present, and the substance of negotiations thus far conducted and agreements thus far reached, testify to governments' uncertainties about deterrence. The international arms control dialogue has continued in bilateral and multilateral form since the late 1940's; and though the results in terms of agreements have not been especially impressive, the superpowers deserve commendation in their determination and abilities to keep disarmament efforts alive throughout the coldest days of the Cold War.

In broad perspective, the history of attempts at disarmament and arms control parallels the history of war. Men in almost every epoch of recorded history have made efforts to protect themselves against hostile neighbors by building bigger and better weapons. But men too have made recurrent efforts to protect themselves against themselves by searching for plans and schemes that would allow them to safely discard their weapons. The earliest arms accord uncovered by the author dates from approximately 600 B.C., when the Chinese states of the Yangtze Valley entered a disarmament league that resulted in a warless

12. Oran R. Young, *The Intermediaries* (Princeton: Princeton University Press, 1967), pp. 206–262.

century for the league's members. Leaping massively over the many minor and short-lived disarmament agreements intertwined in the rise of the Western state system, carries one into the nineteenth century to the Rush-Bagot agreement between the United States and Great Britain for naval limitation on the Great Lakes—the foundation for 150 years of demilitarization along the United States–Canadian frontier. Later, in 1921 and 1922, notable but unfortunately short-lived agreements concerning naval limitations in the Pacific were reached among the British, Americans, and Japanese. The Kellogg-Briand Pact of Paris in 1928 might be looked upon as a "self-control" rather than an arms control accord, but still it reflected the spirit of universal interest in the avoidance of war that motivates the continuing quest for disarmament.

Just as the disaster of World War I and the fear of World War II awakened the search for arms control during the 1920's and 1930's, the disaster of World War II and the fear of nuclear World War III have vitalized disarmament efforts in our era. Journalists' belittlement and pacifists' despair notwithstanding, there have been a number of significant formal arms control agreements since 1945. Austria was neutralized by West-East-Austrian agreement in 1955 so that at least one demilitarized buffer could stand in the path of East-West confrontation in Europe. Moreover, in the same year Western Germany, by international agreement with other Western powers, formalized its commitment to refrain from manufacturing atomic, biological, and chemical weapons. Antarctica was demilitarized by international agreement in 1959. A ban on the atmospheric testing of nuclear weapons was negotiated and signed by the United States, the Soviet Union, and over fifty other countries in 1962. The "hot line" communications agreement designed to alleviate fear of nuclear war by accident was activated between Washington and Moscow in 1963, and since that time a number of other Western capitals have also completed "hot line" links to the U.S.S.R. The United States and the Soviet Union negotiated a treaty for the demilitarization of outer space in 1967. More recent years have seen the negotiation and worldwide ratification of a United Nations nuclear nonproliferation treaty—the most far-reaching global arms control agreement thus far concluded. Another treaty establishing a Latin American nuclear-free zone is gathering ratifications in the Western Hemisphere. Most impressive of all, the United States and the Soviet Union have opened talks directed toward stabilizing the strategic arms race by limiting missile and anti-missile systems.

Disarmament Versus Arms Control. While the continuing dialogue on controlling the arms race has not produced the kind of momentous agreements that idealists might hope for, talking about the arms prob-lem over the years has greatly enlightened governments and nego-tiators concerning its dimensions and complexities. Early in the dia-logue, for example, it became clear that *disarmament* and *arms control* were neither identical phenomena nor interchangeable concepts. *Dis-armament* refers to the reduction of arsenals (i.e., the destruction of national instruments of war). *Arms control,* on the other hand, may encompass disarmament, but more generally it refers to the handling of weapons in such ways as to reduce: (1) the probability of war, (2) the needless prolongation of war, or (3) damage during war. Whereas dis-armament negotiations are bargaining sessions concerning ways and means to facilitate mutual reductions in armaments, arms control ne-gotiations may concern matters such as appropriate military deploy-ments, communications during political-military crises, inspection pro-grams, and guarantee systems. Paradoxically, arms control may even mean agreeing to increase the quality or quantity of weapons in order to buttress deterrence.

The direction away from traditional disarmament discussion toward more imaginative arms control themes was pointed at between 1952 and 1955 when it became clear to both the United States and the Soviet Union that "disarmament" in the nuclear environment had become in-feasible. During this period both countries had stockpiled nuclear weapons to the extent that no nuclear disarmament agreement could possibly have been policed. Neither side could be convinced that the other would refrain from cheating (i.e., hiding a few megatons); neither could be convinced that any inspection system could be thorough enough to uncover hidden weapons (and the Russians were not about to permit inspection anyway); and neither would take the risk of com-pletely disarming its nuclear forces as long as there remained the slightest possibility that the other had cheated. More than this, by the mid-1950's nuclear technology had developed to such an extent in both the Soviet Union and the United States that any temporary loss in capability as a result of an international agreement could have been quickly recouped as soon as international political tensions suggested abrogating the arms accord. Therefore, though the general disarmament theme is still sounded for its propaganda value, it has been clear since 1955 that there is not a great deal of sense in superpowers asking one another to give up nuclear weapons.

The nonproductiveness of the disarmament theme has had two primary impacts upon the East-West arms dialogue. First, when it became apparent that no disarmament arrangement could emerge, and that there thus was little risk of ever having to back words with actions, governments quickly went on record in favor of general disarmament in order to reap the propaganda benefits inherent in the theme. Second, and more significant, quiet efforts were begun to find new, more relevant, arms control themes that might lead to agreements that would stabilize the nuclear deterrent balance and reduce the risk of war.

Current Themes in the Arms Control Dialogue. Two themes concerned with buttressing the nuclear balance have dominated the serious arms control discussions of the 1960's:

I. The nuclear deterrent balance could be stabilized and the risk of war reduced, if arms control measures could be agreed upon that would alleviate reciprocal fears of surprise attack.

II. The nuclear deterrent balance could be stabilized and the risk of war reduced if arms control measures were agreed upon that would minimize the danger of nuclear war occurring by accident.

As noted earlier, skeptics among strategic thinkers are haunted by fears of an aggressive first strike. Some see this coming out of the blue; others expect that it could come in the heat of intense political-military crisis. The fear of surprise attack is considerably more pronounced in the Soviet Union—where idealogues are visited by specters of "war-profiting Wall Street" and "Pentagon militarists"—than in the United States. Still, the reciprocal fear of surprise attack has a spiraling dynamic wherein the United States has reason to fear that the Soviet Union will strike first, precisely because the Soviet Union fears that the United States will strike first. This temptation to preempt the potential preempter builds accumulating tension into East-West political-military relations. Therefore, alleviating the reciprocal fear of surprise attack has become a matter of common superpower concern, and a focal point for arms control discussion.

East-West arms control negotiations directed toward solving the surprise attack problem have produced few formal results largely because the proposals either irritated Soviet sensitivities about inspection, or American sensitivities about overseas military bases. Most American proposals for building mutual confidence in deterrence, such as President Eisenhower's "open skies" proposal of 1955, have called for the mutual or international monitoring of military movements. All have been objected to by the Soviet Union ostensibly because the Russians feel that inspection breeds suspicion instead of creating confidence, but actually because inspection would cancel out any strategic advantages the U.S.S.R. might gain through its ability to shroud its military movements with great secrecy. On the other hand, the Russians have suggested that fears of surprise attack could be minimized if the superpowers denied themselves launching sites and staging areas for such attacks. The U.S.S.R. has, therefore, supported designs for "nuclear-free" zones, in buffer areas between Eastern and Western spheres of interest. Moscow heralded Polish Foreign Minister Rapacki's 1957 plan for a nuclear-free zone in Central Europe, for example. The United States, however, has reacted negatively to such disengagement schemes since most plans of this variety require the abandonment of overseas bases that the United States deems essential to its security.

Though irreconcilabilities have thus far blunted the search for safeguards against surprise attacks, exchanges of views continue. On the American side, at least, there is a new, but guarded, optimism about possibilities for anti-surprise attack arrangements. The optimism stems not from Russian concessions on the inspection issue, but rather from the fact that satellite and other electronic reconnaissance technologies have largely cancelled out early Soviet strategic advantages in secrecy. The Soviet Union has little to fear from international arms inspection now that secrecy no longer yields great military advantage. Moreover, American progress in long-range missile technology has eased our reliance upon overseas bases to the point where United States arms control negotiators might begin thinking aloud about conceding parts of the peripheral system in exchange for positive Soviet moves on inspection or related issues.

Most of the progress in arms control in the 1960's has had to do with alleviating the danger of accidental nuclear war. There are a number of reasons for this. First, there is a strong common interest in preventing a war that nobody wants. Second, unilateral efforts in tightening command and control systems, perfecting delivery and detonation systems, and restraining nuclear proliferation continue in both the United States and the Soviet Union even without formal international agreements. That is, the superpowers find it less difficult to agree to do mutually what they are doing unilaterally anyway. Finally, most arms control measures appropriate for guarding against accidental war have not involved the risks and irreconcilabilities that recurrently surfaced during exchanges concerning inspection and nuclear-free zones.

With the exception of the "hot line" arrangement, which theoretically reduces the danger of inadvertent war or escalation by providing opportunity for communication and consultation before or between nuclear strikes, most anti-accident plans have had to do with nuclear nonproliferation. Here, East-West negotiating problems are reduced somewhat by the fact that the superpowers can focus upon restraining the behavior of nonnuclear states rather than upon restraining their own behavior. East and West find consensus in the belief that nuclear weapons are safest in proven, responsible hands, and in as few hands as possible, and surprisingly, a good many smaller states concur in this ostensibly condescending superpower attitude. Consequently, the first major step toward nonproliferation was the partial test-ban treaty of 1962, in which states voluntarily denied themselves the opportunity to develop nuclear capabilities by denying themselves the right to test weapons in the atmosphere. Meanwhile, the United States and the Soviet Union denied themselves opportunities to pollute the world's atmosphere with radio-active fallout, and, perhaps more important, opportunities to operationalize new technologies that require large-scale testing for feasibility and perfection.

The Treaty on the Non-Proliferation of Nuclear Weapons drafted and signed under United Nations auspices in 1968, may, if ratifications are prompt and universal, prove the most significant arms control step of the 1960's. Above and beyond signatories' commitments to halt the dissemination of nuclear weapons or fissionable materials for military purposes, the treaty assigns surveillance and control functions to the International Atomic Energy Agency; and it also embodies a superpower promise to push forward toward new agreements in arms control:

Article I: Each nuclear-weapon state party to the treaty undertakes not to transfer to any recipient whatsoever nuclear weapons . . . and not in any way to assist, encourage or induce any non-nuclear weapon state to manufacture or otherwise acquire nuclear weapons. . . .

Article II: Each non-nuclear-weapon state party to the treaty undertakes not to receive the transfer from any transferer whatsoever of nuclear weapons or other nuclear explosive devices. . . .

Article III: Each non-nuclear-weapon state party to the treaty undertakes to accept safe-guards as set forth in an agreement to be negotiated and concluded with the International Atomic Energy Agency. . . .

Article VI: Each of the parties to the treaty undertakes to pursue negotiations in good faith on effective measures relating to cessation of the nuclear arms race at an early date. . . .

Just as in the case of the Partial Test Ban Treaty, France and Communist China have refused, for reasons of national security, to consider the nonproliferation treaty. Furthermore, India, West Germany, Rumania, Japan, and others have expressed displeasure with the nonproliferation treaty both because they see in it discrimination against their peaceful nuclear development programs and because they cannot fully accept superpower guarantees for nuclear defense. While the nonuniversality of the nonproliferation agreements certainly flaws the effectiveness of the international arms control systems established, adherence by those states that have accepted the treaties does lessen the threat of nuclear war throughout much of the world.

Emerging Arms Control Issues. As has been the general pattern over the years, arms control themes continue to keep pace with both developments in military technology and with new trends in strategic theory. Presently, for instance, the superpowers stand on the threshold of a significant qualitative escalation in the international arms race. Both the United States and the Soviet Union now have the technological capability to produce and deploy comprehensive anti-ballistics missile defense systems (ABM). Both, as a matter of fact, have already deployed limited, largely experimental ABM networks around their major cities or their important military installations. The purpose of ABM defense is to limit the damage of incoming hostile strikes by intercepting and destroying enemy missiles hundreds of miles from their targets. In offensive technology the United States presently has the ability (and it is likely that the Soviet Union has this ability also) to produce a system of multiple warhead missiles (MIRV). American designs for MIRV call for a "space bus" that would roam over hundreds or thousands of miles of targeting area and periodically release nuclear projectiles. The Soviet MIRV plan, on the other hand, calls for a "roman candle" system in which a primary missile would burst as it approached a targeting area and send out a wide, mathematically plotted spray of secondary projectiles. Limited deployment of American MIRV's has already begun. The result of a MIRV strike would be to overwhelm and penetrate even the most sophisticated of ABM systems simply by putting more warheads in the air than any such system could possibly cope with. Therefore, the next escalation of the arms race can be forecast. If the Soviet Union deploys an effective ABM system, the United States will put a full-fledged MIRV system into operation—or vice versa—and the ultimate outcome will likely be two ineffective ABM systems, two terrifying MIRV systems, two momentous drains on national resources, and no increment in anyone's security. In light of expectations about the inevitable negative outcome of qualitative arms racing, both the United States and the Soviet Union expressed interest in the summer of 1968 in a new round of arms control talks focused on possible arrangements for freezing or deescalating missile development. The common interest in arms control is apparent, as evidenced by the undertaking of the Strategic Arms Limitation Talks (SALT), for example.

Two further potential arms control themes are currently emerging from American thinking concerning the "controlled response" doctrine. First, it is being argued that "controlled response" is itself an arms control doctrine because it has to do with ways for limiting nuclear war. That is, by promising retaliation in kind, as well as selective counter-force targeting, the United States is really promising to control nuclear weapons during combat. Arms controllers are suggesting that if the Soviet Union could be persuaded to accept the idea of limited nuclear war, it might become possible to formalize restraining measures through international agreement and hence to establish an arms control system for minimizing damage during nuclear war.

Second, "controlled response" thinking has raised provocative questions about the termination of nuclear war. Is it possible to stop a nuclear war short of mutual annihilation by some system of prearrangement? For example, in the event that a missile is launched by accident and strikes its target in an antagonist's territory, how could the victim be convinced that the accident was an accident before he unleashes his retaliatory forces? Or how could a superpower step out of an escalatory spiral without losing political face? Or, again, how could a victim of several limited strike-retaliation rounds convince his opponent that he could strike again but would prefer not to if political negotiations could be opened?

"Controlled response" opened official thinking about "unthinkable" nuclear war, but such thinking on the conduct of nuclear war has thus far only underlined the absence of any serious forethought about getting out of a nuclear war once one has gotten in. Several suggestions have been made, nevertheless, for prior agreements to defer settlement in nuclear wars to disinterested third parties such as international organizations, or for prior agreements to permit immediate inspection in cases of accidental firings, or for agreements to use prearranged communications channels for political contact during nuclear wars.[13] In short, the problem of terminating nuclear war is ripe for an arms control initiative. The major drawback at present, however, remains the Soviet Union's official unwillingness to admit the control and termination of nuclear war into arms control negotiations.

THE ARMS CONTROL DEBATE

Though the tone of much of this chapter's discussion of arms control has been such as to suggest that controlling weaponry is both a wise idea and a noble pursuit—especially in our era—it would be erroneous to leave the impression that everyone agrees with this point of view. Above and beyond the semitechnical dialogue concerning appropriate issues and areas for negotiation, there is a continuing fundamental debate over the worth of the whole arms control idea. One of the most fascinating features of this debate in our era is that both advocacy and criticism of the quest for weapons control follow from any number of attitudinal predispositions. Idealists, for example, may favor arms control in the belief that states will settle disputes peacefully when denied the instruments of violent settlement. But, idealists may also point out that self-denial in weaponry becomes possible only *after*

13. *Ibid.,* 50–79.

states have agreed to settle disputes peacefully. Therefore, what one should seek are political conditions for peaceful settlement rather than military conditions for arms control. Similarly, realists may argue that arms control is the only answer to the threat of nuclear war. Without negotiated restraint, the world will remain on a collision course with disaster. But realists have been prone to argue too that sympathy for arms control projects images of "softness" and thereby invites war. Finally, cynics can argue, on a basis of pessimistic interpretations of human nature and world history, that arms control agreements are foredoomed to failure and therefore are not worth the negotiating effort. Still, the cynics have also pointed out that arms control themes make good propaganda.

As Table 12.3 indicates, the arms control debate is structured in a definable set of points and rebuttals, usually based on unstated first assumptions, and all conducive to continuing talk and continuing stalemate.

Most of the entries in Table 12.3 are self-explanatory. We have all heard each of them many times. What is noteworthy however, is the extremely formalistic nature of the arms control debate. Close analysis of the different arguments on both sides of the question reveals that proponents and opponents most often conceive of arms control arrangements only in terms of formal agreements—i.e., official pieces of paper, duly and solemnly signed. It often escapes the debaters that practicing arms control, and signing and abiding by formal arms control agreements can be very different phenomena. There is, for example, a great deal of arms control in contemporary international relations that is informal and unilateral. Both the Soviet Union and the United States restricted atmospheric nuclear testing some time before a formal agreement was signed banning it. Similarly, both superpowers worked unilaterally to control the spread of nuclear weapons for many years prior to the formal drafting of the Non-Proliferation Treaty. Moreover, there are several existing arms control arrangements that depend upon bilateral reciprocity, many of which have never been embodied in international treaties. Both the United States and the Soviet Union refrain from deliberate harassment on the high seas; both refrain from hampering each other's military communications networks; both keep each other appropriately informed about developments in military technology so that exaggerated perceptions do not upset the deterrent

TABLE 12.3. MAJOR THEMES IN THE ARMS CONTROL DEBATE

I. *Critical Positions*	II. *Favorable Positions*
1. Advocating arms control is really putting the "cart before the horse." Military postures and deployments are reflections of political differences and suspicions among states. If political problems were resolved, war could be avoided, and arms control would become a null issue.	1. Arms control should be pursued regardless of underlying political tensions: a. Arms control may "buy time" so that political problems can be resolved. b. Arms control agreements may create patterns of international cooperation and mutual confidence contributive to solving political problems. c. Arms in and of themselves are sources of international tension. Controlling arms therefore eliminates an important source of international danger. d. Arms control may reduce the destructiveness of any wars that do explode from political crises.
2. Arms control is unrealistic in a hostile world. Taking one's guard down invites aggression. Security follows from maintaining military superiority over possible adversaries.	2. Trying to maintain military superiority over potential enemies is unrealistic, especially when antagonists are similarly endowed with power resources: a. Striving for superiority leads only into fruitless arms racing. b. Arms races may provoke preventive wars. c. "Superiority" is actually meaningless in an environment of mutual overkill.
3. Arms control agreements are not worth the paper they are written on. Any state pursuing its self-interest in security would be tempted to cheat on an arms control agreement. Moreover, arms control agreements may ultimately penalize states that respect international law and hence abide by treaties while antagonists gain advantages by cheating.	3. The only possible effective arms control agreements, and therefore the only desirable ones, are those that are founded upon mutual self-interest. If it is in a state's self-interest not to cheat on an international agreement, that state will not cheat. Moreover, a variety of self-enforcing arms control measures can and should be undertaken on the foundation of mutual self-interest.
4. The history of arms control negotiations with the Russians in recent years, and the paucity and relative insignificance of agreements reached, demonstrates	4. One does not move from "overkill" to complete disarmament overnight. Progress toward arms control is, after all, contrary to the entire tradition of relations

what a sham the whole arms control undertaking has been and will continue to be.

among sovereign states. Therefore, progress must be slow and uneven. Thus far it has been slow and uneven, but it has been cumulative. There is every reason to believe that states will continue to build upon the strengthening foundations already completed.

5. Arms control, if it results in reductions in weapons and weapons production, would bring economic recession at least in the United States, where defense spending undeniably buttresses the national economy.

5. With planning the American economy could adjust to greatly reduced defense expenditure. More than this, military spending is a continuing waste of vast resources which could be put to more productive domestic and international uses if arms control permitted both continuing national security and reduced armaments spending.

6. Power breeds status. Military might and display induce deference and respect in the eyes of the world.

6. Arms control is good propaganda. Willingness to halt the arms race and its apparent spiral toward disaster induces deference and respect in the eyes of the world.

balance. Then, too, careful but informal American and Soviet planning and tacit arms control agreements have been parts of all limited war situations in our era. Informal, but nonetheless heeded, rules concerning regional combat delimitation, the nonharassment of supply lines, respect for sanctuaries, and the avoidance of direct battlefield confrontation have been key factors in keeping limited wars limited. While it is true that recognition of informal arms control arrangements has undermined many of the "arms control will not work" arguments, such recognition does not really support the cases of those who favor arms control in the form of legally binding treaties and agreements.

ARMS AND DISARMAMENT IN CONTEMPORARY INTERNATIONAL POLITICS

With a marvelous economy of words, Sir Winston Churchill described East-West nuclear parity as a "melancholy paradox; but nonetheless a comforting one." [14] Most of us can agree that the nuclear era is threatening. Some among us, however, may find the deterrent bal-

14. Winston Churchill, "Defense Through Deterrence," *Vital Speeches of the Day,* XXI (March 15, 1965), pp. 1090–1094.

ance comforting; or at least not as discomforting as alternatives might be. But whether one agrees with Churchill or not, it cannot be denied that the last twenty years of conceptual adjustment to the nuclear age has been a most revolutionary era in modern intellectual history. Interactions among scientists, soldiers, statesmen, and scholars on nuclear questions have been prolific—not only in the United States, but throughout the world. Debates have been intense on questions of nuclear use and nonuse. But these have been highly focused and for the most part productive of understanding. As a result, we think we have learned to live with nuclear weapons. Some believe that we may be able to live with them indefinitely. In addition, we have most certainly learned how to use nuclear weapons if we must. Some of us hope also that we are beginning to learn how to control them.

CHAPTER THIRTEEN
THE CHALLENGE
OF MODERNIZATION

ARGUMENTS and allusions throughout this book have repeatedly linked questions of international stability to problems of political modernization and economic development in Asia, Africa, and Latin America. The fate of current efforts toward modernization in the "third world" will greatly influence the stability of our international system during the next quarter century. For the future, progress or lack of it in underdeveloped countries may make the difference between a new era of relative international calm and a new era of growing chaos, between a mellowing of superpower conflict and an intensified Cold War, and between an era of relations among stable independent states and an era of continuing overlord-vassal interactions.

The problem of modernization in the "third world" has many aspects—far too many to allow a comprehensive discussion here. Moreover, there is a good deal of merit to the argument that the uniqueness of particular countries' special problems defies any attempt to generalize or theorize about economic underdevelopment and political modernization. Still, there are important transnational patterns and similarities in underdevelopment; there are models of premodernity, emerging modernity, and modernity; there are patterns of modernization and development. These general patterns are the focus for discussion in this chapter.

For clarity, problems of the "third world" are grouped here under two headings: (1) economic problems of development, and (2) political problems of modernization. Consequently, efforts below are directed first toward outlining the economic causes and characteristics of lagging growth in per capita income. Then, the problem of economic underdevelopment is broadened by the addition of political factors and by discussions of interrelationships between these and economic conditions. Finally, in a step into prognostication, an attempt is made to sketch possible implications of the underdevelopment problem upon international politics in coming decades.

CAUSES AND CHARACTERISTICS OF ECONOMIC UNDERDEVELOPMENT

Economic development and underdevelopment are most commonly measured in terms of gross national product per capita—i.e., in terms of economic resources available to the average inhabitant in a given year. Typically the lower a state's GNP/capita, the more intense is its economic underdevelopment. In 1950, for example, India's GNP/capita was $70, Burma's was $45, Egypt's was approximately $120. In stark contrast, United States GNP/capita in 1950 was $2300, Canada's was $1750, and Great Britain's was $1200.[1] While it is not wholly accurate to say that the average Britisher enjoyed a standard of living ten times higher than the average Egyptian in 1950, since living styles in the two lands are very different, one can nonetheless observe that the average Britisher was more comfortable and economically secure than his Egyptian counterpart by a factor of considerable magnitude. So too are Americans, Canadians, and Western Europeans a good deal more comfortable and economically secure than most people in most non-Western areas. Notably, things have been this way for centuries.

The Underdevelopment Syndrome. Low GNP/capita reflects rather than defines economic underdevelopment. The measure responds and varies according to a number of interrelated conditions that go to make up what may be described as the "underdevelopment syndrome":

1. POOR ECONOMIC INFRASTRUCTURE. The typical underdeveloped economy lacks an efficient transport system, a rationalized marketing and distribution system, developed sources of energy supply, and perhaps even means of protection against ravages of nature. Lacking in infrastructure, the economy cannot match supplies with demands, cannot monitor itself, and cannot support industrialization. No steel-

1. Bruce M. Russett, *Trends in World Politics* (New York, London: Macmillan and Collier-Macmillan, 1965), p. 110.

producing plant, for example, can function in an economic environment lacking in roads, railways, storage and warehousing facilities, and adequate electric power.

2. SUBSISTENCE AGRICULTURE: PRIMITIVE TECHNOLOGY AND LOW PRODUCTIVITY. Agricultural labor and productivity figures are among the most revealing statistics on economic underdevelopment. One finds in the typical underdeveloped economy that upwards of 60 percent of the labor force is employed in agriculture. (In some countries this figure is over 80 percent!) Furthermore, due to primitive technologies, poor fertilizers, ignorance of conservation practices, and miniscule land holdings divided and subdivided over many generations by family inheritance practices, agricultural productivities per acre and per farmer are often pathetically low. In countries of many farmers and meager outputs, marginal productivity per farmer may be so low that considerable numbers of farm workers can be technically considered unemployed—i.e., making no measurable contribution to output from efforts invested. Low agricultural productivity and rural underemployment result not only in miserable living standards for farm families, but also in limited marketable food surpluses, in consequently limited capital for rural modernization, and in food supplies inadequate to support urban industrialization. Hence, in one of the many vicious circles in the underdevelopment syndrome, low agricultural productivity bars industrialization. Lack of industrialization in turn prohibits rural modernization and perpetuates low agricultural productivity.

3. LITTLE OR NO INDIGENOUS CAPITAL FORMATION. Developing infrastructure, modernizing agriculture, and building industry all require huge initial inputs of investment capital. Moreover, a great time lag must be expected between initial investments and returns on capital. But a root problem in underdevelopment lies in the fact that little or no capital is locally available for long-term investment. Subsistence agriculture generates only negligible savings that can be filtered from rural profits, turned into investment capital, and channeled into rural modernization and urban development. Then too, infant industries in the cities generally yield meager profits for reinvestment, and little in the way of taxable income that can be reinvested by governments. Hence, the underdeveloped economy requires capital for development, but generates almost none locally. States must therefore turn outward for development aid. International private investors, however, recoil

from risks involved in uncertain undertakings and long-time lapses between investment and return. Foreign governments on the other hand, do provide development capital, but seldom without political conditions.

4. LACKING ENTREPRENEURIAL AND TECHNICAL TALENT. The scarcity of trained personnel endowed with skills requisite for economic modernization is acute in most underdeveloped countries. Agricultural modernization is impossible without the assistance and guidance of agronomists, conservation experts, irrigation specialists, meteorologists, and the host of other technicians that must be involved in modern agriculture on a day-to-day basis. Similarly, roads, railways, and factories cannot be built without architects, engineers, and skilled blue-collar corps. Business, whether publicly or privately owned, cannot be run without production engineers, managers, and thousands of white-collar clerks and blue-collar operatives. Banks cannot handle and distribute capital and spur development through investment without a highly skilled professional financial community. Moreover, no one can be too optimistic about the generation of modernization skills in the absence of trained teachers and professors and a developing educational program.

Some authors have argued that the lack of skilled personnel in underdeveloped systems is the single most perplexing "bottleneck" in the underdevelopment syndrome. For example, even if development capital were to become available in adequate quantities, many states would still face the problem of not being able to put the capital to efficient use for want of trained personnel. Therefore, the first stage in many development plans calls for massive investment to enhance education in order to nurture modernization skills. But even here, such plans must include appeals for foreign teachers who will train the native instructors, who will, in turn, train the native technicians. The time lag between input and output in human resource development is immense.

5. FOREIGN TRADE DEPENDENCE AND EXCHANGE INADEQUACIES. Both symptom and cause of economic underdevelopment is the fact that preindustrial economies must turn to the outside world for their manufactured goods—not only for manufactured consumer commodities, but also for the machines to build the machines that will turn out locally produced manufactures. Industrialization must begin with the import of machine tools. But the dilemma here for the underdeveloped

country is that import capability implies foreign exchange reserves, and these in turn imply export capability. What are the underdeveloped countries to export? Some, such as a few countries of the Eastern Mediterranean, are fortunate in their ability to market petroleum in Western Europe. Still, most underdeveloped countries must rely for their foreign exchange upon agricultural sales abroad, and most depend heavily upon sales of a single agricultural export product, such as coffee, bananas, tea, cotton, rubber, rice, or cacao.

The pitfalls of agricultural exporting and single product dependence are many. First, the exporter stakes his hopes for profit upon good weather and favorable harvests. However, when the weather is too good and the harvests too favorable, world markets are flooded with agricultural commodities and prices are consequently depressed to the agricultural exporter's detriment. Then, too, since a good many of the export crops produced by underdeveloped countries tend to be semi-luxury diet items in temperate zone importing countries, purchases can fluctuate markedly in response to booms and recessions abroad. Finally, and perhaps most important, agricultural surpluses for export are dwindling in most of the underdeveloped countries currently under population pressure. In some countries land allocated to export crops is consequently being shifted to the production of locally consumed foods. Other underdeveloped countries have already become net food importers. The result of the exhaustion of export surpluses can only be the drying up of foreign exchange reserves and consequent major setbacks in industrialization.

6. POPULATION PRESSURE. The population explosion was discussed in some detail in Chapter 12. Nevertheless, it must be emphasized that rapid population increase—and especially an increase in economically nonproductive population—is a major factor in the underdevelopment syndrome in Asia, Africa, and Latin America. Very broadly speaking, the major impact of increasing population is the canceling of progress possibly made over a broad range of development efforts. Population increase means increased consumption. It means a shortening of food supplies for urban-based industrialization, and a shortening of surpluses for export. Population increase further means increased importation of consumer goods, retrenched importation of machine tools, and setbacks in industrialization. When there are few local manufacturing facilities for consumer goods, population expansion must mean en-

hancing foreign exporters' markets to the detriment of one's own development. Most important, increased consumption as a result of population explosion means reduced savings, or worse still, net nonsavings where investments are liquidated to support increasing consumption. Reduced levels of savings mean increased capital scarcity and a consequent slowdown in development programs. The only alternative to increased consumption along with population explosion is government enforced austerity. Such measures however are clearly infeasible in countries where significant proportions of the population live at the subsistence level, and there is some question whether they would be politically possible even in some of the relatively better off of the underdeveloped countries.

In overview, the perplexity of the underdevelopment dilemma stems largely from the fact that all of the conditions of economic underdevelopment are casually intertwined in feedback relationships. Each condition hence tends to aggravate all of the others to create vicious circles that either perpetuate stagnation or drive systems deeper into poverty. It is true that launching development means breaking into one or more of these circles and turning the downward spiral in reverse, but to say this is really to utter a meaningless cliché. The problem facing the typical underdeveloped country is that breaking into any vicious circle requires investment capital, and acquiring investment capital implies that at least one such circle has already been broken. In short, at the practical level, there is a world of difference between accurately analyzing the underdevelopment problem and mustering the means to begin solving it.

DESIGNS FOR ECONOMIC DEVELOPMENT

The question of economic development has an important normative dimension. All plans and programs for development are premised on the assumption that economic development is a desirable national goal. But one could ask what value there is in pursuing economic development. Why cannot conditions of economic stagnation that have persisted for centuries be allowed to continue? What is all the urgency about?

An argument could certainly be raised, and documented, to show that economic development disrupts societal tranquility and threatens political order in developing countries. For one thing, development destroys traditional patterns of life, traditional systems of authority, and traditional expectations about rewards from government and economy. Economic development programs accelerate urbanization, require education, encourage media exposure, and generally exacerbate many of the societal conditions believed to contribute to internal disorder in developing countries. Working toward economic development, moreover, raises substantial political risks for the governments of new states because development efforts may well fail after people's aspirations for betterment have been aroused. Even if development efforts succeed, governments in new states may well come under increasing pressure because development invariably creates new social classes, new patterns of socio-economic stratification, new elites, and new and powerful political groups and forces. Hence, a great deal of possible turmoil might be staved off if governments and traditional elites acted to deemphasize, dilute, or delay economic development. Some governments in fact behave precisely in this manner.

The case for economic development, on the other hand, is first a humanitarian one. Why should people live in poverty, misery, and ignorance when it is within men's power to improve conditions of living? Or why should no attempt be made to raise standards of living, even when there is a strong possibility that the attempt will fail?

Humanitarian arguments for development have strong appeal, to be sure, but most ruling elites in developing states tend to pursue economic improvement for additional, and far more pragmatic, reasons. First and foremost, economic development is the key to national independence. As long as a state remains externally dependent for aid and trade (or more desperately, for economic survival), it remains politically exposed to benefactors' requests and demands. To those haunted by specters of colonialism, imperialism, and neo-imperialism, external economic dependence means political subjugation. Hence, the drive toward economic independence is compelling. Moreover, and equally important, most elites in new states have little choice on the development question. Many governments had irreversibly committed themselves to development programs during pre-independence, nationalist agitations. Some aspiring nationalist leaders promised economic utopia after political independence. Then, too, the "revolution of rising expectations" is a transnational phenomenon so that populations tend to become infatuated with aspirations for better living regardless of whether their governments actively promote the development creed. Therefore, with aspirations already so deeply rooted within populations, the political costs from delaying development immediately outweigh the political dangers from promoting it. Finally, and significantly, deemphasizing or delaying development is an unreal alternative in many states because development is the only path away from bankruptcy or famine. The population explosion makes economic stagnation untenable because standards of living within exploding populations cannot stagnate; they can only deteriorate. Therefore, the most compelling answer to the question of development in many countries is that it is desirable because there is no choice save the one between progress or catastrophe.

Heightened Savings and Accelerated Growth. Eloquently stated by Barbara Ward in *The Rich Nations and the Poor Nations,* the central problems of economic development might be summed up as follows:

... how can under-developed countries save upwards of fifteen per cent of their national income when per-capita income is as low as $60 a year? How can the whole field of agriculture, where entrenched ways and ancient methods are most firmly set in popular imagination, be set on a new way of growth? How can farmers be brought to produce more, not only for themselves but for the market as well? Where can capital be found for all the "infra-structure" of industry, for the pre-conditions of growth itself in the shape of roads and power, transportation and harbours? How can manpower and saving be found for the most decisive element of all in infra-structure: the building up of educated manpower? In the field of industrial expansion, given the fact that resources are always limited, which industries should be developed and which should be neglected? ... Should the aim be a high return on capital immediately? Or is there a case for slower returns aiming ultimately at more balanced growth?[2]

All of these questions, as Miss Ward notes, are "perfectly concrete questions which are forced upon the leaders of the under-developed areas." But each of them also underlines the first principle of economic development: *growth follows from capital investment and sustained economic growth in underdeveloped areas requires major increments in capital investment far exceeding that permitted by savings in traditional economies.* The prime problems for developers are then first to

2. Barbara Ward, *The Rich Nations and the Poor Nations* (New York: W. W. Norton, 1962), pp. 83–84.

find new capital for investment, and second to use this capital in ways that will stimulate sustained economic growth.

The reasons for the scarcity of locally generated development capital in underdeveloped countries have already been outlined. Capital available for investment in an economy derives from savings accumulated in that economy—i.e., from profits in agriculture and industry that can be reinvested directly, or that can be taxed and later reinvested by governments. But, as noted, subsistence agriculture yields almost no savings. Nor does infant industry (or nonexistent industry) operate at profit margins sufficient to support significant expansion. Hence, the typical underdeveloped economy lacks the requisite savings to provide the requisite investment capital to sustain economic growth.

How much capital is needed to stimulate and sustain economic growth? Here, estimates vary among different economists; and needs, of course, differ according to local conditions in particular underdeveloped countries. Nevertheless, experience and analysis suggest that an economy "takes off" or moves into self-sustaining growth some time after annual capital investment attains levels ranging from 10 to 15 percent of national income.[3] As Figure 13.1 shows, with a capital/output ratio of 3:1 typical for underdeveloped countries, and an annual reinvestment of between 5 and 6 percent of national income also typical for traditional economies, annual growth in national income is sufficient only to maintain minimal living standards for a growing population. Here we conservatively estimate population growth at 2 percent per year, but it should be borne in mind that some populations in Latin America and elsewhere in the "third world" are already growing at rates exceeding 3 percent per year! The situation illustrated in Part I of Figure 13.1 therefore represents economic *stagnation*. Here, yearly increments in national income are immediately consumed by expanding populations so that no new savings can accumulate to bolster economic modernization.

Part II in Figure 13.1 illustrates economic *growth*. If our assumptions about capital/output ratios and population growth are carried over, an annual reinvestment of between 10 and 15 percent of national income *could* yield new compounded savings for further reinvestment and a consequent acceleration in the growth of national income. We

3. W. W. Rostow, *The Stages of Economic Growth* (Cambridge: The University Press, 1961), p. 37.

FIGURE 13.1. INVESTMENT LEVELS AND ECONOMIC GROWTH PATTERNS

I. STAGNATION

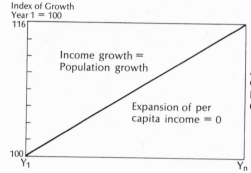

Index of Growth
Year 1 = 100

116

Income growth =
Population growth

Expansion of per
capita income = 0

100

Y_1 Y_n

Annual investment: 6% of GNP
Capital to output: 3:1
Population growth: 2% per year
Growing population
  consumes income increments

II. GROWTH

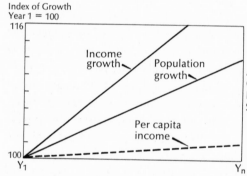

Index of Growth
Year 1 = 100

116

Income
growth

Population
growth

Per capita
income

100

Y_1 Y_n

Annual investment: 10% of GNP
Capital to output: 3:1
Population growth: 2% per year
Savings result from excess income
  growth over population growth

III. DETERIORATION

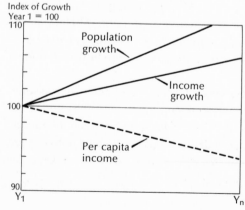

Index of Growth
Year 1 = 100

110

Population
growth

Income
growth

100

Per capita
income

90

Y_1 Y_n

Annual investment: 3% of GNP
Capital to output: 3:1
Population growth: 2% per year
Net dis-saving results from
  excess population growth
  over income growth

underline the conditional here because "takeoff" or movement into self-sustaining growth is contingent upon a number of factors. First, the accelerated accumulation of savings depends upon static levels of consumption. Standards of living cannot be permitted to rise during the early stages of development. Second, national income will not accelerate unless all, or at least most, of the new savings are in fact reinvested in economic expansion. Heightened land rents, Swiss bank accounts, and large military budgets contribute little to economic development. Third, takeoff as depicted in the diagram assumes the maintenance of at least a 3:1 capital/output ratio. This means that rapid acceleration of national income and self-sustaining growth can occur only after most economic infrastructure projects have been completed, since infrastructure investments typically yield very low short-run returns to capital. Nevertheless, once the preconditions for takeoff have been satisfied, positive differences between rates of savings and consumption can project an economy steadily toward modernization.

Finally, the situation marked *deterioration* in Part III of Figure 13.1 needs little explanation. If the growth of national income fails to at least keep pace with growing population and consumer demands, the immediate result must be a decline in living standards. The magnitude of decline that a society can withstand depends largely upon consumption levels attained before the onset of the downward spiral. Developed, industrialized societies, for example, can withstand dramatic cuts in living standards during recessions, depressions, or wars without passing into mass chaos, bankruptcy, or famine. But how much deterioration in living standards can countries such as Indonesia, Egypt, or India withstand? What will actually happen domestically and internationally when and if living standards in parts of the underdeveloped world deteriorate to below subsistence levels? To these questions, unfortunately, we have no satisfactory answers.

Prescriptions for Economic Development. An ideal program for economic development would provide a mechanism for raising local savings toward levels where self-sustaining growth becomes possible despite population increases. It would allow for moderate increases in living standards during early development, but it would nonetheless provide for control over consumption to preserve investment capital. In addition, it would provide for infrastructure development, including education and technical training during the pre-takeoff period, and later for balanced growth in industry and agriculture, and for competitiveness in foreign trade. It would attack barriers to development in traditional attitudes, landholding patterns, conspicuous consumption, and the hoarding of capital. But it would erase traditional society with caution and sensitivity. Finally, the ideal development program would be paced to avoid both the social and political pressures of extremely rapid change, and the frustrations of extreme gradualism.

Needless to say, no plan yet executed has been ideal. There is, however, a great deal to be learned from the successes and shortcomings of various thrusts at economic underdevelopment. Two patterns in particular deserve our attention: (1) Communist prescriptions for rapid development through forced savings and concentration in heavy industry, and (2) Western prescriptions for gradual development through balanced growth. Both of these designs begin with the same basic objective: to raise levels of domestically generated capital. Both, moreover, are sensitive to the same kinds of problems: poor infrastructure, low productivity agriculture, underdeveloped human resources, and traditional economic, social, political, and psychological impediments to modernization. Again, both designs for development have a record of success: impoverished Czarist Russia was transformed into a mighty industrial state in less than forty years; the agrarian United States was transformed into the world's leading industrial power in approximately eighty years. Both designs also have seen notable failures as records of U.S. aid to Latin America on the one hand and the Soviet model applied to Eastern Europe demonstrate. But despite all their similarities in objective and context, Communist and Western plans for economic development differ fundamentally in the means applied to reach economic ends.

The Communist design for economic development follows from three central principles. First, savings, and hence investment capital, can be increased during early development only by restricting consumption, even if such restriction means a short-run deterioration in standards of living. Second, initial capital investment and later reinvestment cannot be left to the uncertainties of private markets and to the whims of private financiers. They must instead be state initiated, carefully planned, and centrally allocated. By way of corollary here, the Communist would argue that *all* savings must be reinvested during development, and to guarantee this no capital can be left in private hands. Third, the Communist key to economic modernization is heavy industry, which must be built first and rapidly regardless of costs that may follow from neglecting light industry and agriculture.

Fashioning means to act out their strategy, Communist developers systematically seize and nationalize all sources of capital available in a society. In practice, and with Marxist ideological justification, this means destroying private enterprise, proprietor classes, and rural landholding strata, and transferring accumulated private wealth to the state. Next, pressure is brought to bear upon agriculture, where imposed quotas and forced deliveries at arbitrary prices (or without payment) feed growing urban labor forces. Workers are then taxed upon their food purchases, and the difference between the minimal payments to farmers and the high government controlled food prices in the cities generates investment capital to be poured into heavy industry. Similarly, all consumer goods and all turnovers in semifinished manufactures are heavily taxed to provide further development capital. The results of these various capital-generating tactics, all planned and coordinated, are first to liquidate private wealth in the society and hence to prevent any leakage of savings into nonproductive channels, next to impose immense burdens upon farmers who are forced to deliver regardless of their own food needs, and then to penalize industrial working classes by restricting consumption with high taxation. Nevertheless, the design does generate remarkable increases in investment capital. During the 1930's, for example, the Soviet Union was reportedly reinvesting between 20 and 50 percent of national income annually. Investment was directed largely into infrastructure and basic heavy industry. In all, though, development under the Communist design is lopsided and it is extremely costly in human resources. But it is impressively rapid.

While many of us in the West may react with some discomfort to the ruthless nature of Communist prescriptions and practices in economic development, it must be recognized that the Communist design holds considerable appeal for modernizing elites in many underdeveloped countries. Its first, and perhaps greatest, appeal lies in the fact that it is not a Western scheme. It does not therefore carry the stigma of Western imperialism. Then, too, it promises extremely rapid industrialization in sectors that are both symbolically impressive and economically strategic where autarky is an important economic goal.

Furthermore, it provides both an excuse and an imperative for eradicating the power of traditional landed and entrepreneurial classes that pose political nuisances for modernizing elites. It complements philosophies and practices of rigid and comprehensive central government control already prevalent in many underdeveloped states. Furthermore, it lends ego-satisfaction to new elites, justifies their exclusiveness, and embellishes their self-styled roles as socio-political guides and controllers. Finally, it offers a way to circumvent agriculture and thereby superficially removes the single greatest stumbling block to economic development.

Most Western designs for economic development, on the other hand, come face to face with the problem of agriculture. Beginning from the first principle that "if you do not change agriculture, you will not change the economy," Western prescriptions call for modernization in the agricultural sector first. Increased rural productivity through land reform, fertilizer, and technology (rather than forced deliveries) feed growing urban populations and generate investable or taxable rural savings. Moreover, agricultural prosperity opens a market for developing light industry, which in turn yields investable or taxable savings for infrastructure development, for expansion into export industries, and then later into heavy industries. In practice, development according to this Western model is seldom a strictly smooth progression from agriculture to light industry to heavy industry. It has jagged edges. Still, investment is patterned to roughly provide for such a progression.

The rub here of course is the question of where initial capital for agricultural modernization is to come from. How is the development spiral to be started? How are the fertilizer plants to be built? Where are the new farm implements and machines to come from? How are the farmers to be educated in new technologies? Most important, who is going to pay the initial bill? If external capital from foreign countries or international organizations is available, so much the better. But external capital is neither a dependable nor wholly satisfying answer to the problem.

Instead, the positive first step should probably be land reform carried out either sensibly by long-term government indemnification of large landholders, or perhaps even ruthlessly by direct expropriation. The impact of land reform is to break a vicious cycle of rural impoverishment wherein farmers annually mortgage significant proportions of their annual harvests against land rents and typically leave themselves only enough for bare subsistence until the next harvest. Landlords in turn market commodities paid to them in rents, and then typically either squander profits in conspicuous consumption, hoard capital in foreign banks, or pour funds into lucrative ventures abroad. Land reform therefore could leave marketable surpluses with farmers, bring profits to farmers, motivate agricultural improvement for the sake of higher profits, encourage agricultural cooperatives and other profit-sharing and joint investment schemes, and gradually bring traditional agriculture into the twentieth century.

But while land reform in many countries would be an act of economic logic, it would also be an act of political courage. Essentially, reforming an underdeveloped country's system of land holding means blunting or breaking the political power of the traditional landlord class—generally the most privileged class of the society. Land reform therefore meets with powerful and often overwhelming resistance, especially where landed interests comprise or otherwise control countries' governing elites. So strong is the resistance to land reform in many countries that land redistribution has become a revolutionary theme. Hence, while the economic promise of land reform is a promise of possible takeoff into economic growth, great political difficulties lend this promise a slightly utopian aura.

If agricultural development cannot be financed from savings generated in land reform, capital must come from control over consumption (through taxation or population control or both), from any slight increase in savings that might be accumulated in propitious agricultural years, from the marketing of export commodities, or from external borrowing. Interestingly, the major countries that have opted for development according to Western designs—India, Pakistan, the Philippines, and Brazil, for example—have combined many methods for raising capital for their initial inputs. India, for one, has experimented with limited land reform, instituted central controls over some areas of consumption, vigorously campaigned for birth control, nurtured export industries, and borrowed heavily from world public and private capital sources. From its combined initiatives India, until recently, has managed to reinvest as much as 13 percent of national income annually and has thereby crept slowly toward takeoff by keeping increments in income somewhat ahead of increments in consumption.

Western designs for development certainly appeal to Westerners nurtured in humanitarian creeds and democratic methods, so much so that grants and loans from the United States and other leading Western industrialized countries have frequently been made contingent upon recipient countries' commitments to Western development designs. Development programs that imply least pressure upon mass populations have found appeal in underdeveloped countries such as India and Turkey, where existing representative political institutions force government responsiveness to short-run popular needs and demands. While central planning and governmental guidance are certainly essential parts of Western designs, private economic decision-making, ownership, and capital control are also called for. Therefore, such plans have found appeal in countries such as the Philippines and Argentina, where private enterprise has been deeply rooted even in the traditional economy.

Still, risks and shortcomings in Western plans for economic development have raised suspicions and hesitations among the leaders of many underdeveloped countries. First, Western developers make no promises about rapid development. They insist, on the contrary, that development must be very gradual, balanced across sectors, and invariably somewhat cyclical. The promise of gradual growth tries the patience of leaders who have raised economic development to the status of secular religion. More than this, the long, slow development process forecast in Western designs implies prolonged external dependence upon industrial and agricultural markets, and stirs suspicions about neo-imperialism. Then, too, Western calls for the preservation of private economic sectors are seen by some leaders in underdeveloped countries as calls for the preservation of bothersome social classes and political groups and other uncontrollable and therefore unpredictable segments of society. But above all, Western development schemes lose appeal from the fact that everything builds from the promise of improved agriculture, and agriculture may well be the one "impossible" sector to modernize.

THE INTERNAL POLITICS OF ECONOMIC DEVELOPMENT

While economists must oftentimes hold noneconomic factors constant to preserve the logic and discreteness of their models, neither students of political science nor development administrators can long allow themselves this intellectual luxury. Economic development succeeds or fails in a social-political milieu. Many of the decisions taken during various phases of development tend to be influenced as much by political appropriateness or expedience as by economic logic. Hence, in the societal setting, the course and fate of economic development are sometimes determined by political adeptness or ineptitude, or, more emphatically, by political courage or cowardliness.

A development plan, after all, represents a series of choices. Fundamental among these are, first, the choice between development and no development; next, the choice between Western and Communist models or their variants, particularly the choice between autarky and prolonged external dependence; and, last, the choice between the incremental gratification of human needs and short-run sacrifice for great improvement in the long run. All of these choices could of course be translated into economic questions of capital accumulation and allocation. But they are seldom viewed in strictly economic terms by elites in "third-world" countries. For men in positions of political responsibility, many of the ostensibly economic choices become in reality choices between secure political tenure and imminent overthrow. They become tactical choices between peaceful evolution and violent revolution, ideological choices between modified Marxism and modified Liberalism, social-structural choices between egalitarianism and elitism, political-structural choices between authoritarianism and democracy, nation-building choices between integration and separatism, and sometimes even international choices between war and peace.

Economic Development and Social Reform. Allusions to the relationship between economic development and social change have already been made in various sections of this book. Still, by virtue of its importance, this relationship deserves elaboration. For a host of reasons most traditional societies are structurally ill-prepared for takeoff into economic development. Most important, typical precommercial societies tend to be highly stratified socially. Wealth is based on landholding and concentrated in small aristocratic strata. Middle classes are extremely small and economically and politically unaggressive. Social mobility based upon material achievement is rare. Moreover, rural and urban sectors of society tend to be mutually ignorant of each other; and regional, provincial, and familial exclusionism are sometimes intense.

Social milieus such as these are characterized by low responsiveness among social sectors, vast and generally accepted gaps between the wealthy few and the indigent many, low premiums upon economic achievement, high emphasis upon primary groups and generally indifferent attitudes towards the society as a whole. Clearly, the foundations of such societies must be shaken before any hope can be held out for even launching into economic development.

As noted in Chapter 12, many of these societies are already "shaking" under the impacts of the pre-independence nationalist agitations and the worldwide diffusion of the revolution of rising expectations. But there are serious questions about whether this shaking will lead to social change. Many leaders in the third world are currently standing upon a precarious political ledge. To push ahead into economic development surely means pushing ahead into social reform, and social reform largely means challenging and overcoming traditional social stratification, opening channels of social mobility based upon economic achievement, making way socially and politically for an emergent commercial-industrial middle class, according social and political status to the peasantry, and breaking the attitudinal and institutional defenses of provincialism and familism. Given the enormity of the change required, few leaders can be expected to engineer even a modicum of social change in the short run.

But, what is more, many leaders lack the political motivation or willingness even to attempt social reform. Political leadership in many underdeveloped areas continues to be either drawn from or supported by traditional aristocratic elites—i.e., those who stand to possibly lose a great deal in the course of social reform. Hence the prevailing tendency in many countries is to combine avid lip service to economic development with profound resistance to social change. The continuation of such patterns invites the likely failure of economic development. It probably also invites increasing recourse to political suppression in the face of unfulfilled economic expectations. Most seriously, it invites the formation of counter-elites drawn from underprivileged strata and strong possibilities of violent revolution under the banner of social reform.

Economic Development and Military Government. The role of armies in leading social reform and economic development in Asian, African, and Latin American countries at first appears somewhat bizarre to Westerners, in whose societies military classes tend to stand in the vanguards of conservatism. But the image of the conservative general (or, more likely, the conservative colonel) hardly stereotypes the typical military officer in the third world. First, by virtue of the demands of modern military technology, military administration, and military discipline, soldiers tend to be among the most "modern" men in many underdeveloped countries. Furthermore, by virtue of their professional responsibilities for national defense and internal order, military classes tend to be among the few elements in typical third-world societies who view national social, economic, and political problems from *national* perspectives. National development, national stability, national prestige, and national power tend to be more salient to professional soldiers than to other elite members, who may hold personal economic and social status, or class or provincial interest above national concerns. If one adds to these factors traditional military suspicions of civilian bureaucracy, inefficiency, and ineptitude, and the fact that military organizations control most of the instruments of violence in most societies, one begins to understand military temptations to seize control of state governments in the name of efficiency, development, and reform. The military coup indeed has become the prevalent form of political succession in the third world.

While it is not difficult to argue that civilian governmental failures in economic development programs and related social repercussions prompt military coups, it is relatively harder to argue that military leadership provides better programs. The grave, and by and large accurate, indictment leveled against military rule is that it tends to be invariably authoritarian and indifferent to the growth of democracy. This is certainly a serious charge on libertarian grounds, particularly in the sense that it denies peoples control over their own destinies. But political democracy may or may not be relevant to economic development. (It was not relevant in the Soviet Union!) In practice, the relationship between military rule and progress toward economic development has been ambiguous. Some military regimes, such as the early Kemal government in Turkey, and Ayub Kahn's regime in Pakistan, have stood out as modernizers, social reformers, and economic developers. Many others, however, such as the parade of military dictatorships that has marched up and down Latin America for the last century, have no records of social and economic progress to offset their political rigidities and authoritarian ruthlessness. Despite initial aspirations for social and economic change military reformers, like civilian revolutionaries, tend to fall into expedient alliances with landlords and other champions of the traditional status quo soon after coming into power. Furthermore, under military regimes extraordinary sensitivities toward external defense and internal policing can result in disproportionate channelings of scarce resources into armaments expenditures, to the detriment of economic development programs. In addition, there is a tendency for military governments to involve themselves in international affairs to a much greater extent than their resources warrant. Again, economic development programs are apt to suffer. Therefore, there is really little reason to believe that military government opens the doorway to social reform and economic development. But still, as long as this doorway remains closed under civilian regimes, aspiring colonels will remain prepared to step in to "save their countries."

Economic Development and Communist Subversion. The argument that economic underdevelopment breeds Communism has been eloquently and reasonably presented so often, that we hardly need repeat it in detail here. Marxism-Leninism provides both an explanation for misery in underdeveloped countries, and a set of promises and prescriptions for economic development with social reform. Economic backwardness, Communists argue, perpetuates as a result of the utter self-interest of the wealthy (either traditional feudal classes or capitalist middle classes). No one in these systems stands and works for the interest of the society as a whole. In the typical underdeveloped society, the Communist points out, the masses sink in poverty while privileged classes enjoy all the luxuries of life. Meanwhile, foreign investors—in alliance with local aristocrats—exploit natural and human resources with indifference to human misery and in opposition to any alteration of the social and economic status quo. Regardless of whether the Communist interpretation of economic underdevelopment is true or false in particular situations, it can be made to appear close enough to reality to generate substantial appeal among indigent populations. Communist appeals strengthen considerably where they are buttressed by the impatience that results from rising expectations and laggardly development, or by hard and real examples of upper-class resistance to change, government corruption, or foreign exploitation.

Communist prescriptions for action are uncomplicated. Development can proceed, the Communists maintain, only after the under-developed society has been socially and politically "turned on its head" through thorough-going revolution. Exploiting classes will never bend voluntarily to egalitarian pressures. Therefore, they must be undermined. Wealth must be seized and redistributed to the poor. Government must be taken from the hands of traditional ruling classes and given over to the whole society. Development can follow only from worker and peasant control over society, polity, and economy. However, worker and peasant interest is best trusted to the guiding hands and "scientific" approaches of the Communist Party. Therefore, the pathway to economic development is opened by a political act—the seizure of power by the Communist Party.

The emotional force of the Communist appeal cannot be underestimated. The revolutionary cries "strike out," "destroy," and "build anew" have radicalized and mobilized the downtrodden throughout history. Emotion, moreover, overwhelms reason. The history of political and economic modernization in the West has in fact been a history of privileged-class acquiescence in emerging egalitarianism. Development in the West is also a story of societal interest rising above self-interest or class interest. Contrariwise, Communist control has not proven a pathway to egalitarianism. If anything, Communism inserts a new all-powerful ruling class in place of traditionally more flexible classes. Moreover, Communism does not necessarily even hold the keys to rapid economic development. Marxist-styled development succeeded under peculiar circumstances in semideveloped Czarist Russia; but it reaped chaos in parts of Eastern Europe, and its results have been anything but impressive in the underdeveloped world, notably in China. Still, the poor peasant and angry worker in the third world are more likely to be swept up in Marxism-Leninism's revolutionary promises, than in the logic of end results. Communism's appeal rests among those whose frustration has blurred their logic. The threat of Communist subversion therefore remains acute in many areas of Asia, Africa, and Latin America.

Economic Development and Democracy. On the basis of Western experience, some theorists of economic and political modernization find important positive links between political democracy and economic development.[4] Economic development, they point out, expands socio-economic pluralism in the form of new classes, new economic interests and interest groups, strong demands for government responsiveness, and strong incentives for participation in government. If emergent socio-economic pluralism during development is not to explode into chaos, then political institutions and processes must function to accommodate, coordinate, and integrate broad ranges of different interests and demands. Democratic institutions and processes provide such functions, and, at the same time, they maximize opportunities for individual and group initiative which some economists deem essential to success in economic development. Therefore, some would argue that tandem movement toward political democracy and economic development is an important part of the recipe for successful, and least painful, modernization.

But while it is certainly true that economic development and democracy have complemented each other in the experiences of several Western states, there remain some questions about both the direction and the necessity of the interrelationship. For example, it could be argued—and this seems closer to actual Western experience—that economic growth somewhat predates the emergence of full-blown democracy, in which all classes attain access and influence government. That is, only after wealth has become sufficiently abundant that it can be shared or redistributed without destroying classes, does it become possible to allocate resources through democratic processes of accommodation and compromise. Democratic institutions and processes may not be able effectively and efficiently to allocate resources in situations of extreme scarcity or in situations where the relatively better endowed classes show unwillingness to bend toward egalitarianism. Hence, democracy seems appropriate only after rigid stratifications and bitter class antagonisms have been significantly dampened by generalized improvements in well-being. In this sense, then, economic development may set the stage for democracy rather than the reverse.

Then, too, while there remains a question about the direction of the

4. Seymour Martin Lipset, *Political Man* (Garden City: Doubleday, 1960), pp. 45–76.

positive relationship between economic development and democracy, there is also some question about a possible negative relationship between the two. Since all societies in the early stages of development find it necessary to curtail mass consumption in the interest of accumulating savings for reinvestment, there is an economic logic in avoiding pressures that would force rising consumption at the expense of savings. Hence, there is a political logic in limiting the governmental access of those forces that would push for higher levels of consumption —i.e., the mass population. This argument is cruelly anti-democratic, and its embodiment in practice could involve social and political costs that far outweigh economic gains. Still, it is a matter of concern to the ruling elites of many underdeveloped countries. Will mass populations, offered political influence over the course of economic development, vote for self-sacrifice in the interest of future ends, or will they vote for the short-run satisfaction of consumer needs? One important answer to this question is being written in India today, where democracy and development are geared in tandem. India's experience could well become the model that other underdeveloped countries will emulate or avoid in the future.

Questions about the nature of the relationship between economic development and political democracy are legitimate, and their answers could be crucial to many countries. But in the midst of preoccupation with positive and negative interactions between development and democracy, one must not lose sight of the fact that there need not be any relationship between the two whatsoever. Integrating and coordinating functions during economic development can be taken over by detailed central planning and tight administrative control. Furthermore, accommodation among interests can be circumvented by suppression. Even private initiative can be replaced by public direction. In short, authoritarian institutions and processes can effectively control a society during economic development. Russian experience shows that economic development can proceed without political democracy; and Russian experience, as well as the experience of Nazi Germany, illustrates that economic development certainly does not have to lead toward democracy. Ultimately, therefore, the relationship between economic development and political democracy depends upon the wills of governing elites during eras of modernization, and especially upon their purposes in pursuing economic development and the means they choose for maintaining societal stability during these periods of rapid change.

Hence, as far as the present-day underdeveloped world is concerned, we must not expect that economic development will necessarily produce a new collection of constitutional democracies. Neither perhaps should we allow our own ethnocentrism to dictate that modernizing means emulating the West. Ruling elites committed to economic development will select and construct political institutions appropriate to the economic tasks before them and to the levels of political sophistication of their mass populations. For the short run, at least, some of these elites will likely find that economic development and political democracy are mutually exclusive alternatives rather than modernizing complements.

ECONOMIC DEVELOPMENT AND INTERNATIONAL POLITICS— CONCLUSION

Despite this chapter's elaborations on development models and its enumerated strategies for "takeoff," none of the information presented should be construed to imply that economic development is easy, routine, or even always possible. Similarly, no bright images projected by UNCTAD, the OECD, the IBRD, and other international development organizations and conferences; by Western foreign-aid programs and by capital flows through the United Nations system, should delude one into believing that economic development in the third world is necessarily the wave of the future. There will be impressive successes in economic development, certainly. Mexico, the Philippines, Brazil, Taiwan, and Turkey are nearing the takeoff threshold; and a number of other countries are making notable progress in infrastructure and human resource development. But, there will also be cases—most likely many cases—where countries will be unable, by any means, to muster the capital necessary to carry them economically into the modern world. Some countries will lose the race with expanding population. Others will stumble in agricultural modernization. Some perhaps will suffocate under the weight of resistance to change among traditional classes.

Implications for international politics follow from both probable successes in economic development in some countries, and from probable failures in many others. Prognostication here is dangerous since the behavior of states depends ultimately upon the decisions of governments and these decisions often defy prediction. Nevertheless, certain international spillover effects of the development drama in the third world are already discernible in present-day international politics:

1. Progress in economic development buttresses national autonomy by lessening external economic and political dependence and enhancing national power. With increased national power comes heightened national self-confidence and related diminutions in fears of Western neo-imperialism and Communist subversion. Such newly gained self-confidence could be reflected in developing countries' revised attitudes toward the external world—i.e., a marked lessening of suspicion and bitterness directed toward industrialized countries, and a related willingness to cooperate with the older, developed countries in efforts to stabilize and regulate the international political system. In short, progress toward economic development could obviate the North/South attitudinal estrangement so marked in world politics today.

2. More than this, economic development and its consequences in enhanced national power and autonomy could help to immunize areas of Asia, Africa, and Latin America against Cold War involvement. Local strength and self-sufficiency in smaller countries could close pathways to Western political and economic penetration and thereby hedge against pressures for alignment westward. At the same time, economic development beyond initial stages of very rapid change could result in increased internal satisfaction and tranquility and much reduced opportunity for Communist subversion. Hence, both West and East could be denied many of the opportunities for intervention and manipulation so readily available in the third world at present.

3. Enhanced power through economic development in the third world could significantly strengthen the United Nations Organization and its operations. Many of the new nations of Asia and Africa are currently among the most steadfast supporters of international organization in general, and the UN in particular. Their influence in the latter, however, is restricted both by their inabilities to back verbal commitments with material support, and by their inabilities to relate to, and hence influence, certain questions of major world concern such as disarmament, international trade, and even international aid. While it

is by no means assured that greater material capabilities among third world nations will make the UN a more effective world stabilizer (quite the opposite is of course possible), it is probable that greater concentrations of power in presently underdeveloped countries will change the nature of the UN. Given presently expressed distastes for "power politics" among new states and their interests in regional integration, nuclear nonproliferation, and superpower accommodation, they may well use their enhanced influence in the UN to push toward a new era of greater international cooperation.

4. Still on the positive side, it is possible that states well along the way toward economic modernization might pour resources into helping regional neighbors who have fallen behind in their development efforts. In this way development capital already flowing from Western countries and the Soviet Union could be supplemented by new aid flowing from within the third world. The probability of such behavior among Asian, African, and Latin American countries is not especially high at present. Nor is it clear that such aid could ever be great enough and come fast enough to make much difference. Still, various infant programs in regional self-help are already in operation. There is hope that these will grow as the relatively more developed countries develop further.

5. Unfortunately, lags and failures in economic development would reverse most of the positive projections listed thus far. First, development failures, increased misery, and greater internal tensions in the third world will widen the North/South economic gap, increase North/South attitudinal estrangement, and embitter the North/South political dialogue. Validly or invalidly, leaders will lay increasing blame for economic failures upon the indifference and exploitive intentions of industrialized countries. Furthermore, continuing external dependence will leave Asian, African, and Latin American countries open to Western pressures for alignment in exchange for aid. By the same token, increasing internal unrest will heighten dangers of Communist revolution. Feeding upon one another, tensions and fears would escalate toward crisis and panic. In addition, lack of progress toward economic development in the third world could stalemate the United Nations system in a morass of indictments and counterindictments all flung amid preoccupation with insoluble problems. Increased tension

would flood the international system as states vent their frustrations upon one another.

This chapter opened on an ominous note: "The fate of current efforts toward modernization in the 'third world' will greatly influence the stability of our international system during the next quarter century." Analysis of the problems and implications of modernization has, if anything, lent deeper foreboding to the opening note. What seems most likely is that the next twenty-five years will be years of continuing instability in the third world. Successes or failures in development efforts will either lessen or intensify this prevailing instability.

CHAPTER FOURTEEN
INTERNATIONAL ORGANIZATION
IN THE CONTEMPORARY
WORLD ENVIRONMENT

SELDOM does a week pass during which one finds no newspaper reports or editorial comments about the activities of the United Nations or other international organizations. Nor is any major foreign policy address likely to omit reference to the UN. The subject of international organization is controversial: some argue that international organizations are making major positive impacts upon the international system; others maintain that international organizations are making negative impacts; some insist that international organizations are making no real impacts upon the international system at all. Nevertheless, considerable governmental and popular attention is paid to international organizations, and reactions to the operations of such organizations are often intense. All of this is testimony to the fact that international organizations are central features of the contemporary world environment. Our system is the most highly institutionalized international system in history.

It would be highly misleading to imply that the topic "international organization" could be covered in a single chapter in one book. The breadth of the topic is enormous: the *Yearbook of International Organizations* for the year 1967 listed 199 intergovernmental international organizations and an additional 1935 nongovernmental organizations with international membership.[1] In membership, existing international organizations range from the bilateral to the universal; in jurisdiction they range from small committees preoccupied with

1. *Yearbook of International Organizations, 1966–1967*, 11th ed. (Brussels: Union of International Associations, 1966), p. 9.

minor technical problems, to regional and world assemblies concerned with critical problems of war and peace; in competence they range from discussion groups lacking even recommendatory power to supranational legislating panels with binding rule-making powers; in capability they range from groups lacking in executive functions to quasi-governments capable of fielding armies. Each organization has a history, each teaches a lesson in international cooperation, and each makes some impact upon the functioning of the international system. Most are worth separate and detailed study.

This chapter, however, must be limited to a few features of a single international organization—the United Nations. Furthermore, since the details of the UN's structure and functioning are already thoroughly elaborated in several major-length textbooks on international organization, attention here can be directed toward some of the more abstract principles and assumptions about international institutionalization that influenced the founding of the UN, toward its structural-functional development through time, and toward its impacts upon world politics and opinion.[2] Accordingly, discussion here develops under three headings: "Approaches to the Study of the United Nations," "The Emergence of the UN Design," and "Structural-Functional Evolution in the UN System." In short, we want to know how to analyze or evaluate the United Nations. We want further to know how the UN is similar to or different from antecedent historical institutions. Most important, we want to know whether and how the organization has evolved in structure and function during the two decades since its formation. Has change within the organization, or in the international system at large affected the relevance of the UN in contemporary international politics?

APPROACHES TO THE STUDY OF THE UNITED NATIONS

The continuing debate over the years about the value and efficacy of the United Nations has been much more a clash of principles and assumptions than a questioning of substance. Different observers tend to hold different expectations about the potential of the United Na-

2. Inis L. Claude, *Swords Into Plowshares*, 3rd ed. (New York: Random House, 1964); Leland M. Goodrich, *The United Nations* (New York: Crowell, 1959); Stephen S. Goodspeed, *The Nature and Function of International Organization*, 2nd ed. (New York: Oxford University Press, 1967).

tions, and these differences, in turn, lead to different criteria for evaluating the organization. Accordingly, optimism or pessimism, and satisfaction or dissatisfaction with the organization follow less from particular successes or failures of the UN than from its ability to meet various expectations.

According to one school of thought—let us call this the *realist* school—the United Nations Organization is looked upon as an instrument of national foreign policy. That is, states use the institutions and processes of the UN as channels and devices for pursuing rather narrowly defined national self-interests. Diplomatic channels and opportunities provided by the UN are exploited by states for purposes of persuasion in the interest of national foreign policies. General Assembly sessions are used for the dissemination of nationally favorable propaganda. Security Council meetings are used by states to mobilize collective international action in their favor, and to debar such action when it appears dangerous to their interests. Similarly, economic distributive and redistributive processes provided by the UN are used by states in their pursuits of economic rewards from the international system. In addition, the totality of the UN mechanism is used by states to nurture international public opinion toward sanctioning and legitimizing narrow national self-interests.

From this instrumental perspective, clearly, the UN can be no more than the sum of its members, and its processes can reflect no more than the relative anarchy of the state system at large. Hence, its policies and actions can embody no more than the lowest common denominator among members' separate interests. Typically, if one views the UN as a mirror of the international system—a reflector of competitive anarchy—one would not expect the organization to accomplish much beyond what might be accomplished in normal relations among states. Moreover, from this perspective, one might not be overly disappointed at the diatribes, diversions, and stalemates that characterize large proportions of the verbal behavior within UN councils.

But while the realists assume away UN action and influence above the level of the lowest common denominator among members' self-interests, others—let us call them *functionalists*—insist that the UN is actually greater than its members, that its institutions are more than merely instruments of national foreign policies, and that the organization influences national policies almost as much as it is influenced by them. Functionalists bow to the fact that states may indeed *try* to use the UN as an instrument of foreign policy. They acknowledge that states often succeed in their attempts self-interestedly to exploit the UN. Still, they point out that the communications channels and sounding boards that the UN provides also influence national foreign policies by making them more informed, more flexible, and often more moderate than they might otherwise be. Some students of the UN have pointed out that UN participation sometimes has the effect of blunting international antagonisms by nurturing interpersonal understanding among statesmen in permanent delegations, by exposing latent common interests among states, and by contributing to awareness of the whole international system above and beyond particular national interest in it.[3]

More than this, the functionalists suggest that the UN as a collective body can act, and has acted, in the interest of the stability of the international system even when such action has contradicted the policy aims of important member-states. The various UN peacekeeping missions exemplify this variety of organizational behavior. Soviet displeasure could not prevent or greatly hamper UN collective security operations in Korea. Nor did Soviet objections thwart the UN peacekeeping effort in the Congo. British and French objections did not bar UN influence in the Suez situation. Nor has American displeasure stifled UN attempts to build a foundation for settlement in Vietnam. Clearly, such initiatives, interventions, arbitrations, and mediations as fall under the rubric "preventive diplomacy" represent UN action well above the level of the lowest common denominator of national interests. It is not entirely clear whether the existence of the UN created the international middleman's role, or whether the prior existence of the role bolstered the independence of the UN. Nevertheless, it is clear that the UN does perform international regulatory functions that cannot be effectively performed by member-states acting separately.

If one accepts the functionalist interpretation of the United Nations, then one's criteria for evaluating the worth and effectiveness of the organization must differ markedly from realists' criteria. First, one can no longer expect that the organization will merely mirror the anarchy of the sovereign state system. Nor can one remain content if

3. Chadwick F. Alger, "Personal Contact in Intergovernmental Organizations," in *International Behavior*, Herbert C. Kelman, ed. (New York: Holt, Rinehart and Winston, 1965), pp. 521–547.

such mirroring is all that the organization produces. The functionalist looks for UN influence over members' policies and evaluates the organization in terms of policies moderated, positions relaxed, and antagonisms blunted. In addition, the functionalist looks for UN action in the name and interest of systemic stability, and evaluates the organization in terms of crises defused, wars prevented or halted, disruptive national policies frustrated, and international settlements or compromises gained through international organizational intervention. The functionalist is pleased to note expansion of the influence of the UN's executive. He is disappointed at members' attempts to hoist national interest above international stability.

The *world federalist* wants even more from the United Nations. From the world federalist viewpoint the United Nations Charter and the institutions that sprang from it should represent steps toward the constitution of a world government. Though interpretations and designs for world government vary, in one way or another most of them imply the suppression of international politics. Under world government, politics among separate sovereign states would be either greatly curtailed or else it would cease altogether. Ultimate authority to regulate, control, and police relations among states would come to rest in a central world government. This government would command a preponderance of military capability; a preponderance of economic distributive capability; and a preponderance of legislative, judicial, and executive authority for the world system. States would perhaps remain as administrative units, and nation-states would persist as ethnic entities. But their independence of action would be curtailed and their war-making privileges proscribed. For the world federalist, world government becomes the ultimate answer to world peace. Therefore, according to the world federalist critique, international organizations such as the United Nations must be evaluated in terms of their contributions to and progress toward the ultimate goal of world government. Where the functionalist looks to international organizations to regulate and moderate the international system, the federalist looks to them to replace it. Needless to say, the United Nations Organization has been somewhat of a frustration to world federalists. Still, the organization represents the greatest institutional step beyond international anarchy ever attempted on a worldwide scale.

While this author leans toward a functionalist interpretation of the

United Nations, no attempt will be made to impose this viewpoint upon the reader. Instead, the reader is invited to explore the bases of his own satisfactions or frustrations with the organization. What must be underlined is that the United Nations will continue to represent many things to many people. The Charter opens abundant interpretative pathways to realists, functionalists, and federalists alike. This is perhaps the way the founders intended it, because only with its potentials blurred could the organization hope to attract nearly universal membership in a fragmented world.

THE EMERGENCE OF THE UN DESIGN

The thinking of the draftsmen of the United Nations Charter as they envisaged their new organization in operation in the post-1945 world, has become a matter of scholastic concern to some students of the world body. Still, no one can know for certain exactly what the founders had in mind. If memoirs and similar bits of recollection are taken as guides, it is more than likely that each statesman at the San Francisco Conference harbored his own image of the new UN in operation. It is likely too that each man worked and bargained to see that parts of his image were codified into the Charter's draft. But still, above the diversities and differences in vision and expectation, a number of common themes did pervade preparatory thinking for the UN. Roughly categorized, the most important of these had to do first with intellectual and historical precedents in international organization, next with specific lessons learned from the functions and malfunctions of the League of Nations, and finally with the functions the new institution was intended to perform.

Institutional and Intellectual Precedents for the United Nations. In structural overview the United Nations binds five major components into a potential world-ordering system. Conventional "separation of powers" categorizations are not wholly meaningful in distinguishing among United Nations organs, since initiating, deliberative, and executive functions tend to be diffused among a number of different bodies and agencies. Still, by the terms of the Charter, international deliberation is the prime prerogative of the General Assembly; international execution is the function of the Security Council; and international administration is the role of the Secretariat, the Office of the Secretary

General, and the specialized agencies of the United Nations system. In addition, adjudication under international law is assigned to the World Court. Each of these institutional components of the UN system has antecedents in traditional designs and devices for world order.

1. *The Security Council* resting at the hub of the United Nations institutional system represents a slight modification of the traditional concept of *concert* among major powers. First articulated in the writings of Immanuel Kant, and later operationalized at the Congress of Vienna in 1815, the idea of concert allots major responsibility for world order to the great powers. The design is elitist, and its execution tends to be reactionary since it institutionalizes and attempts to perpetuate a particular distribution of power in the international system. Nevertheless, it is realistic in that it bows to the *de facto* hierarchical power structure of world politics. Under the concert scheme, the great powers are cast in regulatory roles in the international system, where they lead, tutor, and police lesser powers in the interest of world order.

Underlying the entire concert design is the implicit assumption that major powers can attain harmony in their international objectives, and that they can interact cooperatively toward stabilizing ends. It has never been assumed that major powers necessarily will act in harmony. Indeed, international experience thoroughly documents the contrary. Nevertheless, as noted below, realistic advocates of the concert design note quite simply that if major powers do not act in harmony there can be little hope for world order.

2. The idea of a world forum of nations or an "assembly of peoples," which provides the conceptual foundation for the United Nations *General Assembly,* is the democratic alternative to the concert system's elite design. One finds glimmerings of this "world assembly" idea in the early federationist thinking of William Penn. The idea is also celebrated in the poetry of Alfred, Lord Tennyson. It finds enthusiastic affirmation in the themes of nineteenth-century British utilitarianism and twentieth-century Wilsonianism. The popular assembly design transmits faith in democracy to the international system, where it is assumed that when world order is placed in the hands of the world's peoples, innate pacifism, tolerance, goodwill, and good sense will come to the fore. Peace will then follow from discourse, debate, mutual accommodation, and compromise, and from a free airing of peoples' common sense.

Certainly, the United Nations General Assembly is a rather poor approximation of the mythical "assembly of peoples," since delegates represent and speak for governments rather than populations and since many of the governments represented are only minimally responsive to the wills of their populations. In this sense, the Assembly of the League of Nations, which left millions of people under colonial rule essentially unrepresented, was an even poorer approximation of an assembled world community. Then, too, certainly, there is some question about the validity of assuming the innate pacifism, tolerance and good sense of peoples, especially in a world caught up in nationalist fervor. On the other hand, a case can be made for the understanding and moderation sometimes generated in the General Assembly, as well as for the desirability of universal involvement in questions and problems of world stability. Finally, in a world enamored with egalitarianism, as ours is, it is difficult to conceive of success in any politically oriented international organization where structural and procedural deference to democratic theory is absent. The United Nations may not be more effective because of its "assembly of peoples" but, without this body, it would likely become considerably less effective for want of legitimate authority.

3. Though they are often studied and discussed apart from the political organs of the United Nations, the organization's specialized agencies and commissions—FAO, ILO, WHO, UNESCO, UNICEF, ECE, ECLA, and several more—are integral parts of the UN system. Many of these grew from counterpart agencies created under League of Nations auspices. Others emerged as transnational technical needs in the post-World War II era prompted their creation. They expanded in scope and function as international resources were made available for their operations.

Operations in the specialized agencies follow from several assumptions about the nature and role of technical cooperation in the international system. Many of these were articulated in the works of David R. Mitrany during the 1940's.[4] First, the world community may be subdivided into states and nation-states; but many major problems that confront mankind in the realms of health, food, shelter, enlighten-

---

4. David Mitrany, *A Working Peace System* (London: Royal Institute of International Affairs, 1943); also, Mitrany, "The Functional Approach to World Organization," *International Affairs* (July, 1948), pp. 350–363.

ment, and general human well-being are transnational in nature. They defy unilateral and bilateral solutions. In addition, there are varieties of routine problems concerning communications, migration, sanitation, etc., that could be handled in bilateral relations; but that tend to be handled more efficiently through international administration and standardization. Therefore, there are numerous nonpolitical areas of common interest among states, and these underline functions that could be performed by international organizations.

But while it is essential that international technical agencies be "sanitized" from international politics in the interest of efficiency, the agencies are not intended to remain irrelevant to international politics. On the contrary, many supporters of international technical cooperation hope and expect that cooperative experience gained by states and peoples in common attacks upon common human problems, will feed back or spill over into international politics in a positive way. Habits of collaboration, bonds of confidence, links of interdependence, and satisfactions in mutually rewarding behavior born in technical cooperation are expected both to moderate the tone of international politics and to generate respected procedures for international collaboration over an ever-broadening range of world problems.

The actual political results of technical cooperation under the UN have generally fallen far short of advocates' expectations. Instead of the anticipated spillover from technical cooperation into international politics, it seems that in our ideologically fragmented system the major problem has become one of preventing divisive politics from spilling over into technical cooperation. Once a specialized agency becomes politicized and internally divided along East, West, North, and South ideological lines, its attack upon universal human problems is blunted. Nevertheless, the value and effectiveness of the technical cooperation sponsored by the specialized agencies of the United Nations system should not be belittled. Important progress has been made on a worldwide scale through UN technical guidance in public health, education, civil aviation, and other areas. But even more than this, while technical cooperation has done little to moderate international politics, there is much to be said for its continuation and expansion *despite* an enveloping atmosphere of bitter ideological antagonism.

4. The *Secretariat* of the United Nations evolved from a tradition

of international civil service born under the League of Nations and then kept alive in specialized agencies after the League's eclipse. In theory, and even more so in practice, the creation and operations of an international civil service contradict several of the major themes of twentieth-century international politics. For example, the loyalty and preeminent allegiance to the nation-state so characteristic and valued in international politics are dysfunctional to the operations of an international civil service. The international civil servant may be asked, and must be attitudinally prepared to perform, assignments that may contradict the interests of his own state or nationality. Relatedly, where national bias, nationally constricted perspective, and nonreceptiveness to contending viewpoints may buttress the national diplomat in his assignments and sometimes contribute to his international bargaining capabilities, the effectiveness of the international civil servant depends upon his impartiality, objectivity, and broad world perspective. Any glimmering of bias may alienate an international civil servant from important segments of the international community and thereby diminish his authority and effectiveness. Finally, while national and ideological intolerance and the open castigation of alien ideas and practices have become routine elements in international political dialogue, these have no place either within an international civil service or in relations between international civil servants and the world community. Extreme tolerance or extraordinary abilities for the suppression of personal attitudes are prerequisite for effective international civil service.

Though tradition is of continuing importance in socializing international civil servants to value the impartiality, objectivity, and efficiency requisite to their assignments, the Secretariat of the United Nations—and especially the role of Secretary General—have evolved well beyond their traditions to become unique institutions in the history of international relations. There are, for example, no historical precedents for international executive initiative. Nor are there historical precedents in Charter interpretation by international executives. Nor again is there anything in history that matches the now apparent growth of an international popular constituency to support the office and activities of the Secretary General of the United Nations. The successive Secretaries General of the United Nations, most notably the late Dag Ham-

marskjold, have injected a note of supranationality into world organization heretofore unknown in international relations. Some elaboration
on these points follows later.

The Legacy of the League. There can be no doubt that the experience
of the League of Nations significantly affected the UN design. However, except for some structural carry-over (i.e., both organizations
combined a major-power council with a full-membership assembly,
an international civil service, and a periphery of specialized agencies),
emphasis in the United Nations plan was upon differentiation from the
League rather than similarity to it. This emphasis was deliberate. The
League had failed as an international regulator, not only once, but
several times. It had never aroused the enthusiasm of the United States
government or the American people; it had alienated the Soviet Union
completely by expelling that country; it did little to stop the Japanese
march into Manchuria or the Italian conquest of Ethiopia. Hence, in
1945, there was no lingering reservoir of goodwill and respect for the
League that might have been used to mobilize favor for a new universal
international organization. Therefore, while it is not wholly accurate
to say that the UN actually looks and operates very differently from
the League, it is fair to note that the League's influence upon the UN
design was primarily negative. The draftsmen of the UN Charter
worked to avoid the flaws and pitfalls that ushered the first attempt at
universal organization into oblivion.

Differences between alternative approaches to international organization that produced the League Covenant on the one hand and
the UN Charter on the other, were in part differences in the respective
draftsmen's attitudes, and in part differences in their proposals for
structure and procedure.

To a much greater extent than was the case among the founders of
the League, the designers of the United Nations rejected the idea of
world government. They therefore avoided falling prey to utopian expectations and consequently set their organization into operation at a
level of political discourse substantially closer to international reality
than had been the case with the League. Most telling in this regard were
the UN designers' attitudes toward cooperation among major powers.
The Security Council was not conceived, as the League Council had
been, on the notion that harmony among major powers was likely. Nor
was it assumed among UN designers that an international organiza-

tion would have a major role to play in disputes among great powers. Instead, and much more realistically, the founders of the UN bowed to power in world politics and readily admitted that international organization could be effective only *if* and *when* major powers cooperated. In Inis L. Claude's words: "It was assumed not that the Big Five would maintain their unity, but that the U.N. plan would work if, and only if, they did."[5] Thus, the League's founders took major-power harmony as given, while the authors of the Charter accepted this factor as essential but questionable.

The difference between the former's idealism and the latter's realism produced in the UN plan a good deal more anticipatory buttressing against major-power disharmony than was present in the League system. Not least important in this regard, the unanimity rules in the Security Council (i.e., the veto provision) serve both theoretically and actually to render the United Nations incompetent to take action in major-power disputes. Far from marking a weakness in the UN system, the veto rule is actually a mark of deference to the reality and distribution of state sovereignty and power in international politics. It is both an admission that universal international organization is largely irrelevant to political-military contests among major powers, and a hedge against the destruction of the organization from the shock waves of major-power disputes. When the great powers cooperate, the UN can function at peak efficiency; when major powers disagree, UN action stalls. But here the organization simply steps aside: *it does not disintegrate.* Had the League plan been as sensitive to the realities of power, its contributions might have been more positive.

Relatedly, UN designers took another realistic step away from League idealism when they deliberately decentralized decision-making, operations, and staffing among the specialized agencies of the United Nations system. In this way, the specialized agencies became significantly immunized against political squabbling and stalemate in the main political organs of the UN. More than this, any misfortunes and negative images associated with the main political organs need not necessarily spill over to hamper the operations of the specialized agencies. By contrast, under the League design, where high degrees of administrative centralization bound the specialized agencies closely to the political organs, stalemate in any part of the system brought most

5. Inis L. Claude, *Swords Into Plowshares*, p. 69.

of the system to a standstill. Also, when the main political organs fell into disrepute, the negative image clouded the whole system. Thus, here again, the difference between idealism and realism among the respective designers of the two international organizations produced a difference between frailty and endurance.

But differences in designers' attitudes were not the only factors that differentiated the organization born in 1945 from its counterpart born a generation earlier. Important lessons about appropriate structures and procedures in international organization were learned from the short life and relatively unmourned death of the League. These most definitely influenced the wording and provisions of the United Nations Charter.

Most important, the jurisdictions of the major political organs of the United Nations were made explicit and separate in the UN scheme in a deliberate attempt to avoid the kinds of jurisdictional ambiguities that had hampered the League's ability to act. Under the Covenant of the League, lines of prerogative separating the Council and the Assembly on questions of pacific settlement were blurred. Consequently, under the League design, a party to a dispute could request a transfer of discussion and expedition from the more powerful Council to the less powerful Assembly, and thereby hedge against meaningful League action in the dispute. But under the United Nations Charter, responsibility for pacific settlement is clearly allotted to the Security Council so that opportunities for "shopping around" in search of a sympathetic forum are formally curtailed. (As will be shown below, however, jurisdictional separation between the Security Council and the General Assembly has in fact blurred in UN practice to the extent that "shopping" for a friendly forum has become a prominent feature of organizational politics. Hence, lessons learned from the jurisdictional confusion of the League have been forgotten. Still, in 1945, these lessons were prominent and certainly influential in the shaping of the UN design.)

Similarly, designers of the United Nations were aware of, and concerned with, the impotence of the League in the area of enforcement action. Neither the League's ability to enforce sanctions, nor its ability to hold members to their charter commitments were especially impressive. The Covenant provided for automatic economic and financial sanctions against any state that resorted to war in violation of its commitments to pacific settlement. It also provided the Council with recommendatory power concerning the collective use of military force. But the Covenant left enforcement action entirely to the volition of member-states. In fact, it was left to each state to decide whether an act of aggression had been committed. (Again it was assumed rather unrealistically that states would place the interests of world stability above their own narrower national interests.) Furthermore, the Covenant provided no administrative mechanism for coordinating states' separate voluntary enforcement measures.

With the lessons of the League in mind, the authors of the United Nations Charter determined to put "teeth" into the UN enforcement system. Consequently, enforcement action was assigned specifically to the Security Council. That body was charged with determining the nature of sanctions appropriate in particular situations, with detailing procedures for applying sanctions, and with coordinating enforcement actions. The Charter, furthermore, specifically empowered the Security Council to "take . . . action by air, sea, or land forces as may be necessary," to enter into agreements with member-states for the provision of such forces, and to utilize the expertise of a Military Staff Committee in the planning, preparation, and application of military force. Under certain contingencies the Charter permits the use of international military force; under others it *requires* the use of force. Thus, according to its Charter, the United Nations Organization has "teeth" and a potential "bite" considerably stronger than that written into the League system. Of course again, as outlined below, UN practice has deviated from the Charter design, and actual enforcement actions have proven only slightly more potent than those attempted by the League. Nevertheless, with the lessons of the League in mind, the authors of the Charter wanted a strong international organization and they designed the strongest possible under conditions prevailing in 1945. That the UN has turned out weak in enforcement capabilities and has shown itself unable to aspire to its design, only underlines the shallowness of its members' commitments to international cooperation.

Peacekeeping Under the UN Design. It is sometimes overlooked in discussions concerning formative influences upon the United Nations that the international organization was created to serve a specific central purpose, so that to a significant extent, intended function prescribed structure and procedure. The main purpose of the United Nations Organization—indeed its *raison d'etre*—is to enhance and maintain tranquility and order in the international system. In this purpose, it differs little from antecedent international organizations, real or proposed. Certainly, the UN has additional purposes in supporting the self-determination of peoples; facilitating amicable relations among states; and fostering collective economic, social, cultural, and humanitarian programs on a worldwide scale. But these are all subsidiary, and intendedly contributive, to the organization's central function as an international regulator and conciliator. What is worthy of attention is *how* the United Nations was equipped by its designers to work toward peacekeeping ends.

The UN's peacekeeping mechanism is described in detail in Chapters VI and VII of the Charter. In reading these sections of the Charter, the student should bear in mind that the peacekeeping provisions are not simply recommendations for action handed to states by the sponsors of the UN. *They are commitments to action solemnly accepted and endorsed by each state that signed the Charter.* Hence, shortcomings in the United Nations peacekeeping system should be attributed much more to the false integrity of states than to flaws in organizational design or procedure.

Under Article 33 in Chapter VI of the Charter, international disputants commit themselves to seek solutions to their own problems by peaceful means. They further commit themselves to heed Security Council calls for settlement outside of the UN. Article 34 gives the Security Council authority to investigate any dispute which it deems threatening to international peace, Article 35 invites states to bring their disputes to the attention of the Security Council, and Article 37 *requires* states to bring their disputes to the Security Council should steps toward outside settlement falter. In sum, by signing the Charter, states limited their sovereignties by committing themselves to allow international organizational intervention in their disputes. Most important, they have committed themselves to exhaust United Nations peacekeeping procedures *before* they resort to war.

But commitment to international peacekeeping does not end with Security Council involvement. Under Articles 36, 37, and 38, the Security Council is invited to recommend measures for peaceful solution; and under conditions listed in Article 39 the Security Council is *required* to recommend measures for solution. But even more than this, Article 41 permits the Security Council to enforce its decisions by calling for nonmilitary sanctions, and, as mentioned earlier, Article 42 permits the Security Council to muster and use military force in effecting its decisions. Hence, not only is the Security Council invited into international disputes, but it is also requested to resolve such disputes *even when resolution should require military action.*

Again—and this point cannot be emphasized too strongly—the efficacy of the United Nations peacekeeping procedure rests upon the charter commitments of member-states to respect it, support it, and use it. When states endorse the United Nations Charter, they formally and solemnly discard (or at least agree to postpone) unilateral alternatives to international organizational peacekeeping. The problem in United Nations peacekeeping is not, as some lament, in the absence or misconception of system-level peacekeeping mechanisms. These we have. Moreover, they have proven effective on the few occasions they have been used, as, for example, in Palestine, Kashmir, Suez, the Congo, and Cyprus. Instead, the basis of the problem in UN peacekeeping lies in states' reluctance to use Charter procedures at all or in their unwillingness to use them properly, and in their refusals to respect United Nation's decisions and recommendations. All of this is really to say that the shortsightedness of national interests continues to thwart systemic stability at the international level. UN peacekeeping requires that at least some states at some times rise above their narrow self-interests and work toward broader world stability. The framers of the Charter hoped that the great powers would sometimes behave in this manner. If there are any flaws in the Charter's peacekeeping mechanisms, they show in the designers' reluctance to inject stronger elements of supranationality into their institution at a time when such injection may have been possible. In addition, if there is any flaw in the overall United Nations system, it shows in the system's failure, after more than twenty years, to educate members in the desirability and need to look beyond national interests toward world interests.

STRUCTURAL–FUNCTIONAL EVOLUTION WITHIN THE UN SYSTEM

For all of its designers' wisdom, the United Nations Organization, almost from the outset, was found wanting, structurally and functionally, in dealing with many of the most critical problems of the contemporary era. Changes in world politics after World War II occurred so rapidly and dramatically that the organization framed to deal with the issues of 1945 was already almost obsolete by 1946. United States-Soviet rivalry and the intensifying Cold War immediately stymied the Security Council and thereby practically nullified the core of the UN peacekeeping system. It is true that the designers did not expect perpetual great power harmony and hence foresaw instances where United Nations action would be blocked. But no one expected the wartime coalition of great powers to dissolve in less than one year, and certainly no one expected a break among major powers as utterly complete as that which destroyed Russian-American relations after 1945. Nor, on the other hand, did many expect that the distinction between "great power" and "small power" would give way in the dawning nuclear age to the distinction between "superpower" and "superpower client." Hence, while the Security Council may have been roughly representative of the great powers of the world in 1945, by 1950 it was but a vestige of an old power system all but dissolved. It was no longer a concert of major powers.

Beyond incapacitating the decision-making procedures of the Security Council, the East-West rift rendered enforcement action under the Charter all but impossible. Without superpower cooperation and collaboration, the imposition of UN nonmilitary sanctions would be without decisive impact; and since neither superpower was willing to impose sanctions upon members of its own ideological fraternity, "collective security" rang hollow, and UN enforcement under the Charter was rendered all but meaningless. Moreover, if and when the UN chose to rely upon one ideological camp or the other for enforcement, issues in question automatically became Cold War issues, and consequent East-West polarization about such issues raised dangers of superpower confrontation and general war. In this sense, in all but the historically unique Korean situation, it became almost out of the question for the UN to consider using major-power forces for coercive enforcement. How ironic it is to recall that the authors of the Charter expected that most UN military contingents would be provided by major powers and that the Military Staff Committee would "consist of the Chiefs of Staff of the permanent members of the Security Council or their representatives."

A second sequence of radical changes in the post-1945 international environment, unanticipated and consequently unprepared for by the authors of the Charter, was the rapid dissolution of European colonial empires, the proliferation of new states, and the rapid and vast expansion of the United Nations membership. On the one hand, the expanded membership has introduced elements of unwieldiness into the organization, as reflected in ever-lengthening General Assembly debates and a certain amount of strain on the physical facilities in institutional chambers. But much more seriously, new interests injected by new members have set the United Nations, and especially the General Assembly, directly in the center of the North-South gap in international politics. All too often, the new states have used the General Assembly platform as a springboard for verbal attacks on the older colonial powers, with the result that major powers such as France and the United Kingdom have turned an increasingly colder shoulder toward the UN. The United States too has been made the target of repeated attacks and abuses delivered by new states, who wave the banner of neo-imperialism. As a result of such attacks and in consequence of growing tendencies to form anti-American coalitions along a South-East axis in the General Assembly, American support for the United Nations has waned in recent years to the extent that serious American reconsideration is now under way concerning commitments and contributions to United Nations peacekeeping. None of this is to deny the legitimacy and desirability of universal membership in the United Nations. All states are to be welcomed into the international organization. It remains a fact, however, that the abusive behavior of some of its newer members has seriously diluted former sources of strong support for the United Nations Organization.

UN Adjustments to the Changing International Environment. Along with unanticipated problems for the United Nations after 1945 came also unanticipated opportunities for performing regulatory and conciliatory functions in international politics. It is a credit both to the wisdom of those who designed the Charter and to the courage of those who later interpreted and acted upon it, that the document has proven flexible enough to be fitted to problems of an unforeseen era. Despite the paralysis of the Security Council, and the oftentimes vitriolic clamor of the General Assembly, the United Nations Organization *has* acted to defuse international tensions surrounding a number of disputes. (It has even played a modest part in superpower disputes.)

Moreover, it has acted to impose nonmilitary sanctions pursuant to the enforcement of its decisions. It has stopped wars, and it has fought wars. Some of this was accomplished by raising operative sections of the Charter to prominence and in turn ignoring inoperative ones. Some progress has been made by accommodating and mobilizing the expanded membership of new states. Much has been accomplished through the efforts of men of vision in the Office of the Secretary General. One cannot argue that the United Nations Organization performs ideally, or that it performs in ways intended by its founders, or that it has had or will have decisive impacts on the course of international political history. Still, the organization has played a modest role in the maintenance of international stability. In areas where it could act, it has acted and with some success. Above all, there is something to be said for the fact that the United Nations has not become totally irrelevant to contemporary international politics, especially since the danger of such irrelevance was very high during the early years of the organization.

Redirections in United Nations themes and operations since 1945 fall under several headings, concerned with: (1) the enhanced authority of the General Assembly, (2) the role of "preventive diplomacy," and (3) the supranational functions of the Secretary General. Most of these new departures in UN operations were unanticipated in the Charter. Aspects of each remain highly controversial. Together, though, they underline the creativity and endurance of an international organization enveloped in a highly unfavorable international political environment.

1. NEW AUTHORITY TO THE GENERAL ASSEMBLY. Years of experience, trial, and error have enhanced the international political role and prestige of the United Nations General Assembly. To limit one's positive assessment of the General Assembly to clichés about its usefulness as a disseminator of diplomatic information, its microcosmic embodiment of the hopes and tribulations of mankind, and its uniqueness as an arena where states may relieve frustrations by talking rather than fighting, is to sell the institution somewhat short. Through certain quasi-constitutional developments within the United Nations system, as well as certain attitudinal developments in the international political system at large, the General Assembly has outgrown its singular role as a debating forum and has assumed notable international, executive, and legitimizing functions.

As part of a dominant train of UN efforts to circumvent the veto-bound Security Council, and thereby preserve the organization's ability to act in a peacekeeping capacity, efforts were undertaken in 1950, under the sponsorship of the United States, to transfer peacekeeping prerogatives to the General Assembly. In November, 1950, under fortuitous conditions of a huge pro-American majority, and amidst the clamor for political guidance for UN military forces in Korea, guidance which could not come from the stalemated Security Council, the General Assembly voted itself international enforcement powers. These were embodied in the Fifth General Assembly's "United Action for Peace" resolution.

In substance, the Uniting for Peace Resolution provides the General Assembly with powers to call itself into emergency session at times of international crisis. But much more important, the resolution also provides the world body with (1) the power to consider threats to peace and breaches of peace *when the Security Council does not or cannot exercise its primary responsibility in such matters,* and (2) the power to recommend UN actions, including the use of military force, in response to threatening international developments. In essence, the Uniting for Peace Resolution empowers the General Assembly to act *in place of* the Security Council should the latter become paralyzed in times of international emergency. Furthermore, in a marked step away from Article 11:2 of the Charter ("Any . . . such question on which action is necessary shall be referred to the Security Council by the General Assembly . . ."), the Uniting for Peace scheme permits the General Assembly to recommend action directly to UN members rather than to the Security Council. Hence, with the passage of the Uniting for Peace Resolution, the United Nations, by informal Charter amendment, obtained an alternative emergency decision-making system. Actions under the resolution proved important in the direction of the Korean war, and, in conjunction with the General Assembly's prerogative under Article 22, action under the Uniting for Peace Resolution proved decisive in the Suez Crisis in 1956.

The Uniting for Peace formula was unquestionably controversial and intensely debated at the time of its passage. It was interpreted, and rightly so, by the Soviet Union as an American tactic designed to transform the General Assembly into a reliable tool for American foreign policy. With overwhelming pro-American majorities in the early General Assemblies, any Soviet influence over the UN, positive or negative, was nullified as soon as issues were passed into the General Assembly. In fact, students of international organization have questioned why the Soviet Union maintained any interest at all in the United Nations during the early years, and especially why the Russians persisted in their lonely role after the passage of the Uniting for Peace Resolution. As it has turned out however, the Uniting for Peace Resolution has become a two-edged sword. Since 1960 the influx of new states with anti-Western leanings has undermined the assured American majority in the General Assembly. In the eyes of American policy-makers this has raised the danger that the General Assembly might act under the Uniting for Peace Resolution in ways detrimental to United States interests. Hence, as the General Assembly has outgrown the American pocket, United States policy has gradually swung from encouraging General Assembly action toward revitalizing the functions of the Security Council, where inaction due to Soviet veto is preferable to contrary action from a hostile General Assembly.

Beyond the formal enhancement of its powers under the Uniting for Peace Resolution, the General Assembly has grown in international stature, and therefore in influence, over the years by virtue of its unique ability to function as an international political legitimizer.[6] Because of the deep ideological coloration of most states' foreign policies at present, statesmen tend to invest great effort and many resources in attempts to justify their policies before the world community. Since much of the Cold War under "peaceful coexistence" amounts to respective East and West attempts to make themselves *appealing* to the uncommitted world, images of "rightness," "reasonableness," "justice," and "wisdom" attached to foreign policies have become centrally important to superpowers in their wooing of the "third world." Similarly, among the former colonial countries, great emphasis tends to be placed on efforts to bring moral condemnation down upon traditional imperialistic policies, and to robe their economic demands upon the industrialized world in images of moral obligation and just reward. Hence, in our world of prevailing uncertainty, there exist among states profound needs to secure legitimacy for the international undertakings.

6. Inis L. Claude, *The Changing United Nations* (New York: Random House, 1967), pp. 74–104.

World "public opinion" has become the great legitimizer in contemporary international politics; and endorsement by the United Nations has been, by and large, accepted by states as approval in world public opinion. By the same measure, condemnation by the United Nations has become the mark of international illegitimacy. More than this, it has come to be accepted that the strength of international endorsement or the intensity of international condemnation is proportional to the number of votes obtained or lost in the United Nations General Assembly. The General Assembly, then, has become the world conscience for states' foreign policies.

No one can argue that this is all to the good, since the predispositions of the General Assembly majorities are not always contributive to world stability. Nor must it be assumed that states always, or even most often, tailor their policies with an eye to United Nations endorsement. Still, the very states most critical of equally weighted voting in the General Assembly, and the statesmen quickest to publicly pooh-pooh General Assembly vote counts are frequently among the most vigorous vote-hunters in the corridors, chambers, and lounges of United Nations Headquarters. Indeed, the outcomes of General Assembly votes and the wordings of resolutions passed or defeated need not affect the policies of member-states. But they often do because states, and especially the new states highly committed to the United Nations, have come increasingly to expect they should.

2. PREVENTIVE DIPLOMACY. Where early attempts to keep the United Nations relevant to world politics were instigated primarily by member-states (most notably the United States), more recent efforts in this direction have come from within the permanent staff of the organization. More than anyone else, Dag Hammarskjold, as Secretary General, was responsible for finding a role for the United Nations in contemporary world politics that is commensurate to both the organization's purposes and its capabilities. He labeled his program "preventive diplomacy."

Preventive diplomacy has a dual meaning and hence dual implications for United Nations action. It calls on the one hand for international organizational action to isolate disputes among uncommitted states from superpower intervention. Relatedly, it calls for international organizational action to localize disputes where superpower interest and intervention cannot be avoided. Overall, preventive diplomacy means using international organizational action to minimize the Cold War's disruptive impacts upon international politics.

In Hammarskjold's words:

... Conflicts arising within the non-committed areas offer opportunities for solutions which avoid an aggravation of big Power differences and can remain uninfluenced by them.

.   .   .   .   .   .

This clearly defines the main field of useful activity of the United Nations in its efforts to prevent conflicts or to solve conflicts. Those efforts must aim at keeping newly arising conflicts outside of the sphere of bloc differences. Further, in cases of conflicts on the margin of, or inside, the sphere of bloc differences, the United Nations should seek to bring such conflicts out of this sphere through solutions aiming, in the first instance, at their strict localization.[7]

With reports on efforts at preventive diplomacy so much a part of daily media output, it is easy to pass over the fact that the UN's assumption of the role of preventive diplomat is a revolutionary development in international organization. The Charter's intended enforcement scheme builds from a *collective security* design in which it is supposed that aggression would be discouraged or halted by the UN's ability to pose the collective military might of the world community in the face of an aggressor. Most important, under the collective security design the might of the great powers is pivotal to successful international organizational action. In short, collective security invites major powers into disputes. But in a sense preventive diplomacy, unanticipated in the Charter, is almost the diametric opposite of collective security. Major powers are to be kept out of, rather than invited into, disputes. Peacekeeping forces are to be drawn from the small states instead of the big ones. International forces are to separate combatants rather than bludgeon aggressors. One cannot help but note how very different preventive diplomacy is from collective security. Nor can one fail to note how much more appropriate preventive diplomacy is in an ideologically fragmented system where collective security is clearly impossible.

The techniques of preventive diplomacy are as familiar as the daily

7. Dag Hammarskjold, "Introduction to the Annual Report of the Secretary-General on the Work of the Organization, 16 June 1959–15 June 1960," in *From Collective Security to Preventive Diplomacy,* Joel Larus, ed. (New York: John Wiley, 1965), p. 402.

newspaper. They include UN observation and patrolling activities along disputed borders, within disputed enclaves, and astride tense armistice lines. These are intended first to separate hostile armies so that diplomats may pursue peaceful settlements, but they are intended also to monitor and discourage external interventions into local quarrels. Preventive diplomatic tactics also include offers of international military and police forces to small states threatened or confronted with aggressive acts from neighboring states. The intent in such cases is both to prevent war and to dampen small states' temptations to appeal to superpowers for military aid. Preventive diplomacy of course also includes the provision of mediation, conciliation, and arbitration facilities. Finally, speed in action and dispatch has proven essential for success in preventive diplomacy. To isolate and localize small state conflicts, the United Nations must act quickly to inject itself into situations *before* superpower interests become aroused and superpower actions are planned and executed. This requirement for speed in dispatch, as will be shown below, shifts a great deal of international organizational initiative into the office of the Secretary General.

Hammarskjold's assumptions that disputes among small states can be isolated from the Cold War by UN action have been at least partially borne out in practice on a number of occasions. UNEF in the Middle East facilitated British and French withdrawals from Egypt and saved a great deal of face for the United States and the Soviet Union. Similarly, UNOGIL in Lebanon both facilitated American and British withdrawals and defused a pending U.S.-Soviet confrontation. In the same way, UNFICYP on Cyprus is maintaining an uneasy truce on the island while keeping the Cyprus issue out of major-power bounds. Most important, the ONUC in the Congo successfully, though somewhat chaotically, immunized the turmoil-ridden African republic against East-West cold warfare.

For all of its apparent value, however, preventive diplomacy remains burdened with dilemmas. Most important, Hammarskjold's additional assumption that disputes among small states can be *resolved* through United Nations preventive diplomacy has not been entirely borne out in practice. While disputants have been willing to avail themselves of UN assistance in bringing fighting to a halt and in maintaining armistice lines, they have not, by and large, been willing to use UN conciliation and mediation facilities for resolving underlying political disputes. One result of this ambivalence has been that UN peacekeeping forces once injected into disputed areas cannot be easily withdrawn. If political settlements cannot be gained, withdrawing international forces from tense areas is almost tantamount to inviting renewed violence. Hence, the peacekeepers stay on, sometimes indefinitely, making definite contributions to the reduction of violence in international politics, but relatively few contributions to pacific settlement.

Second, preventive diplomacy has come under strong criticism inasmuch as some have maintained that UN actions dubbed "neutral" are actually partial toward one of the other of the Cold War contenders. This issue has been most highly stressed by the Soviet Union, but it certainly cuts both East and West. Cold War contenders point out, and sometimes rightly, that when the UN acts to discourage political opportunities for one superpower, the organization is really acting in support of the other. Since respective political opportunities for the superpowers are seldom equal in troubled areas, one Cold War contender is invariably penalized more than the other by UN attempts to act impartially. Paradoxically, then, United Nations efforts to keep issues from assuming Cold War overtones have actually heightened superpower interests in the issues. The Congo operation stands as a prime case for reflection in this regard.

3. HEIGHTENED AUTHORITY FOR THE UN SECRETARY GENERAL. One of the most remarkable trends in the evolution of the United Nations over the years has been the steadily increasing authority of the organization's Secretary General. Three factors account in great measure for the rise of the United Nations Secretary General from the role of passive civil servant to that of chief executive and troubleshooter for the world community. First, the paralysis of the Security Council, as already noted, created an "initiative gap" in the United Nations Organization. This gap has been partly filled by the enhanced powers of the General Assembly under the Uniting for Peace Resolution. But it has also been partly filled by the Secretary General, who, in interpreting the Charter broadly, has found means to set the organization into action despite Security Council deadlocks. Second, the foundations for the expanded authority of the Secretary General are actually embodied in the United Nations Charter. Whether intended or not, loose wordings in the Charter have provided handles available for

grasp by aspiring Secretaries General. Third, the uniqueness of the Secretary General's office and its location at the focal point of world attention have offered officeholders important opportunities to establish precedents in international administration. In this way, substantive and procedural innovations under one United Nations administration have carried over to become accepted practices under later administrations.

Articles 97, 98, and 99 of the Charter define the powers and prerogatives of the Secretary General. Article 97 installs him as "the chief administrative officer of the Organization," and the following Article assigns him such functions as he may be asked to perform by the executive and deliberative organs of the organization. Article 99, however, assigns functions to the Secretary General that are not strictly administrative in nature. Under this Article, "the Secretary-General may bring to the attention of the Security Council any matter which in his opinion may threaten the maintenance of international peace and security." Here, clearly, the Secretary General becomes a monitor for world stability—a "watchdog," if you will, who remains alert and reports dangers to international peace.

In ideal circumstances where the Security Council or the General Assembly would be able to arrive at meaningful decisions and to direct the Secretariat in explicit courses of action, independent initiative on the part of the Secretary General would be uncalled for and unnecessary. But "ideal" circumstances seldom prevail at the United Nations. Consequently, evasiveness in the executive organs has prompted the Secretary General to act under Article 99, most notably in the Congo situation; and indecisiveness and ambiguity in these organs have permitted the Secretary General to act with wide latitude under Article 98. When executive organs fail to deliver explicit guidelines for action, as is often the case when resolutions must be reduced to "lowest common denominator" compromises, important policy decisions are invariably left to the Secretary General. More than this, as noted below, Dag Hammarskjold insisted that the Secretary General, as guardian of the Charter, must act in the face of threats to the peace, *even if UN executive organs fail to deliver any directives whatsoever.* In a very real sense then, the strength of the United Nations Secretary General grows from the weakness of the organization's primary policy-making organs.

Added to his unique abilities to step into the "initiative gap" in the United Nations policy-making system, the Secretary General has also enhanced his office by turning his initiatives into precedents and thereby integrating them into accepted organizational practice. For example, nowhere in the Charter is it explicitly stated that the Secretary General should act as a roving diplomat and world troubleshooter. Nevertheless, the demonstrated diplomatic competence of successive Secretaries General and the credibility of their international impartiality, has generated increasing numbers of assignments in international mediation and conciliation. Many such assignments have established precedents that have enhanced the image of the Secretary General as a skilled and disinterested mediator. As precedent has piled on precedent over the years, the ever-open "good offices" of the Secretary General have become special, legitimate, and widely accepted parts of the United Nations peacekeeping mechanism. That these good offices were open during the Cuban Missile Crisis may someday be interpreted as decisive in the course of world history.

Important administrative precedents have also grown from *ad hoc* directives issued by various Secretaries General during United Nations field operations. Since many of the early operations of the UN were "firsts" as far as international organizational activities were concerned, many of the procedures devised during these operations have lingered to become accepted parts of United Nations practice. The so-called UNEF Principles, for example—i.e., the set of operating rules devised by Hammarskjold during the installation of the first UN peacekeeping force in the Middle East—have greatly influenced procedures in all succeeding peacekeeping ventures. Similarly, practices in the far more complicated Congo operation also taught lessons and built precedents for future United Nations undertakings. Since the Secretary General sits at the hub of the United Nations administrative system, operational innovation, prerogative, and hence precedent, are largely in his hands. Moreover, since the United Nations has probably not yet experienced the full variety of challenges that history will thrust at international organization, the current Secretary General and his successors into the foreseeable future will likely have ample opportunity to contribute additional innovations and precedents to United Nations practice.

Finally, Dag Hammarskjold's personal interpretation of the office of Secretary General may well turn out to be the most significant precedent in United Nations development to date as well as the greatest enhancement to the stature of the Secretary General. Hammarskjold affirmed that the first and overriding responsibility of the Secretary General must be to the world organization and its Charter. His interpretation of "responsibility" was broad. Responsibility to the organization implied more than responsiveness toward one or another of its executive organs, and it implied more than the faithful execution of directives from these formal decision-making bodies. Similarly, in Hammarskjold's conception, responsibility to the Charter meant a great deal more than adherence to the letter of the document. Instead, to Hammarskjold, responsibility to the United Nations Organization meant unflinching pursuit of the organization's pacific and humanitarian objectives by any and all means controlled or controllable by the Secretary General. Relatedly, responsibility to the Charter meant, to Hammarskjold, maintaining and projecting the spirit of world cooperation and conciliation that it embodies.

Hammarskjold therefore saw the Secretary General as an executive of the world community and an executor of world peace. He is an official who acts according to the letter of the Charter when such action contributes to United Nations objectives, but a man who acts on independent initiative in the spirit of the Charter when formal procedures fail to carry the organization towards its ends. The organization, Hammarskjold felt, has an existence that is greater than the combined separate views of its member-governments. It embodies an "extranational" or "supranational" impulse. Therefore, the Secretary General, above all, must act to articulate this impulse and bring it "to bear in the prevention of future conflicts." Whether Hammarskjold's philosophy of office will live to become international organizational principle is difficult to determine. However, the next great challenge to the United Nations may well indicate whether the Hammarskjold years set the UN on a course towards an "organized international community," as the late Secretary General himself perceived, or whether these years of dynamic supranational leadership marked an apex in organizational development and a transition into decline.

CONCLUSION

Certain themes that have recurred frequently in this abbreviated discussion of the United Nations Organization deserve a recounting in summary.

First, above and beyond critics' impatience and frustrations with the UN and its operations, few will deny the organization's salience as a part of the contemporary international political environment. Granted, the world body is largely irrelevant and incompetent in the area of superpower competition. Granted also that it is cumbersome in many of its procedures and inconsequential in many of its undertakings. Still, it has a demonstrated relevance in regulating relations among small powers, in influencing relations between great powers and small powers, and in isolating small-power disputes from great-power ambitions. Moreover, its unwieldiness in some undertakings has been more than offset by its efficiency in many others.

Second, structural and functional evolution within the United Nations system has exposed a flexibility and continuing viability that few analysts observed or even expected during the early troubled years of the organization. Pragmatism, improvisation, and creativity mustered at critical junctures by United Nations officials and member-states, have repeatedly carried the organization over formidable barriers. When the organization's primary peacekeeping mechanism sank in the Cold War morass, several *ad hoc* but reasonably effective alternatives were improvised to replace it. When the organization appeared to be losing international political initiative, international civil servants stepped in to fill the "initiative gap." When the organization appeared in danger of drowning in a deluge of polemic and trivia, Hammarskjold emerged to project his vision of world community and to revitalize the purposes of international organization. In all, the United Nations has a demonstrated will to live and capacity to grow.

Finally, what of the organization's potential? It would appear that for the present at least, questions of potential directed toward the United Nations are best phrased in terms of relevance to international politics. That is, while it might be intriguing to ask about possibilities for enhanced supranationality or even world government, such an exercise would be academic in that these possibilities are remote. The central question is: Where, and how well, can the United Nations relate to its surrounding international political environment?

The potential relevance of the United Nations is high because opportunities for such relevance are open. For one, nuclear stalemate and world discomfort with the strategic balance of terror offer the United Nations new and promising opportunities for initiative in the realm of arms control and disarmament. Then, too, the gravity of the problem of economic underdevelopment, the needs and predilections of the newer UN members, and the organization's unique multilateral distributive mechanisms all combine to present the United Nations with a promising opportunity for initiative in the economic development field. The success of early efforts in preventive diplomacy, precedents established, personnel trained in peacekeeping, and reputations for impartiality nurtured, combine to present the United Nations with a promising opportunity in the realm of crisis control. Finally, the growing influence of the world body as a legitimizer of foreign policies presents the organization with promising opportunities in the realm of international legal and moral standards. Hence, the United Nations Organization has considerable potential. A question remaining, however, is whether the international community can attain the maturity necessary to see the potential of the United Nations realized.

CHAPTER FIFTEEN
THE LONG ROAD TO UNDER-
STANDING INTERNATIONAL
POLITICS

THERE is really no appropriate conclusion for this book because it drives not toward an ending but toward a beginning. Reading and reflecting upon its contents should be only the very first steps toward understanding international politics. For the beginning student, these might be steps into the expansive and rich monographic literature of international relations. For the more advanced student they might be steps across one or more of the many research thresholds identified in previous chapters and elaborated in this one. Therefore, rather than to treat this chapter as a conclusion—offering in it only a summary of major points—it is appropriate also to display here some dimensions of the intellectual challenge still before us in the study of international politics.

As noted in the Preface and underlined in Chapter 1, one of my intentions in writing this introduction to international politics was to spark intellectual curiosity in readers, regardless of their previous experience with the subject matter. The beginning student who has read this far must recognize that the most he has gotten from this book, even if he has studied it carefully, is command over a set of tools for international political analysis. He now knows which questions to ask about events in international politics: questions about actors, about goals, about capabilities, and about constraints. In addition, he has become aware of many of the qualities and quantities that he must observe in order to broaden his insights into international political phenomena. Through different chapters of this book, for example, the empirical focus has shifted from the policies of governments, to the

356

perceptions of men, the structure of states, the attitudes of populations, the motivations of men; moving on to the material attributes of states, the personal attributes of statesmen, the mathematical properties of systems, the geometric properties of processes, and to flows of information, trade, people, money, and machines of war. All of these are the data base for international political analysis. Then, too, the student now knows—or should know—something about the causes of international political events.

TOWARD THEORY IN INTERNATIONAL POLITICS

Among advanced students and professional social scientists, acquiring sophistication in understanding within the discipline means moving intellectually toward theory. Most social scientists (save for those who believe that every human event is entirely unique) share the assumption that *kinds of events* are recurrent in human behavior and relations. More specifically, the political scientist applying his expertise to problems in international politics assumes that *kinds of international political* events are recurrent. Each event has some unique features to be sure. But each event—be it a governmental decision, a crisis, a war, an armistice, a treaty-signing or the like—also has enough features in common with other events of its class to lend stimulus and meaning to a search for general explanations or common causes. A theory or set of theories of international politics is the envisaged result of this search. Formulating such a theory would naturally be an achievement in intellectual economy, since a whole realm of human behavior would be rendered understandable in terms of a manageable set of causal principles. Moreover, by injecting at least a modicum of predictability into world events, a general theory of international politics could be a valuable guide for statesmen, and perhaps even a key to peace.

This book, however, has not attempted to offer a general theory of international politics. None in fact exists.[1] Nevertheless, the alert

1. To assert that no general theory of international politics exists is not to belittle the efforts of a number of scholars who have taken important steps in the direction of theory. Among these and their works I would recommend: Raymond Aron, *Peace and War* (Garden City: Doubleday, 1966); Stanley Hoffmann, *The State of War* (New York: Praeger, 1965); Edward H. Carr, *The Twenty Years' Crisis, 1919–1939* (London: Macmillan, 1946); Morton A. Kaplan, *System and Process in International Politics* (New York: John Wiley, 1957); Kenneth E. Boulding, *Conflict and Defense* (New York: Harper Torchbooks, 1963); George Modelski, *A Theory of Foreign Policy* (New York:

reader has no doubt detected and watched this author groping to identify basic components of international politics that might ultimately be welded into a theory. By my definition, a theory of international politics would be a set of generally valid and logically consistent propositions that explain the outcomes of interactions between and among political actors. As such, the theory would contain three kinds of statements: (1) those which identify or take inventory of components and properties of international systems and events, (2) those which identify and describe relationships among the components and properties of the international systems and events, and (3) those which explain or otherwise account for such relationships. In short, I see a general theory of international politics as an inventory of dependent and independent variables, a series of process models, and a set of statements about cause and effect. This book has made some probing moves in all three of these directions. But the net result of these is not a theory of international politics, but more modestly, a framework for analysis that could perhaps yield theory after extensive and systematic empirical investigation.

In broad overview it is accurate to say that the components and properties of international systems and events have been the main foci and overriding concern of this book. Chapter 1 introduced and defined the international system, and explored both its static and dynamic properties. Chapter 2 then focused upon identifying the actors of that system. After the abstraction of "state" was swept away, analysis revealed that actors in international politics are usually small groups of men who speak for states (or other organizations) and whose decisions and directions become their organizations' internationally

Praeger, 1962); Hans J. Morgenthau, *Politics Among Nations,* 4th ed. (New York: Alfred A. Knopf, 1967); Harold and Margaret Sprout, *The Ecological Perspective on Human Affairs* (Princeton: Princeton University Press, 1965); Richard N. Rosecrance, *Action and Reaction in World Politics* (Boston: Little Brown, 1963); Karl W. Deutsch, *The Analysis of International Relations* (Englewood Cliffs, N.J.: Prentice-Hall, 1968); Ernst B. Haas, *Beyond the Nation-State* (Stanford: Stanford University Press, 1964); Arnold Wolfers, *Discord and Collaboration* (Baltimore: Johns Hopkins Press, 1962); Thomas C. Schelling, *The Strategy of Conflict* (Cambridge: Harvard University Press, 1960); Harold D. Lasswell, *World Politics and Personal Insecurity* (New York: The Free Press, 1965); Kenneth N. Waltz, *Man, The State and War* (New York: Columbia University Press, 1959); Quincy Wright, *A Study of War* (Chicago: Chicago University Press, 1942).

pursued policies. In somewhat more formal language we might say that the actors in international politics are *decision-making systems.* Having identified the actors, in Chapter 2 we set about placing them within their local political milieus by surrounding them with political elite comrades, counterparts, and challengers. Chapter 3 added mass populations and public opinion to the local milieus of the foreign policy decision-makers, and charted some patterns of opportunity and constraint that typically arise in relations between government and governed in the foreign policy realm. Clearly, the assumption underlying Chapters 2 and 3 was that attributes of the internal political and societal milieu have bearing upon deliberations and actions in the foreign policy decision-making system. Some of the more obvious relationships between social structure, elite structure, elite preferences, and mass opinion on the one hand and foreign policy decisions on the other were displayed. But a host of more subtle relationships of this nature have yet to be uncovered and explained by empirical research.

Where the first chapters of this book focused on the internal political milieus surrounding decision-makers, Chapters 4–7 sketched the larger world around these men and then inventoried the range of their attempts to cope with it. This larger world—the international political system—was variously depicted as a jungle where the fittest survive; as a market where the adept prosper; as an arena where the mighty, daring, and defiant win acclaim; and as a community where harmony and cooperation intermittently prevail. The most salient theoretical message of Chapters 4–7 was that men's actions in international politics are either initiatives taken to alter or preserve aspects of the prevailing international environment (real or perceived), or else responses to others' attempts at such alternation or preservation. Exactly which aspects of the international environment different actors will attempt to alter or preserve will depend upon different states' relative allotments of rewards and deprivations in the international system, and upon different statesmen's and peoples' relative satisfactions with the pattern of allotment. The motivation to act in international politics, then, follows from dissonance generated by contradictions between reality (as perceived) and ideal situations (as aspired toward), or between reality (as cherished) and threatened change for the worse.

Power is the link between motivation and action in international politics because power is the capacity to act. The message of Chapters 8–10 is a fundamental and long-understood principle of politics: political ends are attempted by allocating resources to their pursuit. These ends are accomplished when such allocations are great enough in quantity and sufficiently superior in quality to overcome all countervailing forces. The inventory of resources required for effective international political action is long, though few entries are surprising or extraordinary. Effective action at the global level requires men, organizations, materials, and machines of high quality in large quantity. By the same token ineffective action and dismal failure in international politics follow from shortages, shortcomings, or breakdowns of men, organizations, materials, and machines. While the meaning and role of power in international politics should not be exaggerated, neither should the basic factors of power be minimized. International politics are indeed "power politics," but so too are all politics.

FROM FRAMEWORK TO THEORY: THE ROAD AHEAD

Isolating the essential components of international politics—systems, actors, motivations, and capabilities—and noting the more obvious and better understood relationships between and among them as I have done in this book, should suffice only to whet the researcher's appetite. With modesty I would assert that a great deal concerning international politics was *described* in the various sections of this work. But with humility I admit that very little beyond the very general about international politics was actually *explained*. Why, when, and how do different kinds of actors mustering different kinds of capabilities, in pursuit of different kinds of goals, converge or collide to produce different kinds of international political events? Phrased differently, what are the permutations and combinations of system attributes, actor attributes, goal attributes, and capability attributes that recurrently generate the variety of international political events? Or, put most simply: What causes wars? What stops them? What preserves peace? Few of these questions were answered in this book to the author's full satisfaction. Even fewer, hopefully, were answered to the student's satisfaction since part of the purpose of this text has been to raise and display unanswered questions in order to encourage new research. Undoubtedly some of this book's inconclusiveness has followed from the difficulty of fully mastering a sprawling discipline. But much more of it stems from the fact that most of the important causal questions about international politics presently rest unanswered. The research frontier in international politics is clearly marked. So too are research pathways leading beyond this frontier.

The next steps toward better understanding in international politics must be large ones. Taking them will require a discipline-wide effort in cumulative and coordinated research by a community of interested students and scholars. Research into the causal dynamics of international politics must move in two directions: first, toward increasing breadth in an empirically grounded search for relationships among international political variables and, second, toward increasing depth in efforts to explain relationships discovered.

Initial effort and resources should be invested in creating a comprehensive archive of systematically gathered data relevant to the study of international politics. ("Relevant" as used here means "informed and guided by a well-conceived framework for analysis.") I lean toward a data-gathering strategy that calls for the collection of information concerning: (1) structural, political, and societal attributes of actors; (2) the nature of actors' goals and aspirations vis-à-vis other actors, kinds of actors, and the international system at large; and (3) the extent of actors' capabilities expressed both in quantitative and qualitative terms.[2] Actor attributes would include notes on the monistic or pluralistic structure of societies and politics, on conditions under which public opinion enters into foreign policy processes in the different polities, on the personalities and backgrounds of statesmen, and other related information on qualities of leadership. Similarly, the motivational inventory would include notes on basic values inherent in different elite and national belief systems; and on states' and statesmen's definitions of security, their ambitions vis-à-vis the international system, and

2. A great deal of data gathering of this nature has in fact gone on in recent years. Cf., for example, Arthur Banks and R. Textor, *A Cross-Polity Survey* (Cambridge: M.I.T. Press, 1963); Bruce Russett, *et al.*, *World Handbook of Political and Social Indicators* (New Haven: Yale University Press, 1964); Rudolph Rummel, *et al.*, *The Dimensionality of Nations* (forthcoming, 1970); J. David Singer and Melvin Small, "Alliance Aggregation and the Onset of War, 1815–1945," in Singer, ed., *Quantitative International Politics* (New York: The Free Press, 1968); J. David Singer and Melvin Small, "The Composition and Status Ordering of International Systems," *World Politics*, XVIII, No. 2 (January, 1966), 236–282; Lewis F. Richardson, *Statistics of Deadly Quarrels* (Pittsburgh: Boxwood, 1960); Quincy Wright, *A Study of War* (Chicago: Chicago University Press, 1942).

their satisfactions or dissatisfactions with characteristics of the prevailing international environment. Entries in "capability" categories would include traditional gross power measures, as well as notes on the performance of governmental organizations in normal day-to-day circumstances and on their performance under stress. Capability entries would also include notes on the legitimacy of regimes in the eyes of populations, on the depth of different peoples' nationalistic or patriotic commitments, on national cohesiveness or fragmentation under stress, and on national reputations and traditions in statesmanship.

Information about participation in various international events that occur within delimited periods of time should also be recorded for each actor. (Was the actor an initiator? What gains was he seeking or what losses was he trying to avoid? Was his participation involuntary? If so, how was he drawn in? Did the outcome of the event reward or penalize the actor? etc.) As will be apparent in a moment, collecting a rich archive of information about international political events and actor involvements is central to launching analysis directed toward theory. Data on all variables should be gathered in yearly sets, each set to include a year's records of actor attributes, actor motivations, actor capabilities, and event participations. In effect, each set of data would, in abstract and coded form, display the international system in a specific year. A sufficient number of such sets could hopefully be accumulated to cover several decades in several historical eras.

Analysis of the data entered in the international politics archive would focus upon recurrent events such as the outbreaks of wars of different kinds and their terminations, the formation of alliances and coalitions and their fragmentation, the signature of agreements and the abrogation of these, etc. The object in analysis would be to isolate and identify patterns of actor attributes, actor motivations, and actor capabilities that emerge before or during the occurrence of events. Here we are seeking more than correlations between attributes and occurrences. What we are rather trying to arrive at are abstract "pictures" (call them *datagrams* if you will) of multivariately defined diplomatic fields on the eve of and in the throes of international events. These might even be visually displayed. Primary focus would be upon *the actors that participated in the events,* with secondary focus upon conditions and configurations prevailing in the larger international system at the time that events occurred. If general patterns of interrelationship among characteristics of international actors, their motivations, their capabilities, and recurrent events are to be discovered, comparison of datagrams for several different occurrences of the same kinds of events should open the way to insight. In all of this, one must not lose sight of the momentousness of the data gathering and analytical tasks involved. If ever attempted on the scale described here, the effort will extend over several years and probably also through a few computer generations. Still, the result of this effort can be an elegant descriptive theory of international politics—a series of statements that describe with precision conditions necessary and sufficient for the occurrence of international events.

The step from descriptive theory toward causal or explanatory theory requires research in depth into the occurrence of specific events that are representative of classes of events. Systematically handled, this would imply a project in comparative case study on a massive scale. Where descriptive analysis yields generalizations about configurations of attributes in diplomatic fields when events occur, depth case studies should yield generalizations concerning *why* and *how* such configurations produce the events, or *why* and *how* the events take place when necessary and sufficient conditions are attained. Anticipatedly, explanation will take the form, "event X happened under conditions Y and Z because . . . ." To hazard a guess, I would suspect that such "because" statements will likely have a great deal to do with men's perceptions, their aspirations, their fears, their reason, their intermittent madness, and other contents of the "black boxes" that so often go unopened and unexplored in political science research. The empirical theorist's hope is that the same or similar answers to "why" and "how" questions will appear repeatedly when successive black boxes are opened, as more and more international events are explored in depth within a common framework.

The road to theory in international politics is a long one. There are no shortcuts. No amount of deduction from untested and untestable first principles, no amount of impressionistically mustered professional intuition, no amount of "on the job experience" in world affairs, and no amount of armchair speculation will substitute for the systematic analysis of a thoughtfully gathered, comprehensive collection of data. These assembled observations on the world are the social scientist's handles on reality. They open doors to understanding, an understanding which—as a key to peace—could well turn out to be the most vital intellectual accomplishment of our century.

INDEX

365